To John Mason

to mark a sad

chapter in the life

for our heritage —

& a very happy stay

in the House.

David Cornack

24 - 1 - 78.

Heritage in Danger

Heritage in Danger

PATRICK CORMACK

NEW ENGLISH LIBRARY
TIMES MIRROR

To Charles and Richard in the hope that they will learn to enjoy their heritage and play their part in preserving it.

First published in Great Britain by New English Library, Barnard's Inn, Holborn, London EC1N 2JR in 1976

Printed in Great Britain by Thomson Litho Ltd, East Kilbride
Bound by Hunter & Foulis, Edinburgh

450030601

Contents

Appendices

Acknowledgements

I would like to extend my warm thanks to all who have helped me during the preparation and writing of this book. Almost everyone to whom I spoke or wrote was very co-operative and it is always invidious to thank only some by name. However, special thanks must go to those who gave me the opportunity to look at their houses and study their accounts and, in particular, to the Earl of March, the Marquess of Tavistock, Commander Michael Watson of Rockingham Castle, and John Chichester Constable of Burton Constable. In addition, and in this context I would like to thank my own constituents and friends, the Earl of Bradford, Peter Giffard of Chillington Hall and Alan Monckton of Stretton.

I have learned much from my friends and colleagues on the Grants Committee of the Historic Churches Preservation Trust and I would like to express my special thanks to the Chairman of the Grants Committee, the Very Reverend Seiriol Evans; the Secretary, Hugh Llewellyn Jones; Raymond Richards, foremost authority on the churches of his native Cheshire, whose work is a mine of information for all antiquaries and church lovers; Canon Ian Dunlop of Salisbury Cathedral; and to Lady Harrod, whose work in Norfolk is a shining example to all.

In Edinburgh I received hospitality and help from Oliver Barrett of the Cockburn Society and Denis Rodwell, who has done so much pioneering work on comparative conservation policies here and in the rest of Europe. In Berwick I was royally entertained by Colonel Jim Smail, newspaper proprietor extraordinary and doughty crusader for his town.

These and many more have given of their time and wisdom, but the book would never have been written in the first place without the convivial hospitality of my friend and fellow campaigner, Hugh Leggatt, around whose ample luncheon table both the Heritage in Danger Committee and this book were conceived. Here, I should also like to pay tribute to Lord Cottesloe, that most distinguished servant of the arts and the Chairman of the Heritage in Danger Committee. He and my fellow Vice-Chairman, Andrew Faulds, are valiant fighters for a common cause and have given me great encouragement.

No book of this nature, however, can ever see the light of day without the devoted hard work and tolerant forbearance of a small band of dedicated helpers. I have particular cause to be grateful to my research assistants, James O'Shea, Jock Black and Ian Stanley, without whose devilling at a time of family illness, I would never have been able to meet a tolerant publisher's extended deadline.

Every married author has reason to be grateful to his wife and I am no exception, for mine typed the original tapes of this book, often under great difficulties, and when they were frequently almost inaudible. The final draft of the typescript was completed with lightning speed, amazing accuracy and unfailing good humour by Dina Hartley.

I am too especially grateful to Lord Goodman who found time in the midst of his incredibly busy life of public service to write the Foreword, and to Mr D. C. L. Holland, Librarian of the House of Commons. He and his staff are unfailingly helpful and courteous and I am particularly indebted to Mr Holland for allowing me to use a Paper prepared by the Library for European Architectural Heritage Year in compiling Appendices 3 and 4.

A major 'thank you' must also go to the Editor of *Historic Houses, Castles and Gardens* and of *Museums and Galleries* (ABC Publications) for permission to draw extensively upon the 1976 editions of these indispensable annual publication in compiling Appendix 1. They give full details of opening times, refreshment arrangements and precise directions for all travellers, and are essential for anyone interested in visiting historic houses, museums and galleries.

To everyone I have named and to all who have corresponded with me, talked to my research assistants, whether at NFU Headquarters, Country Land Owners' Association, or Canterbury Cathedral, I express my most grateful thanks as I do to my publisher's editors, Jane Butcher and Janet Law and to all of those, many already mentioned, who have read all or part of this book in typescript or in draft. I am sure that in spite of the help of all these people, blemishes and mistakes will remain, but for those I accept entire responsibility and merely hope they do not mar the work unduly or invalidate the message it seeks to convey.

Patrick Cormack
Brewood, Staffordshire
1976

Foreword by The Lord Goodman, CH

This book is the expression of one man's love for things of real value in Britain today. It is not in any provocative sense a political work. Mr Cormack is a Member of Parliament and, I have no doubt, belongs to some political party, but the book could be written by any sensitive lover of the countryside, of buildings and articles of beauty, from almost any position in the political spectrum, except perhaps for some on the extreme left who hold the view that a work of art or a thing of beauty ceases to be either if it is not in public ownership.

This is neither the time nor the place to revive the controversies over wealth taxes and other such debates that have caused needless alarm to the community of arts and beauty lovers. Suddenly, people who owned beautiful homes, pictures and other works of art, were made to feel that their motivation was apparently thoroughly discreditable and that they were only concerned to conceal their wealth in some permanent form free from inflationary loss. Thus, the collector—one of the more valuable characters in our society—was suddenly reviled as one who was hoarding beauty away from the eyes of the rest of the community. The magnitude of the rubbish that was voiced, both in and out of Parliament is very clearly evident after a perusal of Mr Cormack's cool, simply written and hopeful book.

Anyone reading *Heritage in Danger* will find much valuable information there that is not common knowledge. He will find a civilised and urbane viewpoint, free from rancour but full of a vigorous determination to defy the erosions of Philistines and political idiots. Those who care for the buildings, the pictures, the landscapes and the countryside for which Mr Cormack cares with such intensity owe him a debt of gratitude for his book and for his other ceaseless labours to retain things of beauty intact, and, above all, to retain the human right to enjoy them.

This book will, I hope, be widely read. I hope equally that it will enlist more people into the ranks of the small but increasing band determined to save what we have and allow it to be enjoyed under the best possible conditions. I hope it will inform an increasing number of people, perhaps for the first time, of the risks to the heritage and the need to preserve it. *Heritage in Danger* will, I am sure, achieve this result and additional gratitude will need to be extended to its author.

A special virtue of Mr Cormack's book is the clear message that a capacity to defend the national heritage cannot simply be an instinct or a reflex. Of course, right-thinking and right-responding people do have both an instinct and a reflex reaction against the destruction and desecration that the insensitive, the foolish and the opportunist frequently achieve. But more is needed, and that is a knowledge of the nature and quality of the things that one seeks to protect and, equally important, a knowledge of the defensive techniques required to protect them.

First and foremost, like the weaker creatures in nature, the community needs a sense of danger. Much that is planned of a destructive and wanton character is planned quietly and without forewarning. But there are people, and Mr Cormack is one of them, whose antennae will respond with sensitivity to a threatening situation before the damage is done. All too often, a planning application, seemingly innocuous, is only the thin end of a hideous wedge. The nation's many sightless planning committees must learn to detect the potential enormity of proposed developments at a very early stage, before permission is granted, no matter how virtuous a building may seem in outline.

Citizens also need a knowledge of how to set about resisting any onslaught on the heritage. The use of organisational power and of individual perception can, and sould, be taught by example. Informed criticism, as opposed to strident vocality, is a much better way of defending the beauty and tradition of the country. Ignorance, blindness and conceit are most often the causes of serious damage; conscious villainy is more rare. The technique for dealing with these needs to be developed. Persuasion can very often do better than a head-on collision, although there are times when nothing but such a collision can, as a last resort, avert disaster.

And, to know what is beautiful and identify what is ugly are necessary concomitants of a civilised community. The town dweller can only know the beauties of the countryside if he visits and examines it. But, strangely enough, the town dweller is no more likely to know the beauties of urban architecture and the splendours of age and antiquity than the man from the country. Children should be taught about these things. The opportunity to see what is worth seeing has, as a prerequisite, the need to be shown what is worth seeing and why. The overwhelming beauty of St Paul's, Salisbury or Canterbury Cathedrals probably needs no architectural explanations, but there are many other buildings less emphatic and immediate in their impact where some explanation is desirable for those coming to them for the first time. Text books provide it but the locality rarely does.

However, these generalised observations are incidental to my praise for this important work, and they are an expression of my gratitude to the author.

Goodman, London, 1976

9

CHAPTER ONE What Is Our Heritage?

Soon after I entered Parliament at the 1970 General Election my wife and I sought a brief rest in Herefordshire, loveliest of counties. One day we visited Abbey Dore in the Golden Valley and looking round that glorious church I suddenly became acutely aware that my children might never have the same privilege. Miles from anywhere, enormously costly to maintain, one marvelled at how the dedicated efforts of the few had ensured its preservation to date, and I came away determined to try to do something to ensure the survival of the thousands of medieval churches which adorn our countryside and give dignity to our towns. It seemed to me then, as now, that they could only be saved for posterity if the nation recognised the importance of making funds available for their repair. That visit was the background to an attempt to get an Historic Churches Bill through Parliament, a Bill which would have made aid available from public funds to assist in the preservation of religious buildings still in use but utterly beyond the capacity of their often tiny congregations to sustain. The Bill foundered but a scheme is now being prepared along the lines that many of us advocated at that time.

Abbey Dore was a catalyst and an inspiration, and during the past six years I have become ever more conscious that almost every part of our national heritage – landscape, buildings, great collections – is at risk. To the natural and inevitable dangers facing anything old and lovely, but often frail, have been added the menaces of twentieth-century civilisation and the urge to change, to modernise, to redevelop. And on top of this is an increasing tendency by Government to impose ever more onerous burdens of taxation upon those on whom the final responsibility for safeguarding the heritage often rests.

When the Labour Government in the summer of 1974 published its Green Paper on the Wealth Tax it became apparent that the heritage, though recognised as being worthy of extra consideration, was not to be exempt from extra fiscal impositions. Many were alarmed and stirred into action and I was one of those involved in setting up a Committee called Heritage in Danger whose aim and object was to point out the danger that a Wealth Tax would impose on the national heritage.

When I am asked to define our heritage I do not think in dictionary terms, but instead reflect on certain sights and sounds. I think of a morning mist on the Tweed at Dryburgh when the magic of Turner and the romance of Scott both come fleetingly to life; of a celebration of the Eucharist in a quiet Norfolk church with the medieval glass filtering the colours, and the early noise of the harvesting coming through the open door; or of standing at any time before the Wilton Diptych. Each scene recalls aspects of an indivisible heritage and is part of the fabric and expression of our civilisation.

Never has there been a wider appreciation of this true quality of life, never a more general determination to preserve and enhance it—and never has each and every aspect of our heritage stood in greater danger. The pressures and the rush of modern life have heightened man's individual awareness of the need for spiritual and cultural enrichment. Yet, at the same time, they have made him collectively responsible for endangering the quiet and beauty of our rural surroundings, of what remains of our urban dignity, and of many great and humble buildings which express as vividly as the words of playwright and poet or philosopher the spirit of a nation.

It is doubtful if there is any country in the world that has more varied rural beauties or more buildings upon which, as Hazlett said, 'the eye may dote and the heart take its fill'. We can lament at what acts of deliberate destruction, casual indifference, or the ordinary ravages of fire and time have removed and we can feel shame at the havoc that has been wrought in the name of improvement and redevelopment even during an era of increased awareness and appreciation. The fact remains, however, that Britain still has an incalculably rich heritage.

The devastation of mining and quarrying, the urban sprawl spawned to house a growing and consuming population, the march of the pylon bringing electricity to the Highlands, the swathe cut by the motorway, all these have reduced the countryside, but not destroyed it. Our landscape remains as varied and as wonderful as any in Europe, from the rugged grandeur of the far north through the romance and drama of the borders, and the bare austerity of the high Yorkshire Dales to the dry golden brecks of East Anglia. The traveller in this island still has, like Johnson, many places he can visit and wonder at, the artist many scenes he can copy and admire. And, although unthinking and haphazard development has suffocated many rural communities in layers of undistinguished suburbia, there are as many authentic villages in England alone as almost anywhere in Western Europe. The Cotswolds, for instance, still house many rural communities and within half an hour's drive of a number of our sprawling cities there are oases of village life. One does not have to go far from Manchester or Birmingham, from Glasgow or Leeds—or even from London itself—to light upon a village scene that many of the more pessimistic doom watchers would claim had disappeared for ever.

Towns, like villages, have often been spoilt. One cannot think of the 'redevelopment' of Worcester or Gloucester without shivers of disgust, dismay and shame running down one's spine. Yet, our urban treasures are by no means all destroyed. The story of Bath is a sad one but we can rejoice that much has been saved, that the developers have been curbed, and their lorries at last restricted in their journeyings. And there are still places like Cirencester and Tewkesbury, Ludlow and Louth, Rye and Berwick, where the developer has been kept at bay, or where civic pride has been mobilised in time to civilise his schemes. Many of our old towns, too, have cathedrals or great churches as their crowning glories and, in spite of the ever increasing difficulties of maintenance and repair, most of them remain in remarkably good order, lovingly cared for, regularly visited and appreciated, and collectively in a far better state than those of almost any other country.

It is perhaps in our country houses and churches, however, that one comes closest to the spirit of England. The exhibition, 'The Destruction of the English Country House', at the Victoria and Albert Museum in the autumn of 1974 showed with dramatic effect just what we have lost, but there remains a wealth of country houses that are lived in and loved. So it is with our country churches. Although the wear and tear of time and inflation, and often dwindling congregations, make their preservation a matter of prime concern, nevertheless there are still nearly eight thousand medieval churches in this country, and almost all could be safeguarded for posterity by a nation that had its priorities right.

And here we come to the nub: the question of priorities. The safe-guarding of our finest buildings can be achieved at remarkably little cost, as can the preservation of our great public and private art collections. The dangers they face are either man-made or assisted by man's indifference. In the chapters that follow, I shall endeavour to spell out some of the dangers and to show how they can be overcome – if we have the will to overcome them.

By touching on all aspects of the visible heritage this book highlights some of the many dangers facing it, and seeks, by taking some brief examples, to 'point a moral and adorn a tale'. Many will be disappointed that gems they value and have strived to save get no more than a passing mention, if that. However, the moral is that our heritage is one and indivisible and that the acutest dangers are of our own creation and could be relatively easily solved by individual and by Government action, or, indeed inaction.

Inevitably, in a work of this nature, there is much reference to what has been lost, but I hope that the message conveyed is essentially one of optimism. It would be a tragedy if in bemoaning what has gone we wasted our time. The best tribute any of us can pay to departed glories is to fight to preserve those that remain.

CHAPTER TWO The Countryside We Take for Granted

The English landscape is at once the most obvious, enjoyed and also the most neglected aspect of our heritage: obvious and enjoyed because of the magnetic appeal of 'the countryside' to an urban population; neglected because that same population takes its presence and its permanence for granted. Hence, 'God made the country and man made the town'—and even an agnostic age instinctively accepts that the natural background and foil for man-made beauties, and escape from man-made ugliness, will always be there.

In a densely populated island such as ours this is a rash assumption. For one thing the pressures of commerce, industry and politics on finite resources of land and beauty are not easily withstood; for another the preservation of the land's natural beauty must be by conscious and deliberate action. That these factors have long been recognised is shown by the legislative sanctification of 'the green belt' and by the proliferation of local and national amenity societies dedicated to fighting insensitive planning decisions, and to achieving the balance between industrial and commercial needs and conservation. But from Dartmoor to the Cheviots the traditional landscape pattern, the beauty we all enjoy and do take for granted, is at risk and only new initiatives on the part of those who exercise a constant vigilance will save it. Though ruins will always have a powerful and romantic hold on our imagination and the presence of vanished villages beneath the furrows has inspired poets, land lost to twentieth-century developers is beauty lost for ever. And land is being lost at a frightening rate.

Between 1945 and 1974 something approaching a million acres was taken out of cultivation and although accurate statistics are hard to find (even the Ministry of Agriculture does not know how many acres of woodland have disappeared since the War) it seems only too clear that approximately 60,000 acres of agricultural land – English landscape – is built on or taken over each year. Motorways and their service areas alone accounted for 25,000 acres between 1960 and 1974. A new electricity generation station requires 500 acres, an oil refinery 1000 acres or more, a North Sea gas terminal about 2000 acres. A thousand acres a year are buried under colliery spoil, and coal extraction affects some 6000 acres a year in South Wales alone, according to the Council for the Protection of Rural Wales. In Bedfordshire, clay production has now consumed almost 2500 acres and this total is increasing at the rate of 50 acres a year.

Of course, it is not just industry that requires land. In 1970, the National Playing Fields Association estimated that the number of people playing golf was increasing at the rate of 9 per cent a year. If taken literally, this expansion would mean we should be requiring four acres per hundred of the population just for golf courses by the turn of the century. Perhaps this gives some point to T. S. Eliot's remark that our only legacy would be 'the asphalt road and a thousand lost golf balls'.

One does not want to be unduly alarmist but anyone with two minutes to spare and a pocket calculator at his disposal can see that by the year 2000 another $1\frac{1}{2}$ million acres will have been occupied and our farmlands shrunk by some 4 to 5 per cent. For green belt notwithstanding, there seems no coherent central plan to halt the urbanisation rate of the countryside. As with most complex issues it is easier to indicate the problems than it is to propound acceptable solutions but if food production is to be given the priority common sense dictates and if 'conservation', 'preservation', and the importance of the 'rural environment' and other clichés are to have any real significance there must be a slowing down in the process of urban encroachment.

In fact solutions do readily suggest themselves, and many have become more attractive in the wake of the energy crisis and attendant economic problems. For instance, though an industrialised country needs good speedy communications these do not necessarily have to be six-lane motorways. It is at least arguable that when those motorways at present under construction are completed there should be an absolute moratorium on motorway building for twenty years and the entire road building programme firmly concentrated on making our towns and villages more habitable. In this way not only would less land be taken up by road works, but there would be less desire to escape and build 'a place in the country' if fumes and noises were reduced within the towns. After all, towns are places for people to live in and they can only have a life and a civilising influence if they house a living as well as a working and shopping community.

Towns and their problems are the subject of Chapters Five and Six but in the present context we can see that both town life and that of the countryside could be improved by a sensible policy of restoring good old houses, and by a more imaginative rehabilitation of derelict sites. It is surely the height of folly to house people at expensive distances from their work and in the process destroy land of great agricultural and scenic wealth when in and around our towns and cities are hundreds of thousands of sound, if dilapidated, houses and tens of thousands of acres of waste land. There were nearly 107,000 acres of waste land in England alone at the time of the last survey in 1974, of which nearly 82,000 were considered to justify treatment. At normal density, these could accommodate nearly a million homes—the land needed for overspill for at least five years. Of course some derelict land could never be built upon, but much could, and most of the rest could be transformed to acceptable park and recreation land, or even returned to farming. For though considerable reclamation has taken place the amount of derelict land has remained frighteningly static for a decade or more. The inland waterway system, too, is almost totally neglected for commercial uses. Although only half its nineteenth-century length, many of the 2000 miles of our canal system could still be used to relieve congestion on the roads of Britain, even though it is unlikely that barge transport could ever assume the same significance here as on the Continent[1]. All these steps would help relieve the pressure on, and reduce the dangers to, the English landscape, but in themselves would not be enough to ensure its survival in anything remotely resembling its present form.

The problems, of course, are not new; they have been developing over the last one hundred and fifty years. Whilst Britain changed from an agricultural into an industrial country, the population grew from a little over 10 million, to over five times that number (1801 census 10.5 million; 1971 census 53.8 million). Early industrial changes brought commercial prosperity, but early industrialists showed scant regard for the countryside, as they built their factories or encouraged the unchecked and destructive development of an urban sprawl around the agricultural hinterland of so many of our towns and cities.

One should not be over-critical about the lack of precautions because the problems of industrialisation had never been faced before. But though commercial opportunities were often commendably exploited, expansion brought not only success but piles of waste, scars across the country, and factories erected regardless of their siting. It was only relatively recently that stringent controls on all this development were imposed. And even with the lessons of the past, we, during the last half century, have allowed a network of pylons to criss-cross the countryside and have disfigured the domestic scene with the ubiquitous television aerial. We have, too, encouraged the development of the cheap motor car, which has brought a new mobility to almost every section of the population.

In the 1920s and 1930s the suburbs grew at a rapid rate, and as a consequence much fine countryside was eroded. In response to this, the idea of the green belt was born with its new stricter planning controls designed to arrest urban spread. But even today, the countryside is not safe in the face of demand and pressure from the huge corporation or from nationalised industry, which can suggest that the development advocated is essential for economic survival, and can then marshal armies of experts to cajole planning departments and impress inquiries. Sometimes the experts are beaten, as they were at the Dulas Valley Inquiry in 1970 when the Severn River Authority was forced into admitting that its estimates for extra water resources were grossly exaggerated. But local opinion is frequently brow-beaten and even

---

[1] This unexploited potential underlines the urgent necessity for a complete reappraisal of our whole transport system, and in particular of the rôle of the railways. It is to be hoped the re-elevation of the Minister for Transport to Cabinet rank and the recreation of a separate Department announced as this book goes to press (September 1976) heralds such a review.

Ministers are often dazzled by the evidence of so-called infallible experts. As I write the battle to prevent building part of the M54 through one of the loveliest remaining parts of Staffordshire goes on, with the Midland Road Construction unit insisting, although most of its estimates have been challenged, that the motorway will be essential, refusing to consider seriously new and telling evidence, and even embarking on expensive preparatory work in advance of the Minister's final decision.

The most remarkable victories over official decisions were those of Stanstead, Cublington and Maplin, over the siting of the proposed third London airport – but they became national campaigns. One of the tragedies is that beautiful local areas rarely incite national fervour, and it is difficult for local amenity societies or other bodies properly to challenge expert evidence. And expert evidence can be misleading. For instance in the 1960s, the figure that was frequently quoted for putting electricity transmission lines underground was over 1 million pounds per mile. What was not said was that this related only to 1400 kV circuits, but at the time this figure was current, the Central Electricity Advisory Board's own booklet (1971 edition) was quoting figures from 120,000 pounds per mile for 132 kV circuits. Richard Crossman surely had a point when he stated in 1965: 'It could be said that by putting them (i.e. cables) underground, we sharply reduce the time taken to invent new methods for reducing that million pound cost to something more reasonable.'

And so the encroachments continue, questionable decisions are allowed to stand and countryside and farmland is lost – at the present rate, an area the size of Nottinghamshire goes every eight years. No one suggests that a proportion of this loss is not inevitable but it is vital to reduce the rate. Certain actions and policies are open to question, for instance the whole concept of the new town – and yet Milton Keynes is going ahead and 22,000 acres of agricultural land will have been built upon and an area at least as twice as large as that adversely affected.

Even when particular bodies are conscious of their 'environmental duties', mistakes are made. The Central Electricity Generating Board, for example, is charged by Parliament 'to take into account any effect that their proposals might have on the natural beauty of the countryside or on flora or fauna, or natural creatures or buildings or objects of special interest'. Nevertheless, they have built a nuclear power station in the Snowdonia National Park and, on a smaller scale, the Iron Bridge power station beside Buildwas Abbey, in the most beautiful stretch of the Severn Gorge. And it is not just the big decisions which are open to question. Much unnecessary damage is done by the widening of country lanes in the interests of convenience and tidiness. Quite often the only result is a spoilt area and more reckless driving.

The picture would, however, be much gloomier had it not been for the doughty campaigning of national and local amenity societies. Among the most vigorous in its efforts and successful in its achievement has been the Council for the Preservation of Rural England. Established in 1926 to combat such horrors as the ribbon development of the 1920s and 1930s, and to draw attention to the defacing of the countryside by long lines of hoardings on rural verges, the CPRE – the brainchild of Patrick Abercrombie – has many victories to its credit. Its agitation, more than anything else, led to the Town and Country Planning Acts of the 1940s which virtually controlled ribbon development; and its persistance was largely responsible for establishing the principle that the restoration of derelict industrial and mining sites should be regarded as normal procedure (although much remains to be done here). It was the CPRE, too, which fought a largely successful battle for Ullswater when Manchester Corporation wished to distort and destroy the whole beauty of the area with its plan for water extraction. The Council has also done much to prevent the proliferation of radio and television masts. At Fort William, for instance, it won the day when it called for one mast to cater for television and VHF, rather than two. There is still much to be done, and it is significant that the Council decided to celebrate its Golden Jubilee in 1976 by launching an appeal for $\frac{1}{2}$ million pounds to enable it to continue its vigilance and campaigning.

Certain parts of the landscape are recognised as being of such importance that special steps must be taken for their preservation. Thus, in 1949, the National Parks Commission was established, and as a result ten national parks were designated: the Lake District, Snowdonia, the Breckon Beacons, the Pembrokeshire coast, Exmoor, Dartmoor, the Peak District, the North Yorkshire moors, the Yorkshire Dales, and Northumberland. The land and the parks generally remained privately owned, but agreements or orders to secure additional public access were made by local authorities. Steps were also taken to preserve and enhance the landscape's natural beauties by high standards of development and control and by such measures as extra tree planting and preservation, and the removal of man-made eyesores.

Under the Countryside Act of 1968, the Countryside Commission replaced the National Parks Commission and was charged with keeping under review all matters relating to the provision and improvement of facilities for the enjoyment of the countryside. Schedule 17 of the Local Government Act of 1972 stated that 'Every Town Planning Board, or National Park Committee established for a National Park shall (a) within three years of the First of April 1974 or of being established, whichever is the later, prepare and publish a plan to be known as a National Park Plan formulating their policy for the management of the park and the exercise of the functions exercisable by them (b) review at intervals of not more than five years the National Park Plan published under this paragraph making any amendments to it which they consider expedient and publish a report on their review and any such amendments.'

All but two of the national parks are administered by the local authorities in whose areas they fall and this has roused considerable criticism because it is often felt that unfortunate conflicts of interest could arise, and indeed some have arisen, over the parks' administration. By common consent the most successful of the parks are those administered by park boards representing a number of authorities, amenity societies and other bodies. No one could seriously challenge the concept of the national parks for they are areas of great importance and great beauty. But by virtue of their very designation they attract enormous numbers of visitors, and balancing the needs of the residents, the demands of amenity and conservation groups and of the visitors, is not always an easy task. One wants to encourage recreation in the countryside and provide facility and opportunity for it, but there comes a point where the number of visitors, by their very presence, destroys the things they come to enjoy. In Snowdonia, for example, which has 210,000 visitors a year, paths and tracks are being worn away by walkers, who, according to the Council for the Preservation of Rural Wales, are 'making a molehill out of a mountain'. The same problems are found on the Pennine Way, where footpaths are being pounded to death, and there are even experiments being conducted on plastic footpaths in certain vulnerable areas. The problems faced by the national parks are faced in a similar measure by the thirty-four areas of outstanding natural beauty (see Appendix 1). These range from the Sussex Downs to Cannock Chase, and include such large areas as the Cotswolds, and smaller ones as Dedham Vale. But their beauty, too, attracts visitors and visitors create difficulties if they come in too great a number, as anyone knows who has visited Flatford Mill on a Bank Holiday Monday.

That people who live in constricted urban areas should have the opportunity for recreation in rural surroundings is beyond dispute. Residents of the Black Country, for instance, tend to look to Cannock Chase as one of their 'lungs'. But the balancing of agricultural needs, environmental preservation and the supply of recreational facilities is a difficult one to achieve. The Forestry Commission has attempted to achieve this balance and in some of its forests has set aside areas where people may picnic and walk, and has attempted to restrict them to places where they will not interfere with, or damage, the forestry. They have also established holiday villages and designated areas for camping and caravanning, which have become increasingly popular pursuits as mobility increases and inflation prices hotels beyond the reach of all but the more affluent families.

Conscious of the difficulties of reconciling recreation with preservation, the Sandford Committee, established in 1971, recommended the creation of 'heritage areas' which it defined as areas where 'the conservation of environmental qualities would be the supreme objective . . . taking precedence over all others'. These areas would contain no large car parks or public lavatories, no refuse bins or refreshments – they would all be sited in surrounding support areas. 'These conservation areas', the Report said, 'are to be kept for quiet and congruous public enjoyment, with access to them to be on foot, bicycle or horse. They should be conserved so as to be handed on unimpaired to future generations.' They considered them to be those rare areas which were especially vulnerable to encroachments and which must be given special consideration and protection if they were to survive. They were, in concept, not dissimilar from the nature reserves, the responsibility of the Nature Conservancy, which in 1974 covered almost 300,000 acres.

But national parks, areas of outstanding beauty, potential heritage areas, nature reserves, National Trust land, and reserves owned by such bodies as the Royal Society for the Protection of Birds, are not *the* landscape, *the* countryside, even though they represent vital and beautiful parts of it which deserve jealous guarding and special treatment. No, the greater part of our landscape is outside such areas of special protection. In Scotland, for instance, there are no national parks, and only 9 per cent of the coastline (of England and Wales) lies within the ten national parks. Indeed, our coastline, with its infinite variety and complexity, a special pride to an island race, is particularly vulnerable, in spite of the valiant efforts of the National Trust's Enterprise Neptune, a scheme devised to bring into Trust ownership some of the most beautiful and unspoilt coastal areas. By far the greater part of the countryside, therefore, is exposed to all the pressures of population growth, industrial exploitation and demand, and developers' dreams. Not that these are the only threats to the countryside.

In spite of all that has been written about the 'silent spring' and the menace of toxic wastes, in spite of the laudable legislative action that has followed public outcry and stimulated further public awareness, pollution remains a threat to the healthy growth of meadow and woodland, to the purity of the air and the life of the water. Industry's pollution of the air is inadequately controlled and while great progress has been made in improving rivers and estuaries, there is much to be done before the work is complete. Our coastal landscape is threatened here, too. Stiffer penalties might have made oil pollution less likely, but penalties cannot prevent determined mischief or genuine accidents and damage done by oil from ship collisions.

But the pollution crises that reach the headlines, such as 'Danger from Radioactive Waste', 'Japanese To Send Atom Waste to UK', 'Cancer Warning on Chemicals', serious and potentially spectacular as they often are, do not perhaps pose the greatest threats to our countryside. It is more likely that they come from the industry which largely created, and still largely controls, the landscape pattern of England: farming. For in seeking to meet demands and at the same time to cope with the problems created by fiscal and other pressures, farming has changed dramatically in the last three decades. The loss of good farmland has underlined the need for a more intensive cultivation of what remains, a need stimulated by a growing population and an ever greater demand to feed it, to make ourselves more self-sufficient as a nation. The increasing sophistication of farming techniques has produced a record of remarkable success in statistical terms. The average yield per acre of wheat in Great Britain was 17.3 cwts in 1885. By 1935 it had risen to only 18.6 cwts. By 1960, it was 28.5 cwts and by 1970, 33.3 cwts. This upward trend cannot be expected to continue in such a spectacular manner and, indeed, the very success that the figures represent must be viewed with some degree of concern, for it has been achieved by an intensification and alteration of farming methods which pose very real threats to the pattern of the English countryside as we know and love it.

Since the Agrarian Revolution and the enclosures of the late eighteenth century, farmers have known that unless waste and crop residues were returned to the land its fertility would deteriorate and yields would decline. Throughout the nineteenth century advanced farmers perfected the techniques of natural fertilising: the ploughing in of the stubble in preparation for the next crop and the spreading of manure from cowsheds and cattle yards on the fields. However, by the middle of the century chemists were discovering that the organic substances used as manures and fertilisers contained a number of chemical elements in common, elements that were essential for plant nutrition, such as nitrogen, phosphorus and potassium. In their organic form nutrients are not immediately available to plants but must be processed by soil microbiorganisms and random chemical reactions so that they are released slowly. Manufactured industrially, however, they can be delivered to the soil accurately and in a form that enters the water held in the soil to form a solution. This makes them available almost immediately and means that nutrients can be fed to the plant when its growth requires them, rather than to the soil.

This knowledge has been harnessed by a farming industry challenged to increase domestic food production. Between 1954 and 1973, the net output of the United Kingdom almost doubled, a rapid increase due to a transformation of British agriculture. Increased use of artificial fertilisers, partly to answer the challenge and partly to answer the problems brought about by the rising cost of labour, played a substantial part in this rise. Thus, the growing availability and use of chemicals, combined with the relative profitability of cereals, persuaded many farms to abandon the practice of ley farming (the seeding of crop land back to grass every few years to rest and allow it to restore its natural structure and fertility). As a result soils in many areas have deteriorated and soil blows, seldom a problem before, have occurred more frequently in areas of East Anglia and the East Midlands.

By the mid-sixties farmers had become concerned themselves by the adverse effects of new practices and the National Farmers' Union conducted a survey to discover the extent of the problem. A full inquiry by the Agricultural Advisory Council followed and, in their 1970 Report, they concluded that modern farming practices were indeed having a detrimental effect on soil structure in some regions. In addition, they claimed that continuous cropping had created serious problems in pest and disease control. In spite of this, pure organic farming has few devotees and very widespread use of artificial fertilisers continues. Most would agree that though artificial fertilisers have a future there is good reason to think that they have an 'addictive' effect altering the ecology of soil population, depressing numbers of those species that make nutrients available in their own waste and decay products. Further, by ending the practice of returning fibrous organic matter to the soil it becomes more difficult for plant foods to reach the soil solution. These adverse effects are accumulative and farmers often find that as the years go by they are using ever increasing amounts of fertilisers to achieve the same yield.

If, therefore, the practice continues, and there is a further increase in the intensity of arable farming, there will almost certainly be further deterioration in soil structure and erosion, probably for only a very small increase in yield. If the process of soil deterioration is to be reversed there must be an increase in the acreage to be sown to grass and a re-integration of livestock and arable farming.

There may be a further restraint on increased fertiliser use. Whereas potash and phosphate, fertiliser compounds, are comparatively stable in the soil, this is not true of nitrogen. In an article in the *New Scientist* in 1972, Dr R. Scorer reported that the number of milligrams of nitrogen, in the form of nitrate, per litre of water at intakes on the Thames and Ley have, since 1972, approached, and in one case even exceeded, the 11.3 milligrams considered to be the safe limit. Above this concentration bottle-fed babies can develop methaemoglobaemia, a disorder affecting the oxygen-carrying capacity of the blood, and above a concentration of 20 milligrams the adult population could also be at risk.

To put it briefly, successive use of artificial fertilisers could well impose extra strains on the biology of farms and gardens which could have a damaging effect on our forests, rivers and waters, but above all on the general appearance of the countryside. Already there has been widespread loss of wildlife in the world through the destruction of habitats and the indiscriminate use of the more persistent pesticides.

But one must take a balanced view. We owe to our farmers the countryside that we enjoy. Its beauties are largely of their creation. For centuries they have looked upon themselves as trustees of the land replacing the resources extracted by their crops and acquiring, gradually, by trial and error, a philosophy of husbandry, largely inspired by their sense of stewardship. Today, farmers are no less responsible for what they have in trust, but the problems and pressures of producing food and earning a living in the twentieth century, and the fiscal inhibitions that a farmer faces, often make him, albeit reluctantly, put financial considerations first. Long-term dangers from fertilisers may be one result. The more noticeably spectacular is the transformation in many parts of England of the traditional rural landscape of chequer-board fields and pastures enclosed by hedgerows.

The hedgerow has long been an indispensable and invaluable feature of the English country scene, a visual break and a shelter for plant, animal and insect life. The uprooting of hedgerows, and the creating of vast prairies in certain areas, has transformed the rural scene more than anything else since the enclosures of the eighteenth century, when most of our 500,000 miles of hedgerow were planted. It is estimated that 100,000 miles of these hedges have been removed in the last twenty years. In East Anglia, nearly half have gone, and the impact of their removal has aroused great criticism from a public often ignorant of farming needs, but deeply attached to the traditional landscape pattern. This attachment dates back well beyond the eighteenth century in many cases, for some of our hedges can be traced to Saxon times. Those who take an objective view appreciate the need for some hedgerow removal, but its scale is enough to disturb even the most farming-conscious naturalist. For the hedgerows are not only valuable and beautiful in themselves. A survey in 1951 found that no less than a fifth of the nation's reserves of indigenous hard woods – oak, ash, elm, beech and sycamore – were hedgerow trees.

Aside from the devastation caused by Dutch Elm disease, every year these hedgerow trees become fewer and many of them will never be replaced because the modern hedgecutting machine cannot distinguish between the unwanted elder sprays and the healthy young leaders of oak, ash, or sycamore that might one day grow into fine trees. Indeed, the very machines themselves contribute to the death of the hedge by failing to remove dead grass heads, brambles and bracken that choke and eventually kill, by not allowing light and air to the rich part of animal life that it sustains. If it continues, this trend will lead to the virtual disappearance from the fields of the blackbird and thrush, the chaffinch and the other hedgerow nesting birds. The hard fact is that because of our taxation system and changes or quirks in Government farming policy, it is often difficult for the farmer to obtain anything like a favourable return on his capital employed and so he saves money where he can and seeks to produce as much as he can. Thus hedges go down to save the bother and cost of maintaining them and to give large units.

Between 1945 and 1970, 4500 miles of hedgerow were removed each year. In that period, Norfolk lost half its hedges and Huntingdon 90 per cent. There are many dairy farmers who are re-organising their holdings by removing hedges, the traditional stock-proof barriers, and creating instead large fields in which the paddocks are wired off. Downland, too, is disappearing before the plough, often for the first time. Half the Winchester Chalk Downs have gone since the War and a quarter of Dorset's over the last fifteen years. Lowland heath, too, is disappearing. These changes not only alter and spoil the beauty of our countryside but they also destroy much of its life. As the cover disappears the balance of nature is upset and animals and birds and plants die. The scale of the damage was such that in 1962 the Countryside Commission set up a study to investigate how agricultural improvement could be carried out efficiently, but in such a way as to create new landscapes no less interesting than those destroyed in the process. The very terms of reference seemed to accept the inevitability of change. Some change *is* inevitable, and many of the more prosperous farmers have replaced hedgerows by clumps of trees for shelter where the fields meet, and those with an interest in conserving game and wildlife often insist on maintaining a few hedges in odd wild corners, even on the arable farm. But every yard of ground sacrificed in this way means a fractional loss in income and not every farmer is willing (or able to afford) to recognise that the future ecological health and balance of the landscape may depend on his making such a sacrifice.

It is not just the removal of hedgerows which has disturbed the appearance and balance of the countryside. Its wildlife has been particularly affected by the widespread use of pesticides. For they are all poisonous to wildlife to a greater or lesser extent even when the manufacturers' instructions are followed carefully. And even while an insecticide may eliminate a pest from a crop, it will also kill many other species which feed on the pest, so that when the pest does return, it can rapidly build up its numbers. This in turn can lead to the creation of new pests, such as the fruit tree red spider mite. At one time this mite, though common, was kept in check by its natural enemies, but so many of these have been killed off by the pesticides, that the mite has now become a serious menace.

The use of pesticides to control weeds is also fast destroying aquatic plants and animals. There was a time when the many pools, lakes and meres and marshes and fens around the country supported distinctive plants and animals. The draining of farmland, the piping of water to fields, has meant that most of these natural habitats have gone, and as the few remaining ditches and ponds are now frequently being contaminated, yet another balance is upset. But is it not just the smaller ditches and ponds that are endangered. The *Observer* for 25 May 1975 carried an alarming report to the effect that the Norfolk Broads, one of the country's most beautiful and popular holiday areas, were at risk. They faced, said Jeremy Bugler '... on a more modest scale, the kind of degredation that has occurred in the great lakes of America'.

The Norfolk Naturalist Trust had produced evidence that rich nutrients from washed-out fertilisers, and from sewage, were flowing into the Broads endangering all aquatic vegetation in eleven of the twenty-eight Broads studied. In another eleven the vegetation had been severely reduced. The article quoted the Trust's Conservation Officer as saying: 'Ten years ago things were very different; you could row across Hickling Broad, lean over the side and see pike swimming across the bottom. Now you cannot see anything; just a muddy, murky gloom.' It is doubtful whether the prime responsibility for this disturbing state of affairs rests with the farmers for using too many artificial fertilisers, or with the holiday makers for throwing refuse and pumping enormous quantities of sewage into the Broads. But the conclusion of the article was that in spite of the new regulations for boats to carry chemical toilets, an increased use of organic fertilisers would be necessary if the Broads were to be saved.

In spite of frequent assertions to the contrary, advanced in some conservationists' lobbies, the farmer *is* concerned with the quality of his environment. The desire to maximise profits is rarely paramount and is balanced by a healthy concern for the countryside and its traditions. The ownership of land is still regarded as a trust, held for succeeding generations and for other members of society who regard the heritage in terms of recreation and amenity. However, today's farmer is under great financial pressure and new forms of taxation will increase this. The temptation is, therefore, to gain the greatest available profit in the short or medium term at the possible expense of the future. The owner-occupier, who for generations has demonstrated a sense of true responsibility, is in danger of being transformed by the actions of the State from the guardian of our agricultural heritage into a potential enemy.

It is easy for a farmer with a relatively modest holding to be a rich man on paper, but the return on the capital invested in farming is a very low one – often as low as 1 or 2 per cent. This is not a new situation, but on top of the normal taxes faced by any businessman or private individual, the farmer has to cope with the prospect of new capital taxes and the threat of a Wealth Tax. All this means that private ownership of land is not in possible danger: it is in peril. In the Budget of April 1976, the Chancellor of the Exchequer gave additional relief to farmers from Capital Transfer Tax, the tax which he had previously introduced to replace the old Estate Duty. The additional relief granted, though it will assist the working farmer with a holding of 1000 acres or less, will in no wise remove the threat to the larger estate – and it is mainly upon the productivity of flourishing large holdings that success in meeting targets for extra food production depends.

This explains why after the Budget there was still a mood of despondency in the ranks of landowners. James Douglas, the Secretary General of the Country Land Owners Association, writing in *Country Life* on 15 April 1976, said: 'The Government is using capital taxation not to raise revenue but to carry out its social policies...when the consequence of investment is a direct increase in the liability for capital taxation – annually under Wealth Tax (postponed but not abandoned by the Chancellor) and once a generation under Capital Transfer Tax, with the break-up of the private land owning business, the virtually certain conclusion—who will invest?' Douglas took a very gloomy view of what the future would hold without further mitigation of the tax burden faced by land owners. 'City institutions will buy some land but they have an overriding responsibility to their shareholders, policy holders or other investors, which it would be unethical for them to disregard. As companies with obligations to fulfil they can normally invest only in land which offers either capital appreciation or a good return... the National Trust for its part has declared that it cannot be used as a receptacle for land that has to be disposed of and no one wants to buy. Only the State or its agents are left.'

Even with the better terms offered in the April 1976 Budget to the working farmer, it is quite obvious that the effect of the Wealth Tax would be to increase the emphasis on short-term considerations at the expense of planning for the future and the same applies to Capital Transfer Tax, even in its modified form. The danger is that the farmer will be obliged to look upon his farm as a purely economic unit to be exploited to the full during his particular ownership. Capital taxation, especially on the transfer of land, will inevitably reduce the interest of the farmer in his holding after his own retirement. And a Wealth Tax would inevitably increase pressure to earn as much money as possible in the minimum amount of time. The National Farmers' Union has calculated that Capital Transfer Tax and a Wealth Tax could together cost the industry over 200 million pounds a year at 1974 prices – a sum which would account for more than a third of gross fixed capital in agriculture at that date. Financial pressures of this sort are bound to increase the damage on the rural landscape and environment. Farm buildings will be reduced in quality; there will be little incentive to use expensive, durable materials, like stone or slate.

The imposition of new forms of capital taxation will also result in the increase in the number of farms held on an institutional basis. And institutional landowners never have the same degree of human care, concern and control that the local farmer or landowner exercises and displays. If present trends continue the great private estate will rapidly become a thing of the past. This is certain to have a very damaging effect on the development of agriculture. Many of the great experiments of the past, the new techniques, have been conducted and perfected on the country estates. The landowner was more likely to have time, energy and resources for experimentation, than an owner-occupier, whose total livelihood depended upon results, and whose resources of capital and land were often insufficient.

It is not just fiscal measures which have a depressive effect on agriculture. The effects of the Community Land Act of 1975 are potentially devastating, the central problem being one of land valuation. The sale of land at development prices did at least serve to put some badly needed capital into the industry – one thinks of Michael Watson, the owner of Rockingham Castle in Northamptonshire, selling land adjacent to Corby New Town and ploughing the money back into the development and sophistication of his estate for the benefit of farmworkers and of the local community.

With the Community Land Act on the statute books the danger is that, in areas threatened with development, land prices will slump and in safe areas will increase. The result would be that the ordinary farmer, whose farm was purchased at use value, would find the money received inadequate to meet the cost of a new farm of an equivalent quality in a 'safe' area. The landlord-tenant relationship will also be disturbed by these latest moves, and by the Government's recently produced and well motivated legislation to ensure the transfer of a tenancy from father to son. With the owner-occupying farmer being the only one to gain significantly from any concessions on Capital Transfer Tax, the temptation will always be to take a farm in hand when it becomes vacant, rather than to let it out again. Therefore, the landowner able to take a more detached and 'global' view of his holding, will be obliged instead to concentrate almost exclusively on the actual business of farming. When one bears in mind how much the moulding of the landscape is owed to the great estate, one can hardly feel confident that the changes will benefit the future appearance of the countryside. Another Government-inspired change that will also have some effects on the balance of farming is the legislation designed to abolish the 'tied cottage'. Lurking behind all these measures, and the changes they are likely to effect, is the fear in the landlord's mind – and in the owner-occupier's, too – that land nationalisation is next. This fear undermines such sense of stability and security as remains in agriculture and the man who does not feel secure is unlikely to allow considerations for the landscape and the environment to loom large in his thinking.

The effects of this attitude of mind have already been noticed in forestry. It takes many years for a tree to mature, a long time to wait for any financial reward to accrue from its translation into timber. The unsympathetic treatment which private forestry has received from successive governments since the War has hardly given heart to those who wish to retain our English woodlands, so many of them planted two hundred or more years ago, so many of them attached to our great estates. It is true that the Forestry Commission has begun to temper its policy of relying entirely on quick growth softwoods and to plant a few hardwoods, at least on the fringes of its plantations. But the traditional contribution of the English deciduous tree, copse and woodland to the landscape is certainly at risk, and it is doubtful whether the devastations of Dutch Elm disease which by the beginning of 1976 had killed an estimated $5\frac{1}{2}$ million elm trees will ever be adequately compensated especially as uncertainty over taxation led to a 40 per cent reduction in private planting in the same year[2].

Farming has always tended to be a traditional occupation and vocation. Those who have lived on the land, and loved the land have wanted nothing more than for their sons to succeed them. This has applied to all levels and stages of farming. Unless current trends are reversed and Governments make a more determined effort to give back to farmers the sense that their efforts will be rewarded by a chance of continuing a tradition, the danger is that the philosophy of the quick return will inevitably dominate the agricultural deliberations where two or three farmers are gathered together. If this is the case, the alteration and deterioration of the landscape will inevitably continue. For personal commitment and loyalty would be more difficult to sustain, and all the efforts of statutory bodies, be they countryside commissions or nature conservancy interests, or an independent organisation like the National Trust, would be able to do little more than ensure the preservation of pockets of traditional England —quaint museum-like reminders of what the countryside used to be.

[2] Some two million trees were destroyed in nurseries because of the lack of confidence of the private sector according to Lord Taylor, Chairman of the Forestry Commission in an article in *The Times*, 29th June 1976.

CHAPTER THREE The Great Estate and the Country House

A nation's history is nowhere more arrestingly or poetically told than in its buildings. Most of our old towns, and far too many of our villages, have been disfigured, and the ever more protective and comprehensive legislation designed to preserve the best of the past has often come too late. Over the last few years there has been an increasing realisation of what not only Britain, but Europe, has lost, and the determination to rescue what remains was most graphically underlined by the designation of 1975 as European Architectural Year. Much was achieved during that year to stimulate public awareness of dangers to the architectural heritage and some splendid rescue projects were launched. However, 1975 also brought sharply into focus – in the midst of public debate on Capital Transfer Tax and Wealth Tax – the problems facing one of our two most important groups of historic buildings: the country house.

These houses are a special public possession for it is in them and in our churches that we perhaps come closest to the soul and spirit of England. Germany has its castles, France its châteaux, Italy its villas and England its country houses. They are a unique and gentle blend of the craftsman's art and rural beauty, filled with the familiar acquisitions of generations: the collections of the dilettanti; the library of the local scholar-statesman; the domestic accumulations which themselves give a living commentary on men and manners through the centuries. Set in their spacious parklands and often containing priceless collections, our country houses are part of the very fabric of our civilisation.

Many of them, of course, have disappeared. One of the most spine-chilling experiences of recent years was to look into the Hall of Disaster in 'The Destruction of the English Country House' exhibition at the Victoria and Albert Museum in 1974, and to see, to the accompaniment of the appropriate 'noises off', the roll-call of the demolition men: 1000 houses, many of them outstanding, destroyed in the last hundred years – some 250 since the end of the Second World War. No one could suggest that every demolition was a national calamity, but equally no one could emerge from that exhibition without a sense of loss and a determination that the remaining treasures must be kept. And much does remain. There is no county without some houses in which it can take pride, but their survival depends upon their owners' ability to maintain them.

In spite of the valiant efforts of some local authorities alone or—as at

Shugborough (Staffordshire) or Tatton (Cheshire) – in conjunction with the National Trust, the rescue potential of the ratepayers' representatives is of necessity strictly limited, as is that of Government. And it should be pointed out that the National Trust, one of the greatest of our national societies, cannot contemplate the cost of taking over more houses unless their owners are able adequately to endow them, and adequately in 1976 means a very large sum of money indeed. Thus, if the country house is not to become a rare and isolated architectural peculiarity, owners must be given every encouragement to remain servantless at the end of draughty corridors, guardians of much that is finest in our heritage.

These owners could more properly be called stewards or trustees. Their special position, and the importance of what they hold in trust for the nation, has been increasingly recognised since the end of the First World War, which marked the end of the great era of country house living. As early as 1923 the National Trust was urging the Chancellor of the Exchequer to introduce legislation whereby the owners of historic buildings could receive tax concessions to enable them to meet the high cost of maintenance. In 1934, at the Annual Meeting of the National Trust, the Marquess of Lothian called on the Trust to extend its protecting arm in a definite and considered manner to the historic country houses of England. Characteristic of this country and unrivalled in any other, they were, he said, under sentence of death by taxation and Estate Duty.

Little was done, however, to assist their owners until the end of the Second World War, when many of the houses, having been requisitioned for national use during hostilities, stood in desperate need of repair. A realisation that this unique English phenomenon was in danger of extinction led Sir Stafford Cripps to appoint the Gowers Committee. Its famous Report was published in 1950, and it signalled a new awareness of the importance of the country house to our heritage. As with most reports, many of the recommendations were ignored, but the Historic Buildings Council was set up and since 1953 grants have been made to the owners of country houses – grants which have often helped to save a house for the nation. One comes again to the phrase 'for the nation', because we are not discussing the distribution of public funds to wealthy individuals. It is for the nation that these houses must be saved. We will come to a detailed analysis of the problems facing owners in Chapter Four, but at the outset it is important to recognise that the country house is just that because it is surrounded by estate and parkland. That parkland, too, is of considerable importance to our national heritage. Indeed, it is arguable that much of what is best in our English countryside has remained unspoilt only because of the existence of the great country estate. For without the estates, there would be little parkland and few sweeping vistas. The works of the great landscape architects of the eighteenth century would be but a memory evoked in old views of 'Gentlemen's seats'. The landowner with 2000 or 3000 acres or more is able to take a slightly more detached view than the ordinary farmer; is able to retain hedgerows and clumps of trees despite a possible reduction in short-term productivity or profitability.

This is something that is not readily grasped even by many of those who appreciate the architectural worth of the houses themselves. These well-meaning preservationists, primarily interested as they are in architectural history or works of art, tend to have little knowledge or experience of the realities of estate economy. What they do not recognise is that giving special legislative protection to the building is a hollow gesture, unless the land and estate surrounding it, and without which its owner could not maintain it, is similarly protected. There must be very careful provision, too, for inheritance, for the problems of the country house are not only fiscal, but physical. The owner has to do more and more physical work for himself, with the result that a large country house is no place for elderly people: hence the need to be able to hand on to the next generation – and the next generation will need just as much income, and probably more, than at present.

What becomes immediately apparent to anyone who starts to look into the question is that no one quite knows how many houses there are. Of course, we all know of the great ones – Chatsworth and Blenheim, Woburn and Longleat – but, although they are of outstanding importance and must at all costs be preserved, they give a very unrepresentative picture of the country-house scene. To save them and to allow the hundreds of smaller houses, often unknown beyond their immediate locality, to fall into disrepair, or worse, would be to change and impoverish the English countryside. It would be similar to maintaining Canterbury, Lincoln and a dozen of our greatest cathedrals, but at the same time allowing the vast majority of our ancient parish churches to fall into disuse, decay and ruin. The tragedy is that such a thing could happen without the public being aware of it.

Awareness would certainly bring protest, for in 1973, according to a British Tourist Authority survey, something like 15 million visits were made to historic houses in this country, 11 million of them to houses and grounds in private ownership. About 15 per cent of the visitors came from overseas – and Britain's tourist industry is now the single most important earner of foreign currency. But the vast majority, 85 per cent, were ordinary British people, most of them seeking escape from the grime of old industrial towns, or from the grim uniformity of the new. They came seeking to enjoy themselves in pleasant rural surroundings, to stimulate their imagination and their taste by looking at beautiful buildings and lovely, interesting objects within them. In 1975, well over a million of these visitors petitioned Parliament to ensure that these houses could remain open.

In his report on the English country house, *Country Houses in Britain – Can They Survive?* (1974), John Cornforth suggested that there are probably 1500 country houses in the United Kingdom of which about 1000 could be considered notable and of historic and architectural importance. Of these about 430 were, in 1973, still in private hands and not regularly open to the public. About 152 were privately owned and open, and about 95 belonged to the National Trust or the National Trust for Scotland. Some 40 belong to the Department of the Environment and to local authorities and most of these are open to the public, and about 225 are adapted for various uses: schools, offices, trade union headquarters, flats and other private and public institutional purposes. These figures in themselves are slightly misleading for, of those 430 houses privately owned and not listed as being open, many are the focus of local activity, regularly accessible to local people. Many, too, are open to the public on numerous occasions during the year, often with the proceeds of the day going to some national or local charity. Furthermore, a number of new houses open their doors on a regular basis each year, and it is a condition of a major grant from the Historic Buildings Council that the public should have reasonable access to these properties.

Michael Watson, owner of Rockingham Castle in Northamptonshire, which dates back in parts to the time of the William the Conqueror, sees his home as 'an active country house performing its rôle in every sense, rather than just a show piece'. Almost all the owners of country houses see their properties like this, and it is important if we are to put the issue in perspective to look at the rôle of the typical country house.

Rockingham is in many respects typical. The house has withstood the changes of fashion, and the ravages of war and now stands on its hill in Northamptonshire, a pleasing blend of medieval, Tudor and post Civil War architecture. It suffered considerably in that war and was altered fairly extensively inside in the nineteenth century. It is not a vast house, not in the same league as Chatsworth, Castle Howard, Blenheim or the other great ducal palaces, but to enter between its twin round towers, to walk through its hall or along its long gallery, or to survey the shires from its tower, is to absorb a vast panorama of English history. And its changes in structure and internal design reflect the changing tastes of generations of owners who have sought to make it more comfortable for themselves and their families. Its furnishings are fascinating, but homely, its portraits and country pictures interesting, in some cases lovely, but in no case of outstanding national importance. Yet no one could argue that England would not be the poorer if the Reynolds or the Marshalls or the lovely Zoffany in the long gallery, or the intriguing portrait of Elizabeth I in the great hall, were lost to the nation. Every year thirty thousand people or more enjoy its sense of timelessness and its tranquil domestic beauty and they can wander through the surrounding parkland. The parkland is important, not only to the house and its setting, but because this is the centre of an important agricultural holding, an estate that includes the village of Rockingham itself and over 4000 acres of agricultural land. The castle is very much the centre of a living community. If it were sold and its contents dispersed, the land bought by some pension fund or industrial organisation – the most likely fate – and the houses in the village were sold off, the whole area would be considerably the poorer.

The owner of Rockingham does not live in any regal splendour. When he inherited the property in 1967 he faced a number of problems, not the least of which was an annual deficit of between 5000 and 10,000 pounds on the running of the estate. But some 250,000 pounds had been spent during the previous twenty years, some 85,000 pounds on the maintenance of the castle alone. This money was mainly raised by the sale of land to the new town of Corby on the fringe of the present estate, and he has now been able to produce a small credit balance, though opening the castle to the public merely covers the cost of employing gardeners to keep the grounds in trim.

Rockingham seems a happy community in which villagers take considerable interest in their work and in their surroundings. The shooting on the estate is run on the basis of a cooperative with workers participating in both the sport and the maintenance, and they are able to shoot at specified times without restriction.

The attitude of the family to their visitors, most of whom are from the surrounding areas, is that each is a guest and should be treated as such. There is no desire here to commercialise. Indeed, if there were it would probably fail, for it is doubtful whether Rockingham could ever become a great national attraction. Northamptonshire, however, is not abundant in museums or places where people can spend an enjoyable, inexpensive day in pleasant rural surroundings, and Rockingham serves a more than useful purpose for those who wish to spend their half-days or Sundays there during the six-month season when the house is open. Michael Watson and his wife, who run the place with the aid of a caretaker and three daily helps, see themselves as very much part of the continuing pattern of the Rockingham story. They have no desire for great riches and certainly will not achieve them, but they have a sense both of history and of stewardship and a genuine feeling for the local people and the local countryside.

So it is with many of the less famous country houses. They stand, often at the end of tree-lined avenues, or on small promontories like Rockingham, up and down the land, centres of local feeling and patriotism and very often 'lungs' for nearby industrial towns. A glance through the list of those open to the public in 1975 reveals an astonishing spread of treasures for people to enjoy: architectural, artistic and rural. Each one is very much the centre of its own local community. Forgetting the large and the dominating, the loss of this random selection of relatively unknown houses which most people will never have seen would be seriously to impoverish the areas in which they lie and would create a local sense of deprivation.

Lincolnshire is a good example of a sparsely populated county with few nationally famous buildings except its supreme cathedral, no important national museum, and yet a number of interesting and some important houses. Houses like Marston Hall, near Grantham, home of the Thorolds since the fourteenth century, smaller than it once was but still a lovely blend of Tudor stone, with family portraits inside, a magnificent painted bedroom (brought from another family home) and a wonderful fireplace in what is left of the great hall, reduced by an earlier generation. And then there is Auborn Hall, near Lincoln, almost certainly designed by the great Smythson. A Tudor building remodelled in Jacobean style, the most outstanding feature is the staircase with open strapwork panels in the balustrade. Belton House, again near Grantham, certainly qualifies as a great house in its architectural splendour – it has been attributed to Christopher Wren – and the importance and beauty of its contents: magnificent Grinling Gibbons carvings, family portraits by Reynolds, and works by Titian, Rembrandt and Canaletto, Van Dyke and Tintoretto. There is a remarkable seventeenth-century bed and some fine and rare silver, including the famous wine cistern presented to Speaker Cust. This exceptional house is well known by connoisseurs but only twenty thousand people visit it each year and its geographical location is such that the number is unlikely to increase beyond fifty thousand.

Most people know of Berkeley Castle in Gloucestershire and it had a hundred thousand visitors by the early 1970s. Edward II was murdered there and Oliver Cromwell battered a breach in the walls. It is a strange blend now of medieval fortress and English country house.

Yorkshire, too, is famous for its houses, but few will have heard of Bramham Park, near Wetherby. No one knows who the architect was, although both Gibbs and Archer (the most likely) have been suggested. It was built between 1698 and 1710 and is a fine example of a Queen Anne country mansion. It contains one of Kneller's portraits of Queen Anne presented to the first Lord Bingley, her Lord Chamberlain, whose descendants still live there.

Travelling from one end of the country to the other, one thinks of Braemore House, near Fordingbridge in Hampshire, built by William Doddington and completed in 1583. It is a typical Elizabethan country house with some fine Brussels tapestries and some Queen Anne chairs. As with Rockingham, there are no outstanding national treasures, although it does contain one of the earliest seventeenth-century English carpets, and Sir Westrow Hulse, who lives there, has gone to great trouble creating a countryside museum for the exhibition of rural arts and agricultural machinery.

The visitor to Dorset can go to Smedmore, an early seventeenth-century house with a later façade, fine panelling and plasterwork, some Dresden and a few examples of the Dutch minor masters. In Oxfordshire, there is Rousham House, a Royalist garrison in the Civil War, which was remodelled by William Kent in 1738. Kent redecorated it although the house does contain some seventeenth-century panelling and an original staircase. There are 150 paintings, mostly portraits, some good furniture and porcelain and a collection of miniatures by the great Samuel Cooper. Outside is an example of the first phase of English landscape gardens, remaining almost as Kent left it, one of the few gardens of that date to have escaped alteration.

These are just a few examples, but to select any is invidious. It is not suggested that they are more important than that considerable number of very famous houses like Burghley, Stratfield Say, Holkham, Haddon (perhaps the most perfect house in all England) and Melbourne Hall in Derbyshire with its glorious gardens and exquisite furniture. Each is an integral part of the fabric of its own landscape and of the history of its corner of England.

Landscape is important to almost every one of these houses but, throughout this century, parks have been disappearing year by year in an unrecorded recession as towns have extended, mines been sunk, gravel worked and as farming has become more intensive. Every landscape park is obviously in some danger because of its age. Capability Brown began his work in about 1750, Repton died nearly a hundred and seventy years ago, and the great majority of the parks that have survived were in fact planted during the second half of the eighteenth century. Many are now past their prime because far too frequently succeeding generations have merely enjoyed what their ancestors planned for them without ensuring continuity by planting for themselves. Cirencester is the outstanding example of a park with a continual process of planting but, unfortunately, it is a rare example. It is not that those who came after the innovators were particularly lax or negligent, but for the first hundred years or so no replanting was necessary and the price of hardwoods took away much of the incentive either to fell or to plant, while growing taxation discouraged landowners from looking ahead. Over the last generation attitudes have changed and a number of parks have been replanted, but it is an expensive process. Even the tree guards which have to be put around every sapling, especially in a deer park, cost upwards of twenty pounds each. And, of course, apart from natural dangers of storm and tempest, such as the dreadful gales of January 1976, there is the twentieth-century problem of personal and corporate vandalism. Perhaps the most outstanding examples of this official corporate vandalism are the proposals for a by-pass and motorway through the superb Capability Brown parks at Petworth, Sussex, and at Chillington, Staffordshire, respectively. At Chillington, permission was given for the motorway almost immediately after the park had been declared a conservation area by the county council.

Landscapes are also at risk from taxation, for such exemptions from Capital Transfer and Wealth Tax as may be granted to historic houses and their contents may not be extended to the parks themselves, even though they must stand or fall together. And, of course, landscapes are not graded like buildings according to their importance, or listed and protected. It is true that the Historic Buildings Council can now make grants towards the preservation of land attached to historic buildings, and under the 1974 Town and Country Amenities Act, grants can be given for the upkeep of 'deer garden or other land' which is of outstanding interest. But the funds are already stretched and it is unlikely that more than a handful of gardens can be helped.

As financial pressures mount it is hard to imagine how many owners will resist the temptation to amalgamate parkland with farms so as to make the land more productive and maximise profits. The plough and the tree-saw threaten and we can only hope that some enlightened Government will allow owners to make a covenant not to alter the landscape and to allow some public access, and that in return they will be granted tax relief for maintenance and grant aid for repair and renewal.

It is a sobering thought that more houses are now under siege than at any time since the Civil War, though the weapons menacing them are fiscal rather than military and those directing them are Government forces.

CHAPTER FOUR The Country House under Siege

The bleak prospect in 1976 for those who treasure our country houses and what they represent and embody, is that there will be almost none in private hands by the turn of the century unless positive action is taken by the Government to help owners with maintenance. If it is thought desirable that they should survive, and if it is accepted that the cheapest way of ensuring their survival as interesting, lively, living-places is to allow their owners to carry on as stewards, then action on the part of the Government is needed. Perhaps we could follow the French example where owners of the more important houses are able to claim tax relief equal to 50 per cent of their expenditure on major repairs and the whole of their annual expenditure on maintenance. For in this country the burden is now a heavy one. As has been mentioned previously, to the weight of income and company taxation has been added the Capital Transfer Tax.

Country houses and works of art accessible to the public will be granted a degree of exemption from Capital Transfer Tax, but the fact remains that houses and contents cannot survive without the estates that sustain them. Only the land which the owner works himself as a farmer will benefit from the April 1976 additional Capital Transfer Tax concessions. This means that much of the estate will be taxed, or face crippling tax on transfer. And still in the wings lurks the threat of a Wealth Tax which will probably be levied along the same lines as Capital Transfer Tax – at the best. All this is not to mention the fact that repairs to historic buildings, far from qualifying for tax relief, *are liable to* Value Added Tax at 8 per cent.

'We have slaved for twenty years to rehabilitate this house, to make it an attraction to the public. We have lived in acute discomfort during that time and I am just not prepared to carry on if there is no chance whatsoever of my child inheriting.' Thus speaks the owner of an important, but not nationally famous, house in Yorkshire. And perhaps the problems facing owners can best be studied from specific examples.

Chillington Hall in Staffordshire stands on the same site as the home of the Giffards for the last eight hundred years. The present house dates in part from the early eighteenth century, but is largely the work of Sir John Soane and is one of his most notable houses. The Hall is the focal point of an agricultural and forestry estate of some 4000 acres. Without the estate the house could not continue as a private home. The

36

present owner, Peter Giffard, who succeeded in 1972, pointed out in a memorandum to the Select Committee on the Wealth Tax that because of the size of the house and many of the rooms, and because of the architectural features, the cost of living in a house such as Chillington must always exceed the cost of living in any house of ordinary size. To keep it moderately warm he needs 5000 gallons of heating oil per year; in a small farmhouse where he lived before he inherited he used 700 gallons. In his former home it took three hours to clean the windows; at Chillington, it takes a hundred.

It follows that if owners like Peter Giffard are to continue to live in and be responsible for houses like Chillington they must, of necessity, have incomes sufficient to support them. Chillington has received a number of grants from the Historic Buildings Council towards the cost of restoration, but even with this help the cost of maintenance is a very heavy burden. In his memorandum Peter Giffard stated that all the income not required for payment of wages, interest and other outgoings has been spent on repairs and improvement to various buildings on the estate. The majority of the farms have had at least one new building, and the cottages and houses have been modernised at the rate of three or four a year over the last decade. These improvements have been financed out of private resources, but those are now exhausted and their source – the sale of some outlying parts of the estate – is exhausted likewise. Future improvements must be financed out of income or borrowing and there are no liquid resources from which to pay any annual capital tax.

Since Peter Giffard submitted his memorandum to the Wealth Tax Committee, there have been some welcome signs of recognition of the problem by Government and during the passage of the 1976 Finance Act the Chancellor introduced a clause to give some relief from Capital Transfer Tax to maintenance funds for historic houses[1]. Unless relief is more far-reaching, however, the problem will still be acute and the threat of the Wealth Tax still hangs over the heads of owners like Peter Giffard. Unless the most sensitive and flexible arrangements are made, owners like him would be placed in an acutely unhappy position for, as he demonstrated in his memorandum, one of the greatest problems facing most country land owners is that they often have little in the way of liquid assets. To put any burdens additional to those imposed already could leave them with little alternative but to forsake their homes and disperse their contents. It would certainly be no adequate solution merely to exempt a building like Chillington

[1] However, the gesture, whilst establishing a precedent, proved to be a hollow one. Any owner wishing to take advantage of this scheme would have to set up a special Maintenance Fund. The capital placed in the Fund would be irrevocable and any family falling on hard times would be unable to reclaim the residue. The Fund could not be used for the maintenance of important chattels and any income from it would be liable for tax. The Fund itself would come under the 'perpetuities rule' and have to be wound up and given to charity after eighty years.

and its contents from additional taxes, for house and estate must stand together.

For the purpose of the rating valuation it is unlettable, as the valuer has to determine what rent it could command as a private dwelling-house on the open market. How many people could contemplate becoming the tenant of Chillington Hall? If, therefore, it is to survive there must be sufficient income from the remainder of the estate to discharge responsibilities for upkeep. The outcry would certainly be long and loud if this oasis, 7 miles from Wolverhampton, and many more miles from the nearest similar collection in public hands, were to vanish.

There is a clear appreciation of this type of situation among those responsible for encouraging and promoting tourism. At the time of the Wealth Tax debates in the summer of 1975, the Director of the Heart of England Tourist Board wrote to the Chancellor: 'It is clear that by encouraging country house owners to retain and properly maintain their property, and to allow public access to it, a great deal more recreational resources, and a great many more works of art and fine craftsmanship would be available to the British people than in any other way. An empty shell is far less attractive than the ensemble of the building, its grounds and its contents, and often also the continued association of its historical owners.'

This latter point was well brought out in the Victoria and Albert's exhibition: 'The Destruction of the English Country House'. The original social and economic function of the country house, as the centre of rural life, activity and industry, may have largely ceased, but the exhibition stressed the beauty of the phenomenon as a whole – house, park, furnishings, community – and how much would be lost if only the building survived, perhaps converted to some institutional use, or even retained as a lifeless museum. That such museums are often lifeless can be seen by anyone who visits Aston Hall in Birmingham. There the local authority has done its best to preserve and maintain an outstandingly fine Jacobean house, but almost all the original contents have gone and the life of the building with them. Drab rooms and sparse furnishings are a poor substitute, and uniformed attendants, however polite and helpful, seem very out of place in a domestic setting.

One cannot help but contrast Aston Hall with places like Weston Park on the Shropshire/Staffordshire border, some 20 miles away. To visit both of these historic houses in a day is a sobering experience. One leaves Aston Hall depressed at what has been lost, though grateful for what has been saved; one leaves Weston Park desperately anxious that what is there should remain. For Weston is not only a house, but a home; beautiful furniture, one of the best collections of Van Dykes in private hands, fine porcelain, silver, tapestry—all beautifully maintained and in bright, spacious surroundings. In 1975, 170,000 people visited Weston. Almost all of them toured the house and to judge from their comments found the experience refreshing. If Weston closed, the Midlands would be much the poorer, even if every object of interest from the house were crammed into one museum or another.

The problems facing all owners are similar, but it is often mistakenly thought that the larger the house the securer the future. That this is not necessarily the case was very forcibly brought home by the Earl of March, owner of Goodwood House in Sussex, in an article in the *Daily Telegraph*, 3 October 1974.

The urgency of the present situation arises from a combination of rising costs and increasing taxation, existing and proposed. The really fundamental problem has always been with us, the sheer size of many of these houses whether or not families are still living in them, or whether they are in reality museums and used for some other purpose. The size and number of the rooms still requires a basic minimum amount of cleaning, heating and light for the place to be habitable and to prevent deterioration and those wages, fuel and electricity bills have been rising faster than ever before over the last two years. Then there are the repairs and maintenance to the building which in an old house is regularly necessary . . . We are not simply trying to hang on to the house and its contents and live in it for our own benefit and enjoyment, we are endeavouring to share it with others and help them to gain as much pleasure and reward from doing so as we do . . . The number of staff we employ is entirely dictated by the size of the house, is mainly taken up with the maintenance of the house and the collection, rather than caring for personal needs . . . I never feel that I am the owner – only a steward for my lifetime, and not principally for the benefit of the family but for the whole community.

The Goodwood statistics are certainly formidable. The house has 9 major state rooms not occupied by the family, and 20 bedrooms, plus 26 rooms used as offices and 5 smaller reception rooms used by the family, and all this despite the fact that 30 rooms were demolished in 1969. The total cost of the house, excluding the direct cost. of opening it to the public, is measured in tens of thousands of pounds a year, for which the gardens, electricity, heating and cleaning account for three-quarters of the total. At Goodwood, the broad distribution of assets is 50 per cent land and cottages, 45 per cent furniture and paintings and only 5 per cent Stock Exchange securities. Thus the gross return, before charging any costs, on 95 per cent of the assets is very small – about $1\frac{1}{2}$ per cent.

Lord March obviously feels a very special responsibility towards all those who live or work on the estate and there is a special written housing policy in which it is stated that, provided circumstances do not drastically change, the company will continue to offer a house for the rest of their lives to pensioners and their wives who have occupied company (estate) houses. In the house itself, every major work of art is available for public view and access to scholars is always granted, whatever the time of year. However, the struggle to maintain the collection is an uphill one and, recently, three pictures have been sold, 50 per cent of the proceeds going to the Treasury. But, in recent years, only one painting and that of historic rather than artistic value, has been added to the collection. To show the dramatic and devastating effect a wealth tax would have on the contents of the house, Lord March stripped a room bare in the summer of 1975 and asked his visitors whether they approved of the results. They did not.

In Yorkshire one can see the problem facing the owner of a house of middle rank by going to Burton Constable. Though not the most famous Yorkshire house, it is a great Elizabethan mansion and the contents, though not of Woburn or Chatsworth standard, are fine, too; there is much original Chippendale furniture. It had been virtually derelict for a generation and John Chichester Constable and hs wife have struggled over the last fifteen years, with the aid of the Historic Buildings Council restoration grants, to make it an enjoyable place for people to visit from Hull and the surrounding countryside. That they do find it enjoyable is proved by the fact that 70,000 visitors come every year. But as with any vast house, there are constantly recurring problems of roof leakage, dry rot, and all the other accompanying ills that affect ancient buildings. The chances of the Chichester Constables being able to maintain the struggle during the next decade would be very remote if additional taxes were imposed. As the owner of Eastnor Castle, Mrs Hervey-Bathhurst, said: 'Even with the grant the cost of borrowing the 50 per cent that remains is almost impossible to find.'

One thing that emerges very clearly from studying the remarks of owners is how deeply they feel their sense of responsibility, but how pessimistic many of them are. As Michael Watson of Rockingham put it: 'By drawing on the moral responsibility that we feel for our inheritance, the Government has in us, the owners, the cheapest caretakers, but they must be in no doubt that if the pressure becomes too great many of us, particularly the younger ones, will not be prepared to sit it out.'

What also emerges very graphically in any study of the English country house is the way owners do struggle against adversity and in much discomfort to rescue what is in danger. Burton Constable furnishes an admirable example of this. Brympton D'Evercy in Devon another. There the contents of the house were sold to pay death duties and the house was then let to a school. The present owners managed to remove the school – which had not paid the rent – and they are turning the house back into a stately home.

We, ourselves, decorated the seven state rooms open to the public and by furnishing the rooms with the few pictures that remained, along with a few purchases, we have managed to get the house back some of the way to what it looked like. But we have gone against all the advice of trustees and solicitors trying to keep the house in one piece. We know the place cannot be sold – the probate was put at 4000 pounds – or let – the school could not find its rent for the last six years. The local authority already have one property in ruins and certainly would not like to be landed with another. We cannot pull the house down since it is scheduled Grade 1. I feel very strongly that unless we make the effort the house has no future. As it is we know we are running against the tides of time and will probably be the last generation to live here – but if we don't try no one else will.

What comes out time and time again in the words of those who own these houses is the fact that their visitors 'seem to enjoy seeing round a house that is well and truly lived in'; equally clear, is the fact that so many owners cannot afford any living-in, or in some cases even daily, help. 'In the winter we cannot afford to heat the three rooms with the wonderful ceilings. The garden was lovely but now instead of a full-time gardener and a pensioner we just have a pensioner for four hours a day.' Many owners have turned in despair to the National Trust.

I tried to give the castle to the National Trust for Scotland but they said they would need an endowment of 80,000 pounds which we could not provide, so now if we are taxed out of the house we have no option but to try and sell it, or take the roof off. We are very pleased to show it to the public but no one could say it was a paying proposition as they cause a lot of wear and tear. I am not really complaining but if one is not allowed enough of an income to keep it up what good is it going to be to posterity? We come under the heading of unearned income but I feel we should get tax relief to heat and repair the house.

Another owner writes: 'Every visitor without exception has been a simple town and country person and this is a point never taken by those who want to destroy our heritage. We have had fishermen, firemen, labourers, farmers and one man arrived last Sunday from the East End of London. He had cycled here (70 miles).' And from another letter: 'Nearly everybody comments on the completely different atmosphere of a house that is virtually a museum, and the general comment is that this one feels alive and much more interesting.'

The constantly repeated theme is one of public enjoyment and it is undeniable that museums, and particularly provincial museums with their scanty resources and almost complete lack of national financial support, are unprepared to take a flood of works of art when any such house closes. 'It is folly to attempt to foist a national responsibility on to local authorities' shoulders without preparation or calculation of the consequences', wrote the Director of the Brighton Art Gallery and Museum in *The Times* in 1975, 'nor can I believe that my fellow curators would welcome acquisitions, however magnificent, that had been acquired at such a cost. English country houses and collections are entities far more coveted and of historical significance and it should be the national policy to preserve them as entities.'

Perhaps the greatest attribute of country houses is the opportunity they give to countless visitors to see and enjoy works of art amid pleasant surroundings, and this at a time when even national museums find it impossible to display many of the treasures that they already have. This makes it the more tragic that current tax laws act as a positive disincentive to owners to make the architectural heritage more widely accessible to the public. Only about twenty-five of the greater houses, such as Woburn and Longleat, are treated like other leisure industries and allowed to set the cost of maintenance against tax. Other houses open to the public are only allowed to set the actual cost of opening – guides, guide books etc – against income. Things are ordered differently in France where the more a building is open to the public, the more the cost of running it can be set against tax. In 1974, in the Province of Auvergne alone, more than sixty houses opened to the public for the first time. In Britain, in 1975, Architectural Heritage Year, eighty-five fewer historic gardens were opened than in the previous year. It is, nevertheless, encouraging to note that 1976 did see the opening for the first time of a number of houses of great importance: Drumlanrig, Dumfriesshire; Plas Newydd, Anglesea; Houghton, Norfolk; Boughton in Northamptonshire; Chicheley, Buckinghamshire; and Pencarrow, Cornwall – to name just a few of the most significant.

But even the greatest show places, and there are very few which can offset all their operating costs against tax, have their difficulties. At Woburn, perhaps the most outstanding example of a great country house and popular attendant attractions, to which almost ¾ million people go each year, there are still problems. In a place that costs 400 pounds a time to clean the windows, 2000 pounds a year in materials alone to maintain the wall around the park, 10,000 pounds on heating, and where some 250 people are directly employed for most of the year, there is no overall profit shown. Even the Game Park, the biggest single attraction, does not pay its way, although obviously it is of value in bringing visitors to the estate.

The picture, however, is not one of unrelieved gloom. The Historic Buildings Council has been responsible for channelling grants of some 4 million pounds to historic houses over the last twenty years. But grants in themselves are not enough. Sometimes, as at Stonor Park, where 60,000 pounds of public funds were spent on maintenance and repair, the struggle was still too great and the owner had to give up. There is no certainty that the house will survive.

The story of Stonor is a melancholy illustration of what can happen to a great country house when its owner is no longer able to face the battle to maintain it. We must hope that it is not a forerunner of similar sad episodes and perhaps a brief outline of the Stonor history will both reinforce an argument, and act as a warning to those in positions of public authority, or those who have some chance of influencing national policy. Towards the end of 1975, Lord Camoys announced that he could no longer afford to live in Stonor or keep the house open to the public as had been his intention – an intention he had planned and worked towards for over twenty years. Instead the house was to be offered for sale and its contents dispersed separately.

Stonor Park is not a Knole or a Blickling, but its surroundings are glorious: a landscape park, now a nature reserve containing a herd of deer which was recorded here as long ago as the fourteenth century, and its history is as romantic as any in England. The house, with its elegant Georgian façade, bears traces of almost every period of domestic English architecture. Until Lord Camoys moved out it had been occupied by his family since the twelfth century and has one of the longest unbroken records set in the male line. Its particular importance, however, is as a Catholic shrine: the chapel at Stonor is one of only three in the country where Mass has never ceased to be celebrated. It has close links with Edmund Campion, the Jesuit martyr, and the most important recusant library in existence.

Its furnishings were not original, the vast majority of the contents having been auctioned in 1938. The tragedy, however, was that after that disastrous dispersal, the late Lord Camoys, who died in March 1976, decided to refurnish and restore the house after it had been derequisitioned at the end of the War. From 1955 he pursued his aim of making it into a house that would be interesting and attractive to visitors. He spent over 100,000 pounds, to which the Historic Buildings Council of England added a further 60,000 pounds in grants, and it was during the restoration that much evidence of so many periods of English architecture came to light. What had been casually assumed to be a Georgian house was seen to have traces of every period from Norman to Gothic behind its façade. While the restoration progressed, Lord Camoys collected as many suitable furnishing as he could including a fine collection of eighteenth-century Gothic furniture.

In 1975, however, the family's financial situation was such that he had no alternative but to put Stonor, its park and its contents up for sale. Before doing so, he had offered them to the National Trust, but the Trust could not accept this proposition without a large endowment which circumstances made it quite impossible to supply. Lord Camoys then offered the house to the Government through the Land Fund, but the Government turned this down because it has been the policy of all Governments not to take on historic houses unless they are in immediate danger of collapse or decay, or there appears to be no alternative prospect of saving them.

In January 1976 the sale took place and the contents were dispersed. At the time of writing, April 1976, the house stands empty, and no buyer has apparently come forward. One can only hope that, in the near future, Stonor's future will be secure. Be that as it may, the moral of the story will still hold good. When Lord Camoys made his offer, would it not have been better for the Government to have accepted, making the house accessible to the public rather than to see it used for institutional purposes, or sold to a foreign buyer? It would surely have been better for Stonor to have been retained, as Heveningham, with as much furniture as possible, and opened either by the Department of the Environment or endowed by the Government and given to the National Trust. Obviously, a State ownership solution did not commend itself to a Government which had proclaimed itself determined never to acquiesce in the dispersal of the heritage and to ensure 'that it becomes more readily available to the public generally'.

The nation did, however, accept Heveningham in Suffolk in lieu of Estate Duty as a charge on the Land Fund and the Department of the Environment now runs it as a country house. But vast Government departments are not geared to this sort of operation and one cannot envisage it happening in more than isolated examples.

Local authorities, too, find their resources stretched. Tatton Park in Cheshire, which is in many ways a great success story, and is run by the Cheshire County Council in conjunction with the National Trust which owns the property, still costs the ratepayers of Cheshire 100,000 pounds per year. How could a county like Yorkshire, still less a sparsely populated county like Norfolk, take on even half a dozen of its finest houses, if the owners departed?

One frequently hears the comment 'hand it over to the National Trust', but the Trust has repeatedly stressed, as it did to Lord Camoys, that it cannot afford to take on properties unless they are properly endowed. In 1975, in addition to Stonor, it had to turn down the offer of Arundel Castle, an important house by any standards, because the new Duke of Norfolk was unable to provide the necessary endowment. In almost every county there are similar stories of properties that the Trust has officially or unofficially been invited to take an interest in, but the financial resources available for maintenance were insufficient for it to do so. No one could fail to marvel at the magnificent job done by the Trust and the superb and efficient and very homely way in which it runs the many properties that it now owns. The 'National Trust solution' is a good one if an owner has to go but the key phrase here is 'if an owner has to go'. The National Trust has stated repeatedly, and especially during the last two years of financial debate, that the ideal solution is for the owner to be encouraged and indeed, helped, to stay. Their pleas and entreaties in this regard have not fallen on deaf ears as far as the general public is concerned. This was evident from the remarkable response to the petition to Parliament organised by the Historic Houses Association during the summer of 1975, which called on the Government to recognise the unique position of historic house and the needs for special provision to be made for their survival. This petition, which was on show in most houses open to the public, was signed by 1,116,253 people, plus 200,000 from 57 overseas countries (9 from behind the Iron Curtain!). It was presented to Parliament by Mr Ted Graham, the Labour Member for Enfield/Edmonton, the first

Chairman of the all-party Heritage Committee in Parliament. It was certainly the most public and probably the most successful enterprise undertaken by the Historic Houses Association.

The Association had its origins in 1966 in a committee of the British Travel Association, which in 1969 became a committee of the British Tourist Authority – the Historic Houses Committee. In those days it consisted of a small group of owners including the National Trust and the National Trust for Scotland, with an observer from the Department of the Environment. That it should have been instigated by national bodies responsible for tourism was an indication of how those entrusted with the development of this industry regarded our historic houses as one of our greatest tourist magnets.

In 1972, the Committee commissioned Mr John Cornforth to conduct an independent survey of the country houses of Britain and the problems facing their owners. This invaluable document, a mine of information for everyone interested in the country house problem, was published in October 1974 – entitled *Country Houses in Britain – Can They Survive?* By 1973, however, the Historic Houses Committee of the British Tourist Authority had been joined by a powerful new Historic Houses Association, with its own executive committee and executive secretary. It now represents over 400 owners of country houses most of which are regularly open to the public. In the spring of 1976, it launched an imaginative scheme for associate membership whereby members of the public could become 'Friends' and, in return for an annual subscription, be granted free admission to all but a handful of the houses in membership of the Association.

The Association campaigned vigorously during the debates on the Wealth Tax and Capital Transfer Tax and must indeed have been largely responsible for the detailed and unemotional arguments which led the Government to accept a number of its proposals during the passage of the Finance Act of 1975, whereby exemptions for transfer on death from the Capital Transfer Tax were granted for historic houses, their contents and surrounding land and other land of scientific or scenic interest. These exemptions were extended to lifetime gifts in the April 1976 Budget, but the criteria for determining eligibility were, according to the Chancellor, to be extremely strict.

Throughout, the Historic Houses Association has tried to make it plain that it has not been seeking preferential treatment for a selected group of people but for a selected group of properties, which not only form an integral part of our heritage but are a major source of attraction for native holiday makers as well as tourists. Its contention, like the National Trust's, is that these houses are best and most cheaply maintained by their owners. But it has sought to demonstrate – and the Cornforth Report did this most effectively – that very few houses in private ownership make a profit from visits, and if they do, it is invariably used for restoration. The Association suggests that, with limited tax concessions, and those already granted are for this purpose too limited, more houses, particularly the smaller ones – which make up the majority – would be opened to the public and stand a much better chance of survival. Successive governments have in their halting way recognised this since Sir Stafford Cripps set up the Gowers Committee in 1950, but now the danger is that the shutters will go up in many of the finest houses during the course of the next decade as owners die, or decide that the game is not worth the candle. The Historic Houses Association has been able to show just how much more costly it would be for the nation if Government now reversed the trend of past policies and accentuated economic difficulties so that owners did give up their struggle. Even to keep a few of the more spectacular and idiosyncratic houses inevitably would be a continuing drain on public funds. Even Heveningham Hall which the State bought through the Land Fund for 300,000 pounds costs the tax payer 30,000 pounds a year to maintain.

The Historic Houses Association made forceful representations to the Select Committee on the Wealth Tax and it was noticeable that the Committee in its Report took a very constructive approach to the problems facing the heritage, for instance, recommending that conditional exemption from Capital Transfer Tax and Wealth Tax should apply to maintenance funds on the same conditions as for the houses, subject to control and supervision. The Chancellor of the Exchequer, however, announced that he would not be bringing in a Wealth Tax in 1976 although he still intended to proceed with such a tax at a slightly later date. The Association's campaign therefore continues for this further threat still hangs over the heads of many owners.

Everything therefore points to the fact that if the siege of the country house is to be lifted, the Government must lift it. Some enterprising owners might find ways to stave off impending doom; some might persuade local authorities or other bodies to assist them; some might be able to afford to give their houses to the National Trust; some might be able to set up country house trusts. But the vast majority of houses, great and small, will close once and for all during the next twenty years, unless Government is prepared to give a generous measure of exemption from current fiscal burdens and to remove the threats of new ones. It is up to those in authority to decide whether the English country house is worth keeping or not. By the year 2000, the country house as we know it could either be a fond memory, or the majority of those still standing could be open and making as vigorous and as vital a contribution to the cultural and social life of the nation, and to the tourist economy, as they do today.

CHAPTER FIVE Urban Dignity, Decency and Decay

Though there are still breathtaking exceptions, our larger towns and cities are something of a disappointment to the visitor. The city, which ought to be the highest expression of man's civilised moulding of his environment, is too often ugly, out of scale and out of sympathy with the requirements of civilised living and the demands of the cultured mind. This is not merely because of insensitive redevelopment since the Second World War. Thirty years ago, the first Lord Kennet, writing in *Character of England* (1947), remarked that: 'The spirit of our towns is a dejected spirit . . . our countryside is a success . . . but our towns on the whole are a failure. They are not beautiful, and they are not convenient. They are not even cheap. Large sums have been wasted on them on ornament which does not beautify, and display which does not impress.'

Unfortunately, what was appropriate to an historical analysis in 1947 is even more true today. The years since the War have seen a distortion of scale and a disturbance of symmetry that has gone far to ruin such urban treasures as we had. Nowhere is this truer than in London itself. The London which replaced the city devastated by the Great Fire in 1666, enhanced and adorned by Georgian developers, was not long inviolate. So great was the havoc caused during the first confident urban treatures as we had. Nowhere is this truer than in London itself. The London which replaced the city devastated by the Great Fire in 1966, enhanced and adorned by Georgian developers, was not long south-west corner of Trafalgar Square. By 1877, William Morris had founded the Society for the Preservation of Ancient Buildings. This in itself was two years after the Society for Photographing Old London had been established because so many of the ancient buildings were being demolished, buildings such as the last of the sixteenth-century galleried coaching inns in the City.

The later years of the nineteenth century witnessed something of a battle between developers and conservationists, but although the developers triumphed the scale of their buildings was limited, largely by the London Building Act of 1888. This restricted the height of buildings to 80 feet, or the width of the street on which they stood, a restriction which played a crucial part in the development of London until it was removed in the 1950s. It meant, for instance, that although such glories as Nash's Regent Street, Norfolk House, Devonshire House, Grosvenor House, the eighteenth-century Grosvenor and Berkeley Squares, and the great Adelphi Terrace itself, were all replaced by impersonal and undistinguished slabs like those on Park Lane between the Dorchester and Grosvenor House, the scale of the new buildings was not so over-powering as to shadow totally such gems as remained.

During the War our enemies became the allies of those for whom age meant decay and among the thousands of buildings destroyed was nearly a third of the City. There was thus a great excuse for those who advocated another and wider rebuilding programme. The first years after the War were years of controlled rebuilding of bombed buildings and government offices, although the meticulous and brilliant achievements of the Poles and Russians in rebuilding Warsaw and Leningrad were not emulated here. By 1954, when the building licenses were removed, the bulldozers were able to encroach in force, and the last twenty years have seen a total transformation of the London scene and skyline. One has only to look at some of Canaletto's views, at nineteenth-century aquatints, or even at photographs taken up to the outbreak of the War, to realise that more has been done to alter the face of London in the last twenty years than in the previous two hundred. Although each change has brought new and more vigorous protest, the prospect is that the next ten or twenty years will see a greater transformation yet.

The conservation movement has come into its own, but for London it may well have come too late. If fifteen years ago it had been agreed to keep the centre of London low-scaled and to preserve the façades, as in Rome, Paris and Amsterdam, perhaps it would have been otherwise. However, a survey of some of the things that have happened in London might perhaps point some useful lessons for the future, and even reinforce the somewhat slender chances of success which the conservationists have in prospect.

One of the main factors in the destruction of much of London's architectural fabric has been the ease with which official bodies have been able to redevelop. For instance, in the squares of Bloomsbury, the London University bulldozers have plied remorselessly along the course laid down by Sir Leslie Martin in 1959. A catalogue of what has gone, and what is still threatened, makes gloomy reading and any Rip Van Winkle returning to town after a twenty year slumber, would find himself adrift in a London he would hardly recognise! No longer could he even go into the stores that were the Mecca of so many shoppers as recently as the 1960s: no Maples, Marshall and Snellgrove, Gamages, nor Army and Navy; these and many more have either gone forever or been redeveloped.

Over thirty Victorian churches and some earlier ones, perhaps not distinguished in themselves, but local landmarks of great prominence, such as St Stephen's Rosslyn Hill, or Holy Trinity in Bishop's Bridge Road, have been closed or demolished. The very stations where the visitor alights have, in some cases, altered beyond recognition, expecially Euston[1]. Covent Garden market has been taken across the river, and nearby there are nine separate schemes which will eventually result in the removal of three-quarters of the existing buildings in Charing Cross Road, to be dominated by Town and Cities' massive tower block on the north-east corner of Cambridge Circus. These tower blocks – Warren Street, Centre Point and the grotesque one at the Elephant – dominate London and make one fear for posterity's regard for the twentieth century. They represent neither good working environments, nor good planning decisions.

In 1973 Christopher Booker wrote that: 'It seems that the tide of conservationism has now broken through to become a major factor in shaping London's future.' Certainly things have been done to arrest the onward march of the developer. In Covent Garden extra buildings have been listed – a quadrupling of the old list of 82, of which 48 were threatened with demolition. The scheme for Piccadilly Circus has been delayed, while the City of Westminister Council seeks a greater degree of public participation. And in general, it is harder to get schemes passed by more vigilant local authorities.

But the difficulties facing the conservationists were well illustrated in August 1975, during the saga of Tedworth Square. The Cadogan Estates sold large parts of the Square, and the north-east side was due for demolition. The Kensington and Chelsea Planning Committee put the houses into the Royal Hospital conservation area and the GLC backed their plans. Unfortunately, the Council mislaid the GLC's reply and during the intervening altercations over what could and could not be done before specific committees had had their official meetings, the demolition men moved in and were only restrained by the concerted efforts of the residents.

Local authorities within the Greater London area have varying reputations[2]. Sometimes the same local authority is both guilty of enormity and also responsible for achievement. One would have thought that the bleak areas of Gospel Oak would have persuaded the Camden Borough Council to preserve its fine nineteenth-century streets wherever possible. Yet one finds its Housing Development Committee taking, and then, after being challenged, reaffirming, a decision to tear down a large part of Fitzroy Road in the Primrose Hill environmental area, in order to put up a new row of flats, a decision opposed by the local civic society and the local ward Labour Party. In spite of the latter's intervention, Camden Council still seems to stigmatise pressure groups as representing 'the middle class comfortably off'.

And yet the same Camden Council is responsible for the most sensitive restoration of Keats's house at Hampstead, on which it lavished 70,000 pounds and took advantage of the fact that a decorator's order book

[1] Currently there is a great battle to save Liverpool Street.
[2] The GLC itself does have a well run Historical Buildings Division staffed by intelligent, sensitive people and with some outstanding schemes to its credit.

of 1820 made it possible to choose not only wallpaper patterns that
were in existence at the time, but also those that were popular in the
sort of circle in which Keats and his friends moved. They collected period
furniture and restored the library and altogether gave an excellent
example of how a local authority can make significant achievements in
conservation.

However, important as it is that individual houses, such as Keats's,
should be preserved, it is the conservation of whole areas of perhaps
individually undistinguished houses that so often is the key to safeguarding atmosphere and maintaining the warmth, unity and humanity
of scale which has so often been destroyed in new developments. This
is why it is comforting to know that the Grosvenor Estates have
committed themselves to the preservation of 200 acres of Belgravia.
One hopes that they will be able to withstand the pressure to redevelop,
for the whole area is of interest and Eaton Square and Belgrave Square
themselves contain perhaps the finest remaining examples of late
Regency architecture in London.

Preservation and conservation not infrequently make good economic
sense and one can only trust that the financial constraints of recent
years will make councils think again before tearing down property that
could easily be brought up to a high standard of comfort and convenience
at much less cost than erecting an impersonal modern house or flat. An
example of this is provided by Hackney Borough Council's decision in
May 1975 to knock down fifty early Victorian houses in Shepherdess
Walk, Hoxton. Over half of these were listed buildings, but the Council
claimed that they were not worth rehabilitating and that they should
be removed in order to extend the neighbouring park. Opponents of the
scheme claimed that the houses could be renovated at a cost of about
10,000 pounds each, whereas the park could be extended by taking over
a derelict factory site. Bearing in mind the fact that the average cost of a
two bedroom council flat in Greater London is now (1976) some
30,000 pounds, one finds it difficult to justify this sort of decision from
the guardian of the public purse.

Not all redevelopment is unnecessary or insensitive. The Victoria
Street changes, providing as they have a new view of Westminster
Cathedral, are a case in point. But this well mannered exercise is,
alas, not typical. Far too often scale is sacrificed for pseudo-grandeur
and everything subjugated to the new. Nowhere is this truer than in
the City itself. The square mile known as the City was, until the War,
basically a medieval town with its courts and alleys following the
pattern laid down centuries ago. It was a place of great contrasts
ranging from churches to merchants' houses, and Georgian livery
stables. It survived changes of generations and parts of it even escaped
the Great Fire of 1666. Parts of it, too, escaped the Blitz, when a third of
the City was laid waste, but after the War, the authorities were determined that the City should not be rebuilt piecemeal and early post War
planning legislation facilitated comprehensive development, if necessary

through compulsory purchase and drastic alteration of traffic routes and rights of way. No longer in the parts due for rebuilding was there the centuries old discipline of permanent streets, frontages, public thoroughfares. All could be modified by local or national decree.

What could have been an opportunity, unfortunately came at a time when architects were at their least inspired. As a result, we had the total destruction of the scale of intimacy which had marked the old city. Tower blocks dominate the skyline even within yards of St Paul's itself. The trend has continued, though occasionally local pressure saves a particular landmark. A visit to the City is a depressing experience for anyone who possesses either a memory or a book of photographs of what was there before. And the process of change has also been a process of depopulation, for hardly anyone lives in the asphalt and concrete jungle of the square mile. That a place, which still prides itself – and quite rightly – on its maintenance of ceremonial tradition, could have encouraged one of the most wanton acts of architectural devastation in the history of man is one of the more curious paradoxes of the twentieth century, and shows that taste and discernment and wealth do not always go together. For the sadness is that hardly a building erected in the City since the War deserves more than a passing glance, nor is it likely that many will be regarded with affection by future generations. Perhaps recognition of this is in part responsible for the spectacular success of the St Paul's Cathedral appeal for 3 million pounds for essential restoration work. At least we have the consolation of knowing that Wren's masterpiece is likely to remain, even if it is hemmed in by the grotesque buildings that cluster around. For it can not be seen from many of the old familiar places and, indeed, can scarcely be discerned at all, until one comes upon it, noble, grand and glorious, submerged in the architectural debris of the twentieth century.

The urge to modernise, to improve, to redevelop, to change, is not a peculiar twentieth-century one. Without it, no city would ever have progressed beyond the meanest dwellings and we owe to it many of the charms and much of the dignity for whose loss it is now responsible. The tragedy of the twentieth-century application of the urge lies in the dearth of inspired architects around at the time when so much money was available to indulge the whims and the fancies of those who would improve and change. As we have seen, London has suffered incalculably as a result. And not just London: Newcastle, Birmingham, Manchester, Liverpool, Glasgow, have suffered too, but, with the exception of Newcastle, which until the reforming zeal of Mr T. Dan Smith was unleashed upon it was a charming Georgian city, gracious and well planned, most of the others do not evoke so many sadnesses.

Before looking in detail at some of the other black spots and some of the challenges that lie ahead, it would be as well to consider the dilemma which has faced so many local authorities since the War. These local authorities are important because, for better or for worse, Parliament has vested in English local government an almost total power over planning. True, the Secretary of State for the Environment has the opportunity to overturn planning decisions, but only if they are appealed against and the difficulties of coordinating strategy, and the frequent absence of local information, have very often acted as deterrents to would-be objectors. And even when an objection is lodged and an appeal heard, the expert evidence and official figures, on which decisions are said to have been based, give the local authority a considerable advantage and often lead to the Minister – who cannot know each local area – deciding in favour of local government.

But what is the nature of this dilemma? Local authorities need money to supply essential services, money depends upon the rateable value of their areas, and with the decline in population in city centres, the most valuable parts of their areas, they depend increasingly upon commercial ratepayers. Because old buildings are sometimes inconvenient and old streets sometimes over congested, there is often a great temptation to pull down the one and widen the other. The revenue generated by development companies is an added attraction. So one finds that those in the local council chamber, frequently persuaded by self-styled experts on design and taste, are cajoled into thinking that they are serving posterity as well as the individual ratepayer, and voter, by allowing wholesale change to take place.

And so many of these changes took place before the individual objections of the articulate became the outraged protest of groups of civilised people. Nowhere is this truer than in Bath where a perfect Georgian city, one of the supreme cities of Europe, was vandalised before the conscience of the nation was awakened to what was happening. Bath will provide an interesting study, but first, it might be as well to establish certain general facts and factors in the changing urban scene.

As a result of the Parliamentary initiative of people like Lord Duncan-Sandys, the concept of the important (listed) building and the need to treat certain areas as 'conservation areas' has been firmly established in law and is increasingly recognised by planning authorities. There are now some three thousand conservation areas and something like 3 million pounds is spent annually on grants and loans for their care. Within and outside them are 240,000 listed buildings which have statutory protection from arbitrary alteration and demolition. However, in spite of such welcome legislative developments and the growing awareness of what is in peril which has inspired so many able young people and which led, for instance, to the continent-wide European Heritage Year, the devastation and destruction is not at an end.

The foremost reason for this is financial. Although governments of both political persuasions have shown an increasing appreciation of the need for adequate and comprehensive conservation policies and have sought, as in Chester, Chichester, York and above all, Bath, to work with local government, the amount of money made available centrally for conservation in general and the preservation of old buildings in particular, is very small indeed and in the context of gross national expenditure totally insignificant.

Substantial sums, however, are needed to cope with one of the central problems facing those who have responsibility for our towns' and cities' transport. Most of our urban centres were based on an elaborate railway system fed by horse-drawn vehicles and the basic form of most cities and towns, and even villages, is unsuited to the general use of the motor car and the lorry. Although some might argue that cars themselves are an unsuitable form of transport for general use in town centres, either accommodating or excluding the car and the delivery vehicle does present problems. That they can be solved in a fairly novel and exciting way can be seen to some extent in York, where a whole area of the old city has been given over to pedestrians, a solution seen perhaps at its most spectacularly exciting in Copenhagen. But no one can pretend that the 'pedestrians only' idea is easy and even the 'park and ride' schemes as operated in Oxford present difficulties, not least that of consumer resistance when it was first suggested.

London with its massive traffic flow and almost eternal congestion has this problem, as most others, in major degree. Some Londoners feel that London is a worse place to live in than ever before. As one of them said to me, 'The Planning Departments march across town and country-side, building huge roads, spoiling communities and dumping people in the barren wilderness on the outskirts, miles from their own jobs and friends.' Some of the greatest controversies in the capital in recent years have concerned the three ringways. These motorways, consisting of two inner ringways (1 and 2) and an outer orbital route, were approved in principle by the Conservative Government in February 1973, but the Labour Party on the GLC was pledged to revise this decision. It did so, with considerable sighs of relief in many political quarters, soon after it was elected in April 1973. The 'Homes before Roads' campaign had won a signal victory. However, Ringway 3, renamed the Outer Orbital Route, remains a firm proposal and the present Government has on numerous occasions stated its commitment to giving it a higher priority in the roads programme. Though there are those who support this there is undoubted concern at the demolition and destruction that will be necessary if it is built, much of it many miles into the countryside.

Many local authority officials see themselves being used as whipping boys and resent it. They point the accusing finger at Government and say it is all very well to be encouraged to go in for conservation and improvement of the environment, but where is the money coming from? Their cry is not entirely unreasonable for although the Treasury has provided help from time to time, for example during Operation Eyesore in 1972, its generosity has been intermittent to say the least. Operation Eyesore was a Government financed plan to clean up the debris of industrialisation and had some spectacular successes: in Manchester and Newcastle, old Victorian buildings positively gleamed, though in Newcastle, admiration of what has been achieved is overshadowed by recollection of what was pulled down before. In Glasgow, there has been a special Government grant of 5 million pounds for environmental improvement. But Glasgow is a city of problems and has suffered considerably from the property developers' tendency to move in and build, and then happily leave office blocks empty because rates are not due and losses can be offset against other investments. In Glasgow, for instance, in 1975, there were 2 million square feet of empty office space – the equivalent of ten Centre Points. Manchester, too, had a precinct centre 75 per cent empty in the same year. Instead of too much money chasing too few goods, it is often too many shops chasing too few people.

But just as local authorities have genuine problems, so do owners, corporate and individual. One can sympathise considerably with those responsible for maintaining the buildings housing London clubs. In a *Country Life* article in February 1976, Marcus Binney pointed out that the London club was becoming one of our fragile national institutions. The last half of 1975 saw the closure of the United Service Club, the St James's Club, and the Guards' Club moving from its own premises to join the Cavalry Club. In January 1976, there were fifty clubs belonging to the Association of London Clubs and pessimists were suggesting that by 1986 there would be no more than ten surviving. If this happens, the nation will be left with a series of 'architectural albatrosses'. For no less than seven of the Clubs are listed as Grade 1 buildings, and another four are Grade 2 – and even some of those that are not listed, such as the Constitutional, are not without their attractions and importance to the streets in which they stand. The loss of Decimus Burton's Athenaeum or Barry's Reform Club, would be even more significant and regrettable than the demolition of the Euston Arch. The importance of the Clubs is all the greater because London has so very few important town houses left, and many of the City livery halls were damaged or destroyed during the War. To quote *Country Life* again, 'The principal rooms of the major clubs form an unrivalled series of nineteenth-century interiors and many contain either original or very appropriate furnishings or paintings... Many have major collections of books on particular subjects... In present financial circumstances, all these must be threatened by attrition.' Rising staff costs together with the general inflationary spiral are making it more and more difficult for the clubs to put up subscriptions without losing too many members. The future is bleak and their listing may not save them.

It is possible that these, and other buildings, will feature in a future edition of that alarming book *Goodbye London* (1973). Happily some of the book's warnings of what was at risk were heeded, but there are still in 1976 hundreds of plans large and small affecting every part of the city; and that in London and elsewhere listing is not a sufficient protection is most graphically illustrated in the Save Report. Save Britain's Heritage, a committee inspired by, and largely consisting of, environmental journalists, was formed during Architectural Heritage Year to give publicity to proposals for demolishing historic buildings, and although its activities were not without success, their Report published at the end of 1975 showed that we were still destroying officially listed buildings at the rate of one a day.

In the first six months of 1975, Heritage Year itself, permission was given to demolish no less than 182 buildings in England and Wales, and hundreds more were partially demolished or drastically altered and their setting ruined. The Report says, 'Even given the facts that more buildings are being placed on the lists each year, the loss suggests a disturbing inability to protect the very buildings that they have singled out to be worthy of preservation.' Its obituary on Heritage Year is perhaps a little unkind but its strictures should not go unheeded.

Heritage Year has possibly been unfortunate in coinciding with a year of economic recession unprecedented since the Second World War. And as a result, many local authorities simply abandoned their Heritage Year projects. But the Department of the Environment which has so ardently supported the idea of Heritage Year found itself effectively ordering local authorities to ignore it under the guise of cutting out all unnecessary expenditure. The list of projects put forward to celebrate Heritage Year, projects which in any civilised society should have been normal civic activities, makes pathetic reading. The emphasis on spending public money on superficialities was fundamentally mistaken and the campaign should have pressed instead for the use of legal sanctions that now lie dormant and for fiscal reforms that would encourage owners to maintain and use their buildings in the public interest ... The local authority and the public corporation have assumed the grim mantle of vandalism which once lay on the shoulders of the property developer. For given an alert public opinion and a determined local authority there is precious little which a private property developer can get away with, yet Britain is, alas, cursed with some of Europe's most philistine public officials.

Perhaps some of these words are a little harsh, for the sanctions that can be invoked against those who either pull down listed buildings or allow them to decay were not until very recently at all daunting. But the Save Committee's criticisms are difficult to ignore as one looks through the photographs of some of the buildings which were pulled down during Heritage Year. The Tapestry Factory at Streatham Street, London, pulled down by Town and City Properties; the Church of the Saviour, Bolton, pulled down by the Church of England; Nile Street, Birmingham, pulled down by the Corporation; the former town hall in Leominster demolished by the Council; the Queen's Hotel, in Micklegate, York, demolished by its owner; Wellington House, Westminster, pulled down by Land Securities; the fabulous nineteenth-century St Enoch's station in Glasgow, destroyed by British Railways; and the loss of the Westminster Palace Hotel, once the finest and largest hotel in London. So the grim list continues with photographs of buildings from Swindon to Aylesbury, Stroud and Wootton-under-Edge, all gone or under threat.

The Save Committee quotes the injunction laid down for German Master Masons: 'When a master dies and another comes he shall not remove the first master's masonry already set nor throw away the unset but hewn stones, that the master whose work has been interrupted by death may not be put to shame.' When one sees the striking Hylands House in Chelmsford dating from the early years of the nineteenth century and forming the centrepiece of a Repton Park and learns that its owner, the Chelmsford District Council, no less, is allowing it to decay and has refused three private schemes for restoration, one could hope that those words from medieval Germany would be heeded in some of the Council Chambers in the land. For Hylands House is not alone. Buckingham Town Hall was in similar danger at the end of 1975 as was Sedbury Park designed by Smirk, and Prince Street, Hull – a listed street in a conservation area and one of the few remaining small scale streets in the city centre – is still threatened with demolition rather than rehabilitation. And so one could go on, through Berkhamstead; the Beaumont Cavalry Barracks, Aldershot; Scotch Street, Carlisle, to Merthyr Tydfil (where the council had plans to demolish all but two of the town's listed buildings) to Sutton Coldfield, Northampton and Leicester, Reading and Plymouth and Denby and Bristol. The catalogue is unending. Perhaps the work and warnings of the Save Committee will have borne fruit in some cases by the time this is published. What is certain is that many of the buildings they sought to preserve will have disappeared in a pile of rubble.

And there are many piles of rubble to testify to past destruction. A book about them was published in 1975 – *The Rape of Britain* by Colin Amery and Dan Cruickshank. In his foreword, John Betjeman remarks, 'In my mind's ear, I can hear the smooth tones of the committee man explaining why the roads must go where they do regardless of the old towns they bisect. In my mind's eye, I can see the swish perspective tricked up by the architect's firm to dazzle the local councillors.'

The scenes of rape from Aberdeen to Truro are startling, a dreary commentary on the activities of the soulless and the insensitive. Nowhere have those activities had a more devastating effect than in Bath. Bath was the Queen of English cities and indeed, unrivalled in Europe as a surviving example of an elegant age, planned with symmetry and sensitivity and nearly untouched for two hundred years until, in the 1950s, a development plan was drawn up. Today the results of that plan tower over Bath: an austere, impersonal, square and scaleless hotel squats ugly and depressing on the river bank above Adam's Pulteney Bridge, one of the last of Europe's old town bridges. Where eighteenth-century houses once stood, a modern technical college now dominates. New blocks of flats have replaced Georgian homes, which could have been restored at much less cost and provided more human and attractive dwellings for their occupants, and shopping arcades which might have graced Wigan Pier have replaced bow-fronted stores. As Lord Goodman remarked in the foreword to Adam Fergusson's *Sack of Bath* (1973): 'It is incredible that a city so loved for the character and beauty of its buildings should have suffered the indignities already inflicted on it and should remain exposed to increasing and even lethal risks. If this can happen to Bath, there is no architectural shrine safe from violation.' John Betjeman writes:

> Now houses are units and people are digits,
> And Bath has been planned into quarters for midgets...
> Goodbye to old Bath. We who loved you are sorry.
> They've carted you off by developer's lorry.

But so much was there that in spite of acres of Georgian rubble and in spite of the distortion of scale that has been inflicted upon a gracious city, much does remain. Although 3000 listed buildings have been pulled down there are well over 20,000 left. Bath, one of the towns singled out by Government in 1966 for a special conservation study now has one of the most vigorous local amenity societies in the land, the Bath Preservation Trust. Under the chairmanship of Sir Christopher Chancellor and led by Pamela Lock, an Australian Boadicea, the Preservation Trust has achieved much. Every plan is monitored, logged and listed and every application carefully studied and where necessary challenged. Bath City Council has been persuaded that destruction and redevelopment is not the answer to every problem. In 1968 the Buchanan Conservation Study of Bath said: 'In no case has the Corporation bought an unfit dwelling for occupation or re-occupation ... the emphasis is on closure with a view to demolition. Of course, some of the houses pulled down were in a bad state, but many of them could have been rehabilitated and were far from slums. There were small proud Georgian homes, the kind that many people would sacrifice their savings for.'

In spite of the successes of the Preservation Trust in helping to create a new attitude even the Trust was not immune from dissension. In 1975 there was some quarrel about its aims and objectives when there was a move to expel a member whose firm was demolishing a house which the Trust had asked the Department of the Environment to list. There was danger of the Trust losing support as two groups quarrelled amongst themselves, the 'conservation at any price' lobby likely to deter the more objective and discerning supporter.

Though there is far too much urban destruction and decay, and though visitors to Gloucester and Lincoln and Bristol who knew the towns only a few years ago throw up their hands in horror at what has gone, every story is not one of disaster. Though the character has been ripped out of towns as different as Worcester and Grimsby, the conservation movement and the coming of the conservation area has brought a new appreciation of our heritage.

The Civic Trust which began in Norwich (where, appropriately enough, one of the most outstandingly successful of Architectural Heritage Year schemes, the Winsom scheme, has brought new life and beauty to an old and neglected area) has burgeoned during the last two decades and been given great encouragement by the passing of the Civic Amenities Act. Indeed it was the President of the Civic Trust, Lord Duncan-Sandys, who piloted that Act through Parliament and whose persistence as much as anything else was responsible for the Town and Country Amenities Act – the logical successor passed in 1974.

There are now local civic societies in all parts of the country and a list of them is given in Appendix 2. The Civic Trust makes awards and holds conferences to discuss what is being done. Its publications record some refreshing achievements, such as the protection of traditional street character side by side with new and up-to-date living accommodation in Cirencester, or the way in which the Hammerson group of companies has redeveloped a whole block of shops and offices in the centre of Salisbury and the revival of the Barbican district of Plymouth.

It is perhaps in Edinburgh that one sees the most startling contrast of failure and achievement. There the south side of the city, including much of the medieval town round the castle and the land immediately to the south of it, seems to have been regarded as expendable in the interests of academic expansion and road engineering. The University redeveloped most of George Square and its surroundings and did not exactly put harmony of old and new and the preservation of all that was best at the head of its priorities. The rest of the area was allowed to deteriorate while the ring road controversy continued and the city was unable to decide on an overall shopping policy. At the end of the War many structurally sound and architecturally pleasing houses were allowed to decay and be demolished purely because they did not have bathrooms when their modernisation could have been achieved at a fraction of the cost of new houses and the city's appearance, as well as the comforts of residents, would have gained immeasurably. To walk round the old town is to have dismal reminders of what has gone and what is almost certainly going. But the active campaigning of the Cockburn Association – the oldest of all the civic societies – has drawn not only local, but also national, attention to what is at stake and there is a hope that much of what remains of the old town will still be saved. It is incomprehensible that the old town, an essential foil to the new, and containing some architecture of equal distinction, should be neither a conservation area nor a Heritage Year project. Across the city, however, in the New Town, the finest Georgian city in the country after Bath, the story is happily different.

This spacious classical area, designed to accommodate the wealthy citizens of Edinburgh and their servants who wished to move out of the overcrowded medieval city clustering around the castle, remains a living city. Its regularly patterned streets, squares and crescents laid out on sloping ground have a compelling beauty. Charlotte Square was designed by Robert Adam and much of the rest of the new town, almost all designed by Scottish architects, is worthy to rank with the work of the master. By 1970 the condition of many of the buildings after two centuries of northern weather was perilous indeed and in that year the Scottish Civic Trust organised a remarkable conference on the conservation of Georgian Edinburgh. Their initiative was supported by local associations, residents and representatives of the Government and the Corporation and the conference was addressed by, among others, John Betjeman, Professor Buchanan, Lord Halford and Count Sforza, who indicated that Edinburgh was as important to the culture and the civilisation of Europe as Venice and said that he had never attended a meeting of similar character that had gathered so large an audience. It was as a result of this conference, that highlighted both the treasures and the problems of retaining them, that the Edinburgh New Town Conservation Committee was formed. The funds were provided, two thirds from the Government one third by the Corporation, for distribution by the Committee for owners to restore walls, roofs and external features.

The largest grants were offered to owners restoring properties with low rateable value. For most of these properties were on the 'scattered fringe' of the New Town where decay was most apparent. Residents were circulated with information such as a leaflet called *Your House Is a National Treasure* and inviting applications for grants for restoration. At the headquarters of the Committee, presided over by a genial Dubliner, Desmond Hodges, advice was given on fixtures and fittings from fanlights to door-knockers and every scheme for restoration was carefully examined to make sure that what was done would be authentic. In order to provide a focal point for interest an example of Georgian Edinburgh at its elegant best, 7 Charlotte Square, has been opened by the National Trust for Scotland to show the domestic social conditions of the eighteenth century. An audio-visual show tells the story of the New Town and of the development of Georgian architecture.

The Committee procedure for giving a grant is extremely thorough. When the inquiry is received the property is inspected by the Director or one of his staff. The net annual valuation of all affected properties is listed and averaged (for grant purposes). The category and historical notes of the property are then extracted from the statutory list of buildings of architectural and historical importance and a summary made of all visible defects in the external structure and of all deviations from the original design. When a number of owners are involved in an application a meeting is held and the Director goes through his preliminary reports, discussing the desirable work and explaining the types of grants that might be offered. The applicants themselves are advised to appoint a committee with authority to commission architects and quantity surveyors with a view to finding out exactly what is needed.

The procedure is meticulously set out in a series of guide sheets issued by the Committee and the very professional approach to the problem is certainly justified by the results so far achieved. In Fettes Road, for instance, where the pilot conservation scheme was launched, some 43,000 of the 49,000 pounds total cost was furnished by the Committee. At 2 Scotlands Street, the Committee provided 116 out of 199 pounds. Grants can be as low as 40 pounds because the Committee works on the basis of 'a stitch in time'. If it is allowed to continue its work – financial stringency threatens here as elsewhere – the future of the New Town will be assured, tremendous impetus given to Scottish craftsmanship and a model conservation project will continue to be an inspiration and example to the rest of Europe.

South of Edinburgh and just over the border lies one of the most historic towns in England. Berwick-upon-Tweed, today a town of 12,000 people, has a unique and colourful history. It has been fought over and 'owned' both by the English and the Scots. Because it was normally specifically mentioned in treaties, but was omitted from that which concluded the Crimean War, a local legend persists that the town is still at war with Russia. Border feuding and exciting history apart, Berwick, with its massive walls and fortifications, is a town of enormous charm. One in ten of its houses is listed as being of architectural or historic interest, a higher proportion than anywhere else in the country. Yet Berwick, with its strategic position and its three bridges had the problems of traffic and industrial stagnation common to many towns of similar size. As the town's fortunes declined, so did the state of its buildings, and many of the citizens moved out to the initially more comfortable housing estates beyond the walls. The process continued without exciting undue attention until, in the early seventies, it was realised that unless something was done to arrest the process of decay and deterioration, the attractions of Berwick would be memories rather than realities. Luckily the realisation did not come too late, although inevitably some demolition had occurred. A Town Preservation Trust was established to arouse public interest, improve standards of planning and urge local authorities to come to the assistance of the preservationists with enlightened planning and financial aid. A sum of 45,000 pounds was spent on restoring the Georgian Town Hall and many of the fine town houses were renovated and repaired with the aid of grants. A special headquarters was set up for the Trust in the old barracks and spurred on by local newspaper proprietor, Jim Smail, a New Zealander but with Berwick blood in his veins, the properties around the wall were systematically tackled. Today Berwick presents not only a more pleasing but a more hopeful aspect than a decade ago.

But Berwick is not by any standards a large town and it is perhaps understandable that some of the more notable achievements in conservation have been accomplished in towns of more manageable proportions. There and elsewhere perhaps the greatest contribution towards safeguarding the heritage would be an intensification of the demolition controls that at present exist. For every day up and down the country listed buildings are still being demolished without permission and the fines levied are still an insufficient deterrent. A more effective sanction than the fine might be the French system of refusing any subsequent planning for a site where a building had been demolished without consent.

Another loophole in the legislative protections that has been created is that a building, even if part of a conservation area, is exempt from protection if planning permission was obtained prior to the designation of the conservation area.

It is lack of safeguards such as this that make any visitor to Britain's remaining historic towns and cities change his expression from delight to dismay as he travels on.

CHAPTER SIX Village and Country Town

Most of our larger towns have lost much of the character they once possessed. The pressures of expansion, redevelopment and commercial life have seen to that and the struggle to retain such fine buildings and noble streets as remain is not an easy one.

The larger the town the greater the difficulty of adopting and adapting the old street patterns and buildings to the pressures of modern life. One sees this even in our larger university and cathedral cities and mention has been made of the pillage of Worcester and the rape of Gloucester. Of our two ancient English university cities, Cambridge, which did not suffer massive industrialisation, has escaped this process much more satisfactorily than Oxford. However, it would be churlish to deny the magic of an early morning or late evening walk through parts of the old university city, or to withhold unstinted admiration for the spectacular successes of the Oxford restoration scheme of the 1960s, a model of living conservation in action and a stimulating example to everyone who cares about old buildings and their maintenance.

If our smaller towns have mercifully fared much better, this is partly because the changing pattern of industrialisation created quiet urban backwaters where life could go on much as before. Indeed, most of our recognised 'historic towns' are county towns, serving rural districts as their market and banking centres with perhaps a little light industry on the fringes, but at the same time retaining a sense of community. Not that we can complacently give thanks and think that all is well, for even in Berwick, given as an example in the previous Chapter, it took great effort to stir civic pride into civic action. A graphic brochure was issued with large scale photographs of a crumbling façade and a questioning title, *What Is So Special about Berwick?*, emblazoned across the front. Yet, in spite of the success achieved, Berwick is still not immune from problems created by road widening schemes and supermarket development projects.

For though tourists love to wander through quaint streets and admire the scale, proportion and beauty of the buildings, there is not always the same local appreciation of the distinctive or the distinguished. Familiarity in this, as in so many things, can breed indifference. Harassed by a reporter from the Architectural Press, one local mayor exploded, 'I am sick and tired of people going on about the period shop fronts. I see no interest in them. Architecturally they leave me cold.' But even where this attitude does not prevail – and all too frequently it is just beneath the surface – one must have some sympathy with the task of the smaller council elected to administer an historic town, but obliged to satisfy many twentieth-century whims and fancies.

On the very last day of 1975, *The Times* carried a report that an historic coaching inn of Newark, Nottinghamshire, the Old White Hart, might be acquired by the local council unless the owner, the National Coal Board, carried out urgent repairs. The council had decided to apply for a compulsory purchase order, as it is entitled to do under the Civic Amenities Act, after its architect described the building as totally unsafe for use, the owners having failed to comply with the repairs notice. The Coal Board had said that the repairs were the responsibility of the tenants, a multiple store. Whatever the moral rights or wrongs of the situation may be, the fact was that an outstanding building in a town of great charm and character was in dire danger. Sir Nikolaus Pevsner himself has described the Inn as: 'One of the paramount examples of fourteenth-century timber-framed domestic architecture in England.' It stands in the corner of the market square that has been designated a conservation area and, after the Parish Church and the ruined Castle, is the oldest building in the town. In taking action the council certainly seems to have displayed a proper sense of civic pride and duty, but the necessary repairs were estimated at over 60,000 pounds and inevitably a district council faced with this bill would have to curtail or postpone other important schemes.

Historic towns have modern problems in large measure. The enormous increase in road transport and the decline of the railway have brought heavy and inappropriate traffic streaming through their centres, a threat not only to lives and limbs on the narrow pavements but to the foundations, and even the superstructures, of many buildings. Not all traffic damage is as spectacular and tragic as that caused by the fish lorry that demolished the only remaining Roman arch in the country – the Newport arch in London – in 1967[1]. But damage occurs and often noise, dirt and poor access to old houses along heavily used streets in ancient towns have made those houses unattractive, and understandably so, as homes. This factor has often been the cause of poor maintenance and the reason why the fabric of buildings has begun to decay thus stimulating demand for redevelopment. These demands have been easy to sustain by those who have argued that the medieval street pattern is inconvenient to modern commercial life and that old buildings cannot easily be converted. By the time these arguments have been advanced the charm and individuality of the area in question has often begun to fade, and this has reinforced the contentions of those who want to demolish and start again.

Smaller historic towns while they have not escaped unscathed have fared much better than larger centres. Their future, too, is brighter, in

[1] It has since been meticulously reconstructed.

spite of the financial difficulties involved, and in spite of the obvious necessity of ensuring that market towns remain market towns and are not just conserved as pretty museums of a departed way of life. Fareham in Hampshire furnishes an excellent example of how an historic main street can be conserved alongside a developing shopping centre. The old High Street follows a medieval line, although its buildings are mainly Georgian. It still contains a number of excellent shops, mostly specialised, a club, an hotel and a private school in three of the finest Georgian houses, offices in other converted houses, a pub, and some residential accommodation. Here is a high street conforming to something of a traditional pattern, a community street in the true sense of that much maligned and over-used word. But, not all high streets have been as effectively maintained. Far too often a single blot, like an incongruous modern supermarket, spoils the scale and pattern as in Kinver in the southernmost tip of Staffordshire.

Sometimes the solution for modern problems is to restrict traffic, or even create a pedestrian precinct, as at Harlow Old Town, Essex, where all the old houses have been renovated and repainted. The street is well paved and spacious, the shops inviting and the area served by a well planned but unobtrusive car park. Far too often, though, main routes take passing traffic through the midst of towns and it is heartening to know that even at a time of economic stringency, when, quite rightly, decisions have had to be taken to cut back the road programme, the Government has indicated (White Paper on Public Expenditure, February 1976) that schemes for the by-passing of historic towns should be given priority. This is a wise, human decision, and also a wise economic one. The more attractive the town, the less passing traffic that disturbs it, and the better car parking facilities that serve it, the more tourists will come to see it. And because of the scale and size of these towns parking and walking present few problems as parks can generally be fairly close to the hub of the town's activities.

It is important that those in charge of county structure plans should, so far as possible, ensure that large scale development takes place away from historic towns. However, at the same time there should be positive encouragement given to as much residential reconversion, in-filling and rehabilitation as possible, for a town is not a town if people do not live in it and a proper community spirit and sense of civic pride and dignity are the best safeguards for these places in the future. An active local community is much more likely to fight not only against insensitive redevelopment but also against the distortion of the old town or village street. By distortion I mean that artificial pattern where one sees nothing but over-restored antique shops selling over-restored antiques cheek by jowl with boutiques and craft shops and with never a grocer, newsagent or greengrocer in sight. That the boutiques and antique shops should be there is natural enough, and without them many of the finest buildings would have gone before now, but one does not want an artificial atmosphere created by people who have no roots in a place and no real opportunity to sell to the community in whose midst they operate.

Ludlow in Shropshire is one of the best examples of a town which escapes this artificiality. With its dominating position, its fine church of St Lawrence, and its famous and imposing Castle where Prince Arthur died, where the Lords of the Marches held their Court, Ludlow must be on any list of the ten most fascinating and romantic towns in the country. Commanding the wooded valley of the Teme, Ludlow is an enchanting place, with its wide streets of gracious, Georgian town houses, small rows and courts with lesser cottages leading off, a market-place which hustles and bustles with life and real shops selling real things to real people. A day there is a most refreshing urban experience, and one cannot help but think of Houseman's 'Shropshire Lad':

> Oh, come you home of Sunday
> When Ludlow streets are still
> And Ludlow's bells are calling
> To farm and lane and mill.
> Or come you home on Monday
> When Ludlow market hums
> And Ludlow chimes are playing
> 'The conquering hero comes'.

The town is full of history and full of life: a happy and uncommon combination. Of course, Ludlow has antique shops, including an outstanding one run by Paul Smith. Perhaps the essence of the place is summed up by a visit to his charming shop in a quaint alleyway by the church. Here is a man who sells furniture because he knows and loves it and who is not interested in a mere quick profit from trade deals. He has made his home in the town and served on its council, and became Chairman of the Friends of the Parish Church, even though a Roman Catholic. In his shop you have service with integrity, based on a sound knowledge of the thing sold. And perhaps it is integrity more than anything else that is the hallmark of Ludlow itself: a town which has mercifully escaped the attention of the developers, and which although it would certainly benefit from a by-pass, has a street pattern which to some degree has enabled the local council to protect the centre from the shakes and the exhaust fumes of a traffic-ridden age.

Shropshire is fairly rich in small towns of character – Bridgnorth, clinging to its cliff above the Severn, the half-timbered Much Wenlock with one of the most romantic ruined priories in England; and Bishop's Castle, and Clun. Unfortunately, the county town, Shrewsbury, does afford a desperately sad example of how character can be torn out of the centre of even the smaller English town. As for Wellington, that has become the nucleus of the new town of Telford, perhaps the most frightening example of the triumph of the accommodation unit and the planners' whims and fancies over people, scale and needs.

On the other side of England, in Lincolnshire, is Louth, once described by Sir John Betjeman as the most beautiful town in England. Nestling in

the Lincolnshire wolds and overlooking the coastal marshes, the town
has much to preserve. It is rich in historical associations, from the
Pilgrimage of Grace, to the boyhood of Tennyson, who attended its
ancient grammar school and lived a few miles away in the still lovely
hamlet of Somersby, where his eccentric scholar father was rector.
Everyone who knows and loves English churches knows Louth, with its
majestic spire, but it is the rows of distinguished Georgian houses that
are its special claim to distinction. Wandering down Westgate calls to
mind Keats's memorable description of Winchester in September 1817
when he was writing his 'Ode to Autumn'. Rich in buildings of
character, it retains its medieval street pattern. Luckily, too, the centre
does not bear the brunt of passing traffic and is a charming oasis just
a few yards from the coastal road. Many houses and shops are the
subject of conservation orders and a number of owners have taken
advantage of grants to repair them. But even in Louth there has been
some despoilation. As I write, the fate of the splendid Wesleyan Chapel
hangs in the balance and the skyline, which was once solely dominated
by the soaring spire, now has been marred by a gigantic box-like
factory. But Louth is beautiful and those who know it and love it rather
relish the fact that its beauty is not more widely known.

England's country towns are certainly the jewels of a rather tarnished
urban crown, many of them worthy of whole chapters in themselves. To
spend a day in Cirencester or Tewkesbury, to go to Rye or to
Oakham or Olney, Woodstock or Chipping Norton, or Chipping
Campden, Southwell or Ripon, is to savour a form and pace of life which
is rapidly becoming extinct. To select like this is bound to provoke the
wrath of many people who feel that their particular favourite has
passed unnoticed. But these are merely quoted as an indication of some
of the richness that does remain. Mercifully, their future is probably
better secured than most parts of our heritage, although even here
there are dangers, for the preservation of our country towns depends not
only on vigilant local civic societies and enlightened local councils, but
also on the ability of owners to maintain the buildings which give
them character. A Wealth Tax which assessed dwellinghouses as wealth
(as has been advocated) and began at 50,000 or even 100,000 pounds
could have serious effects in the future. Already, however, these
owners have to grapple with such problems as VAT on maintenance,
and old buildings always require more maintenance than new. It
would indeed be a great incentive and encouragement to those
contemplating taking on a bedraggled house in an old town if there could
be some easing on the limit of improvement grants. These grants, which
have been responsible for the conservation of many neglected buildings,
and their restoration to the housing stock, have been restricted to houses
below a certain rateable limit and, such has been the increase in property
values, that already even modest houses in London and the larger cities
are above that limit. The country town could be the next on the list.

At a time when there are some 1¼ million unoccupied or derelict houses in the United Kingdom, many of which could be restored and make a significant contribution to our housing shortage, everything possible should be done to encourage their purchase and restoration. How much better the old, small restored house in Bridgnorth to the worker in nearby Telford than one of the accommodation units into which our families are being decanted in that obnoxious new town seven miles away.

We should not be complacent in any way about the future of country towns, for as was indicated at the beginning of this chapter, they know pressures too. Devizes, for instance, always a market town and still retaining the charm of a town closely allied to the land, has been for five years a place of controversy and acrimony over a proposed road scheme which would destroy a number of important buildings. Here and in many other such towns a local authority is struggling to satisfy legitimate conservation arguments, whilst seeking to maintain the commercial centre.

Commercial development brings particular problems to the smaller historic town: for the illuminated or plastic sign, which might pass unnoticed in the centre of Manchester, would be most incongruous on a shop front in Dorchester. Within conservation areas, especially, a stringent policy to cover such things as the replacement of windows and door fittings and the colours in which shops and houses are painted, is essential to the maintenance of character and charm. The more intimate the town the easier it is to disturb it and to ruin its atmosphere.

Austerity and charm rarely go together. This is perhaps why so many old Scottish towns seem to have been transformed for the worst in an excess of Presbyterian zeal, which has put utility before character. There are, of course, exceptions, and the university and cathedral city of St Andrew's is a notable example. It is one of the most attractive of Scotland's old towns. In its courtyards, garden frontages and the interiors of its buildings, St Andrew's has some of the best examples of Scottish domestic architecture. A local preservation trust was founded as early as 1937, and has undertaken some remarkable preservation of traditional Scottish buildings threatened with destruction. Many others have been saved by individual initiative and enterprise and, during the period from 1970 to 1973, the Town Council reconstructed houses in South Street, which dated from the early years of the nineteenth century, in order to provide small flats for elderly people. Not only was the scheme successful in itself, but it has important social implications through showing how old buildings can be renovated for new purposes to the benefit of the community.

It is in Scotland that one sees one of the most spectacular and successful schemes for restoring and rehabilitating old houses: the Little Houses Improvement Scheme, promoted by the National Trust for Scotland. Believing that Scotland's lesser buildings were as significant and evocative in their way as the castles and great houses and that, since they were the homes and stores of merchants, artisans and fishermen and their families, they should be preserved, the National Trust for Scotland started its Little Houses Scheme in 1960. The scheme put to use a new concept based on the purchase of appropriate buildings for restoration and subsequent resale. In 1961, with the aid of the Pilgrim Trust, a revolving fund was established to launch the project. Since then, the fund has increased almost tenfold, refreshed by donations, interest-free loans, legacies and profitable sales. The Trust's objective remains the same: to conserve and assist private owners and local authorities to preserve the best of Scottish vernacular architecture for which there can be a use in the future.

Using what they call 'a country-wide intelligence network', the Trust seeks to identify suitable houses then, taking into account their intrinsic architectural and historic value, the price and the cost of restoration and their potential saleability, it prepares to acquire the property. A building may be purchased from the Trust and restored by a client using his own architect, but he must observe the Trust's general specifications. Alternatively, a purchaser may invite the Trust to become his restoring agent. In urgent cases – when the building is particularly outstanding – the Trust will immediately undertake restoration at its own expense and rely on the ultimate sale to cover the cost of purchase and work done. Sometimes, it has been assisted by the Historic Buildings Council for Scotland making a special grant. But, whatever method is adopted to restore the property, the eventual purchaser is required to enter into a conservation agreement with the Trust in order to ensure the integrity of the building for the future.

By the end of 1975, the Little Houses Scheme had been instrumental in restoring nearly one hundred and fifty old houses, principally in Fife. In addition to this, the National Trust for Scotland had made various interest-free loans to enable local conservation societies to undertake similar work.

Scotland also has perhaps the most moving example in the whole country of a community restoration project launched on the initiative of private individuals with a mission. In the middle of the thirteenth century, just a few years after the death of St Francis of Assisi, the Franciscans came to Haddington in Lothian and built there a 'church of wonderful beauty', the choir of which became known for its elegance, clearness and light as the 'Lamp of Lothian'. A century later, when the Lothians were laid waste by the English armies, the church was destroyed in the 'Burnt Candlemass' of 1356. Another church, St Mary's, was built in its place, but during the 'rough wooing' of 1548, when Henry VIII sought the hand of the infant Queen of Scotland, the church was damaged and the choir ruined. For four centuries it remained roofless, until, in the mid-1960s, the Duchess of Hamilton, who lives in nearby Lennoxlove, one of the most romantic and loveliest of Scottish houses, inspired a local project to restore the church to its former glory as the focus of a revived and reinvigorated community.

The success story of the 'Lamp of Lothian' Project, as it came to be called, is one of the most remarkable in the history of restoration and renewal. Now, the church, derelict for four hundred years, is almost fully repaired with walls, roof and windows restored. The project has brought a new sense of purpose and determination both to the immediate community and to a much wider area. Not only has the church itself been recalled to life, but a group of important buildings around have been tackled with similar zeal. Haddington House, close by the church and built in 1680, had stood derelict for some years. In 1969, it was taken in hand and has now been completely renovated to become the home of the Lamp of Lothian centre, housing the office from which the centre is run. There are rooms for recitals and exhibitions, and even accommodation for visiting artists and musicians. Across the road, Poldrate Mill has been restored to provide a concert room and art gallery, and a youth centre has been established in the seventeenth-century mill workers' cottages that were abandoned and on the point of collapse as recently as 1967.

The whole story has brought a vigorous new purpose to the community and the centre acts as a focus for people from many miles around. More than that, it provides an inspiration, both to those who know that conservation is not a barren exercise undertaken for its own sake, that old buildings can have new life and new uses, but also to those haunted by the seemingly daunting task of raising vast sums in small communities for ambitious projects. The secret of the Haddington scheme – which is continuing with exciting plans for seventeenth-century gardens and other ventures – is leadership, in this case provided by the Duchess of Hamilton, a woman of great determination and great faith. This, in itself, illustrates how important the connection between small community and big house can be, even in 1976.

Nowhere is local patriotism stronger than in Wales and it is surprising that, as late as 1974, there were no civic societies in Monmouthshire, Radnorshire, Newport or Methyr, except for the latter's exceptional society at Abervan. In Pembrokeshire, outstanding towns such as St David's, Fishguard, Newport, Haverfordwest and Pembroke itself – all scheduled by the Council for British Archaeology – remained virtually unprotected. At that stage, only one district council in Tenby seemed fashionably interested in conservation. It contained all eight of Pembrokeshire's designated areas and for years had spent 2000 pounds or more on conservation of the town wall and had asserted powerful development control in its capacity as ground landlord of much of the old borough. This was regarded as a sensible investment in the discriminating type of tourism on which it pinned its future. One can only hope that, although late to enter the conservation stakes, Wales will make rapid progress in the latter 1970s.

In all conservation projects, especially in smaller towns and villages, the ingredient of local pride and patriotism is essential. But much invaluable work is still done by national amenity groups and preservation bodies, such as the Georgian Group and the Victorian Society. The latter has a particularly exciting record and has done sterling work in drawing attention to the large number of nineteenth-century buildings which have a special distinction, but, until recently, were totally unregarded and unappreciated. Both the Society and the Georgian Group adopt modern methods of painstaking research. They list developments and potential developments, monitor planning appeals, submit cases and submissions, and, in short, do everything possible to mobilise public opinion, local and national, when retrograde planning decisions have been taken or are seen as about to be taken. Over the years, their annual reports catalogue cases in which they have been involved and furnish model and invaluable documentation: classic case studies of battles won and lost.

Looking at recent developments, one often thinks that there should be an English village and cottage preservation society dedicated exclusively to those objectives. The fate of many English villages has been a less happy one. Of course, England does still have rural communities which preserve a village character and atmosphere and where many of the inhabitants still look to the land for their livelihood. But this rural orientation of community is becoming increasingly rare, as Robin Page wrote in *The Decline of the English Village* (1975):

> The whole structure and nature of village life is dying and in many villages the old ways and the old character have gone; gardens have now been sold off to squeeze in another building plot and lose their country flavour; there are street lights, footpaths, garages instead of garden sheds; and every Sunday morning, worshippers with wash leather and plastic buckets bow down before their new chromium-plated God. Work and entertainment is found mainly in the towns with the village a dormitory empty during the day and dead during the night.

This dismal epitaph on the English village is all too frequently true, and many villages have been swallowed up in the urban sprawl. To say this, and to lament it, is not to suggest that villages should be preserved in aspic, as it were, or that councils should not give planning permission for new buildings in any circumstances. When a community ceases to grow, it begins to die, but too many councils have in the past forgotten that most important word 'scale', which applies not only to the size and height of buildings in town centres, but also to the number of dwellings in rural communities. They have been far too ready on occasions to shrug off responsibilities and allow featureless houses and flats to replace old cottage homes. The disappearance of the English cottage would be an economic and environmental tragedy. Local authorities could, like St Andrews, make use of their old homes, and convert them into accommodation for old people, young marrieds or those who do not want a large house. Many politicians see people in their advice bureaux who would relish the thought of a cottage rather than a unit in a tower block.

If nothing is done positively to encourage retention, restoration and rehabilitation, the cottage will become either a memory or the exclusive preserve of the rich, weekend commuter. Cottages are for people to live in and work from. In England, every parish has its church and generally its manor house, and beyond are the homes of the estate workers, farmers, artisans and craftsmen, sometimes grouped around a green, sometimes straggling along the main road. They could still be used for homes and wherever possible their retention should be encouraged. As Alec Clifton Taylor in his brilliant analysis, *The Pattern of English Building* (1972), points out, 'every part of Britain had its own type of cottage, every community and sub-region, studies in a rich vernacular shelter'.

Perhaps the most authentic villages in scale and size are those which are owned by single families. This is not to suggest that rich men should buy up villages and rename them. But, if one wants to study the English village, one could do far worse than go to Rockingham, Northamptonshire, where development has been carefully controlled, plans vetted and scale maintained, or to a little village like Langton-by-Spilsby, Lincolnshire. Langton is not attached to any big house. The last member of the family to hit the headlines was Bennet Langton, and then only because he was a friend of Johnson's, who stayed with him in 1764. It is not necessary to advocate feudalism to appreciate this sort of system or to wish for it to remain. The chances of its doing so, however, are remote. As the owner of one of these villages wrote: 'While the estates of these families are small, I do not see how continuity can be maintained, with the imposition of Capital Transfer Tax and the Wealth Tax to follow. By working myself and drawing little to date from the income of the estate, I have managed to tidy up the small village which is in an area of outstanding national beauty and I would like to proceed further.' The great value of this type of association is that, where people care deeply for something, they generally work hard to cherish it. One would like to think that they would be encouraged to continue.

For better or for worse, however, few people will have the opportunity of that sort of landlord and, for better rather than worse, more people, one hopes, will come to own their property and will need advice and encouragement on how best to maintain it and ensure that the area in which it is situated is itself properly regarded. For these people and for local community societies, the Civic Trust has been a great guide, philosopher and friend, doing much to draw attention to improvement schemes and showing how to make something of the apparently most drab town or village street. Owing to its inspiration, buildings all over the country have been scrubbed, houses painted, trees planted, gardens created, rivers and canals cleaned up and obtrusive advertisements removed, in fact, eyesores of all kinds eliminated. Abandoned vehicles have been cleared away, street parking reduced and pedestrian precincts established. In 1972, the Trust published *Pride of Place*, a stimulating little book, which brought together ideas and practical experience of the previous decade and gave advice to those who wanted to improve the appearance and quality of the places where they lived. As the book observes, 'Britain can boast not only of a great wealth of architectural masterpieces, but at a lower level, a great number of wonderfully agreeable houses, farms, and groups of town or village buildings . . . In the last fifty years, this heritage has been grievously eroded and only since the middle 1960s has public opinion generally shifted to recognise conservation as desirable and necessary.' That it is desirable and necessary, most readers of this book will readily agree, and that its effect can be spectacular and heartwarming on village green or in old country town, is beyond dispute.

CHAPTER SEVEN The Medieval Legacy

On a late September morning in 1975, the Vicar of Brewood in Staffordshire noticed a fungus-like growth along the base of the wall in the north aisle of his church. Within a few days, his worst fears had been confirmed. There was extensive dry rot and the parochial church council, which had taken good care of the fabric and had reckoned that no major repairs were on the horizon, suddenly found itself facing bills of some 8000 pounds. Brewood is a fairly large parish of about two thousand souls, so the task of raising the money locally was not an impossible, though it was a formidable, one. What was certain was that the money had to be raised quickly if one of the most important of Staffordshire's churches was to be maintained in good repair and preserved for future generations of worshippers.

Brewood's crisis is typical of many that occur every week throughout the year, for architecture, unlike any other form of art, requires unceasing and costly maintenance. Because the greater number of our cathedrals and churches date from medieval times, the problems caused by crumbling stonework, rotting beams and timbers, and subsiding foundations, are common. Surveying the vast wealth of English church architecture, and its importance to landscape and townscape, and reflecting on the costly problem of maintenance, I am reminded of a passage from one of Solzhenitsyn's stories from *Stories and Prose Poems*:

Travelling along country roads in central Russia you begin to understand why the Russian countryside has such a soothing effect. It is because of its churches. [He talks of them in loving terms, but then goes on] As soon as you enter a village you realise that the churches that welcomed you from afar are no longer living. Their crosses have long since been bent or broken off; the dome with its peeling paint reveals its rusty rib cage; weeds grow on the roofs and in the cracks of the walls... People have always been selfish and often evil. But the angelus used to toll and its echo would float over the village, field and wood. It reminded man that he must abandon his trivial earthly cares and give up one hour of his thoughts to life eternal... The tolling of the eventide bell... raised man above the level of a beast... Our ancestors put their best into these stones... all their knowledge and all their faith.

Let us hope that no English writer has to pen such an elegy on England's churches. Today they still ensure that the English countryside has the soothing effect of which Solzhenitsyn speaks, an effect which is not dissipated as one enters them. True, England has its ruined churches – there are two hundred and fifty in Norfolk alone – but for the most part our churches are 'lived in' and loved. For all this, however, there is a frightening chance that many of them will have crumbled into decay and stand neglected and open to the elements twenty years from now.

England's finest architectural heritage and legacy is in our cathedrals and churches. If the cathedrals bring to life much of the pageantry and high drama of some of the greatest events in our history, the daily round of generations of citizens and villagers, whose lives are the social history of England, is brought to mind in the simple quiet of many a village chancel or in the more spacious and grander naves of the great town churches.

No one knows quite how many churches there are in England but there are over ten thousand listed as being of architectural or historic interest, and most are medieval, as are the greatest of our cathedrals.

The problems of maintenance and preservation are seen most dramatically in our great medieval cathedrals. There are twenty-six of these and, until this century, they were not only the greatest but the largest public buildings in the land. They are still the supreme examples of the English architectural genius. All well merit visiting and to select is always to be subjective. However, few could deny that many of our medieval cathedrals stand comparison with any of the great buildings of the world and must be ranked among the noblest works of man in Europe.

There is the mother church of the Anglican communion at Canterbury, with its wonderful Norman crypt, superb medieval glass, the wall paintings in St Gabriel's and St Anselm's chapels and a wealth of fascinating and evocative monuments. Its central tower is the finest in the land and its lantern has quite exquisite fan vaulting. Winchester, the longest of our cathedrals, has a slightly austere exterior, but a magnificent nave and transcepts, a lovely Perpendicular reredos, three sets of medieval wall paintings, a font of Tournai marble, and fourteenth-century choir stalls with sixty small but exciting misericords. An hour's drive away is Salisbury, one of the most famous and most remarkable buildings in England, with its marvellous spire rising above the tower.

Each of these cathedrals has known its problems. Salisbury imposed an entrance charge for visitors in an attempt to meet the ever increasing costs of daily maintenance. There was something of an outcry at the time (1973), but the practice is rarely challenged. It is surprising that more cathedrals have not followed Salisbury's example. Surely,

Canterbury must be tempted to do so. This vast and glorious building is at present in considerable danger and, if some 3 million pounds of repairs are not carried out in the next few years, some at least of its outstanding glass will probably be beyond saving.

As at Canterbury, so at Lincoln. A glory both inside and out, this is perhaps the finest building in England, perched on its limestone ridge and visible for miles around. Yet Lincoln has twice had to launch appeals in recent years. Much of the structure is unsafe and passers-by are warned to beware of falling masonry. Almost everything here is of priceless excellence. The misericords, the carved corbels, the soaring beauty of the angel choir, the thirteenth-century glass and the noble chapter houses all contribute to a masterpiece which challenges any of the great continental cathedrals, and which only Chartres surpasses.

Norwich, with its graceful spire, elegant nave and splendid presbytery; Ely, with its enchanting lantern tower; Peterborough, one of the least altered of our great Norman churches; Wells, which has been called 'the most poetic of the English cathedrals... the queen among cathedrals'; Exeter, with its 300-foot ribbed vault, among the greatest creations of Gothic architecture in Europe – all make a stunning and unique contribution to our heritage.

No reference to English cathedrals could be complete without mentioning York, not only a masterpiece of medieval architecture, but now a masterpiece of the restorers' skill and the engineers' genius. For, at the end of the sixties, York was discovered to be in imminent danger of collapse. The foundations were giving way. For a generation, the west front had been sheathed in scaffolding but the Minster was gradually sinking into the ground and, as it did, was being shaken by the thundering of lorries as they drove within feet of the walls. A massive rescue operation was launched. Two million pounds were raised, new foundations were pumped in. Stainless steel and concrete came to the aid of medieval stone and wood and now York looks better than at any time in the last three centuries. One can go north from York to Ripon and Durham, the finest Norman building in England and probably the finest Romanesque church in Europe. With a site to rival that of Lincoln, it broods with massive majesty over the Weir.

The three cathedrals, known for the Three Choirs Festival – Hereford, Worcester and Gloucester – must be visited by any serious lover of cathedral architecture or by any student of music. It is not only the cathedrals themselves which are fighting for survival in an expensive and inflationary world, but many of the traditions they embody and enliven, and especially church music. Music plays a vital part in the life of all cathedrals and, without the daily sung services, they could easily become lifeless monuments. English church music is an important contribution to the arts, and the excellence of its accomplishment owes much to the choir schools attached to most of our cathedrals and to many of the colleges of Oxford and Cambridge. These schools are suffering the pressure felt by all small institutions with limited resources, and they also face an uncertain future as Government policy seeks to sweep aside the old educational system and dispatch into oblivion anything considered to be elitest. The problem of the future of our choir schools is felt acutely by all those who value their standards, and anxiety has not been dispelled by the threatened closure of Westminister Cathedral Choir School, the finest of Roman Catholic musical establishments.

However, the difficulties facing cathedrals are to some extent mitigated by the success of appeals. This does not mean that one can take a detached and relaxed view, for there are more and more good causes clammering for the fewer pounds left in the wallets of the over-taxed. Surely, though, no government could allow Canterbury or York, Durham, Salisbury or Lincoln to collapse.

But if it is unthinkable to contemplate an England without her cathedrals, it is as painful to imagine her without her ancient parish churches. At their greatest, they bring an almost miraculous glory and dignity to town centre or country scene; and even the humblest furnish an oasis of simple reverence and timeless beauty in a troubled world. But the ravages of time and inflation have not passed them by, and, though their plight may not be as dramatic as that which faces the cathedrals, in many ways it is worse; many of them lack the national fame and prominence that enables public, and even international, appeals to achieve, as at York, spectacular success. Our parish churches including, as they do, almost all our medieval buildings still in use, are a national treasure collectively; and individually, almost every one gives a special dimension to the town or village it serves. Many of these churches are, by any standards, great buildings. Some, like Cirencester and Boston, St Peter's, Wolverhampton, and Holy Trinity, Hull, are well known. Others, of equal beauty and importance, like Louth in Lincolnshire, its spire second only to Salisbury in height – and perhaps even more beautiful in proportion – are less so. Lincolnshire, being a sparsely populated county, with a long and fairly rich history, has some remarkable churches, none more so than Stow, the finest Norman parish church in England. But Stow is relatively unknown, and certainly off the beaten track, and any need for massive funds could hardly be met from the very limited local resources of the small, scattered rural population. The same is true of Abbey Dore in Herefordshire. Betjeman calls it a perfect example of early English architecture with seventeenth-century fittings and yet, surrounded by the small orchards of the Golden Valley, this survival of a great Conventual church of the Cistercian Order, miles from anywhere, must be in danger.

Indeed, of all the churches mentioned here, the only one able to summon large sums with relative ease has been Boston, whose success has arisen from its American connections. And, whilst it is delightful to think that this grandest of parish church owes its sound condition and beautifully decorated interior to the Americans' acknowledgement of their heritage, it is of small consolation to those hundreds of incumbents and church councils struggling to maintain the fabrics for which they are responsible. That this should be the fact comes as a surprise to some, who talk glibly of 'the church commissioners and their millions'. It is true that the Church of England has fairly substantial resources and investments, but the income from these is devoted exclusively to the religious work of the church and, in particular, to paying the stipends of the clergy, and no one could argue that they are among the better paid members of the community. So, if the money cannot be centrally provided for the restoration and maintenance of our churches, local vicars and congregations have to raise it as best they can themselves.

The recent plea of the vicar of a locally notable, but nationally unknown, medieval church – one of three in his charge – is all too typical:

New wooden floors have been put in the nave and in the vestry owing to dry rot. We have had to put a drainage trench round part of the outside wall to cure rising damp. I had hoped for a better response from the parish, and some more should come from our appeal, but agriculture and other businesses are not doing very well at the moment. We shall continue trying, for later we shall have to replace tracery in some of the windows.

This type of problem is geographical as well as financial, for the parish churches of England are suffering from the population shifts that have taken place during the last century. The movement away from the centres of our towns and cities has left parishes depopulated after office hours. In this regard, one thinks of Holy Trinity, Hull, or St Peter's, Wolverhampton, both churches of the first importance but neither with a sizeable resident congregation within the parish. Many of our small villages, also, have parish churches big enough to house, not only the whole population of their village, but of the last three and the next three generations as well; and even small churches have difficulties. At Aston Eyre, Shropshire, a population of fifty-three and a worshipping congregation of about fifteen suddenly had to raise 6000 pounds to save the tiny thirteenth-century church, with its quite magnificent Norman tympanum. Problems like this have to be tackled, not only against the background of a changed population, but at a time when churchgoing has declined. Although most of our parish churches ring to the voices of the occasionally faithful – the festival Christians at Easter, Christmas and Harvest, or on occasions of private joy or grief – they are almost empty for the rest of the year. And so, the band of willing workers who launch and conduct appeals is often a fraction of a congregation, which itself is a fraction of the population served by the church. This is a very far cry from the early sixteenth century, when the great church of Louth, Lincolnshire, was rebuilt of Lancaster stone between 1501 and 1515. The church wardens' book tells us, 'For fifteen years, with scanty labour and scantier means, the work was carried on. They borrowed from the Guilds and the richer inhabitants, they pledged their silver crosses and chalices. From the richest to poorest all seem to have been affected with a like zeal.'

Nowadays more and more people are 'appreciative' of our old churches. They exercise an affectionate hold on many people who, when they come, expect to find the brasses bright and ready for rubbing, the floors polished and the stonework clean. Their protestations would be heartfelt if signs of 'danger' and 'keep out' barred the way to occasional conformity, or to historic or artistic pilgrimage. But few of the visitors, whether infrequent worshippers, eager tourist or both, leave much token of their appreciation. That is why so many of these churches are in danger, not of immediate destruction or sudden collapse, but of the slow and total destruction of decay. It is only the faithful and continuing struggle of often tiny groups, sometimes sustained by the generosity of bodies like the Historic Churches Preservation Trust, that has kept England's medieval heritage intact so far.

Aston Eyre is one of the many churches which has been rescued by grant and loan from the Trust, although its own parishioners made very prodigious efforts and raised well over half the money needed. A glance through some of the Trust's files reveals the true extent of the problem. There is hardly a county in the country that does not contain churches which have been helped by the Trust and recent applications show that problems are increasing rather than diminishing. Some of the churches applying, like Holy Trinity, Elsworth, Cambridgeshire, are not spectacular, but Elsworth is a fine fourteenth-century church in a parish of six hundred, forty of whom go to services. If its roof is not restored, it will gradually decay, and it can only be repaired if 6000 pounds is produced. St Mary's, Kempley, Gloucester, turned to the Trust when it had to find another 3000 pounds for repairing its roof: a large sum for a population of two hundred and forty, an even larger one for the average congregation of twenty. And Kempley's population is mainly agricultural with no wealthy landowners to show an interest in the church. St Mary's Church, Clifton, Nottinghamshire, a church of mainly twelfth-century origin, but with additions dating from the fourteenth, fifteenth and sixteenth centuries and with a fine series of monuments and tombs, found that it needed 3750 pounds to replace large areas of eroded stonework and to relead the roof. The population was two thousand five hundred and the average congregation one hundred and twenty, so the task was perhaps slightly easier than that facing the parishioners of All Saints, Hopton, in Suffolk, where three hundred and sixty people, twenty-five of whom go to church, had to find 2000 pounds. Week after week, applications from churches all over the country flood into the Trust. Often, the Trust is able to help them but its assistance is, of necessity, limited. And the other bodies, such as the Friends of Friendless Churches, and the many county trusts throughout the country, although they have wonderful achievements to their credit, cannot arrest the surging tide of dilapidation and decay. For the sums needed are frequently in local terms, tremendous and inflation adds to them daily – as does VAT. One fails to see how some of the necessary jobs that are in hand can ever be completed: 20,000 pounds to replace the parapet of a city church when most local effort is understandably directed to saving the crumbling cathedral; 5000 pounds for roof repairs to a fourteenth-century country church in a parish of fifty souls; 3000 pounds for essential first aid to a Norfolk church in a village of sixty people.

It is in Norfolk that the problem is most acute. In medieval times, East Anglia was the richest part of England and the great wool merchants and clothiers gave testimony to their wealth and their faith, and sought to ensure a speedy passage through purgatory, by endowing churches. Throughout Norfolk, Lincolnshire and Suffolk, the great churches rose: Boston, Lavenham, Long Melford, Clare, Salle, Blakeney, Cawston, Cley-next-the-Sea, Great Snoring, Great Walsingham, Erpingham, King's Lynn, Snettisham, All Saints, Sheringham, Walpole St Peter's – perhaps the finest of them all. All but the first four of this list are in Norfolk and they represent but a small proportion of the six hundred and fifty-nine medieval churches in the county. As John Betjeman wrote in *Norfolk Country Churches and the Future* (1973),

Their profusion is their greatness...Some are miracles of soaring lightness with wooden angels in their high-up roofs; some of painted screens or Georgian box pews; some medieval carved bench ends or ancient stained glass. Each is different from its neighbour even if it is miles off or in the same churchyard. None is without a treasure of some sort be it in wood, stone, iron, tile or glass. Some are famous throughout Britain. Lovers of the Norfolk churches can never agree which is the best. I have heard it said that you are either a Salle man or a Cawston man. Others say that Walpole St Peter's bears the palm. Norfolk would not be Norfolk without a church tower on the horizon or round the corner of the lane. We cannot spare a single Norfolk church. When a church is pulled down the country feels empty like a necklace with a jewel missing. Every Norfolk church that is left standing today, however dim, neglected and forgotten, its looks are loved by someone, or it would have disappeared long ago.

That is certainly true, for in addition to the six hundred and fifty-nine to which John Betjeman refers there are two hundred and fifty which are in ruins. It is because of this local recognition and love of the County's churches, that the Norfolk Society's Committee for Norfolk Churches came into being. A small group of people, led by the indefatigable Lady Harrod from Holt, and fired with a determination to ensure that as many churches as possible should be enjoyed and worshipped in by future generations, set about the task of raising money, fighting suggestions of redundancy, giving encouragement to local efforts and stimulation to local enthusiasts. The Committee has produced booklets on the problem in general and on the glass and the furnishings of the churches. Lady Harrod states her aims in simple but moving terms,

> We feel, that with the rapidly increasing population of East Anglia, the enormous interest in church architecture, and the new and strongly expressed desire for religion on the part of young people, there are real indications that all our major churches should and could be kept for religious use ... We can offer legal advice, practical suggestions for money raising, historical research, manual work and even a little money to prime the pump. We are involved already in rescue operations for six churches.

One of their great successes has been Warham St Mary Magdelene. Let Lady Harrod tell the story in her own words:

> At Warham there are two (churches) both medieval and both of interest. All Saints had very thorough late-Victorian restoration and has lighting and heating. St Mary Magdelene has a Georgian interior but no lighting. If any church could be called 'superfluous' it was this one; so it is not surprising that in 1960 when the architect's estimate of 3450 pounds for repairs was received, a suggestion was made to close it. No doubt the very fine stained glass, and the three-decker pulpit could have been transferred elsewhere but a committee called the Friends of St Mary's was formed and the required money was raised. In order not to deprive All Saints, no general appeal was made in the village, though a few devoted families there gave time and money. The Historic Churches Preservation Trust made a grant of 250 pounds and the Pilgrim Trust paid 1100 pounds for the restoration of the glass. The rest came from families who had ancestors or friends connected with the church. Endowments from these families, added to the donations of patron, worshippers or visitors, and the sale of leaflets enables us to keep the church in proper repair. It is used throughout the year, twice each month for the weekday service of Holy Communion, and there is always a festival evensong for the Saint's Day in July. The box pews keep us warm in winter when the service is read by candlelight, and there are always 'two or three gathered together', to carry out the purpose for which our ancestors build this beautiful little place.

Lady Harrod and her Committee are motivated by love and scholarship. They love the churches for their own sake and for what they represent, for the faith they have kept alive and can still sustain. But their approach is far from sentimental. They see themselves as guardians of an ecclesiastical architecture of national importance. They recognise how vital it is that methods of building should be fully understood and are anxious that research should be done on the relationship between the great cathedral churches and the abbeys, priories and the parish churches. 'Our understanding of such major and internationally important buildings would be greater if the work of known masons can be more clearly defined.' Above all perhaps, they see themselves as trustees of wood and stone and glass for future generations. Their work is echoed in Norwich itself – outside their scheme of things – where the ancient city, with its many fine churches, has its own preservation committee. In Norwich, the local authority has worked with the committee, and local authorities do have power to assist with grants. Some, notably the GLC, have very good records; others, such as Staffordshire, have acknowledged their county responsibility, albeit only in small measure. But local authorities are generally reluctant to commit the ratepayers' money to what they think will not be a very popular cause. What is needed is State aid for churches in use. At the time of writing, the Government has agreed to a scheme whereby the equivalent of a million pounds a year, at 1973 prices, will be made available for religious buildings of all denominations. But details of administration of the grants have still to be finalised. It is hoped they will be worked out quickly, for it would be a sorry commentary on our sense of priorities if more churches were reduced to selling their treasures. Not only do the treasures, principally plate, have an intrinsic aesthetic importance of their own, not only were they given to be held in perpetuity by particular churches, but once sold, they are gone for ever, from the church and, probably, from the country, too. In a letter to *The Times*, in March 1976, James Lees Milne reflected sadly on the church treasures that filled market stalls in Italian towns as parish priests obeyed the dictates of guilt-ridden superiors. Let us hope that no American tourist in the Portobello Road will be able to pick up Georgian or Victorian chalices sold for a pittance to mend a hole in the roof.

Today the State can only step in if the church is declared redundant under the Pastoral Measure of 1968. And, whilst one rejoices at the success of the Redundant Churches Fund in rescuing fine old churches, no one has suggested that the number ultimately in the Fund's care can grow to more than four hundred by the end of the century. The process of declaring a church redundant is long and complicated and mercifully few of our parish churches are truly redundant. There is, indeed, considerable resistance on the part of many people to see the process accelerated. The fear of what redundancy could mean was spelled out by Lady Harrod,

Until now, churches could slumber away in their churchyards looking very picturesque until they crumbled away to romantic ruins like Egmere or were restored to life like Bramford (and many others). But now under the Pastoral Measure all that has changed. Once a church has been made redundant if it does not qualify for preservation by the Redundant Churches Fund and if no suitable alternative use has been found it must, by law, be demolished. The waste of this asset would be regrettable, but if a church is converted to an alternative use such as a dwellinghouse, what has been saved? The landscape value, hopefully the tower, walls and windows, but not the setting – the graveyard must go – not the furnishings, not the monuments, nor carved grave slabs, nor the historical links. Not, in fact, the essence of the church which is its intrinsic worth.

It is easy to agree emphatically with Lady Harrod and to welcome the sort of suggestions that her committee has put forward for creating pilgrim churches, for instance (that is, retaining the exterior characteristics of the building and as much as possible of the interior and using it as a centre for 'pilgrim holidays' for Christians). However, the Redundant Churches Fund has significant achievements to its credit. The object of the scheme for redundant churches is to ensure that, where a church is no longer ministering to any proper congregation, and where there are too many parishes in a small town, the building can be retained. It can be devoted to alternative uses – much easier in a town, where churches might lend themselves quite readily to museum purposes, or, as in St John's, Smith Square, to concerts and meetings – or retained as a religious building in the care of the Fund. The Fund can then ensure that such churches are available on occasions for the holding of services, as well as being accessible to those interested in them for the sake of their architecture and their fittings.

In an article in *Country Life*, March 1976, Marcus Binney surveyed the progress of the Fund to that date. By then, eighty-four parish churches were being looked after by the Fund:

> Already there is an impressive geographical spread and the fact that there are more Fund churches in the province of Canterbury than that of York largely reflects the larger concentration of churches in the south. The most appealing to visit are those romantically situated in remote stretches of country. Shotely, in Northumberland, has to be approached on foot across fields; Upton Cresset lies in a quiet and lonely valley in Shropshire; St George on the Isle of Portland stands isolated in an enormous graveyard; Friarmere, Yorkshire, is built on a windswept Pennine hilltop; Skidbrook is set in a clump of trees in an empty expanse on the Lincolnshire marshes while St Peter the Poor Fisherman in Devon has a breathtaking view over Stoke Bay.

But the Fund cannot provide the answer for most of these churches, and we should remember that we are not just talking about the medieval ones. There are many fine seventeenth- and eighteenth-century churches that are in danger, and, indeed, a wealth of churches whose architectural distinction is now being recognised, date from the last century. The Victorians may have over-restored many of the churches they inherited, but they also contributed much to town and village scene and it would be a tragedy if the masterpieces of Butterfield and Street and Pearson were allowed to fall into decay.

The simple brutal fact in 1976 is that there are many hundreds, if not thousands of churches, that are in danger. These churches are among our foremost architectural assets. They are centres and places of pilgrimage, they form focal points in town and country. In a very real sense they embody the soul of England. They must not be allowed to fall down.

CHAPTER EIGHT Artists and Craftsmen — the Rescue of the Past

No Act of Government, however harsh, can quench the creative spirit of man. The arts will survive, however 'cabin'd, cribb'd, confin'd' so long as man survives. Our ancestors adorned their caves with colourful and ritualistic paintings and, even if a nuclear holocaust engulfed us, the last survivors in the fall-out shelters would no doubt do likewise. But, though the creative spirit will persist, the arts need encouragement and stimulation in order to flourish; and individual crafts and techniques, unless they are sustained and the knowledge behind their execution kept alive, will die.

Genius and penury have often gone together and the artist needs recognition and patronage if he is to escape poverty. There are probably fewer full-time artists of repute today – artists earning a living entirely from their creative works – than for many decades. This is sad, for while it is by no means destructive of talent that an artist should spend some time in teaching, if he is to pursue his skills with any degree of commitment he must have time to devote exclusively to art. That time can normally only be paid for by those who purchase his works and it would be a grim prospect, indeed, if the sole purchasers were institutional ones, right as it is that industrial patronage should be encouraged and that public institutions should show the works of living artists. The collector, who relies on his knowledge, judgement and discernment, and that almost indefinable attribute we call taste, is a very necessary being in the field of patronage.

On 10 September 1975, thirty-three of Britain's foremost artists wrote to *The Times* urging the Minister for the Arts to intercede with the Chancellor so that the Wealth Tax should not apply to them. Their reason was a fear that:

It (the Wealth Tax) will discourage discriminating patrons from purchasing the works of any artists if an enhancement in their value – even if the purchaser has no intention of selling the work – involves taxation. Survival of an artist is difficult enough without the creation of new difficulties and problems by the very Minister that should regard himself as charged with the duty of aiding and not impeding their careers.

These artists recognised from common, and no doubt often painful, experience that without the private collector prepared to take a chance and indulge a fancy many a career would have been blighted. Thus it has been through history, and, indeed, it could be argued that the private patron can save the public purse, for his judgement may be rejected by the 'experts', and far better that his money should be spent than the public purse raided.

In their letter to *The Times* the artists, who included Francis Bacon, Reg Butler, Frederick Gore, Ivor Hitchens, Henry Moore, Ben Nicholson, Victor Pasmore, John Piper, Ruskin Spear and Feliks Topolski, observed that:

The Minister has made a point that the works of young artists are not purchased by people of wealth. It is happily the case that quite a number of people of limited wealth do buy the works of young artists and have always done so. It is also the case that wealth by no means destroys taste or discrimination and a number of people of considerable wealth continue to support young artists. Artistic discrimination is not a matter of money or speculation.

At a time when increased economic pressures no doubt seduce many an embryonic artist from his course, it is depressing that any Government should take steps further to discourage or penalise artistic progress. What is needed is a positive encouragement, to both individuals and institutions, to purchase the works of artists and it would be no bad thing if fiscal incentives, such as are available in the USA, were introduced into this country. There, the patron who wishes to give to a public institution can offset the purchase price of the work against his tax. Alas, the chances of such a scheme being introduced in this country do not seem very great.

Of course, some artists are in a worse situation than others. The work of a young silversmith, for instance, is liable for $12\frac{1}{2}$ per cent VAT. From April 1975 until April 1976 he had to pay 25 per cent, a figure that made the 8 per cent that other artists have to charge seem like a positive blessing, although that VAT should be applied to the work of any living artist is unfortunate. One might argue that the silversmith is a craftsman rather than an artist but, whatever the outcome of such a debate, one thing is abundantly clear: many of the crafts are in acute danger of disappearing. One of the more depressing ironies of recent years is that, although the conservation movement has grown, the supply of craftsmen has tended to diminish. One faces the absurd prospect of a situation where the crafts and skills necessary for the effective discharge of a sensible conservation policy will not be available. For automation, which has brought many blessings in its wake, has also produced casualties, and far too often the craftsman is the first of these. The 'true' craftsman loves his work and lavishes thought and care upon it, as the craftsmanship of the past (often executed in the face of extraordinary odds) testifies. Perhaps British craftsmanship is at its best in our great cathedrals, but if these buildings are to be preserved, more young men will have to be recruited and trained in ancient crafts.

The recruiting and training of craftsmen is a slow and laborious process. Craftsmanship itself can never be hurried and is therefore expensive in time and materials; and in much of twentieth-century architecture, not needed. The individual who cherishes his work, loves and knows his materials and solves the problems that arise in their use, is not required on most modern building sites. Since the end of the Second World War, methods and techniques of production and materials have changed and superseded traditional skills. As a result, most skilled craftsmen are in the last years of their working life and the new generation of builders and carpenters – even though they may have served apprenticeships – is rarely proficient enough to cope with the intricate problems of repairing and maintaining historic buildings. The trend towards industrial building is bound to continue and so the conservation craftsman will become a special creature whose work will have to be valued for its own sake.

Bernard Fielden, who has done more than almost any other man to pinpoint the need and suggest solutions, has for several years now been urging the recognition of these facts. He acknowledges that the few craftsmen to be found in modern firms, generally retained for special assignments, are often an uneconomic proposition as far as their employers are concerned. As he sees it, 'The problem is twofold, firstly, to organise a steady supply of work and secondly to find means of paying for the cost of any craft work or to make this cost more palatable to the 'public.' Bonus schemes and work study techniques are almost impossible to apply to the case of craftsmen. He suggests that the level of demand for each trade in each region should be assessed and that there would be a case for setting up regional or national crafts trusts on a trade by trade basis. He instances the York Glaziers Trust, established to cope with the enormous problems involved in the maintenance and restoration of the medieval stained glass of York.

The cathedrals could well provide an ideal basis for regional craft centres. Like the Forth Bridge, they are in constant need of attention and so many. of the skilled crafts are constantly called for that a cathedral base would be both sensible and economical. Craftsmanship is always bound to be expensive, and with so many intensive labour activities, it is in danger of being priced out unless some form of sensitive subsidy scheme can be devised.

All this is not to suggest that nothing is being done. There are a number of cathedrals with their own resident staff, though the inflationary pressures of recent years have already led to some redundancies. Perhaps the whole subject, with the problems and the achievements that are possible, can best be understood by looking in some detail at the restoration of a great cathedral. The story of Canterbury is less well known than that of York, but it provides an almost equally good example of the restoration drama and the central rôle of the craftsman: the stone-mason, who must replace features eroded by pollution, shattered by water and frost and split by iron; the cathedral plumber, who has to be a specialist in working lead, responsible for roof coverings and dispersal of rainwater; the carpenter, who has to work in the maze of medieval beams and struts; the glazier, who has to cope with the problems caused by the eroding iron bars which hold the great windows together.

Canterbury is the Mother Church of the Anglican Communion and the cradle of English Christianity, and also one of the largest and loveliest of our cathedrals. Its Norman crypt is England's best and its stained glass ranks with that of Chartres in quality, if not in quantity. The central tower is the finest in the land and the nave a masterpiece of earlier Perpendicular style. Long a place of pilgrimage, its history and associations still hold a powerful fascination for all Englishmen with a sense of history, and for Anglicans throughout the world. The history of the cathedral itself mirrors much of the turbulence and joy of our chequered past. The first cathedral was consumed by fire in 1069 and the second was the work of the great Lanfranc, appointed by the Conqueror. On 5 September 1174, just four years after the murder of Becket, his cathedral, too, suffered the ravages of fire. A detailed description of that catastrophe was written by one of the monks, Gervase, and so Canterbury is better documented at the time of destruction and rebuilding than any other English cathedral.

Fire has always been a hazard—even in recent years—and most English cathedrals, at some stage in their history, have suffered from it to a greater or a lesser degree. The destruction of Canterbury was in 1174 when 'the grief and distress of the sons of the church were so great that no one can conceive, relate, or write them; but to relieve their miseries they fixed the altar, such as it was, in the nave of the church where they howled, rather than sang, matins and vespers'. (This quotation is from a translation by Charles Cotton of Gervase's record.)

In place of Lanfranc's church there rose one of the glories of early English Gothic architecture. Under William of Sens the choir was built and then another architect, known as William the Englishman, built eastwards, transepts, Trinity chapel, corona. It was to this new cathedral that the remains of the canonised 'holy, blissful martyr' were carried in 1220 and placed in the shrine, which became one of the greatest places of pilgrimage in the medieval church. This was the shrine of which Erasmus wrote in 1512, 'I saw St Thomas's tomb all over bedecked by a vast number of jewels of an immense price...The holy man, I am confident would have been better pleased to have his tomb adorned with leaves and flowers.' A quarter of a century later the jewels had gone and the religious houses of England were dissolved and plundered. History was rewritten, Becket proscribed, the monastic foundation destroyed, and in its place the Dean and Chapter established.

Canterbury's treasures were further plundered during the great rebellion of the seventeenth century. Glass, statues, vestments and rich hangings perished and the inadequate work of replenishment at the Restoration cost some 10,000 pounds. But, through trials and tribulations, the cathedral has survived. As John Shirley wrote, 'The cathedral has stood through the changes and chances of this mortal life, sometimes damaged, sometimes near destroyed, whether by fire or invading armies or the zeal of reformers and iconoclasts. Today it stands in all its calm majesty witnessing to the spiritual and the eternal, as it stood in the fateful first week of June 1942 when fifteen high explosive bombs were rained on its precincts and many hundred incendiary bombs.'

Now, in 1976, Canterbury faces perhaps its greatest danger, for it is struggling with the problem of preservation, a problem consequent upon the erosion of decades and exacerbated by mounting inflation. To rouse the nation, and the Anglican community, to the dangers faced by glass, stone and timber, and in the knowledge that there would be no money forthcoming from Government sources to help maintain this famous and valuable national asset, a Cathedral Appeal Trust Fund was set up under Lord Astor of Hever. The trustees include the Prince of Wales, Lord Armstrong, the former head of the Civil Service, Lord Selwyn Lloyd, the former Speaker of the House of Commons, Lord Clarke (of *Civilisation*) and Lord Hailsham of St Marylebone. The special needs were outlined by the Dean: 'The preservation and conservation of the stained glass, the restoration of much of the fabric, and the establishment of adequate bursary funds for apprentices in our glassworks and masons' yard, and for the forty-four members of the musical foundation.' The intention of those responsible for the Appeal was to ensure that there would be adequate craftsmen to maintain the building well after the immediate dangers had been removed and also to ensure that the living heritage of music, to which the English church has made such a valuable and individual contribution, should continue.

Overall responsibility for the restoration rests with the Surveyor to the Fabric, Peter Marsh, a highly qualified professional architect and surveyor, who stresses that the immediate problems, though grave, are not the consequence of past indifference or neglect. Canterbury has been lovingly cared for through the centuries and, because it was built over a period of four centuries, the deterioration and decay does not affect every part of the structure to the same degree. The greater part of the cathedral is faced with Caen stone, brought from Normandy by boat in the Middle Ages, and used throughout south-eastern England as it was generally more accessible than the stone from most of our own quarries. Today, Caen stone is hard to acquire and, although Clipsham stone provides a good substitute and has been used in the restoration of Canterbury and other cathedrals, the policy of saving materials to save costs has been adopted at Canterbury and wherever possible, the old stone is re-used. Indeed, no piece of masonry is discarded out of hand: recycling is the order of the day. After all, those entrusted with restoring a great cathedral must be cost conscious. Labour costs in particular are daunting and far outstrip that of materials. In the old days, the reverse was true.

The task faced by the Surveyor was a daunting one. The stonework had been badly affected by corrosive elements. Outside, crumbling masonry was everywhere apparent, even to the casual observer; inside, there was evident damage to upper stonework and the ribs of the vaults were in an uncertain condition in many places. There were cracks in the south-east tower and the south-east transept and, although the whole interior needed to be cleaned before the full extent of the damage could be ascertained, it was quite clear that only the most comprehensive programme of cleaning and repair, stone replacement and maintenance would ensure the preservation of the building. Repairs to Bell Harry Tower were started as early as 1963 after inspection had disclosed that the tower, though structurally sound, was suffering from erosion of the stone facing – the core was of English brick – and that this was endangering the roof of nave and transept. Initially, Clipsham stone was used for replacement, but this was believed unsuitable, and so the quarries of Normandy were surveyed and stone imported, which it was hoped would nearly match the original Caen stone of William of Sens. The work on Bell Harry took some nine years and occupied the attentions of five masons and four apprentices under the supervision of a head mason. It became increasingly apparent that the cathedral could not expect to find a body of skilled craftsmen in the future and they took active steps to encourage the training of apprentices. Working conditions within the precincts were unsuitable and so the Dean and Chapter established a masons' yard a mile and a half away at Broad Oak. Here, there was plenty of space for the delivery, storage and working of stone. Given the success of the current Appeal, the cathedral should now be able to have a continuing supply of skilled masons to ensure proper maintenance for many years ahead, but the capital outlay on a project such as this is considerable.

An even greater problem facing Canterbury is the preservation of the incomparably beautiful stained glass windows, which constitute the finest body of medieval glass in the country. This glass has survived the dangers of war and iconoclasm and now faces the much more perilous hazards of decay and corrosion. These windows, which include the genealogical sequence depicting the descent of Christ from Adam, the Apse windows with scenes from Christ's life and Passion, were begun in 1178. They told some of the great Bible stories to the untutored pilgrims in medieval times, and represent as varied and as historically important a collection as in almost any cathedral outside Chartres.

In the early 1970s, it suddenly became apparent that this unique collection was so mutilated by the passage of time and the pollution of the modern atmosphere that its survival was at risk. The extent of the damage only became apparent after scaffolding had been erected for a close inspection of the west and south-west transept windows in 1970 to 1971. As a result of this inspection, it was arranged that the eighth

colloquium of the Corpus Vitrearum Medii Aevi, the greatest
concentration of international expertise on medieval glass, should be
held in part at Canterbury to examine the windows. The genealogical
panel, 'Adam Delving', and one window from the south choir clerestory
were taken down and mounted in frames in the crypt, where they were
scrutinised by seventy of the leading scientists, historians and restorers
of Europe and America. Other early windows were examined from the
scaffolding inside the cathedral at clerestory level. The unanimous
decision of the delegates was that the condition of the early glass was
critical. Dr Frenzel of Nuremberg called it 'catastrophic' and added
that the glass could not survive in its present state for twenty years.
Another German expert said that none of his European colleagues had
ever seen glass in such poor condition. The rapid decline during recent
years is very largely due to the accumulation of chemicals in the
atmosphere. The combined effects of sulphur dioxide, together with a
moist climate, had created a corrosive acid that had eaten into the
surface of the glass, a problem, of course, not unique to Canterbury.
At Augsburg, photographs taken in 1947 revealed little more than slight
blemishes to the surface of the glass, but, by 1972, this was so deeply
eroded as to be almost opaque and four panels alone would, it was
estimated, take four years to stabilise and restore at a cost of 40,000
pounds.

At Canterbury, the decay is worse even than that of Augsburg and the
area involved some fifty times greater, yet the problem is being tackled.
A modern studio workshop is established in the precincts and glass in a
dangerous condition is restored in a thermostatically controlled strong-
room and treated by the most modern scientific techniques and aids. A
Stained Glass Advisory Committee has been appointed, consisting of
experts from Europe as well as from this country, and including cathedral
officials, and help is being sought from leading specialists in glass history
and glass technology. The idea is that some of them will be invited to
become research Fellows.

Faced with the task of establishing an order of priorities, the salvation
of the glass is of necessity first on the list. However, unless work on
the fabric is maintained, its condition could be as grave as that of the glass
ten years from now. And, added to the problem of arresting decay and
disintegration, there is the ever present worry of future damage and the
Surveyor is especially concerned about fire risks. Every large and old
building is at risk from fire, as the fire at Malines in Belgium sadly
emphasised. As part of the current programme, therefore, Canterbury
is taking urgent measures to reduce the possibility of outbreaks and to
contain them if they should occur.

Of necessity, any major restoration project must depend to some
degree on outside contractors, working on particular tasks and the
whole operation must be planned with military precision. In Canterbury,
a comprehensive plan has been evolved which will take the restoration
and conservation up to 1982. The work is all concurrent, designed to

save costs and to make the most flexible and practical use of available labour. The hope is that, by 1982, the urgent tasks will all have been accomplished and then the permanent staff will be able to concentrate on the continuing problems of routine maintenance. A project of these dimensions affords opportunity for research and development of techniques which can be of use to other cathedrals and great churches. Although, luckily, Canterbury does not face such grave problems as there were at York, where the whole foundations were at risk, design faults are constantly being discovered and research into their correction carried out. Scientific research and application has been concentrated upon the need for discovery of new materials with weathering properties to help prolong the life of the stone. The use of plastics is being investigated, particularly with regard to whether they can help protect the windows from pollutants. To date, these materials have shown a tendency to yellow in time and plain glass protection is out of the question as it would seriously detract from the artistic glories of the medieval glass.

Canterbury, because it is a national and international symbol, found that its Appeal met with initially striking success. By 12 February 1976, some 1,878,000 pounds had been raised or promised. The target, however, is over 3 million—at 1975 prices. The burden of cost is becoming increasingly heavy and even Canterbury may be glad of some Government aid. Surely, no Government could deny the request if it were made, but in fact, there is no criticism of Government for not stepping in immediately. There is indeed deep feeling that spontaneous giving and local control over spending is of fundamental importance. Peter Marsh fears that any legislative intervention could lead to 'less interest, love and care'. There would seem little danger of any diminution of love and care at present. The case for Canterbury has been put with force and public figures of great eminence have rallied to support, not only in Britain, but elsewhere, irrespective of religion. There is, too, a happy relationship with local voluntary pressure groups, such as the Canterbury Amenity Group and the local archaeological trust.

The media have all been helpful in publicising the dangers to the cathedral. The Prince of Wales went on television to talk about it and there is a fervent hope among those conducting the Appeal that anything that they may achieve will help other cathedrals with similar problems. Peter Marsh is confident of succeeding. As he told me, 'We are getting on top of the problem. Until the Appeal we were losing out.' He sees his task in graphic terms: 'We have no option in my view. We are the caretakers of our heritage. We must see to it that we pass it on in the state we inherited it. The sum of money can do more than just ensure speedy repairs. It can enhance the quality of the building if it is spent wisely.' The two and a half million people who pass through Canterbury every year must surely share his determination and pray his optimism is justified.

CHAPTER NINE Treasures on Earth— Private Patrons and Public Collections

Man's acquisitive instinct is as old and as natural as his desire for security and, from the earliest times, those in positions of authority and responsibility have sought to surround themselves, both in life and in death, with the most beautiful objects their fellows could create. Perhaps the most remarkable collections of ancient times were those which the Egyptian pharaohs accumulated to support them in the next world and everyone who has seen just something of the fabulous treasures of Tutankhamen which have survived the pillaging of grave-robbers, must be grateful to the religious beliefs of Ancient Egypt.

Collecting for collecting's sake, however – the acquisition of works of art and beautiful objects to attract and adorn – began on a significant scale in Greece and by the second century BC, had spread to Rome. Throughout the period of the Roman Empire there was a constant searching of the East for masterpieces of great art, for their possession was a proud symbol of prestige with wealthy Romans. Many of the most notable figures in Roman history were avid collectors of Greek art – Atticus, Pompey and Julius Caesar, and those equally remarkable but very different Emperors, Hadrian and Nero. Rome itself produced a fine flowering of artistic elegance, and sometimes genius, as any visitor to Rome or Pompeii, or a thousand outposts of the Roman Empire, can testify. But the desire to collect is universal and the hallmark of every civilisation; long before the concept of fine art was recognised in Europe, the Chinese Emperors were amassing vast collections of objets d'art. Unfortunately, many of these collections perished with the overthrow of the dynasty that had accumulated them. The Greek and Roman empires passed away but the successive civilisations of China went on while Europe was plunged in the Dark Ages. And, during that same period, great collections were made in Japan. On another continent and in a third world, the royal rulers of Ife and Benin in Africa employed artists to adorn and beautify their courtly surroundings. In medieval Europe the great patron was the Church, and the monasteries of Italy, France and England became the treasure-houses of western Christendom, full of paintings and sculptures, rare and beautiful manuscripts, sacred relics, precious stones, and all manner of lovely and curious things. War and religious upheavals led to the dispersal of many of these treasures, but in Aachen and Cologne, and in some of the individual glories of the medieval age, one senses just what richness did belong to monasteries and churches throughout Europe.

Among the earliest secular collectors of precious objects were the Dukes of Burgundy but it was in the Italy of the Renaissance with the glittering acquisitions of the humanist princes – the Medici, the Este, the Gonzaga, and many of the Popes – that the first great collection of post-medieval times came into being. This is not the occasion to dispute their morals or politics, but it is indisputable that these men, both as collectors and as patrons, helped to create a whole new civilisation and attitude of mind.

England's Elizabethan Renaissance, also, depended largely on the discernment and vanity of the private patron and benefactor, but one of the first important English collectors was Charles I. He bought most of the paintings and antiquities that had been gathered together by the Dukes of Mantua, but his collection (one of the finest that Europe had ever known) hardly outlived him, and the stern rulers of the Commonwealth were glad to disperse it for cash to Mazarin, Philip IV of Spain, the Archduke of Austria and many others. With the Restoration, collecting again became an acceptable and fashionable pursuit and paved the way for its greatest age in England: the eighteenth century.

The succession was assured, internal strife – save for two brief flurries in 1715 and 1745 – was over and, as great magnate and local squire settled down in an attitude of national and parochial superiority and turned their attention to their houses and estates, they also turned their minds to beautifying and adorning them. By the middle of the century the Grand Tour was beginning to be thought of as the natural conclusion of any young gentleman's education; and when he travelled he bought, and brought back, antiquities, pictures and other things that took his fancy. If his scholarship was real, or he was well advised, he collected masterpieces, but whether his foreign acquisitions were genuine or dubious, he turned his attention to housing them properly and giving them a setting worthy of their true or alleged lineage. He patronised the great cabinet-makers of the day, silversmiths who had come over from France when Louis XIV revoked the Edict of Nantes, and the new generation of portrait painters. Every family had to have its likenesses displayed on the walls. The public museum was on the way because, proud of what he had gathered, the duke, or even the squire, was often eager that his collection should be accessible to an interested public, and by the middle of the century some of the more spectacular country houses were open on specific days of the week.

Not all looked upon patronage kindly. We all know of Johnson's unhappy experience which led him to write one of the bitterest and saddest letters in the English language to the Earl of Chesterfield, when he spurned that nobleman's tardy recognition of his genius and wrote that a patron was, 'one who looks with unconcern on a man struggling for his life in the water and, when he has reached the ground, encumbers him with help'. A patron, he thought, was 'commonly a wretch who supports with insolence and is payed with flattery'. But Johnson's experiences were not, happily, universal.

One would have thought that patron and collector would have had their day with the growth of public galleries and museums in the nineteenth century. However, not only were most of these galleries and museums indebted for their very existence to private benefaction, but the continuing existence of the private collector was never more important than when 'official taste' dominated the selection and display of pictures and works of art in public places. Academic judgement is often blinkered, and committees seldom make adventurous decisions. It is therefore sad, but understandable, that almost all the creative movements in the arts in the nineteenth century took place in spite of public patronage rather than because of it. The arch example is that of the Impressionists, and the Post Impressionists, who were excluded from official exhibitions. They and their successors depended almost entirely on private buyers, and sometimes on dealers, and their works found their way into public collections only after their position had been established, and then only because there were private holdings of their works to be donated for public display.

The rôle of the private collector was not restricted to his patronage of contemporary art. His was the interest that focused attention on Japanese colour prints, African sculpture, pre-Columbian American art, in fact, on almost everything that added to the aesthetic vision of the nineteenth century. It was he who created a new awareness for some of the more obscure periods of European art. Fifteenth-century Italian paintings were in private hands long before any national gallery was interested in them. Collectors, such as Sir Hugh Lane and the famous Misses Davies, owned superb French nineteenth-century paintings, which official hands were reluctant to take when offered. In this century the same trends have continued and it is to collectors and scholars, led by Denis Mahon, that we owe the rediscovery of Italian seventeenth-century paintings, and most of the celebrated collections in that field are still in private hands.

So it is in Britain today that many of the most distinctive and stimulating collections are not owned by the State, local authorities or other public bodies. This fact is recognised and positively welcomed by the directors of almost every public gallery and museum. They, above all, know that the private collection of today may well become the public collection of tomorrow, and they know, too, that without the private collection most of the exhibitions which attract attention to their galleries could never be held. Also, of course, the public itself has a greater chance of seeing beautiful things, in a variety of settings throughout the country, if collections are preserved and the private collector encouraged. Many of our greatest private collections are on display for at least half the year for anyone who wishes to see them and there are very few which cannot be viewed by the serious student at any time, provided adequate notice is given and proper arrangements made. It is this accessibility in the stately homes and country houses of England

Above: A beauty spot after contact with twentieth-century civilisation: Box Hill after a Bank Holiday *(Dudley Styles, for the National Trust)*

Below: Traditional landscape: a scene on the Yorkshire Wolds near Huggate, looking east *(A. F. Kersting)*

Top: 'Song of Summer'. Norfolk: a wayside scene in the East Anglian region of wide horizons *(Kenneth Scowen)*

Above: The product of one civilisation threatened by the product of another: Capability Brown's magnificent pool at Chillington, Staffordshire, which may soon have a motorway within half a mile *(Peter Gifford)*

Left: The gentle woodlands: autumn in the Buckinghamshire woods near Turville *(A. F. Kersting)*

A great house threatened: Stonor Park, for nine centuries the home of the Stonor family, vacated by Lord Camoys in January 1976, its contents dispersed and its future unknown *(Alex Starkey, for* Country Life)

A great house saved: the east front of Erddig, one of the most recent acquisitions of the National Trust, remarkable for its contents, but in very poor structural condition when the Trust accepted it *(National Trust)*

Opposite: The Stone Hall, Houghton Hall, Norfolk, opened to the public for the first time in 1976 *(Sydney W. Newbery, for* Country Life)

Leeds Castle in Kent, newly opened to the public *(Country Life)*

Georgian elegance replaced by twentieth-century ugliness. Southgate, Bath *(William Morris)*

The monstrous Beaufort Hotel, an intruder in a graceful townscape, Bath *(William Morris)*

A view of John Slessor Court, Bath *(William Morris)*

The archway to the famous Vanburgh Barracks at Berwick, the oldest in the country still in use. They are the Regimental Headquarters of the King's Own Scottish Borderers and the headquarters of the Berwick Preservation Trust *(Tweeddale Press Ltd)*

Above: St Mary's church, Louth, seen from Westgate. Only the television aerials are visible intrusions of the twentieth century *(Northgate Studio)*

Below: The ruins of Berwick Castle. Both the castle and walls of Berwick have been imaginatively preserved *(Tweeddale Press Ltd)*

Before the 100,000 pound scheme for restoration at Pan Ha', Dysart, Kirkcaldy *(National Trust for Scotland)*

After the six derelict seventeenth-century houses had been restored, plus five new ones, Pan Ha' is a new community *(National Trust for Scotland)*

Another example of the National Trust for Scotland's Little Houses Scheme: before the restoration *(National Trust for Scotland)*

After restoration: the house of John McDouall Stuart, the explorer *(National Trust for Scotland)*

Above: The church of St Margaret Cley-next-the-Sea, Norfolk, is typical of many such in Norfolk, serving a small community *(Eastern Daily Press)*

Right: The topping out ceremony on a 'new' medieval tower at Wyghton, Norfolk. The old tower collapsed, but, thanks to a Canadian benefactor, was replaced *(Eastern Daily Press)*

Above: The church of St Faith, Little Witchingham as the Trust found it *(Peter Newbolt, for the Norfolk Churches Trust)*

Left: After part of the medieval wall paintings had been discovered *(Peter Newbolt, for the Norfolk Churches Trust)*

The Lamp of the Lothians: Haddington church, East Lothian, from the south east, before restoration *(A. F. Kersting)*

Haddington church, now almost totally restored, is the centre of a reinvigorated community *(A. F. Kersting)*

Below: The magnificent baroque church of Great Witley, Worcester *(Vicar and Churchwardens of Great Witley)*

Above: The interior. Despite having a tiny parish, by 1975 half of the money needed for restoration had been raised and spent *(Vicar and Churchwardens of Great Witley)*

The great enemy of old woodwork: death-watch beetles crawling over an oak beam *(Heather Angel)*

Detail of galleries and borings made by the beetle *(Heather Angel)*

Natural disaster: one of two spirelets of Peterborough Cathedral blown down by the great gales of January 1976 *(Dean and Chapter of Peterborough Cathedral)*

The ravages of time: stained glass from the panel, 'Adam Delving', showing the damage caused by acids from atmospheric pollution *(Canterbury Cathedral)*

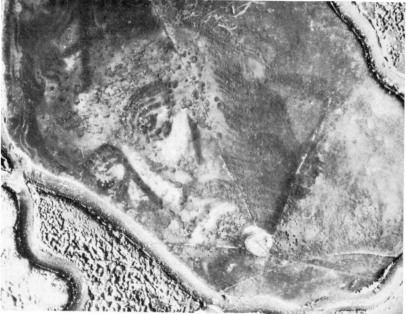

The face of Adam from the same panel shows pitting, erosion and fracturing *(Canterbury Cathedral)*

Craftsmen at work restoring Canterbury Cathedral, carving by hand
(Canterbury Cathedral)
The head mason, Keith Newing, makes zinc templates, or patterns, to enable the masons to fashion each block of replacement stone to the shape of the old
(Canterbury Cathedral)

Craftsmen working slate to re-roof the market hall at Chipping Campden, Gloucestershire *(National Trust)*

The art of re-moulding at Blickling in Norfolk *(National Trust)*

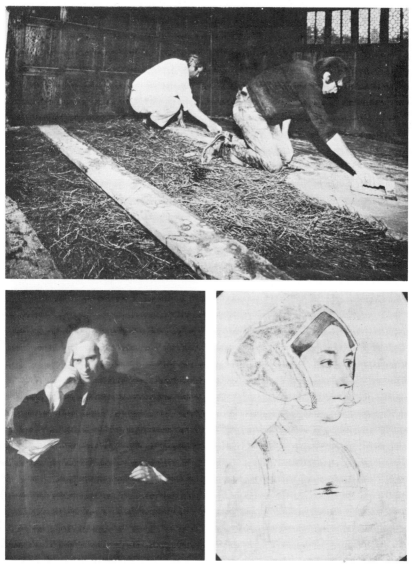

Top: Craftsmen laying a new floor at Little Moreton Hall, Cheshire *(National Trust)*

Above left: A treasure saved for the nation: Reynolds' portrait of Laurence Sterne, bought in 1975 for 50,000 pounds *(Trustees of the National Portrait Gallery)*

Above right: Holbein's drawing of a lady of King Henry VIII's court, sometimes said to be Anne Boleyn, bought by the British Museum for 70,000 pounds in 1975 *(Trustees of the British Museum)*

Opposite: The techniques of a new age used to preserve the beauties of an old: work on the new foundations of York Minster *(Shepherd Building Group Ltd)*

Lost from English collections because our national museums were unable to
raise funds **Top left:** the famous Velazquez sold to New York in 1970
Top right: Rembrandt's portrait of a boy, sometimes identified as his son Titus
Above: Bassano's 'Flight into Egypt' sold to the USA *(Christies)*

A superb example of medieval craftsmanship in silver,
the Savernake Horn, purchased with a grant from the National Art
Collections Fund in 1975 *(Trustees of the British Museum)*

Stubbs' masterly painting of the Millbank family, saved for the nation in 1975, is now in the National Gallery *(Trustees of the National Gallery)*

One of a pair of unique Queen Anne silver chandeliers which were exported to Switzerland because no museum could raise sufficient money *(Christies)*

Above: A treasure at risk: 'Racehorses Exercising' by Stubbs, who painted many pictures while staying at Goodwood in 1759-60. Having always hung in the Long Hall, the room for which they were painted, they should not be lost from there *(Trustees of the Goodwood Collection)*

Below: The Earl of March sits in an empty room, demonstrating the devastating effect taxation could have at Goodwood *(The Earl of March)*

that gives them such a special status.

Much has been said about the English country house already, but two points can readily be made here. First of all, it is surely not desirable that works of art should only be accessible in the big cities, and in London in particular. Far better that there should be beautiful things to see, and in beautiful, non-institutional settings, in obscure corners of Lincolnshire, Shropshire, Suffolk and Bedfordshire than that everything should be displayed in the often clinical atmosphere of a museum or gallery. Secondly, not everything that gives pleasure and enchantment in a country house would be suitable for a museum. Vast numbers of topographical pictures and family portraits are interesting and enlivening in their natural setting, but are often of very little interest when removed from it. That many will be moved, together with their surrounding domestic trappings, the unrivalled collections of English furniture and porcelain, silver and tapestries that make up the contents of so many of our country houses is only too likely. Throughout the twentieth century, country houses have been abandoned and their contents dispersed. We have seen, too, how the threat to the houses is greater than ever, but if the threat to the houses is great, the danger to their contents is acute. For who, faced with the necessity of maintaining a family, would sell a productive field or woodland in order to retain a Rembrandt or a Reynolds?

It is this threat of extinction by taxation that faces the private collection, and continuing private patronage, and calls for the most spirited defence of collections and collector. Such a defence can best begin by a careful examination of just how dependent our public collections have been upon private benefaction and loan and how dependent they still are on these sources. In a recent paper submitted to the Select Committee examining the proposals for the Wealth Tax, the Museums Association, which represents the governing bodies of the country's museums and art galleries, and also the staff working in them, pointed out that there are some 950 public museums and galleries in this country and that just under half of these are administered by national or local government bodies. Their acquisitions have been built up to a large extent by outright gifts from private collections. One thinks instinctively of the Wallace Collection, the Iveagh Bequest at Kenwood or the Courtauld Gallery, but these are in a special category and recognised as such – they were bequests to the nation. It is when looking at the country's other museums that one becomes aware of how vital a rôle private benefaction and private loan has played in their growth.[1] For instance, in Wolverhampton 75 per cent of the works on show have been given; in Liverpool the Walker Art Gallery, one of the most important provincial galleries in the world owes 90 per cent of its works to private generosity and private purchase appeals. In the Ashmolean, Oxford, 90 per cent of the coin room has been given, 80 per cent of the antiquities, 98 per cent of the Eastern art, 95 per cent of the silver, 80 per cent of the paintings. From Bristol to Leeds, Manchester to

[1] See Appendix 5.

Hull, in all of these places the figures are startling. And, even where the objects themselves have not been given, it is private endowment that has enabled the museum to continue. In Hull, for instance, 80 per cent of the purchases of the Ferens Art Gallery have come from an endowment fund established by Thomas Ferens when he founded the gallery. These figures illustrate just how little of the purchase money comes from public sources. The Fitzwilliam Museum in Cambridge, for example, one of the finest of all university museums, has official annual purchase funds of less than 10,000 pounds.[2]

Apart from provincial collections that owe either their existence or their chief attractions to non-public sources, of the 5890 works owned by the Tate Gallery 71 per cent were bequeathed or given, 1049 purchased with Government money and 593 bought out of privately subscribed funds. In the National Gallery, founded with a private bequest, 55 per cent of the paintings have been given or bequeathed. At the National Portrait Gallery the figure is almost as high. At Edinburgh, the National Gallery of Scotland is heavily dependent upon the pictures lent by the Duke of Sutherland and at Cardiff in the National Museum of Wales, 95 per cent of the ceramic collection, 90 per cent of the glass, 83 per cent of the Impressionist and modern paintings, have been given or lent. The same applies to the recently established specialist museum, such as the National Army Museum, or the RAF Museum, which rely very heavily on material and financial help from private sources.

In 1975 there were only two local authorities, Birmingham and Manchester, which gave their galleries and museums purchase funds of 20,000 pounds or more and if that be thought to indicate that all was well in Birmingham and Manchester, it should be noted that only 9 of the 17 picture galleries in Birmingham are available for display of paintings and barely a quarter of the collection of oil paintings can be shown at any one time. Three galleries have in fact been converted into store-rooms, but even these are insufficient to house the paintings under tolerable conditions and many pictures are on long-term loan to offices and colleges for want of adequate storage. This highlights the fact that, if there were a flood of acceptable works of art released on to the market by owners who could no longer afford to hold them, and if Government refused to allow any of them to be exported, very few could be displayed. There is a real crisis of accommodation in the nation's museums and many notable works of art hardly see the light of day from one decade to the next. Even if the maintenance of museums and art galleries to a defined minimum standard became a statutory liability upon local authorities, it would be at least a couple of generations before those works already owned could be properly displayed, let alone quantities of new ones. It is not only a question of storage and display;

[2] At the time of going to press the Museum was struggling to raise 200,000 pounds to prevent Van Dyck's 'Madonna and Child', long on loan on its walls, from being shipped to America – an early casualty of excess fiscal repression.

perhaps the most acute crisis facing provincial museums is the problem of conserving their collections. There are almost no galleries which have sufficient conservators on their staff adequately to maintain them.

All of these facts underline the importance of enabling collections in houses as different and as far apart as Belton and Woburn, Castle Howard and Goodwood, Weston Park and Lennoxlove, to be maintained—maintained by their owners without the public purse being embarrassed in any way. Not only are the Woburn Canalettos as well preserved and displayed as ever they could be in their historic setting, and visited by as many people as would see them in any public gallery, but also there is surely no point in seeking to take them into public ownership while eight galleries in Birmingham remain closed, the Tate has an enormous store of paintings never on public view, and while the new extension at the National Gallery can hardly cope with those which it already has to display. It is for these reasons that, when the Select Committee on the Wealth Tax was receiving submissions and hearing evidence, the almost unanimous plea, not only from collectors but from those knowledgeable about the state of our national museums, is that the private collector has a continuing rôle to play in maintaining and enhancing our heritage.

The Museums Association, for instance, made the point that loans from private collections are vital, for in many instances the loans are semi-permanent and if withdrawn can have a devastating effect on a collection (as would have happened if the Harewood Titian had not been bought by the National Gallery in 1974). Of course, if fiscal impositions mount, an owner would be sorely tempted to sell something that is not even adorning his own walls as the line of first resort when confronted with a tax bill. Mr Hugh Leggatt, who owns the famous Beechey portrait of Nelson on show in the National Portrait Gallery, has made it plain that, much as he would like that picture to be regarded as a permanent part of the heritage, it would be one of the things he would sell first if he were in dire straits as a result of the taxman's incursions. Many short-term loans form the basis of exciting and unique exhibitions. Without the willing private lender, the Tate could not have held the superb Constable bicentenary exhibition in 1976, nor the Royal Academy the Turner exhibition of 1975. In the field of contemporary art, especially, the private collector is often prepared to take risks in his purchases which public museums, accountable to the public purse, may not feel justified in taking. With the extraordinary nature of much 'Modern Art' this is a good thing in more ways than one. For example, those who deplored the Tate Gallery's acquisition of a pile of bricks for a sum reputed to be well over 1000 pounds in February 1976, would merely have raised their eyebrows or shrugged their shoulders had some eccentric made the purchase out of his own pocket.

The Museums Association warned about the possible outcome of Wealth Tax and suggested that it would result in the depletion of existing private collections, the withdrawal of loans from museums and the drying up of private patronage, not to mention the end of outright gifts of money and objects. One of the Association's prime anxieties was that the operation of export controls as such works came on the market would be inadequate. They felt it likely that, wherever restrictions were introduced, there would be a considerable increase in the activities of overseas buyers. And it must not be forgotten that, currently, the Reviewing Committee on the Export of Works of Art cannot consider objects costing less than 4000 pounds, and many of those can have either a local or a national significance.

All of these points were underlined, and many more made, in the submission produced by the Standing Commission on Museums and Galleries itself. This Commission, whose members are appointed by the Prime Minister, and which reports to the Secretaries of State for Education for Scotland and Wales, has a statutory duty to advise generally on questions 'relevant to the most effective development' of museums and galleries of all kinds. It was set up 'to stimulate the generosity of those who aspire to become public benefactors'. In its Report the Commission said:

> The rôle of the private collector can never be replaced by the State. This is even the case with old master works which are subject to fashion... But it is illustrated most clearly in the case of modern, and especially contemporary art. In comparison with Germany, Switzerland and the USA, this country is not rich in pictures and sculptures of this and the late nineteenth century, particularly the works of modern foreign artists. If it had not been for the gifts and bequests of Sir Hugh Lane and Samuel Courtauld to London and the Misses Davies to Wales and Alexander Aitkin to Scotland, the country would have owned virtually no Impressionist paintings.

The Standing Commission's conclusion, also, was that a Wealth Tax, in conjunction with a Capital Transfer Tax, even with some sort of exemption for chattels, would deplete existing private collections of museum objects. The museums could only benefit from this if their funds for purchases, exhibition and conservation were most substantially increased and this, in turn, would involve considerable expenditure from public funds. They went on to say that the definition of a museum object, given the needs of different museums both now and in the future, was bound to be arbitrary and affected by changes in fashion, and the application of the definition to many thousands of objects year by year would be difficult, uncertain and irksome. It would be far better to exempt all art and scientific objects or archives whatever their individual merit. Since this would include furniture and silver, as well as pictures, books and manuscripts, it would probably mean exempting all household goods.

All of this was reinforced by a letter to the Chancellor of the

Exchequer by the Chairman of the Standing Commission: 'The past importance of private collections to public collections cannot be overstressed.' He then quoted some of the examples already mentioned and made the additional point that all the great foundation collections of early books and manuscripts in the British Library became public property as a result of private generosity. He also observed, that, 'The future importance of private collections at home is no less vital for our public collections as future acquisitions from abroad are now virtually impossible.'

That such a Commission should have to spend its time urging Government not to do what it recognised should not be done when it appointed the Commission in the first place, is particularly absurd, the more so in that in recent years there has been an increasing recognition in Government circles of the importance of private benefaction. This was recognised when gifts of property and other bequests to public collections were exempted from Estate Duty and Capital Gains Tax. When these concessions were made, many felt that the way was open for an adoption of the American fiscal incentives, whereby those giving money or works of art to museums are allowed to offset their expenditure against taxable income. If such a system were adopted here it would undoubtedly act as a spur towards an industrial participation in the arts, which has in this country been lamentably behind that of many of our neighbours, and is in any event almost entirely restricted to sponsorship of the performing arts. One cannot but think that, if the incentive were there, more companies and individuals would feel inclined to be generous. Then we might see an early implementation of some of the Gulbenkian and Wright Reports' recommendations on conservation and the display of collections. The record of public subscription to meet existing contingencies, let alone to enhance our collections, has not been notably spectacular in recent years. The Radnor Velazquez would, probably, have remained in the country if contributions towards its retention could have been offset against tax and, if that sort of concession had been allowed, the National Gallery would not have had to pawn its future purchasing grant to retain the Titian.

The Reviewing Committee on the Export of Works of Art feels alarmed about recent fiscal developments. In 1975 they said, 'We feel that the threat of such a tax (i.e. the Wealth Tax) may at any moment start a rush to sell which could lead to chaos in the world of art and scholarship, and to the breakdown of the present control system with greater or lesser national treasures leaving the country never to return.' Certainly, the art market has not suffered from the fluctuating fortunes of the Stock Market or the property market and there has been an increasing number of foreign buyers during the last three years. That London should continue to be the centre of the art market is obviously desirable from every point of view, whether one looks at it through the spectacles of scholarship, or is motivated by concern for the balance of payments. In the past, however, a vast amount of the goods bought in the London auction houses were bought by British dealers and came to rest in British homes, but 1975 and 1976 saw a distinct change in this pattern. More and more works were being bought for foreign buyers, especially in the Middle East.

This disturbing trend is likely to continue, and the fears of the Reviewing Committee realised, unless there is a very sharp change in Government policy, for, although the Budget of April 1976 gave extended Capital Transfer Tax exemption to works of art, the exemptions only applied to works of art owned for twenty years. There could be hardly less of an inducement to the British collector of today than this. Again, the exemption would, at the time of writing (April 1976), only seem to apply to works of art readily accessible to public view. Whilst one can understand the reasons behind such a policy, it must be recognised that not all collectors live in mansions and that, there are, as that great scholar collector, Denis Mahon said in a letter to *The Accountant*, April 1975:

> ... innumerable collections or even more or less isolated objects, situated (in very considerable quantities in the aggregate) in houses or indeed flats, which cannot reasonably be expected to be accessible on a similar basis to those in the great historic houses... Moreover there exist great quantities of works of art and items of cultural and historic importance which ought not to be dispersed overseas but which are of interest to specialists rather than to the general public. This would include, to take but a single category, manuscripts, archival material and libraries. These have problems of conservation as do, for example, certain drawings (and particularly water colours) which can be quite literally consumed if they are subjected to light on more than infrequent intervals.

Many of those who would support the 'qualified' exemptions would do so because of a mistaken idea that most people who buy works of art at the present time are speculators and investors assisted by avaricious dealers but, although this is a travesty of the truth, that has not prevented its being given circulation in numerous agitatory articles. It is undeniable that some people buy works of art because they believe they keep their value better than other things, but very few people buy them purely as investments. The great auction houses and well established London and provincial dealers represent a core of men and women whose integrity and contribution to the heritage is considerable, and without them most of the great collections of the twentieth century would never have been assembled. A healthy and flourishing art market, organised by people who know their subjects and care for them, is an integral part of a cultured community. Without the pre-eminence of Christies and Sothebys, the fame and often the altruism of the great dealers, many of Britain's public institutions would be poorer and great works of art, which we now accept as integral parts of the heritage, would never have reached this country, or would have left it for ever. In spite of all the uncertainty, great works do still pass from the private to the public collection, for example the National Portrait Gallery's acquisition of Reynolds' portrait of Sterne and the British Museum's acquisition of Holbein's portrait of Anne Boleyn in 1975. But both of these were acquired for the public as a result of the willingness of their owners to forego the possibility of a spectacular price, accepting the very limited advantage of the tax concessions that the State currently allows. The portrait of Sterne was acquired for 50,000 pounds and that of Anne Boleyn for 70,000 pounds. In the open market 'on a good day' the Reynolds could well have reached 200,000 and the Holbein substantially more. The temptation to go for the big price will increase as the fiscal burden on owners becomes heavier. A Wealth Tax, coupled with the Capital Transfer Tax, could quickly reduce our remaining great collections. As one museum director remarked to me:

No one is going to hold on to and retain works of art either by heritage or by purchase to pay rent to the State and finally as a gracious gesture be allowed by the State to wipe out his tax arrears by giving it to a museum. It is astounding that words such as 'encourage' and phrases such as 'it is highly desirable to ensure that the rich benefit which public collections have attained from private munificence be continued' can be used in a series of proposals designed to produce precisely the opposite effect.

With the exception of a few Marxist art historians, everyone giving evidence to the Select Committee on the Wealth Tax agreed that the future of the private collection and the private patron is gravely in doubt because of the oppressive level of current taxation, and the threats of new taxes. Recognition of the realities by a sensitive Government would go far to remove the threat and restore incentive to collectors, and thus provide an investment for the public collection of the future. The Government of the Republic of Ireland seems to have recognised this, for its Finance Act of 1975 contained provisions for a wealth tax that would exempt all works of art to which there are reasonable facilities for viewing by members of the public or recognised bodies. And reasonable facilities should not be taken to mean constant availability or display. For much has been achieved by the small collector devoting his time, talents and resources to the acquisition and study of works that would otherwise have been lost or forgotten. As the then Chairman of the National Arts Collection Fund said in 1975, 'Great wealth is not essential for the creation of outstanding collections but if a collector happens to be wealthy this does not preclude that he may be a man of taste, a man with an eye, or a man with a sense of public responsibility to boot.'

This view is not shared, of course, by those who see any possessions, particularly durable ones, as evidence of some sort of social immorality. During the debate on the Wealth Tax, one of the leading advocates of

its application to works of art was a certain Marxist art historian called
Peter Fuller. He and a group of colleagues said that they took their
stand, 'Because such a measure would be in the social and cultural
interests of the majority of the population of this country. We are also
certain that it will advance the interest of the increasing number of people
who enjoy looking at painting and sculpture rather than hoarding them
or trading in them...' It was very sad that the only person who was
seen to accept this line of argument was the then Minister for the Arts,
Mr Hugh Jenkins. But Fuller was a political nonentity, and one can
only hope and indeed trust that his view of the heritage will never
prevail. If 'public wealth' in the arts is an object of those who
devise Government policy for the Arts, there must be a conscious and
determined effort to safeguard not only the great private collections but
the collecting instinct as such. That is surely a view that must be shared
by the citizens of Warwickshire, who can view a magnificent collection
in Warwick Castle while having to read that one of their public museums
may have to sell valuable possessions for their own protection after
damage by rain and rats.

CHAPTER TEN A Wider Heritage

The heritage that we cherish in Britain is part of a wider heritage, that of western Christendom, which itself has cultural roots in Greece, Rome and Judaism. The pattern of our landscape, the temples of our faith, and houses great and small, all have a distinctive native quality about them, yet they are none of them insular in the fully isolated sense of the word. Though Romanesque architecture evolved far from the banks of the Wear, we owe to it Durham Cathedral. To the brilliance of the ancient world filtered through the Italian Renaissance, we owe the Banqueting Hall in Whitehall. To the acquisitive instinct in action of the Grand Tour, we owe many of our finest collections of works of art. Indeed, there is hardly a notable expression of our civilisation that does not betray, if not portray, its European roots: though the plants may be indigenous to our soil the seeds were nurtured across the Channel.

With more and more people from these shores flocking to the Continent every year, our television screens making many of the landmarks of Europe as familiar as our own and Britain now firmly involved in the European Economic Community, it is appropriate to look briefly at some aspects of this wider heritage and to see how problems common to its effective appreciation and preservation are dealt with in other European countries. And it is particularly appropriate, in the aftermath of a European Architectural Heritage Year, which saw a common expression of concern, a desire to educate, and a desire to co-ordinate and concert effective action to preserve the best of our architectural heritage. That many of the problems are common, and that each nation can teach its neighbours something about effective solutions, was most graphically demonstrated in the Architectural Heritage Year film, *Europa Nostra*. But it is surprising, when one comes to look in detail at the question, how little work has been done of a comparative nature, seeking to analyse the approaches to heritage problems in neighbouring countries. Much of what follows will, in so far as it concerns architecture, lean heavily on the work of Dennis Rodwell, a young Scottish architect who has done some of the most valuable pioneering work in this field.

'Out of evil cometh good.' This has certainly been true of the way in which the efforts of civilised men and women all over Europe have been directed in recent years towards saving Venice. 'Venice in Peril', an international fund, has focused attention on the dire plight of this European city, whose influence as a city state reached out across nations and frontiers and touched indirectly the life of so many courts and communities in the fifteenth and sixteenth centuries. When it became widely known that Venice was in danger of sinking beneath the waters that have given it its distinctive and unique character, the common cry went up, 'Venice must be saved'. Funds were established and in many countries, scholars, connoisseurs, architects, restorers (including some from the Victoria and Albert Museum) and statesmen have been at work to assist the efforts of the Italian Government. Unfortunately, whilst this united action was a moving testimony to international co-operation, it became increasingly obvious that all would depend upon the will of the Italian Government, in its determination in imposing, and its financial commitment in underwriting, a solution which would preserve Venice into the twenty-first century.

The problems facing any Italian Government are enormous as Italy has so much of the European heritage, not only in Venice; Florence, Rome, Assisi, Piza and Naples and ... one could go on through a whole catalogue of historic cities and noble buildings, all of them important landmarks in the history of European civilisation. Provisions for safeguarding them are enshrined in a series of laws passed between 1892 and 1971. As a result of these, about a hundred thousand individually important buildings have statutory protection and may not be altered or demolished without permission. This provision is separate from those seeking to guarantee the protection and restoration of certain important historic towns. They are safeguarded by separate legislation; for instance, there are special laws for Venice itself and Assisi and Siena, and Urbino. Under a law of 1968, regional authorities are given power to establish strict regulations for safeguarding historic zones within their areas and there is provision for the awarding of grants. Over and above the statutory protection that is afforded and the grants that are made available – up to 50 per cent for restoration to listed buildings – there is the powerful pressure group known as Italia Nostra, founded in 1954, and now having over a hundred local branches or chapters, and a membership of some 20,000 in Italy and 50,000 abroad.

Some of the successes and failures, and continuing problems, facing the planning authorities are most clearly seen in Naples. The hills around the city bear witness to the inadequacy of past Italian planning regulations. They have been defaced and despoiled by thousands of featureless slabs of housing blocks. Historic and romantic landscape has gone for ever, buried under the undistinguished architectural excreta of the post-War developers. The heart of the old city, however, remains, dowdy and dingey, but largely inviolate and, though the vagaries of

Italian drivers make a walk through the narrow courts and alleys a hair-raising experience, the street patterns and buildings have for the most part survived. But enormous sums of money will have to be spent if they are going to last beyond the end of this century. The city, however, pulsates with life and there seems an encouraging resolve that the ghastly mistakes on the hills around, based on a fraudulent falsification of the 1939 city plan, should not be repeated. The new city plan, resembling in intention that of 1939, limited the city's population to 1,100,000 and has among its features an intention to remove oil refineries and chemical works from the city. All remaining open spaces are to be preserved and the conservation area within the city enlarged from 170 hectares – the ancient centre – to 750 hectares, to protect the Spanish, Baroque and nineteenth-century extensions.

There is, though, all the difference between a plan and an achievement, especially in Italy, and the latest plan has not been widely accepted, still less welcomed in every quarter. But plans are important. They show that people who care think, and they can often point the way for others in similar circumstances and in different countries. The low-cost housing plan in the historic centre of Bologna has many features which could commend it to local authorities throughout Europe. The idea is based upon a belief that the town depends for its life on people of all classes being able to afford to live in it. The Bologna Council considered this an indispensable element in the active preservation of the centre of their city and wisely sought the co-operation of small proprietors, so that there would be no danger of their selling out to speculators, and no need for compulsory acquisition, which always slows up any work, in order to restore and conserve.

With a population of 13¼ million and an expenditure of some 84 million guilders on preservation and restoration projects in 1975, the Netherlands have one of the most encouraging records in the field of heritage, preservation and protection. A Government Commission was founded to prepare an inventory of historic monuments as long ago as 1903. The State Office for the Protection of Monuments was founded in 1918, and laws to ensure their protection were passed in 1940 and 1950, though the present comprehensive system was enacted as recently as 1965. Overall responsibility for the preservation of historic buildings and of town and village views rests with the Ministry of Cultural Affairs, Recreation and Social Work. Working through the State Service for the Preservation of Monuments and advised by the Monuments Council, an independent body established by Statute, the provincial authorities are responsible for the provision of grants and the general maintenance of monuments within their territory. A number of the provinces have special by-laws for the purpose, and have also appointed local qualified inspectors to supervise their implementation. A similar situation exists in regard to the larger towns, and special restoration departments have in fact been established in some of these, such as Amsterdam, Haarlem and Utrecht. In the Netherlands, there is a proliferation of voluntary organisations working closely with local and central government. As in Britain, some of these organisations are of a general nature whereas others are specifically concerned with certain types of monuments, such as castles or windmills, and some restrict their activities to specific regions or towns. The State Service for the Preservation of Monuments is concerned with the grading of restoration projects and the provision of expert advice in cases where alterations to buildings are envisaged. It acts as a clearing-house for applications and gives information to applicants on how to obtain grants for maintenance, conversion and alteration. It has been instrumental in the establishment of a Documentation Centre on Dutch Architecture in Amsterdam, which is intended to form the nucleus of a future national museum of architecture. The Service has on its staff not only inspectors, but architects and town planners, art historians, artists and craftsmen and other specialists.

The Monuments Act of 1961, which the Service seeks to interpret and enforce, specifies monuments as 'those objects and sights, no less than fifty years old which are of public interest because of their beauty and significance to science, ethnological value or historical association'. Under the Act, not only single monuments but groups of buildings can be designated. All the buildings listed under the Act are entered into a Monuments Register, which in 1975 contained some 40,000 entries, ranging from 27,800 private dwellings to 135 inns and including Government buildings (600), churches and other ecclesiastical buildings (2200), castles (250) and diverse monuments (a special category covering statues, gates, signposts, etc). In 1974, an additional register was compiled, which included 136 churches and 18 railway stations built between 1825 and 1924, as well as 25 archaeological sites in Friesland. Once a building has been listed, the owner is subject to certain restrictive provisions and must obtain permits for alteration or demolition. Similarly, he is eligible for grants of up to 70 per cent towards the cost of approved restorations.

As a result of these carefully constructed and monitored provisions, many thousands of houses throughout the Netherlands are restored each year and the budget for grants is certainly high compared with other countries. In spite of this, funds are not adequate to cover all authorised restoration projects and there is a substantial backlog of work. However, projects are always tackled with a typical Dutch thoroughness and this is no doubt why so many Dutch towns preserve an individual identity very much more successfully than those in neighbouring countries. One of the by-products of the Dutch policy has been the discovery, as in the ancient city of Middleburg, that renewing a modest residential heritage can cost far less than its demolition and replacement by new accommodation. Tourists sometimes criticise Dutch restoration as being more in the nature of complete rebuilding but the results are so pleasing to the eye that most would discount this criticism as academic. They have also been particularly adept at finding new uses for old buildings, as in Amsterdam, where the round Lutheran Church, a fine example of Dutch classicism, has become a reception centre for a new hotel. They have set great store on maintaining the scale of street building, too, so that old and valued scenes are not unduly distorted by a skyline dominated by out-of-scale buildings.

As long ago as 1950, the famous Gowers Report on English Country Houses carried a special appendix on the protection of historic buildings and their contents in France. This pointed out that among other things the most important of French châteaux, *monuments classé*, qualified for repair grants of up to 50 per cent and could claim 50 per cent relief on tax on repair and maintenance expenditure. The owner of a major French château is in a more advantageous position with regard to tax than the owner of a British stately home, but although the French system affords considerable protection to the greatest of its ancient buildings, many of the rest are in a somewhat dilapidated state.

France appointed its first Inspector General of Historic Monuments in 1830 and established its first Historic Monuments Commission in 1837. The original list of such monuments was drawn up in 1840 and, by 1841, a framework of control and grants to major cathedrals and other large monuments had been prepared. In this century, a whole series of laws has been passed between 1913 and 1975. The Historic Monuments Law of 1913, the basis of all subsequent legislation, provided for the strict control of a limited number of buildings and enacted the grant and tax provisions which the Gower's Report extolled. Under this law, some 75,000 moveable objects – paintings, sculptures, etc – were also listed. In 1930, a Sites Law, which established a list of protected town and country sites and parks, eligible for grants, and which restricted development and building heights, was enacted and in 1945 came the concept of a protected zone of up to 50 metres radius around all designated monuments and sites. The seminal act of recent years was the Malraux Law of 1962 which designated some 50 protected areas and 23 action areas for which detailed conservation plans had to be drawn up and implemented. Loans of up to 60 per cent and a further grant of 20 per cent in the case of the action areas were made available and under this law some 5300 buildings have already been restored at the cost of some hundred million francs in special grants. In France, all is very much under the eye of the central authorities and every action is carefully logged and monitored. The work that has been carried out, especially since the Malraux Law, has often been fascinating and spectacular. In Chartres and in Lyons, whole streets have been completely restored and in Paris, Marais *hotel particuliers* have been transformed from objectionable and filthy slums into luxurious apartment buildings and museums.

The disadvantage of the French system, however, is that, while certain selective buildings are subjected to the most thorough and comprehensive treatment on restoration, many pleasant and important vernacular buildings, such as the less important châteaux, and many villages and farm buildings, are left entirely without protection and are in danger of disappearing altogether. There is also a noticeable lack of public participation and involvement in conservation: either the State does it or no one does. There is, therefore, an urgent need for a reappraisal of the system which will enable more buildings to be helped and private initiative to be encouraged. Another criticism is that the expensive restoration often results in a situation whereby the working people who lived in an area cannot afford to return to their old homes at the new rents.

The contrasting of Ghent and Bruges shows the patchiness of approach and success in Belgian conservation issues. In Ghent, a project supported by the Ministry of Transport and the Ministry of Public Works among others, envisaged the filling-in of 10 kilometres of waterways to allow for the construction of an express highway through the city. This, in spite of the fact that the beauty of Ghent relies on the association of the buildings with the water. The same is true of Bruges, but there a beautiful and ancient city has been very successfully safeguarded. Canals in the centre of the city have been cleaned and the residential quarters attained a new attraction. The local authority is now backing the scheme, initiated by a private trust, and at present newly restored houses can be rented, but not bought, so that the authority has a tighter control over the character of the residential population. Belgium, however, is not a success story in the sphere of conservation. A law of 1931 does provide for the protection of monuments and sites and includes provisions for control and grants for a limited number of the more outstanding buildings, but with notable exceptions, such as that of Bruges (and at Louvain where the Grand Beguinage has been restored for use by the university). Belgium has few outstanding successes of which it can boast.

The Federal Republic of Germany, too, presents a strangely disappointing picture. One always thinks of Germany in terms of efficiency and, of course, some of their restoration projects, such as the *Rathous* in Bonn have been remarkably successful. However, there is no special protection for monuments in the federal laws although there are sections in the Federal Building Law which require developers to take into account 'cultural necessities' when producing plans. A number of the German Landes have no statutory provision for the protection of buildings either (Berlin, Bremen, Hamburg, Lower Saxony). In general, there seems no appreciation or implementation of the conservation area approach and towns as famous as Lubeck and Heidleberg seem remarkably vulnerable. In Lubeck there is already much disruption of the scale of the centre of the town by inappropriate modern building, and at Heidleberg little seems to have been achieved in the way of permanent protection save the listing of some of the more important buildings.

In Bavaria, the picture is much more encouraging. Although, until recently, the protection of historic buildings had been achieved largely through voluntary agency, the State authorities have a record of consistent sympathy with conservation and the State has some examples of which any country could be proud. In the historic town centre of Nuremberg, where 90 per cent of the 2560 historic buildings were destroyed, there has been a painstaking reproduction of the old; there have been some magnificent reconstructions of War-damaged cathedrals and churches and castles; the old town of Rothenburg, a notable centre, has been exceptionally well preserved. Regensburg is another notable example of a revived and attractive historic city and Munich itself has been pedestrianised to a greater extent than almost any other major European city.

The most outstanding examples of complete reconstruction, however, come from behind the Iron Curtain, and no story is more moving than Warsaw's. Warsaw was devastated during the Second World War and, in 1945, half the population was living in tents or rubble houses but at this point, and with hunger bordering on famine proportions, it was decided to rebuild this historic capital of Poland. It was seen as a national gesture of faith and the results have been remarkable. With painstaking accuracy, whole areas arose with their former glories and the opportunity of rebuilding allowed for more open space and therefore a better setting for many of the great public buildings. The Russians adopted a similar policy, especially in Leningrad, and the opportunity has been taken to encourage craftsmanship and to inspire the young with a particular regard for the treasures of the past. There is something contrived and clinical in all this rebuilding but the results have been astonishing and ought to act as a spur to those of us in the West who have so many genuine old buildings that merely demand our careful attention if they are to be safeguarded and appreciated into the next century. We also have the added incentive of being able to restore buildings that are still being used for their original purpose. If a purely aesthetic appreciation of what is pleasing and a dispassionate regard for certain versions of the nation's history is sufficient to prompt the Russians to erect their wooden churches in open air museums, then our motivating force should be even greater with the opportunity to preserve a living history and tradition. But this should not allow us to belittle the achievements of Eastern Europe, nor to denigrate the genuine regard which has prompted these feats of rebuilding, restoration and preservation.

Whole volumes could be written on this subject, and this one can only afford the passing reference. A similar reference, however, must obviously be made to the United States of America where in the bicentenary year of 1976 a cherishing of the past and a re-enactment of selected portions of it have become both a national preoccupation and a national industry. The lavish protection afforded to the great national shrines in and around Washington is second to none and the loving care with which chapters of the nation's past have been rebuilt at

Jamestown and Williamsberg is quite remarkable. Williamsberg, in particular, is a startlingly successful recreation of an old colonial capital, based on the restoration of what had survived and the rebuilding of what had been lost. This centre of national pilgrimage and historical entertainment could easily have become trivialised, especially as all the restored shops do business and all the inns serve food and drink. But restrained good taste prevails and to walk through the town is like taking a step back in time and to have an acuter appreciation than anywhere else of just what the eighteenth-century colonial capital was like. There is certainly nothing quite like this anywhere in Europe. However, the concept of preservation in the USA has only recently begun to replace the old frontier mentality of exploiting resources and then moving from one locality to the next without much regard for what was left behind. Now, prompted by such bodies as the Council for Environment Equality, established in 1970, there is a concerted attempt to ensure that what remains of the American past is properly regarded and maintained. In 1975, Senator Henry Jackson promoted a Land Use Bill which had, as its major objective, a regulation of the somewhat chaotic planning structure, the establishment of an order of priorities which would obviously go far to safeguarding the best of the past.

The problems of the USA over conservation of historic buildings are small in comparison with those faced by most European nations. However, it is in America that one sees twentieth-century civilisation at its ultimate, with all the benefits and pitfalls that its impedimenta generates, and much of the American experience can act as a warning to all of us who lag behind in adopting the gadgetry and gimickry of a 'throw-away' society. Perhaps the acutest twentieth-century problems with which Americans have to cope are those of pollution. The average American family produces 4lb of domestic refuse per person per day, twice the current British rate, and in many parts of the USA, and indeed in almost any town of any size, the problems of pollution are manifest and manifold. (One does not merely have to think of the Los Angeles smog or the stagnant waters of the Great Lakes.) Both Federal and State authorities have, in the last decade, begun to battle with some success on the pollution front and thus water and air pollution control legislation, which includes provision for 'citizen participation', are now on the Federal Statute Book.

Parts of Europe can make us feel fairly satisfied with the level of our own pollution problems and the measures taken to redress them. The Mediterranean, for instance, is a heavily polluted zone along much of its coastline and, although those like Lord Ritchie Calder and Jacques Cousteau are perhaps unnecessarily pessimistic in forecasting doom and stagnation for this brightest of European seas, the debris of the industrial civilisations brand its shores – sewage, oil and industrial waste – which cause disease and destroy marine life do present enormous hazards. It is reckoned, for instance, that 90 per cent of all sewage flowing into the Mediterranean is untreated, that 300,000 ton of oil is dumped into the Sea every year; that the Rhône alone discharged 500 ton of pesticides and 1250 ton of detergent each year. It would be unjust to suggest that the Mediterranean countries are doing nothing, but their programmes do seem to lack a necessary degree of international co-operation and urgency. The magnitude of the problem, though, is illustrated by the fact that the new sewage plants for the Bay of Naples alone cost something over 100 million pounds.

Britain's record, in comparison with her neighbours, is not a bad one but much can be learnt from the thoroughness with which the Dutch tackle their problems. In the Netherlands, there is a greater emphasis on the importance of history and appreciation of art, and secondary school pupils are given a thorough grounding in these subjects. As a result there is a close liaison between schools and museums, and the directors of the national museums and representatives of the Department of Archaeology and Nature Conservation and the Ministry of Cultural Affairs Recreation and Social Work meet several times a year to discuss common interests and how they can best work together. But of the 400 museums in the country only 18 are national museums and the Government provides advisory services and grants to many of the rest. There is a Government Inspector for National Works of Art and his office makes recommendations to the governing bodies of these museums and galleries not owned by the State. It acts as an information centre, organising travelling exhibitions and, in its registry, records works of art that are not housed in State museums but which belong to the State. In addition, the office functions as a centre for the collection of works of art that were recovered from Germany after the War and which could not be returned to their original owners. The registry is also responsible for paintings and drawings and other works of contemporary artists who receive financial assistance from the State. The Netherlands, too, is a pioneer in the concept of the open air museum. Near Arnhem, a large and representative collection of Dutch buildings that would have otherwise been lost – windmills, houses, shops, etc – have been reassembled in open air settings and have for many years given not only delight, but a clear insight into methods of building and types of housing fast disappearing in parts of the country.

There are now open air museums in Britain and perhaps our most spectacular venture is at Iron Bridge on the Severn Gorge. This exciting experiment in industrial archaeology, a new but an increasingly fascinating and, until recently, a sadly neglected field, is attracting considerable numbers of visitors. A similar attempt to preserve the industrial past of the nation can be seen at Engelsberg, a tiny village of about two hundred inhabitants some 160 km north-west of Stockholm. This is in Bergslagen, the traditional centre of the Swedish mining and iron-working industry. A number of buildings have been preserved, renovated and restored and Englesberg has been declared an historic area under an Act of the Swedish Parliament of 1960.

There is, in this part of Sweden, the potential for a vast industrial museum where appropriate historic monuments in their original settings could illustrate the old techniques and the development of the mining and metal-making process. Although some of the installations and buildings have been listed as monuments, and some converted to other uses, many of the old workshops and houses are derelict and in danger of demolition and others are falling down as the result of years of neglect. This is something of a tragedy, for Sweden has more monuments connected with the mining and metal industry than any other in Europe, an industry going back to the twelfth century and reaching its climax in the nineteenth.

As elsewhere, sophisticated techniques and the march of technology had their casualties and the reminders of the foundations on which the Swedish iron industry was built diminished rapidly in number during the last century, although the last charcoal furnace did not cease operation until 1966. And so, as the iron industry progressed, the old iron works were abandoned or closed down and reminders of a former greatness disappeared. Still, Sweden is rich in monuments and many of them are worth maintaining, because of their intrinsic attractiveness as buildings and because they form a vital part not only of Swedish but of European industrial history. Alas, their future is far from secure and therefore Englesberg was chosen as one of the pilot projects in European Architectural Heritage Year in the hope that it would stimulate debate on the necessity of retaining the whole Bergslagen district as a vast conservation area. In this, as in so much else, finance plays a vital part. Many of the buildings and installations in question are still the properties of industrial companies and of necessity their first priority must be towards production and continued prosperity and, with a government decision to reduce the contribution from central finance for all conservation work, the Swedish situation,one of considerable doubt and difficulty.

Throughout Europe, adequate conservation of the heritage depends on effective partnership of government and private, individual and industrial co-operation. There is need for harnessing business and commercial sponsorship of the arts in all their forms. And there is a need for giving adequate incentive and special consideration to those who, through accident of birth and inheritance, have the duty of guarding much of a country's history and heritage. Although this is recognised by many European governments in their taxation structure, it is particularly depressing to note that, whereas this country has more of its heritage dependent on an enlightened guardianship, and where the record of that stewardship is second-to-none, the burdens of taxation on the stewards are administered in a heavier and more insensitive way here than almost anywhere else in the free world.

Most governments do not create the same fiscal problems for the agriculturalist, the owner of the country house or the collector of works of art as does the British Government. For instance, the highest rate of personal Income Tax in the United Kingdom is 98 per cent, whereas in Germany it is 56 per cent, in France 60 per cent and even in Italy—our closest challenger in this field – 82 per cent. And it is not just in Income Tax that the United Kingdom heads the league. In March 1975, the Chancellor of the Exchequer was asked if he would set out a table showing the maximum rate of tax on a gratuitous transfer of capital by a man on his death to his son, for Germany, Belgium, France, Holland, Italy and the UK. The table produced in answer made fairly stark reading. In the UK the percentage could be as high as 75 per cent whereas in Belgium and Holland the highest rate was 17 per cent, in France 20 per cent, in Germany 35 per cent, and in Italy 31 per cent. Similar figures apply to lifetime gifts.

On top of Britain's penal rates of Income Tax and high level of Capital Transfer Tax, it is the intention of the British Labour Government in 1976 to introduce a Wealth Tax during the course of the next year. Many countries already have such a tax and in Belgium the rate can be as high as 72 per cent and in Ireland 70 per cent, down to Denmark, where it is 39.6 per cent. However, Denmark, the Netherlands, Sweden and Norway give total exemption to works of art and Germany partial exemption. Favourable treatment, too, is given to the owners of historic houses. In Denmark, the only part of the house taken into account is that which is actually lived in; in Germany, houses and estates which are open to the public are exempt and other historic houses are charged at 40 per cent of the full rate. In the Netherlands, estates designated as preservation areas and open to the public are charged at 25 per cent of the value of the parkland and, in Sweden and Norway, there are no special concessions, but Wealth Tax valuation on historic houses is very low and there is exemption in Norway for land that is under statutory protection by reason of scientific or historic interest. Agriculture, too, has special treatment in Denmark, Germany, the Netherlands, Sweden and Norway. Comparative figures and tables are always difficult to compile, for they do tend to change from year to year, but what emerges quite clearly, from even the most perfunctory study, is that the incidence of taxation in the UK is already much higher than in most of Europe, even without the added imposition of a Wealth Tax. It is equally apparent that most European countries make more concessions for the heritage than Britain does.

One of the other keys to the preservation and survival of the heritage is the adequate encouragement of conservation techniques and of those who practise them. The inadequate facilities in most European countries for the training of architects and craftsmen in conservation is alarming. In an admirable article in the Heritage Year publication, *Architectural Conservation in Europe* (1975), Bernard Fielden, the saviour of York Minister, and Derek Linstrum of York University make this observation:

Taking it (conservation) in its widest architectural sense, as the method of ensuring continuity to a building, it is clear that whether this is achieved by preservation, restoration, consolidation, adaptation, rehabilitation (or even at times reconstruction or imagination), that it must be a part of a large number of general architectural purposes and should be regarded as a normal professional skill which might need at times a specialist's knowledge and experience. It is equally clear that the conservation of great monuments, cathedrals, castles and ruined abbeys, country houses and public buildings, is another professional obligation. Whether it is undertaken by public or private practice, it must continue as a service to the public.

Fielden and Linstrum, surveying the provision of training facilities available to undergraduate architects in Europe come up with the depressing information that 'only in ˋLouvain, Delft, Copenhagen, Aarhus and Stockholm are there facilities for the study before graduating of the restoration of historic monuments or the problems of historic town centres'. Bearing in mind the vast dimensions of the problem, and the number of historic buildings which need expert attention, this is a depressing statistic and it is made all the more so when one considers that there are few post-graduate courses on conservation either. France has its well established ones in the *Centre d'Etudes Supérieures d'Histoire et de Conservation des Monuments Anciens*, whose qualifications are essential for any wishing to practise in the field of conservation. There are also post-graduate courses in Madrid, Segovia, Copenhagen, Rome and Naples. Most of these courses are intended to serve the countries in which they are situated but, as Fielden and Linstrum point out, none is exclusively national and they suggest that a possible new rôle for UNESCO could be in co-ordinating and strengthening the links already existing between these courses and those in Britain and North America and, potentially, in central and South America as well. The situation in architecture is mirrored in the state of craftsmanship in general throughout the Continent. Because the building industry has become ever more dependent on the techniques of mechanisation, the need for higher standards of workmanship has tended to diminish, and so the truly proficient carpenter, bricklayer, mason, plasterer and glazier are in very short supply.

The old-fashioned edifice of the City and Guilds Craft Training and the five years' apprenticeship has been simplified and condensed by the wishes of the building industry. The skills required by the present day building industry are now inadequate for conservation work, where the craftsman needs the ability to be able to think out problems for himself, based on the knowledge of traditional techniques and materials.

Fielden and Linstrum suggest the whole organisation and incentives of the construction industry militate against the encouragement of craftsmanship, and this is a European problem.

This chapter has merely touched on some of the problems, but what it has possibly illustrated is that the problems are common, and that, although some other nations might in certain directions have things that they can teach us, especially in the way most of their tax systems operate, the difficulties facing the heritage are similar throughout Europe and demand the same blend of sensitivity and patience and positive devotion if they are to be solved. The wider heritage is worth fighting for, and all over Europe there is a greater realisation of this fact. European Architectural Heritage Year was not an unqualified success, but that it ever happened at all should give cause for rejoicing and some optimism to all of those new people who now realise that without their active interest and their constant cajoling of government, their heritage will not merely be in danger – it will disappear.

CHAPTER ELEVEN Some Solutions— the Preservation of the Heritage

It would be very easy to end on a gloomy and despondent note. Much of the finest of our past has disappeared and the threat of decay or destruction hangs over much of what remains. But much does remain and there is no reason why, given public will and Government resolve, our heritage should not be progressively enhanced and our descendents two centuries from now have as rich and varied an inheritance as we enjoy today.

Enhancement implies addition and it would be a mistake to think purely in terms of preserving monuments and works from the past. A heritage, if it is to have meaning and inspire affection, is something that is being added to constantly, and added to not only by acts of preservation but by new works of creative genius.

Though the dedication of individuals and the activities of voluntary societies, and schools and other institutions will always have a vital part to play in the conservation field, the central rôle inevitably, if regretfully, belongs to Government. Given the backing of authority there is little that cannot be achieved, but if Government is negligent or disinterested the erosion of our history, the impoverishment of our landscape, and the disappearance of our finest buildings will continue. Understandably, the provision of hospitals and schools, roads and sewers and other public services will always take priority over the preservation of the landscape and historic buildings, or the encouragement of the arts. But these are not the only amenities essential to the living of a well ordered and comfortable life.

One of the phrases politicians are particularly fond of using is 'the quality of life'. If challenged. most of us would say that it is our duty to protect quality where it exists and to promote it where it does not. But definitions of this 'quality' are not so easily supplied. Pledging oneself to protect and promote the quality of life must mean something more than the incantation of a favourite slogan. It must mean, in particular, having a clearly developed strategy for the defence of the national heritage and promotion of the arts. For much that is best and most enjoyed in this country is symbolised by, and enshrined in, the landscapes and buildings and great collections that constitute our heritage, and much that is most excellent and vigorous in our national life is represented by our achievements in the arts.

To say that Government must have such a strategy is in no way suggesting that it should be the rôle of any politician to advocate the creation of an all-embracin g ministry of culture on the Eastern European model with the unhappy and stultifying connotations of 'State Art' that such a creation brings to mind. But politicians do have it in their power to create conditions where things can happen, and it should be a foremost aim to create conditions where things that are excellent are safe from harm, and talents that are creative and imaginative are positively encouraged. In no field of policy are such conditions easier, or cheaper, to create than in that of the heritage and the arts, and nowhere is it more important that they should be created, and created quickly. That things could so easily be put right – and at little cost – is both a tragedy and a challenge. A sensitive and imaginative Minister could do for the nation what Myra Hess did for Londoners during the last War – lighten the darkness and inspire the weary. But the most sensitive and imaginative of people can only be an effective Minister if he has the authority to reveal his sensitivity and the opportunity to display his imagination.

That is why we should be thinking in terms of appointing a Cabinet Minister with total responsibility for the heritage and the arts, a Minister with the chance to formulate a strategy and the muscle to ensure its effective execution. At the moment, much of the heritage is in the hands of the Department of the Environment and most of the arts are under the jurisdiction of the Department of Education and Science. The junior Ministers who, often valiantly, fight for both can easily be divided and conquered, or just ignored, by a Chancellor besieged by Cabinet colleagues with demands on more spectacular fronts. Even within their own departments the responsibilities of these Ministers are often reckoned to be of relatively minor importance.

A Minister who had an overall responsibility for seeing that Canterbury cathedral did not collapse nor Wilton House become a deserted ruin; that London remained the theatre capital of the world; that true craftsmanship and artistry was stimulated; and that our great collections did not evaporate before the dragon breath of the taxman, would be in a powerful position when arguing with his colleagues. He would be powerful not only because of the obvious and recognised importance of his job, but because he could discharge his responsibilities to much benefit at little cost.

The benefit is not difficult to demonstrate. Forgetting for a moment the vital educative and civilising rôle of the arts in any society, and the importance of a national heritage to a nation's culture, it does not take much forensic skill to argue that our heritage and arts represent much of our wealth in the full financial sense of the word. Tourists who come to Britain, and without whose money we would already be both the poor and the sick man of Europe, do not come especially to bask in our sunshine or sample our cuisine. They come to marvel at our history and share in our heritage, and to enjoy, in London in particular, our drama, our opera, and our ballet. In 1975 alone, overseas visitors spent something over 1000 million pounds within the UK and another 300 million in fares on British air and shipping lines. Total tourist earnings for the year were 1400 million pounds – an increase of 30 per cent over 1974. The visitors themselves increased by some 11 per cent to 8,800,000[1].

Our earnings from these visitors amounted to some 4 per cent of our total exports, both visible and invisible, which means that 4p in every pound earned overseas in 1975 was earned through tourism, which accounted for 11 per cent of all invisible exports. The British Tourist Authority estimated that 1976 would see 9,600,000 visitors coming to Britain with an increase in their internal spending of some 300 million pounds.

Tourism is, in fact, one of the fastest growing earners of foreign currency for Britain and all sections of the community benefits from tourist spending. Yet it is not only overseas tourists who help to prime the pump of the national economy. In 1975, 48 million holiday trips of four nights or more were undertaken by British citizens and 40 million of those were taken within the United Kingdom. British citizens spent some 1250 million pounds on these holidays and many of them included in their itinerary at least one historic house or museum or cathedral; 14 million separate visits were paid to historic houses in private ownership during 1975.

It is surely quite extraordinary that, given these figures, we should have a situation where many of the attractions that delight these tourists should be fighting for survival. What then should be the policies and priorities of a Government enlightened enough to create an important and co-ordinating Ministry for the Heritage and the Arts?

Its responsibilities for the landscape would inevitably not be absolute for, as we have seen, the landscape depends so much upon farming and farming obviously would remain the responsibility of the Ministry of Agriculture. However, there is no reason why the Minister for the Heritage should not have an overall responsibility for the national parks and for the designation of areas of national beauty. He could do much, too, to encourage those industrialists and architects who are becoming increasingly aware of their responsibility towards the creation of a pleasant environment for industry by supporting the technically feasible and generally very successful large tree transplanting operations which have already done much to transform the landscape in industrial areas. He could also, no doubt in concert with the Minister of Agriculture, realising how much the landscape depends upon the farmer, encourage the Chancellor to provide a legislative framework for an owner of agricultural land to 'dedicate' it for agriculture on the lines of the forestry dedication scheme and receive tax concessions if he did

[1] During 1974 total Government expenditure on the Arts was some 52.9 million pounds and, some 2.5 million pounds was spent on grants and loans for the repair of historic buildings and for the preservation and enhancement of conservation areas. Local authorities spent a further 300,000 pounds. Total national and local authority expenditure on conservation since 1953 amounts to some 20 million pounds. These figures do not include expenditure on buildings and monuments in the care of the Department of the Environment.

so. The advantage of such a scheme would be to give inducement to landscape preservation to owners who now find themselves preoccupied with fiscal worries.

One also finds it difficult not to believe than an active Minister for the Heritage would not have sought to inspire a more active Government fight against the scourge of Dutch Elm disease as it ravaged and rampaged through most of England. Certainly he could have a stimulating rôle in ensuring that proper encouragement and incentives were given to farmers and landowners, both public and private, to replace with good English trees, as so many have done, the elms that have been lost. This Minister could work closely with the Countryside Commission and do much to encourage such valiant and imaginative schemes as Enterprise Neptune, one of the most splendid ventures ever promoted by a non-Governmental agency or association. Enterprise Neptune has already added 175 miles of outstanding coastline to the 190 in the possession or the protection of the National Trust. But many more hundreds of miles are in danger of despoilation or 'threatened' with improvement and they surely constitute an emotive and valuable part of the heritage of an island race.

He could stand up, too, for the National Trust in its struggle to preserve the principle of the inalienability of National Trust land, endangered again at the end of 1975 by the West Sussex County Council's plan to relieve Petworth's town traffic problem by building a by-pass through the grounds of Petworth House, so threatening with destruction perhaps the finest surviving example of Capability Brown's genius. For such a Minister could do much to ensure that the powers of local authorities were supervised and controlled in a field where they have so frequently been misused by the shortsighted, the indifferent, or the frankly hostile.

These attitudes have taken their toll of some of our finest townscapes and buildings, and there is certainly a need in this regard for a stronger Governmental presence. Perhaps the Government should give serious attention to designating some of our finest remaining towns as 'heritage towns', so as to ensure that special resources are made available to assist in their preservation and that not all of the decisions about their future are left to local councils, for local councils can, as we have seen, make great mistakes. Although there has been a considerable extension of sensible and protective legislation over the last few years there are still grave threats facing many of our historic buildings, and of these perhaps the gravest is the cost of maintenance and repair.

The Historic Buildings Council administers Government grants and loans toward the upkeep of Grade 1, and sometimes Grade 2, buildings, and buildings in outstanding conservation areas. Owners of other Grade 2 buildings, however—those buildings often of vital importance to the preservation of a whole street or town or village scene—do not normally qualify for any assistance, despite current legislation that can prevent them from demolishing or altering a building they cannot afford to maintain. A Minister for the Heritage would obviously have some added weight if he sought to widen the Historic Buildings Council's terms of reference so that proper assistance could be given to Grade 2 buildings, and indeed there is something to be said for the theory that the very act of listing could include some entitlement to a grant.

It might be argued, of course, that the Local Authority (Historic Buildings) Act of 1962 was intended to help the owners of any historic building, and especially those outside the scope of the Historic Buildings Council. In fact, local authorities very rarely use their powers to give grants; there always seems to be something more pressing on the agenda and more justifiable to the ratepayer. The present author sought to introduce an Historic Churches Preservation Bill in successive sessions of Parliament and this did include a clause to enforce the provisions of the 1962 Act. The Government felt unable to accede to it, then, but perhaps this is something that could be achieved with an Exchequer subsidy towards local authority expenditure, along the lines of the successful 'town schemes' in which central and local Government pay joint grants towards the repair of buildings and selected urban areas of outstanding interest. Some of these schemes are unfortunately likely to be casualties of cuts in public expenditure. At the time of writing (April 1976) York's Historic Buildings Committee has warned that city centre property owners would be unable to pay for renovations without the help of grants which had recently been drastically cut by the Department of the Environment, the North Yorkshire County Council, and the City Council.

But provision of extra Government finance, as desirable and welcome as it would be, is not necessarily the most important form of aid and incentive that could be given. As long as 1950, the Gowers Committee's Report recommended that owners of historic houses should be entitled to certain types of tax relief if they opened their houses to the public, including income tax and surtax in respect of expenditure on the house and relief from death duties on the house, land and property, to provide an income for maintenance. Although they have frequently been advocated these recommendations have never been implemented[2].

Now we have seen that with the additional burden of the Capital Transfer Tax, and the still present threat of Wealth Tax hanging over their heads, the owners of historic buildings are in a siege condition. They certainly need a powerful Minister to point out to his colleagues that it would cost little to achieve much, to ensure that neither Capital Transfer Tax nor Wealth Tax so distorted social priorities that in seeking equality they destroyed what all our people now have the opportunity to enjoy: Britain's country parks with their houses and the collections they contain. The National Trust would certainly be the first to pass a vote of thanks to any Minister who achieved this for, as they said in their annual report for 1975: 'Believing that the private owner looks

[2] Changes introduced in the 1976 Finance Act do not begin to tackle this problem effectively.

after these properties best, and at the lowest cost, the Trust will continue its efforts to ensure that the issues at stake are fully understood and will press for policies that will make this possible.'

The further fiscal burden that menaces not only private owners but those entrusted with the preservation of our ancient churches is that of VAT. This is chargeable on the repair and maintenance of buildings and it has been calculated that if it were lifted in respect of historic buildings in order to help owners and others to keep them in good condition the total cost to the Government in lost revenue would be very modest. It is difficult to justify a situation where those who give—many of them are small givers—to bodies like the Historic Churches Preservation Trust, are inadvertently supporting the Chancellor of the Exchequer, and it is ridiculous that grants from the Historic Buildings Council should be diminished in their value because of the imposition of VAT on the repairs they make possible.

One would also like to see a more flexible use of the Land Fund. This was established by Dr Dalton in 1946 with 50 million pounds from the sale of War stores, the idea being to create a fund which could be used for a variety of purposes connected with the preservation of historic buildings and landscapes of outstanding natural beauty. He thought that it would be 'A thank-offering for Victory and a War Memorial which, in the judgement of many, is better than any work of art in stone or bronze.' Unfortunately, this imaginative idea has not lived up to the hopes of its founder and although the Fund has been used for the acceptance of chattels and a number of fine houses, the legislative rules which hedge its operation prevented it, for instance, from being used by the Treasury to save Stonor Park – a fact which was made crystal clear by Parliamentary answer to the author in January 1976. One would like to see it extended into becoming a true contingency Fund fed by annual grant and available to ensure that no outstanding building crumbles into ruin for lack of assistance and no outstanding work of art leaves these shores for lack of funds. The emphasis, of course, would have to be on 'outstanding', but certainly, if such a fund existed, Stonor Park's future would not be in doubt and the Radnor Valesquez would be hanging in the National Gallery.

However, listed buildings are still being demolished without permission because fines for demolition, although they can be severe, are in practice rarely penal. A more effective sanction might be the adoption of the French system of refusing any subsequent planning permission for a site where a building has been demolished without consent. There is another loophole in the law in that a building, even though it is part of a conservation area, is exempt from protection if planning permission was obtained prior to the designation of the area. This means that a building totally out of scale and character can sometimes be erected after the importance of an area has been officially recognised.

Other threats to conservation areas are the building of roads or motorways, as has been seen at Petworth, and at Chillington – perhaps the classic case. There, a six-lane motorway is to be driven through the finest Capability Brown park in the Midlands, even though the local authority, Staffordshire County Council, had the imagination and foresight to declare the whole of the Chillington grounds a conservation area, and even though the Inspector at the Public Inquiry acknowledged that enormous environmental damage would be done and recommended the consideration of alternative routes.

In London a listed building can still deliberately be neglected by an owner in order to redevelop the site. Under the London Buildings (Amendment) Act if a building is declared unsafe and a Dangerous Structure Notice is issued by the District Surveyor, a court can order its demolition regardless of every protection given by planning laws. In 1975, Sir George Dobry's final Report on 'The Review of the Development Control System' emphasised the need for tighter control in special environmental areas, including conservation areas. It was recommended that this control could be achieved through a more extensive use of existing powers, although the same Committee's interim report on Control of Demolition suggested that some further control was necessary.

The Save Report in December 1975 suggested that listed buildings should be presumed 'innocent' and condemned only if an overwhelming case against them had been proved: 'Otherwise they should be discharged unconditionally. The burden of proof should rest with the applicant who should be required to give reasons for demolition – the test should be why demolish? not, why save?' Another deficiency in the present system highlighted in the Save Report is that the public notices for an application to demolish need be only a small notice outside the building in question, and a paragraph on the announcements page of the local newspaper. It is very rare that photographs of the threatened building are published, or even available for inspection, and owners and architects can, and frequently do, refuse the Press permission to reproduce plans of such new buildings or alterations as are proposed. The Report suggests that all notices of applications for listed building consent should be accompanied by proper photographs.

It is in matters like this that Government direction is needed for most of the laws relating to historic buildings are administered by local authorities and the powers they have, though extensive, are rarely used. A Minister for the Heritage could take a much stronger line on these matters and could perhaps do something to ensure that where local authorities fail to discharge their obligations they are called to account. The very last thing a Minister for the Heritage would do would be to imply, by suggestion of Government omnipotence, that voluntary effort was neither required nor necessary. Nowhere is this truer than in the case of historic churches. Here it is vital that communities should contrive to have a congregational responsibility and voluntary aid should continue side by side with State aid. Churches must not become mere museums because of State intervention in restoring them. It would be advisable if there could be representatives from concerned and knowledgeable bodies on any State committee administering aid.

There is definitely a vital rôle for Government in ensuring that this priceless heritage of largely medieval architecture survives. One often ignored factor is that our churches contain within them some of the most interesting and irreplaceable parts of our heritage and the national funding of a survey and the listing of individual objects of special merit in parish churches, as is the practice with historical monuments in France, has much to commend it. The present intention is not to assist cathedrals with State funds but government aid in the setting up of cathedral workshops that would combat the serious shortage of craftsmen would be a welcome step. Indeed, Government encouragement and subsidising of regional craft workshops based upon our cathedrals would be a constructive move. But these buildings are of supreme national importance and must have a properly recognised eligibility for assistance from central funds. State funds are, of course, already provided for redundant churches but so far only for the Anglican ones. As Marcus Binney recently suggested, the fund could well be extended to become a National Trust for Churches. Its aid could then be available to unwanted churches, chapels and kirks of all denominations throughout the United Kingdom and it could recruit members to augment its resources and to enlist public support of a voluntary nature.

There is something very sad, however, about the word 'redundant' when applied to churches and with the proper encouragement of bodies such as the Historic Churches Preservation Trust and the Friends of Friendless Churches and with fiscal aid (by the removal of VAT) to local congregations, and a provision of State aid in cases of real need, the redundancy solution would not be invoked as lightly as it has been in some dioceses. Imaginative alternative uses such as the transforming of suitable churches into concert halls should continue to be encouraged but it must be recognised that churches of significant value architecturally are frequently unsuitable for conversion; those that are and cannot be kept in a state of good repair by the Fund should be allowed to fall into ruin rather than be bulldozed into oblivion as the present regulations demand. There are, of course, a number of ruined churches and where these are of any worth they could be registered with the Ministry of the Heritage as ancient monuments and opened to the public in the same way that our ruined abbeys and castles are.

As long ago as 1971, the Civic Trust approached the Department of the Environment and advocated the setting up of a National Building Conservation Fund. It pointed out that the initiative for setting up such a fund would have to come from the Government and suggested as a first step exploratory consultation with such bodies as the British Tourist Authority and the CBI, leading chambers of commerce, building societies and insurance companies. There is a rôle for such commercial and industrial involvement and recently an Association for Business Sponsorship of the Arts, under the Chairmanship of Lord Goodman, was established. It should be encouraged in every possible way[3]. It should not need Government funds, but it could do much to encourage commercial and industrial participation in the preservation of the heritage and the patronage of the arts. Whether we will ever adopt in Britain the full range of fiscal incentives that exist in the USA, where it is permissible to deduct from taxable income the value of donations of money or works of art to public institutions, is possibly doubtful. But it is noticeable that the American scheme has played a very large part, and a very constructive part, in the establishment in the United States of some of the finest collections in the world. It is surely not anti-social or reprehensible to give tax concessions to those companies and individuals who are prepared to support public projects and adorn public collections. The sponsorship of the performing arts and the collection of objects of beauty should be seen as laudable aims in themselves—as laudable as any other form of industrial or private investment or saving.

Both sides of industry could play a particularly valuable part in helping our public museums to maintain and increase their collections. The grants for extensions to museums and for acquisitions of new works are, as we have seen, grossly inadequate. When a great work comes on to the market, a public appeal is invariably the one means of saving it for the nation but what incentive is there when, as in the case of the 'Donatello Relief', saved for the Victoria and Albert Museum in the early part of 1976, an appreciable part of the money subscribed finds its way back to the Exchequer? In this instance, a commercial concern produced silver replicas of the relief and the entire profits were given to the purchase fund. However, silver is liable for $12\frac{1}{2}$ per cent (25 per cent until April 1976) VAT and so far from giving money towards the purchase the Government found itself 26,000 pounds the richer as a result[4]. A strong and central Ministry could surely do something to ensure that this sort of anomaly did not exist; and to ensure that local authorities did not starve, or treat as mere Cinderellas, the museums and collections in their care—in short, that standards of excellence were nationally and rigorously upheld.

The condition of our museums causes concern to everyone with an intimate knowledge of the arts and an appreciation of the vital rôle which the public museum and gallery must play in preserving the heritage and in educating people so that they can enjoy it to the full. The great national museums in London are models of what museums should be but they are not exactly over-burdened with resources by generous governments. For instance, between 1965 and 1975 the total expenditure

[3] In a letter to the *Financial Times*, 29 May 1976, Brenda Capstick, Secretary of the Museums Association expressed the need for private and business sponsorship and welcomed the idea of lotteries to provide 'desperately needed' additional funds for provincial museums and galleries.

[4] In 1975/76, VAT receipts from the sale of antiques and fine arts, and the sales of works by living artists, authors, and composers amounted to 8 million pounds—over three times the amount the Government spent on grants and loans to historic buildings.

on acquisitions by all our national collections amounted to a fraction over 12 million pounds—perhaps the value of the collection at Chatsworth—an interesting thought for those who would like to see the State take over out great houses. Furthermore, although the National Gallery has recently opened a spendid new extension there is no exhibition space spare in any of our national museums or galleries.

Our national museums have, however, achieved remarkable success and attained a new popularity during the years since the Second World War, partly owing to the splendid occasional exhibitions that they have staged. In this context, one cannot escape mention of the invigorating presence on the museum scene of Dr Roy Strong who, first as Director of the National Portrait Gallery and now as Director of the Victoria and Albert Museum, has been responsible for some of the most vital and lively presentations ever seen in this country – exhibitions such as 'The Age of Pepys' at the Portrait Gallery, 'The Destruction of the English Country House' or, the less significant, but captivating display of English fashions in the early decades of this century at the V & A. The Tate staged a series of set-piece exhibitions which linger in the memory of those who were fortunate enough to see them: exhibitions such as 'The Age of Charles I', 'The English Landscape', 'Hogarth' and, most recently, 'Constable' – perhaps the finest exhibition ever devoted to a single artist. The Royal Academy also, has played a great part in the exhibition field. Perhaps its most spectacular success – vying in popularity with the Treasures of Tutankhamen at the British Museum – was its presentation of 'The Arts of Ancient China' in 1973.

Although the national museums have their problems, it is the museums in the provinces which give cause for alarm. It is not that they are staffed by unqualified unimaginative people: quite the contrary. Whether one is thinking of the great provincial and university museums, or the local collections of limited interest but of importance to understanding the English past, the truth is that many are starved of resources and administered by authorities which place them very low in their order of priorities.

A Minister of the Heritage could give special status to the great provincial museums. These are exceptional by virtue of the excellence of their collections and often, too, by virtue of the difficulties under which they operate: Bristol, with an art gallery and museum crammed onto one site; Birmingham, with display facilities of some 20 per cent less than at the end of the First World War; Manchester, where an extension has been deferred since before the First World War; Leeds, where the buildings are unsafe[5]; Glasgow and the Ashmolean at Oxford, both severely under-financed; and the Fitzwilliam at Cambridge, faced with a serious problem of staff and display facilities. These and the other important provincial museums, Liverpool, Leicester, Norwich and Sheffield, deserve to be elevated to become National Museums in the

[5] There is a novel plan for a small extension over a basement pub but Leeds' major galleries have been closed since 1974 and are likely to remain so for many years.

Provinces, given a proper degree of Government support, and administered under a trustee system (with, of course, local government representation) as our other great national museums are.

But beyond these outstanding museums, it would be advisable for local authorities to be obliged to have an efficient museum service, administered preferably at county level, and possibly supervised by a national n.useums council. Far too often museums are merely part of a local authority's leisure services and a poorly regarded part of them at that. A capital and central fund of as little as 1 million pounds a year to provide grants for improving facilities, to encourage the development of conservation scholarships and conservation centres, within the context of a ten year plan designed to bring all museums up to minimum acceptable standards, would revolutionise the museum world. And if it were allied to a new and improved system of training, designed to provide a national career structure (where there could be a staff interchange, of a regular nature, between national and provincial museums) the museum service would offer an attractive and challenging career to the able and industrious undergraduate. Unless steps along these lines are taken, the danger is that all but a few of our museums will by the turn of the century be slum depositories of objects badly secured, inadequately housed and conserved, and poorly displayed[6].

Great as the need is for a more forceful co-ordinating Government strategy for the preservation of the heritage and the encouragement of the arts, there is a limit to what Government can do, and rightly so.

'At a stroke', Government could remove the threat that is posed by the ubiquitous VAT and it could do much to generate the development of policies already suggested, but at the end of the day without a lively and widespread public concern and participation the rôle of Government could become an oppressive and directional one. Without vigilant local amenity societies we would have very little heritage to safeguard and the price of our heritage, as of our liberty, will increasingly be eternal vigilance on the part of these bodies. It is heartening, however, to read about the number of rescue and restoration stories that are already shining examples of what local effort and initiative can achieve. One thinks of the restoration of Bateman's Mill recounted in a recent issue of the National Trust Newsletter:

Kipling's Mill, celebrated in Puck of Pook's Hill is busy again after seventy years disuse... During its long idleness the whole of the mill's ground floor had disappeared, the wheel pit was full of mud and rubble to shaft level and the evidence of the ravages of the woodworm and beetle was everywhere. An outside inspection revealed considerable damage to the lower part of the mill where the brickwork

---

[6] In 1976 local authorities spent a total of 214,915 pounds on conserving their collections. National collections employed only one hundred and twenty five conservationists with a further thirteen in training.

had collapsed. In addition, the mill leaked. The mill pond and tail race were blocked with silt and the river bank and its surroundings overgrown with luxuriant vegetation ... The primary need was for repairs to the building's structure so that volunteers could work without fear of injury. The crumbling brickwork was restored, a complete ground floor laid, new roof joists fitted to the west roof, the rickety stairway renewed ... undergrowth was removed from banks and approaches, the silt removed from the pond and mill and the sluice put in order. Now the streams are filling the pond at need ... and the mill which 'has ground their corn and paid their tax ever since Doomsday Book' will be grinding and paying once more.

Jobs that can be done by volunteers of all ages whose enthusiasm is harnessed to a common cause, are innumerable. Even the dearth of expert craftsmen can in some cases be compensated for by the activities of devoted and conscientious volunteers. The National Trust's Annual Report for 1974, dealing with textile conservation, observed:

A number of the Trust's properties contain fine textile hangings and furnishings. Their condition is delicate and they are now increasingly threatened by the effects of light and dirt. A scheme was devised at Knowle to make a systematic start on the restoration of the famous gold and silver thread and other furnishings in the King's Room. The task is being carried out by a large number of volunteer embroiderers who have generously put their time and skill at the disposal of the Trust to work under an expert supervisor.

Much can be done to arouse the interest of schools and one of the pleasantest and most successful features of Architectural Heritage Year in this country was the way in which the enthusiasm of youth was channelled and directed. There was a series of awards sponsored for youth groups which furthered the aim of the Heritage Year. In Winchester the famous College, in conjunction with St Swithin's Girls' School and the Winchester Consumer Group, planned a Town Trail. At Stow, the boys helped restore the famous Kent and Capability Brown landscape gardens. The Department of Education and Science sponsored a special course at Bath College of Education and the National Institute of Adult Education held courses aimed at increasing the number of tutors in environmental and architectural heritage studies.

The Chiltern Society, one of the largest and most enthusiastic of local amenity societies, set up a Chiltern Conservation Volunteers Bureau in 1975 and in the first ten months of its existence it had offers of help from sixty-two organisations, including twenty-five schools and twelve scout groups. Indeed, most of the offers came from young people and youth organisations—all of them anxious to improve the Chiltern countryside. The vice-chairman, Mr Don Gresswell, in a letter to *The Times* in August 1975 said:

There is great scope to carry out projects that would otherwise never be accomplished. Our society has never sought to 'save the rates' but to do those tasks that the authorities would not tackle, e.g. surveying and clearing 1500 miles of Chiltern footpaths, restoring a windmill, both taking five or six years to accomplish...I am sure that the youth of this country would welcome the spirit of adventure and the feeling of comradeship and opportunities to improve our environment and our countryside and this would bring no additional cost to the taxpayer.

Don Gresswell's words should remind us that there is still a rôle for the individual. By joining societies such as his, any man or woman can play a part in preserving and enhancing what he values. And the individual, too, can, without the backing of societies or even membership of them, be vigilant and speak out through the columns of his local press or in letters to his Member of Parliament or to his local amenity society if he sees trees being needlessly sawn down, cottages vandalised, hedges uprooted. Perhaps his initiative will not be rewarded, but a danger foreseen can often be a disaster prevented.

The increase in membership of conservation and amenity societies and the number of extremely imaginative new societies and groups that have been set up has been heartening in recent years. Perhaps the most exciting of these has been the Landmark Trust, the brainchild of John Smith, former Member of Parliament for the Cities of London and Westminster. The Trust set out to rescue smaller but significant buildings which would otherwise crumble into decay and to make them available for people to live in and enjoy for holiday periods. Now, a Martello Tower at Aldeburgh, the Gothic temple at Stow, an abandoned railway station at Alton in Staffordshire and Clytha Castle in Wales are booked up through the year by people who enjoy a period of peace and recreation, and a chance to appreciate their heritage.

There is certainly scope for the Landmark Trust to increase its invaluable work and plenty of scope for other similar trusts. In the Netherlands they have played an invaluable part in the rehabilitation of many noteworthy buildings and have done so for many years. The first in the field there, the Hendrick Dekyser Association was founded in 1918 and today has some 2500 members and donors and owns about 200 buildings, 67 in Amsterdam and the remainder in 54 other towns and cities. Then there is an investment company specialising in the restoration of old houses in which the Amsterdam City Council itself has a shareholding. It owns over 200 houses in Amsterdam alone, many of them on important corner sights on the central canals. These and other trusts have undertaken some vitally important conservation work, work which would almost certainly not have been done by central or local government agencies. The most distinctive contribution has been the way they have restored to entirely suitable modern uses ancient and apparently obsolete buildings.

It is this sort of work—for instance, the restoration of a group of seventeenth-century Dutch alms houses into a quarter for students, flats for single teachers and a few homes for old people—which is the best type of answer to those who are sceptical of the value of conservationists. These people, and there are many of them, tend to decry the desire to conserve because they see it as a desire to preserve every scrap of existing fabric no matter what its potential use or worth. Their attitude was well summed up in an article in the journal *Built Environment* in January 1975: 'The idea of function has a very different meaning in the vocabulary of the environmental critic from the connotation which would be familiar to a Social Scientist. Thus New Scotland Yard for all that it is unusable as an office for ordinary people to work in, must at all costs be preserved as a monument to Norman Shaw.'

In fact, the north Norman Shaw building has already been completely restored and transformed and now provides the best offices available for Members of Parliament and their secretaries—and this at a fraction of the cost that would have been incurred had the grandiose project for a new parliamentary building been allowed to proceed. That building, with its acres of tinted glass, sauna baths, and luxurious facilities, would not only have been difficult to justify to the taxpayer; its size and construction would have been totally incongruous in Parliament Square.

It is appropriate to end in Parliament Square. The decisions of Government touch our lives more nearly, and more often, as each year passes and it is these decisions which can do most to increase, or to remove, the many dangers to our heritage.

Those who care should strive to influence those who decide; to impress upon Parliament and, through Parliament, upon Government, the need to maintain those things that are 'honest, lovely and of good report'. It is a cause that can succeed for it is capable of arousing great passions – without party rancour.

Those who know Kilvert's *Diary* – one of the best of all bedside books – may remember a joyful description of a cloud that hung heavy over Clyro till it became a rainbow. There is really no reason why the cloud that hangs heavy over our heritage should not be similarly transformed.

Countryside Conservation
(courtesy of the Countryside Commission)

HERITAGE COASTS

Defined completely

1 Sussex

Defined laterally

2 North Northumberland
3 Suffolk
4 Tennyson
5 Hamstead
6 Vale of Glamorgan
7 Gower
8 South Pembrokeshire
9 Marloes and Dale
10 St Bride's Bay
11 St David's Peninsula
12 Dinas Head
13 St Dogmaels and Moylgrove
14 Leyn
15 Aberffraw Bay
16 Holyhead
17 North Anglesey
18 Great Orme

NATIONAL PARKS

AREAS OF OUTSTANDING NATURAL BEAUTY

LONG-DISTANCE FOOTPATHS AND BRIDLEWAYS

DEFINED HERITAGE COASTS

The Heritage County by County

A list of national parks, officially designated areas of outstanding natural beauty, historic houses and castles, gardens and public museums and galleries. The new (post 1974) boundaries have been used throughout with apologies to those who abhor the demise of old Lincolnshire and Somerset etc. The list brings out clearly just how many areas would be impoverished if houses in private ownership were closed.

*denotes open by appointment

ENGLAND

AVON
OUTSTANDING NATURAL BEAUTY

COTSWOLDS (part)
MENDIP HILLS (part)

HISTORIC HOUSES AND CASTLES

BADMINTON HOUSE, Badminton (His Grace the Duke of Beaufort, KG, GCVO)
Built for the 1st Duke of Beaufort in Charles II's reign. Altered by Kent circa 1740.
CLEVEDON COURT, Nr Clevedon (National Trust)
A 14th-century manor house incorporating a 12th-century tower and a 13th-century hall with terraced 18th-century garden, rare shrubs and plants.
DODINGTON HOUSE, Chipping Sodbury (Major S. F. B. Codrington)
The last great 18th-century classic house to be built. Magnificent staircase. Architect James Wyatt. 700 acres of parkland lanscaped by Capability Brown.
DYRHAM PARK, Nr Bristol and Bath (National Trust)
Late 17th-century house in remarkable setting. Blathwayt furniture and Dutch paintings in a fine series of panelled rooms.
HORTON COURT, Horton (National Trust)
Cotswold manor house restored and altered in 19th century. 12th-century hall and Renaissance ambulatory.

*LITTLE SODBURY MANOR, Chipping Sodbury (Gerald Harford, Esq)
15th-century manor house with fine great hall and scenes of William Tyndale work.
No 1 ROYAL CRESENT, Bath (Bath Preservation Trust)
Georgian house as it was when built by John Wood the Younger in 1767.
ST VINCENT'S PRIORY, Clifton (G. Melhuish, Esq)
A small Gothic revival house, built over caves which were traditionally once a
Christian sanctuary.

GARDENS

*VINE HOUSE, Henbury (Professor and Mrs T. F. Hewer)
2 acres. Trees, shrubs, irises, water garden, bulbs, naturalised garden landscape.

MUSEUMS AND GALLERIES

AMERICAN MUSEUM IN BRITAIN, Claverton Manor, Nr Bath
The American decorative arts (from late 17th century and mid-19th century) seen
in a series of furnished rooms and galleries of special exhibits.
BATH ROMAN MUSEUM, Abbey Churchyard, Nr Bath Abbey (Bath City Council)
Adjoins the extensive remains of the Roman baths, and includes material from
that and other Roman sites.
BLAISE CASTLE HOUSE MUSEUM. Henbury, Bristol (Bristol Corporation)
Collections in an 18th-century house, dealing with objects illustrating English life.
BRISTOL CITY ART GALLERY, Queen's Road, Bristol 8 (Bristol Corporation)
Permanent and loan collections of paintings; applied art with particular emphasis
on English and Oriental ceramics.
BRISTOL CITY MUSEUM, Queen's Road, Bristol 8 (Bristol Corporation)
Collections of Egyptology, British archaeology, ethnography, industrial history
and technology, natural history, with geology. Chief attention is given to the
history and natural history of the West of England.
CHATTERTON HOUSE, Redcliffe Way, Bristol (Bristol Corporation)
Birthplace of Thomas Chatterton.
GEORGIAN HOUSE, 7 Great George Street, Bristol (Bristol Corporation)
A Georgian House exhibiting furniture and fittings of that period.
HOLBURNE OF MENSTRIE MUSEUM, Great Pulteney Street, Bath (University of Bath)
Exhibits displayed in an elegant 18th-century building.
MUSEUM, Burlington Street, Weston-Super-Mare
Local history including archaeology, folk-life costume and natural history.
Frequent special exhibitions.
MUSEUM OF COSTUME, Assembly Rooms, Bath (Bath City Council)
Founded on the world famous collection of Mrs Langley Moore. The exhibition
comprises every aspect of fashion from the 17th century to the current year.
THE RED LODGE, Park Row, Bristol (Bristol Corporation)
Elizabethan house with early 18th-century alterations and furnishings of these
periods.
ST NICHOLAS CHURCH AND CITY MUSEUM, St Nicholas Street, Bristol (Bristol
Corporation) (A redundant church)
Church plate and vestments, water colours and medieval antiquities related to
local history. Also the Hogarth altarpiece.
VICTORIA ART GALLERY, Bridge Street, Bath (Bath City Council)
Exhibitions from permanent collections changed monthly.

BEDFORDSHIRE
OUTSTANDING NATURAL BEAUTY
CHILTERNS (part)

HISTORIC HOUSES AND CASTLES

LUTON HOO, Luton (Wernher Family)
Exterior commenced by Robert Adam, 1767. Interior remodernised in 18th-century French style early this century. Art collection includes Fabergé jewels and unique Russian collection. Park landscaped by Capability Brown.

WILLINGTON DOVECOTE AND STABLES (National Trust)
16th-century stables and stone dovecote, lined nesting-boxes for 1500 pigeons.

WOBURN ABBEY (Trustees of the Bedford Estates)
The great 18th-century house remodelled by Flitcroft circa 1747 and Henry Holland 1802. Famous collection of paintings together with collection of French and English 18th-century furniture and silver. 3000 acres of park designed by Repton. Also large game reserve.

GARDENS

STAGSDEN BIRD GARDENS, Stagsden (Mr and Mrs R. E. Rayment)
A large bird zoo and breeding establishment for birds. Collection of shrub roses.

WREST PARK, Silsoe (Department of the Environment)
Fine example of a formal canal garden.

MUSEUMS AND GALLERIES

BEDFORD MUSEUM, The Embankment, Bedford
Important collection of local antiquities, local history and national history.

THE BUNYAN COLLECTION, Public Library, Harpur Street, Bedford
Library and exhibits devoted to life and works of John Bunyan (the Mott Harrison Collection).

THE BUNYAN MEETING LIBRARY AND MUSEUM, Mill Street, Bedford (Trustees of Bunyan Meetings)
Containing all surviving personal relics of John Bunyan. World famous collection of Bunyan's works in 165 languages.

CECIL HIGGINS ART GALLERY, Castle Close, Bedford
Exhibits include English and continental porcelain and outstanding collection of English watercolours. Handley-Read collection of Victorian and Edwardian decorative art.

ELSTOW MOOT HALL, Bedford
Medieval market hall containing 17th-century collections associated with John Bunyan.

LUTON MUSEUM AND ART GALLERY, Wardown Park (Borough of Luton)
Bedfordshire archaeology and history, rural trades and crafts, social and domestic life, furniture, woodwork, decorative and fine arts. Costume, needlework accessories. Doll and furniture collection.

THE SHUTTLEWORTH COLLECTION, Old Warden Aerodrome, Old Warden
Some 40 specimens of historical types of aeroplanes, cars, carriages and bicycles – many unique and in flying and running order.

BERKSHIRE

OUTSTANDING NATURAL BEAUTY

NORTH WESSEX DOWNS (part)

HISTORIC HOUSES AND CASTLES

*No 25 THE CLOISTERS, Windsor Castle (Dean and Canons of Windsor)
Medieval house, privately occupied, with remains of medieval wall painting in main bedroom.
SWALLOWFIELD PARK, Swallowfield (Mutual Households Association Ltd)
Built by the 2nd Earl of Clarendon in 1678. Now converted into flats.
WINDSOR CASTLE, Windsor (Royal Residence)
Largest inhabited castle in the world. It is largely medieval, Stuart and Regency. The state apartments contain many historic treasures.

GARDENS

SAVILL GARDEN, Windsor Great Park (Crown Property)
35 acres of woodland garden. Large range of plants throughout the season, of horticultural and botanical interest.
VALLEY GARDENS, Windsor Great Park (Crown Property)
300 acre woodland garden adjoining Virginia Water lake.
WEXHAM SPRINGS, Wexham (Cement and Concrete Association)
Large informal garden with mixed shrubs and lake. Formal area with courtyards, terraces, patios, walling and paving.

MUSEUMS AND GALLERIES

ETON COLLEGE NATURAL HISTORY MUSEUM, Eton
Collection of British birds, entomological specimens, mammals, reptiles and fossils.
THE GUILDHALL EXHIBITION, High Street, Windsor
Collections including implements, documents, pictures. The Guildhall, dating from 1689, contains a collection of royal portraits.
HENRY REITLINGER BEQUEST, Oldfield, Riverside, Guards Club Road, Maidenhead
Chinese, European, Italian, Persian pottery. Paintings, sculpture, drawings and glass.
MUSEUM AND ART GALLERY, Blagrave Street, Reading (Reading Corporation)
Natural history and local archaeology. Roman collection from Silchester. Changing art exhibitions each month. Thames Conservancy collection of pre-historic and medieval metalwork. Historical collections.
MUSEUM OF ENGLISH RURAL LIFE, Whiteknights Park, Reading (University of Reading)
A national collection of material relating to the history of the English countryside.
*THE MUSEUM OF GREEK ARCHAEOLOGY (FACULTY OF LETTERS), Whiteknights, Reading (University of Reading)
A collection of Greek antiquities, mainly pottery.
NEWBURY MUSEUM, Wharf Street, Newbury
Local collections covering Paleolithic to Saxon and Medieval to recent periods, natural history.
STANLEY SPENCER GALLERY, King's Hall, Cookham-on-Thames
Paintings, drawings, sketches and personalia of the artist, including some letters.

BUCKINGHAMSHIRE
OUTSTANDING NATURAL BEAUTY
CHILTERNS (part)

HISTORIC HOUSES AND CASTLES

ASCOTT, Wing (National Trust)
Anthony de Rothschild collection of fine pictures, French and Chippendale furniture, exceptional Oriental porcelain. 12 acres of grounds. Garden containing unusual trees, flower borders, topiary sundial, naturalised bulbs and water lilies.

CHICHELEY HALL, Newport Pagnell (Trustees of the Hon Nicholas Beatty)
Beautiful Baroque house and gardens built 1719–23. Fine panelling, naval pictures, and momentos of Admiral Lord Beatty. Open for the first time in 1976.

CLAYDON HOUSE, Middle Claydon, Nr Winslow (National Trust)
Built in mid-18th century as an addition to an earlier house. Magnificent rococo state rooms, including Florence Nightingale Museum, her bedroom and sitting-room.

CLIVEDEN, Nr Maidenhead (National Trust)
Fine tapestry and furniture. Gardens contain temples of Giacomo Leoni. Box paraterre, fountain, formal walks. Historic open air theatre, water garden, rose garden, herbaceous borders.

HARTWELL HOUSE, Aylesbury (House of Citizenship)
Jacobean with 18th-century front and decorations.

HUGHENDEN MANOR, High Wycombe (National Trust)
Home of Benjamin Disraeli. Small garden. The Disraeli Museum.

LONG CRENDON COURTHOUSE (National Trust)
14th-century building where the manorial courts were held from reign of Henry V until recent times.

MILTON COTTAGE, Chalfont St Giles (Milton's Cottage Trust)
Preserved as it was in 1665, this is the cottage where Milton completed 'Paradise Lost' and began 'Paradise Regained'. Contains many relics and a library with first and early editions.

NETHER WINCHENDEN HOUSE, Aylesbury (J. G. C. Spencer Bernard, Esq)
Tudor manor house with 18th-century additions. Home of Sir Francis Bernard, Governor of New Jersey and Massachusetts, 1760.

PRINCES RISBOROUGH MANOR HOUSE (National Trust)
17th-century red brick house with Jacobean oak stairs.

WADDESDON MANOR, Nr Aylesbury (National Trust)
English, Dutch, Flemish and Italian paintings, French decorative art and drawings from 17th and 18th centuries and other works from earlier centuries. Momentos of the Rothschild family. Grounds include 18th-century aviary and small herd of Sikka deer.

WEST WYCOMBE PARK (National Trust)
Palladian house with frescoes and painted ceilings. 18th-century landscape garden with lake and various classical temples.

WOTTON HOUSE, Nr Aylesbury (Administrator Mrs Patrick Brunner)
Built 1704 on the same plan as Buckingham House. Interior remodelled by Soane in 1820. Wrought iron by Tijou and Thomas Robinson. Capability Brown landscape.

GARDENS

BOARSTALL DUCK DECOY, Nr Brill
An ancient working duck decoy in natural surroundings.

DORNEYWOOD GARDEN (National Trust)
Given to the Trust as an official residence for a Secretary of State, or Minister of the Crown.

STOWE (STOWE SCHOOL), Buckingham (Governors of Stowe School)
Famous 18th-century house (not open). Garden and garden buildings by Bridgeman, Kent, Gibbs, Vanburgh and Capability Brown.

MUSEUMS AND GALLERIES

BUCKINGHAMSHIRE COUNTY MUSEUM, Church Street, Aylesbury (Buckingham County Council)
Displays illustrating county geology, natural history, archaeology and history; new rural life gallery; costume; small collection of paintings. Temporary exhibitions.

COWPER AND NEWTON MUSEUM, Market Place, Olney
Personal belongings of William Cowper and Rev John Newton, manuscripts and other items of local interest.

WYCOMBE CHAIR AND LOCAL HISTORY MUSEUM, Castle Hill, High Wycombe (Wycombe District Council)
Collection of chairs of most periods, but mainly directed to the Windsor chair. Unique collection of local tools and equipment, Bucks lace and local items.

CAMBRIDGESHIRE
HISTORIC HOUSES AND CASTLES

ANGELSEY ABBEY, Nr Cambridge (National Trust)
Founded in the reign of Henry I. An Elizabethan manor created from the remains by the Fokes family. Contains Fairhaven collection of art treasures. About 100 acres of grounds.

HINCHINGBROOKE HOUSE, Huntingdon (Hinchingbrooke School)
Early 13th-century Nunnery converted mid 16th-century into Tudor house with additions, late 17th-century and 19th-century.

KIMBOLTON CASTLE, Kimbolton (Governors of Kimbolton School)
Tudor manor house, completely remodelled by Vanbrugh.

THE KING'S SCHOOL, Ely (The Governors of King's School)
Built in 12th and 14th centuries.

NORTHBOROUGH CASTLE, Northborough (Mr Roy Genders)
Early 14th-century house with great hall and solar. Rose garden and herbaceous borders.

PECKOVER HOUSE, Wisbech (1722) (National Trust)
Important example of early 18th-century domestic architecture. Victorian garden contains rare trees, flower borders, roses.

UNIVERSITY OF CAMBRIDGE (In most Colleges, only the Chapels and Halls are open)
    GONVILLE AND CAIUS COLLEGE, Trinity Street (1348)
    CHRIST'S COLLEGE, St Andrew's Street (1505)
    CLARE COLLEGE, Trinity Lane (1326)

CORPUS CHRISTI COLLEGE, Trumpington Street (1352)
DOWNING COLLEGE, Regent Street (1800)
EMMANUEL COLLEGE, St Andrew's Street (1584)
JESUS COLLEGE, Jesus Lane (1496)
KING'S COLLEGE, King's Parade (1441)
MAGDALENE COLLEGE, Magdalene Street (1542)
PEMBROKE COLLEGE, Trumpington Street (1347)
PETERHOUSE, Trumpington Street (1284)
QUEEN'S COLLEGE, Queen's Lane (1448)
ST CATHARINE'S COLLEGE, Trumpington Street (1473)
ST JOHN'S COLLEGE, St John's Street (1511)
SIDNEY SUSSEX COLLEGE, Sidney Street (1596)
TRINITY COLLEGE, Trinity Street (1546)
TRINITY HALL, Trinity Lane (1350)

GARDENS

UNIVERSITY BOTANIC GARDEN (Cambridge University)
Fine specimen trees and shrubs. Founded 1761.

MUSEUMS AND GALLERIES

CAMBRIDGE COUNTY FOLK MUSEUM, 2—3 Castle Street, Cambridge
Museum occupying the former White Horse Inn, contains domestic and agricultural bygones.
FARMLAND MUSEUM, High Street, Haddenham
Agricultural implements, rural crafts.
THE CROMWELL MUSEUM, Market Square, Huntingdon (Cambridgeshire County Council)
Concerned with the Cromwellian period, displaying contemporary portraits, Cromwelliana and documents.
FITZWILLIAM MUSEUM, Trumpington Street, Cambridge
Picture gallery of old and modern masters. Collections of antiquities, ceramics and applied arts, coins, drawings and prints. Collections of music and medieval manuscripts and art library.
NORRIS LIBRARY AND MUSEUM, The Broadway, St Ives (St Ives Town Council)
Local collections. Prehistory to bygones. Local literature.
PETERBOROUGH MUSEUM AND ART GALLERY, Priestgate, Peterborough (Peterborough City Council)
Local archaeology, history, geology and natural history. Small collection of paintings and ceramics.
THE SCOTT POLAR RESEARCH INSTITUTE, Lensfield Road, Cambridge
Current scientific work in the Arctic and Antarctic. Expedition relics and equipment. Eskimo and general polar art collections.
SEDGWICK MUSEUM OF GEOLOGY, Downing Street, Cambridge
Fossils and subordinate collections of rocks, building stones and ornamental marbles.
UNIVERSITY ARCHIVES, University Library, West Road, Cambridge
Manuscripts dating from 13th-century. Charters of privilege, statutes, Royal letters and mandates, Grace books, matriculation books, university accounts and many other classes of records.

UNIVERSITY COLLECTION OF AERIAL PHOTOGRAPHS, 11 West Road, Cambridge
A collection of aerial photographs illustrating different aspects of agriculture, archaeology, geography, geology, history, vegetation, and the social and economic past and present of the United Kingdom.

UNIVERSITY MUSEUM OF ARCHAEOLOGY AND ETHNOLOGY, Downing Street, Cambridge
Archaeological collections illustrating the Old Stone Age in Europe, Asia and Africa, Britain from Prehistoric to Medieval times, Prehistoric America, Ethnographical material from America, Africa, South East Asia and Oceania.

UNIVERSITY MUSEUM OF CLASSICAL ARCHAEOLOGY, Little St Mary's Lane, Cambridge
Representative collection of casts of Greek and Roman sculpture.

UNIVERSITY MUSEUM OF MINERALOGY AND PETROLOGY, Downing Place, Cambridge
A comprehensive collection of minerals and rocks.

UNIVERSITY MUSEUM OF ZOOLOGY, Downing Street, Cambridge
A collection of zoological specimens used in teaching and research. Normally opened to visitors.

WHIPPLE MUSEUM OF THE HISTORY OF SCIENCE, Free School Lane, Cambridge
Collection of historic scientific instruments mainly of the 16th, 17th and 18th centuries.

WISBECH AND FENLAND MUSEUM. Museum Square, Wisbech
Fenland and Natural History, Archaeological and Antiquarian Collections. Pottery and porcelain, bygones.

CHESHIRE
NATIONAL PARKS
PEAK DISTRICT (part)

HISTORIC HOUSES AND CASTLES

ADLINGTON HALL, Macclesfield (Charles Legh, Esq)
Great Hall dates from about 1450. Elizabethan half-timbered 'black and white' portion 1581.

CAPESTHORNE, Macclesfield (Lt Col Sir Walter Bromley-Davenport)
Believed to have been built by John Wood of Bath in 1722, with later alterations by Blore and Savin. Pictures, furniture, Americana.

CHURCHE'S MANSION, Natwich (Mr and Mrs R. V. Myott)
A unique Elizabethan tanner's half-timbered mansion house, built by Thomas Clease in 1577 for Richard Churche. Original plan. Fine oak panelling.

GAWSWORTH HALL, Macclesfield (Raymond Richards, Esq)
Tudor half-timbered manor house with tilting ground. Former home of Mary Fitton, Maid of Honour at the Court of Elizabeth I, and the supposed 'dark lady' of Shakespeare's sonnets. Pictures, sculpture and furniture.

LITTLE MORETON HALL, Congleton (National Trust)
16th-century moated half-timbered building. Remarkable carved gables.

LYME PARK, Disley (Leased to Stockport Metropolitan Borough Council by the National Trust)
House dating from Elizabethan times. Impressive Palladian exterior (1720) by Giacomo Leoni. Home of Leghs for 600 years. Grinling Gibbons carving. Extensive garden. Park of 1320 acres. Herd of red deer.

NETHER ALDERLEY MILL, Nether Alderley (National Trust)
15th-century corn mill used until 1939 and now restored.

PEOVER HALL, Over Peover, Knutsford (Randle Brooks)
Dates from 1585. Tudor stables, famous magpie ceiling.

TATTON PARK, Knutsford (National Trust [financed, maintained and administered by the Cheshire County Council])
Seat of the late Lord Egerton of Tatton. Georgian house by Samuel and Lewis Wyatt. 2000 acre park. 50 acre garden.

GARDENS

ARLEY HALL GARDENS, Northwich (Viscount and Viscountess Ashbrook)
Topiary, rhododendrons, azaleas, herbaceous border, shrub roses.

MUSEUMS AND GALLERIES

GROSVENOR MUSEUM, Grosvenor Street, Chester
Roman antiquities from the legionary fortress, including a large number of inscribed and sculptured stones. Special gallery illustrating the Roman army. Natural history and bygones.

KING CHARLES TOWER, City Walls, Chester
Dioramas and exhibits illustrating Chester in the Civil War.

MUSEUM AND ART GALLERY, Bold Street, Warrington (Warrington Borough Council)
General collections of natural history, botany, geology, ethnology, anthropology, bygones and small arms. Art gallery contains permanent collections of early English water colours, pottery and porcelain and local glass. Frequent temporary exhibitions.

NORTON PRIORY MUSEUM, Warrington Road, Runcorn (Norton Priory Museum Trust)
Recently excavated remains of monastic house. Set in woodlands and gardens.

THE SHAW MUSEUM, Cross Street, Runcorn (Halton District Council)
Pictures and photographs of Runcorn and some excavated historical objects.

WEST PARK MUSEUM AND ART GALLERY, Prestbury Road, Macclesfield (Macclesfield Corporation)
Important Egyptian collection, local exhibits, oil paintings and water colour drawings including sketches by Landseer, and oil paintings and sketches by C. F. Tunnicliffe, ARA.

CLEVELAND

NATIONAL PARKS

NORTH YORK MOORS (part)

HISTORIC HOUSES AND CASTLES

ORMESBY HALL, Nr Middlesbrough (National Trust)
Mid-18th-century house. Contemporary plasterwork. Small garden.

MUSEUMS AND GALLERIES

BILLINGHAM ART GALLERY, Billingham New Town Centre (Stockton Borough Council)

A modern and forward-looking gallery with monthly changing exhibitions.

CAPTAIN COOK BIRTHPLACE MUSEUM, Stewart Park, Middlesbrough (Middlesbrough Borough Council)
Illustrating Cook's life and adventures, Australasian ethnography and natural history.

DORMAN MUSEUM, Linthorpe Road, Middlesbrough (Middlesbrough Borough Council)
Featuring the social, industrial and natural history of the area. Changing exhibitions, specialist collections.

GRAY ART GALLERY AND MUSEUM, Clarence Road, Hartlepool (Hartlepool Borough Council)
19th- and 20th-century paintings, oriental antiquities. Museum displays illustrate the archaeology, social history and natural history of the district.

MARITIME MUSEUM, Northgate, Hartlepool (Hartlepool Borough Council)
Maritime history of the town. Displays include simulated fisherman's cottage and ship's bridge, and an early gaslit lighthouse lantern.

MIDDLESBROUGH ART GALLERY, Linthorpe Road, Middlesbrough (Middlesbrough Borough Council)
Permanent collections including some good examples of contemporary British paintings. Monthly changing exhibitions.

NEWHAM GRANGE FARM, Off the Parkway, Middlesbrough (Middlesbrough Borough Council)
Leisure-educational farm, featuring agricultural museum and interpretive centre.

PRESTON HALL MUSEUM, Preston Park, Eaglescliffe, Stockton-on-Tees (Stockton Borough Council)
Arms, armoury personalia, local pottery, toys, ivory period rooms.

REDCAR MUSEUM OF SHIPPING AND FISHING, King Street, Redcar (Borough of Langbaurgh Museum Service)
Graphic and three-dimensional material, illustrating the history of Tees shipping and fishing, including ships and *The Zetland*, the oldest surviving lifeboat in the world.

STOCKTON AND DARLINGTON RAILWAY MUSEUM, Stockton-on-Tees (Stockton Borough Council)
Sited where the first ticket office stood, the museum contains historic pictures and relics of the world's first paid-passenger railway.

CORNWALL
OUTSTANDING NATURAL BEAUTY
CORNWALL (part)

HISTORIC HOUSES AND CASTLES

ANTONY HOUSE, Torpoint (National Trust)
The home of Sir John Carew Pole, Bt. Built for Sir William Carew from 1711 to 1721. Unaltered Queen Anne house, panelled rooms, fine furniture.

COTEHELE HOUSE, Calstock (National Trust)
Fine medieval house. Former home of the Earls of Mount Edgcumbe. Armour, furniture, tapestries. Terraced garden falling to the sheltered valley, ponds, stream, unusual shrubs.

EBBINGFORD MANOR, Bude (Mr and Mrs Dudley-Stamp)
Typical Cornish manor house dating from 12th century with a walled garden.

GODOLPHIN HOUSE, Helston (S. E. Schofield, Esq)
Tudor House. Colonnaded front added 1635. Former house of the Earls of Godolphin.

LANHYDROCK, Nr Bodmin (National Trust)
17th-century picture gallery. Fine plaster ceilings. Family portraits 17th to 20th centuries. Formal garden laid out in 1857.

MOUNT EDGCUMBE, Nr Plymouth (City of Plymouth and County of Cornwall)
Home of the Earl of Mount Edgcumbe. Fine gardens and park.

PENCARROW HOUSE AND GARDENS, Bodmin (Molesworth-St Aubyn Family)
Georgian mansion. Fine collection of 18th-century paintings. English, French and Oriental furniture and china. Large formal garden and woodlands, with granite rockery, ancient encampment and lake. Noted specimen conifer collection.

PENDENNIS CASTLE, Falmouth (Department of the Environment)
Castle fort built by Henry VIII circa 1540.

ST MICHAEL'S MOUNT, Penzance (National Trust)
Home of Lord St Levan. Medieval and early 17th century, with considerable alterations and additions in 18th and 19th centuries.

TINTAGEL, OLD POST OFFICE (National Trust)
A miniature 14th-century manor house with large hall.

TRERICE, St Newlyn East (National Trust)
Small Elizabethan house, plaster ceilings and fireplaces, in a newly planted garden.

TREWITHEN, Probus, Nr Truro (Mrs G. H. Johnstone)
Early Georgian house occupied by same family since 1723. Internationally renowned landscaped garden of camellias, magnolias, rhododendrons and other rare plants.

GARDENS

GLENDURGAN GARDENS, Helford River (National Trust)
A valley garden overlooking the estuary, with fine trees and shrubs. Giant's stride and maze.

TRELISSICK GARDEN, Nr Truro (National Trust)
Beautiful wooded park at head of Falmouth harbour. Woodland walks. Particularly rich in rhododendrons and hydrangeas.

TREMEER, St Tudy (Major-General E. G. W. Harrison)
6 acre garden with water, closely planted with rhododendrons, camellias and other shrubs. Aviary of budgerigars.

TRENGWAINTON GARDEN, Penzance (National Trust)
Large shrub and woodland garden. Fine views. A series of walled gardens containing rare sub-tropical plants.

MUSEUMS AND GALLERIES

CORNISH ENGINES, East Pool Mine, Pool, Cambourne (National Trust)
The 30 in rotative beam winding engine (1887) and the 90 in beam pumping engine (1892) stand complete in their houses.

THE CORNISH MUSEUM, Lower Street, East Looe (Museum Enterprises)
Representing life and culture of Cornwall, including unique collection of relics dealing with witchcraft, charms and superstitions.

COUNTY MUSEUM AND ART GALLERY, River Street, Truro (Royal Institute of Cornwall)
Local antiquities and history. Ceramica and art. World famous collection of Cornish minerals.

HELSTON BOROUGH MUSEUM, Old Butter Market, Helston
Folk museum dealing with all aspects of local life in the Lizard Peninsula.
LAWRENCE HOUSE, Castle Street, Launceston (National Trust)
Local museum.
WAYSIDE MUSEUM, Old Millhouse, Zennor
Archaeological collection of West Cornwall origin. Folk collections.
NEWLYN ART GALLERY, Newlyn
Exhibitions of contemporary works by leading West Country artists. Also permanent collection of Newlyn School paintings, 1880–1930.
OLD MARINERS CHURCH, Norway Square, St Ives (St Ives Society of Artists)
Exhibitions of the St Ives Society of Artists.
PENLEE HOUSE MUSEUM, Penlee Park, Penzance
Archaeological, local history and tin-mining exhibits.
PUBLIC LIBRARY AND MUSEUM, The Cross, Cambourne
Collections of archaeology, minerology, local history and local antiquities.
TOWN MUSEUM, Bodmin
Local history collection.
VALHALLA MARITIME MUSEUM, Tresco Abbey, Tresco (Isles of Scilly) (R. A. Dorrien-Smith)
Figureheads and ships' ornaments from ships wrecked in the Isles of Scilly.

CUMBRIA
NATIONAL PARKS
LAKE DISTRICT (part)
YORKSHIRE DALES (part)

OUTSTANDING NATURAL BEAUTY
ARNSIDE AND SILVERDALE (part)
SOLWAY COAST

HISTORIC HOUSES AND CASTLES
CARLISLE CASTLE, Carlisle (Department of the Environment)
Earliest remains of keep circa 1170. Outer gatehouse construction 13th century. Regimental museum.
HILLTOP, Nr Sawney (National Trust)
17th-century house where Beatrix Potter wrote the Peter Rabbit books. Contains her furniture, china, pictures, and some original drawings.
HOLKER HALL, Cark-in-Cartmel (Hugh Cavendish)
Dates from the 16th century with 19th-century additions. Exhibition, gardens and deer park.
LEVENS HALL, Kendal (O. R. Bagot, Esq)
Elizabethan house with fine plasterwork, panelling and notable furniture. Famous topiary garden laid out in 1689.
MUNCASTER CASTLE, Ravenglass (Sir William Pennington-Ramsdem, Bt)
Seat of Pennington family since 13th century. Famed rhododendron and azalea gardens. Superb views over Esk Valley.
RUSLAND HALL, Nr Ulverston (Mr and Mrs J. Birkby)
Early Georgian house with later additions set in 4 acres of landscaped grounds. Recently restored contents include mechanical music and mechanical curios.
RYDAL MOUNT, Ambleside (Lt Cdr and Mrs P. P. R. Dane)
Wordsworth's home from 1813 to his death in 1850. Family portraits, furniture, many of the poet's personal possessions, and first editions of his works. $4\frac{1}{2}$ acre garden with rare shrubs and trees.

SIZERGH CASTLE, Kendal (National Trust)
Home of the Stricklands for 700 years. 14th-century Pele tower. 15th, 16th and 18th-century additions.
TOWNEND, Troutbeck (National Trust)
17th-century lakeland farmhouse with original furnishings. Home of the Brownes for 300 years.
*WHITEHALL, Mealsgate (Mrs S. Parkin-Moore)
14th-century Pele tower.
WORDSWORTH HOUSE, Cockermouth (National Trust)
Built 1745, birthplace of Wordsworth. The garden is referred to in his 'Prelude'.

GARDENS
ACORN BANK, Temple Sowerby (National Trust)
Spring bulbs, walled garden with herbaceous plants, herb garden. Red sandstone house, part 16th century (*not* open).
GRAYTHWAITE HALL, Ulverston (Major M. E. M. Sandys)
7 acres of landscaped gardens. Rhododendrons, azaleas and other shrubs.
LINGHOLM, Keswick (Viscount Rochdale)
Large rambling garden, woodland, rhododendrons, azaleas, etc. Exceptional views of Borrowdale.
STAGSHAW, Ambleside (C. H. D. Acland, Esq)
Woodland garden started 1959, bulbs, trees and shrubs. Views over Windermere.

MUSEUMS AND GALLERIES
ABBOT HALL ART GALLERY, Kendal (Lake District Art Gallery Trust)
Contains 18th-century furnished rooms and modern galleries with pictures, sculpture, furniture and pottery. Changing exhibitions.
ABBOT HALL MUSEUM OF LAKELAND LIFE AND INDUSTRY, Kendal (Lake District Museum Trust)
Contains period rooms, costumes, printing, weaving, local industries, farming.
BARROW-IN-FURNESS MUSEUM, Ramsden Square, Barrow-in-Furness (District Council)
Illustrating all aspects of the area. Vickers-Armstrong collection of model ships. Findings from prehistoric sites, mainly Bronze Age. Lake District bygones.
BRANTWOOD, Coniston
The home of John Ruskin from 1872 to 1900. Large collection of pictures by Ruskin and his associates, his coach, boat, furniture and other associated items.
DALTON CASTLE, Dalton (National Trust)
14th-century Pele tower houses collection of armour and documents.
DOVE COTTAGE, Grasmere
The early home of Wordsworth from 1799 to 1808.
FITZ PARK MUSEUM AND ART GALLERY, Station Road, Keswick
Original Southey, Wordsworth and Walpole manuscripts. Local geology and natural history.
HAWKSHEAD COURT HOUSE, Hawkshead (National Trust)
Building dating from 15th-century now used as museum of rural life.
HELENA THOMPSON MUSEUM, Park End Road, Workington
Local material mainly of family association.
KENDAL BOROUGH MUSEUM, Station Road, Kendal (Kendal Corporation)
Outstanding collection of mammals and birds, area geology and Kendal bygones.
MILLOM FOLK MUSEUM, St George's Road, Millom (Millom Folk Museum Society)
Unique full-scale model of a drift of the former Hodbarrow iron ore mine.

MUSEUM AND ART GALLERY, Tullie House, Castle Street, Carlisle (Carlisle Corporation)
Jacobean town house with Victorian extension having regional collection rich in prehistoric and Roman remains, Lakeside birds, mammals and geology. Bottomley Bequest of Pre-Raphaelite paintings, Williamson Bequest of English porcelain.
PRIORY GATE HOUSE, Cartmel (National Trust)
Used as gallery and local Museum.
THE RUSKIN MUSEUM, Coniston
Illustrates the life and work of John Ruskin. Also local history, scenery and industries.
THE WORDSWORTH MUSEUM, Grasmere
Manuscripts, first editions and a collection of objects illustrative of rural life in Wordsworth's time.

DERBYSHIRE
NATIONAL PARKS

PEAK DISTRICT (part)

HISTORIC HOUSES AND CASTLES

CHATSWORTH, Bakewell (Trustees of the Chatsworth Settlement)
Built by Talman for the 1st Duke of Devonshire between 1687 and 1707. Splendid collection of books, furniture, pictures and drawings. Gardens with elaborate waterworks surrounded by great park.
FOREMARKE HALL, Milton (Governors of Repton School)
Georgian house built 1762 by David Hiorns. Now a school. School museum by appointment.
HADDON HALL, Bakewell (His Grace the Duke of Rutland)
Fine example of medieval and manorial house. Terraced garden noted for wall and bed roses.
HARDWICK HALL, Nr Chesterfield (National Trust)
Built 1591–97 by Bess of Hardwick. Notable furniture, needlework, tapestries. Gardens with yew hedges and borders of shrubs and flowers. Extensive collection of herbs.
KEDLESTON HALL, Derby (Viscount Scarsdale, T.D.)
Probably the finest Robert Adam house in England, with unique marble hall, contemporary furniture and fine pictures.
MELBOURNE HALL, Melbourne (Marquess of Lothian)
Important collection of pictures, furniture and works of art. Famous garden by Wise, in style of Le Nôtre. Wrought iron pergola.
SUDBURY HALL, Nr Uttoxeter (National Trust)
17th-century brick built house with plasterwork ceilings, Laguerre murals, staircase carved by Pierce and overmantel by Grinling Gibbons.
WINSTER MARKET HOUSE, Nr Matlock (National Trust)
A stone market house of the late 17th or early 18th century.

GARDENS

EDNASTON MANOR (S. D. Player, Esq)
Originally formal garden more recently developed with wide range of interesting trees, flowering shrubs and roses, including collections of acers, sorbus, rhododendrons, azaleas, climbing and old-fashioned roses.

LEA RHODODENDRON GARDENS, Lea (Mrs Tye and Miss Colyer)
Large garden, extensive collection of species and hybrid rhododendrons and azaleas in woodland setting.

MUSEUMS AND GALLERIES

BUXTON MUSEUM, Terrace Road, Buxton (Derbyshire County Council)
Local history. Pleistocene and later animal remains from local caves. Local rocks, minerals, fossils and stones. Blue John and Ashford Marble ornaments. Paintings, prints, pottery, glass.

DERBY MUSEUM AND ART GALLERY, The Strand, Derby
The museum: archaeology, social history, ethnography, coins and medals, zoology, geology. Bonnie Prince Charlie Room (1745 rebellion). Art gallery: paintings by Wright of Derby, Derby porcelain, costumes.

*THE HEATHCOTE MUSEUM, Birchover, Matlock
Finds from the Bronze Age barrows on Stanton Moor.

INDUSTRIAL MUSEUM, Silk Mill, off Full Street, Derby
Rolls-Royce collection of historic aero engines and an introductory gallery to Derbyshire industries.

LECTURE HALL, Library Centre, New Square, Chesterfield (Borough of Chesterfield)
Exhibitions of art, photography, etc.

THE OLD HOUSE MUSEUM, Cunningham Place, Bakewell (Bakewell Historical Society)
Early Tudor house. Costumes, kitchen utensils, craftsmen's tools, etc.

REGIMENTAL MUSEUM, The Strand, Derby
9th/12th Lancers.

REVOLUTION HOUSE, Old Whittington, Chesterfield (Borough of Chesterfield)
An old inn connected with the plotting of the 1688 revolution. 17th-century furnishings.

THE TRAMWAY MUSEUM, Matlock Road, Crich, Nr Matlock (Tramway Museum Society)
Unique collection of horse, steam and electric tramcars and associated equipment.

DEVON
NATIONAL PARKS

DARTMOOR (part)
EXMOOR (part)

OUTSTANDING NATURAL BEAUTY

EAST, NORTH AND SOUTH DEVON

HISTORIC HOUSES AND CASTLES

ARLINGTON COURT, Barnstaple (National Trust)
Regency house furnished with the collections of the late Miss Rosalie Chichester, including shell, pewter and model ships. Display of horse-drawn vehicles. Victorian formal garden.

BICKLEIGH CASTLE, Nr Tiverton (Mr and Mrs O. N. Boxall)
Medieval romantic home of the heirs of the Earls of Devon. Great hall, armoury. Thatched Jacobean wing. Early Norman chapel, moat and garden.

BRADLEY MANOR, Newton Abbot (National Trust)
Small, roughcast 15th-century manor house with great hall, screen passage, buttery and perpendicular chapel.

BUCKLAND ABBEY (National Trust, administered by Plymouth Corporation)
13th-century Cistercian monastery altered by Sir Richard Grenville in 1576. House of Drake. Drake's relics. Folk gallery.

CADHAY, Ottery St Mary (Lady William-Powlett)
An Elizabethan manor house built about 1550. A charming 'lived in' house.

CASTLE DROGO, Nr Chagford (National Trust)
Granite castle designed by Sir Edward Lutyens. Standing at over 900 feet, overlooking the wooded gorge of the River Teign. Terraced gardens and miles of splendid walks.

*CASTLE HILL, Filleigh, Barnstaple (Lady Margaret Fortescue)
Palladian mansion built circa 1730–40. Fine 18th-century furniture, tapestries, porcelain and pictures. Ornamental garden, large shrub and woodland park, and arboretum.

CHAMBERCOMBE MANOR, Ilfracombe (Mr and Mrs H. R. Sirett)
Small 14th- and 15th-century manor house. Mainly Tudor and Jacobean furniture. Early Benz motor car, date approximately 1889. 1½ acre garden in beautiful setting.

COMPTON CASTLE, Nr Paignton (National Trust)
Fortified manor house. Restored great hall.

DARTMOUTH CASTLE, Dartmouth (Department of the Environment)
15th-century castle designed for coastal defence.

FLETE, Ermington, Ivybridge (Mutual Households Association Limited)
Built around an Elizabethan manor.

KIRKHAM HOUSE, Paignton (Department of the Environment)
Interesting example of 15th-century architecture.

KNIGHTSHAYES COURT, Nr Tiverton (National Trust)
Large garden of interest at all seasons. House by William Burges (1870) decorated by J. D. Crace.

*LEE FORD, Budleigh Salterton (Mr and Mrs N. Lindsay-Fynn)
Georgian house in 40 acres of parkland. Adam pavilion.

POWDERHAM CASTLE, Nr Exeter (Earl and Countess of Devon)
Medieval castle built circa 1390, damaged in the Civil War, and restored and altered in the 18th and 19th centuries. Music room by Wyatt. Park stocked with deer.

SALTRAM HOUSE, Plymouth (National Trust)
George II house built around and incorporating remnants of late Tudor house, in landscaped park. 2 fine rooms by Robert Adam. Furniture, pictures, fine plasterwork and woodwork. Garden with orangery and octagonal summerhouse.

SHUTE BARN, Nr Axminster (National Trust. Tenant: Patrick Rice Esq)
Remains of manor house built over centuries and completed in the 16th century.

TIVERTON CASTLE, Nr Tiverton (Mr and Mrs Ivar Campbell)
Historic fortress of Henry I. Joan of Arc Gallery. Clock collection. Chapel of St Francis.

WATERSMEET COTTAGE, Nr Lynmouth (National Trust)
Fishing lodge furnished in 1832, used for recruiting and information.

YOULSTON PARK, Nr Barnstaple (J. J. C. Clarke, Esq)
A former Chichester home. 18th century with fine ceilings and staircase and Chinese wallpaper. Lake and woodland garden.

GARDENS

BICKHAM HOUSE, Roborough (Lord Roborough)
Shrub garden, camellias, rhododendrons, azaleas, cherries, bulbs, trees.
COMBE HEAD, Bampton (Mr and Mrs A. D. Baxter)
Aboretum begun in 1963 in 25 acres of fine old trees and walled garden.
THE GARDEN HOUSE, Buckland Monachorum, Yelverton (Mr and Mrs L. S. Fortescue)
Trees, lawns, terraces in attractive Devon landscape. Up-to-date collection of flowering shrubs, ornamental cherries etc.
KILLERTON GARDEN, Nr Exeter (National Trust)
Lovely throughout year. 19th-century chapel and ice house.
MARWOOD HILL, Nr Barnstaple (Dr J. A. Smart)
Collection of camellias, daffodils, rhododendrons, flowering shrubs, rock and alpine garden, rose garden and waterside planting.
ROSEMOOR GARDEN CHARITABLE TRUST, Torrington (Col J. E. and Lady Anne Palmer)
Graden started in 1959. Rhododendrons, ornamental trees and shrubs, primulas, species of roses, scree and alpine beds.
TAPELEY PARK GARDENS, Instow (Christie Estate Trust)
Home of the late John Christie, founder of Glyndebourne. Italian style garden.
WOODSIDE, Barnstaple (Mr and Mrs Mervyn Feesey)
Plantsman's garden in 1½ acres with outstanding collection of ornamental grasses and sedges. Wide range of dwarf shrubs, conifers, rock plants and alpines, rhododendrons, foliage shrubs and trees, many variegated.

MUSEUMS AND GALLERIES

ASHBURTON MUSEUM, 1 West Street, Ashburton
Local antiquities, weapons, period costumes, lace, implements, lepidoptera, American Indian antiques, bygones.
BICTON COUNTRYSIDE MUSEUM, Bicton Gardens, East Budleigh (Clinton Devon Estates)
Items dealing with the countryside.
BIDEFORD MUSEUM, Municipal Buildings, Bideford (Bideford Town Council)
Samples of North Devon pottery, shipwright's tools, geological specimens, maps and prints.
BURTON ART GALLERY, Victoria Park, Kingsley Road, Bideford
Contains the Hubert Coop collection of paintings and other objects of art.
CITY MUSEUM AND ART GALLERY, Drake Circus, Plymouth (Plymouth Corporation)
Collections of paintings and English porcelain. Cottonian collection of English and Italian drawings. Reynolds family portraits and early printed books. Local and natural history collections. Ships' models.
COOKWORTHY MUSEUM, The Old Grammar School, 108 Fore Street, Kingsbridge
William Cookworthy and the story of china clay. Victorian kitchen and scullery. Local history. Trade and shipbuilding tools, rural life, early photographs, costume and prints.
THE ELIZABETHAN HOUSE, 70 Fore Street, Totnes (Joint Committee)
Period furniture and costumes, local tools, toys, domestic articles and archae-ological exhibits. Documents from local collections. Computer exhibition. Local reference library.

ELIZABETHAN HOUSE, No 32 New Street, Plymouth (Plymouth Corporation)
16th-century house in Plymouth's historic quarter, furnished according to period.
EXETER MARITIME MUSEUM, The Quay, Exeter (International Sailing Craft Association)
A unique collection of working craft, many afloat, from all over the world, constituting the finest collection in Europe.
GUILDHALL, High Street, Exeter
One of the oldest municipal buildings in the country. Main structure medieval, Tudor frontage, and oak door added in 1593. City regalia, silver and historic portraits.
HONITON AND ALLHALLOWS PUBLIC MUSEUM, High Street, Honiton
Collections of local interest including Honiton lace, local implements, and a complete Devon kitchen; bones of hippopotamus, straight-tusked elephant, ox and red deer, all 100,000 years old unearthed from Honiton by-pass in 1965.
ILFRACOMBE MUSEUM, Wilder Road (opposite Runnymeade Gardens), Ilfracombe
Collections of British botany, North Devon birds, reptiles and insects. Early engravings, pictures, maps, arms, Victoriana. Ships' models and marine life.
MORWELLHAM QUAY, Morwellham, Nr Tavistock (Morwellham Recreation company)
Historic river port on the Devon bank of River Tamar. Museum of industrial archaeology, copper port of the 19th century with incline planes, harbours, quays and water wheels. Audio visual 'Introduction to Morwellham', self-guided trails.
THE NORTH DEVON ANTHANAEUM, The Square, Barnstaple
North Devon geological specimens. Cryptograms, local antiquities, and library.
ROUGEMONT HOUSE MUSEUM, Castle Street, Exeter
Important collections of archaeology and local history from Exeter and Devon.
ROYAL ALBERT MEMORIAL MUSEUM AND ART GALLERY, Queen Street, Exeter
Important collections of English paintings, watercolours, ceramics and glass, Exeter silver, costume, natural history and anthropology. An active programme of temporary exhibitions.
ST ANNE'S CHAPEL MUSEUM, St Peter's Churchyard, High Street, Barnstaple
Antiquities and exhibits of local interest.
ST NICHOLAS PRIORY, The Mint, Fore Street, Exeter
Fine monastic guest house including a Norman crypt, and a 15th-century guest hall.
SHARPITOR, Salcombe (National Trust)
A museum of local interest and of special appeal to children. Gardens.
SOUTH MOLTON MUSEUM, Town Hall, South Molton (South Molton Town Council Friends of the Museum Committee)
Local history, pewter weights and measures, documents, bygones.
TOPSHAM MUSEUM, 25 The Strand, Topsham, Exeter
History of the port and trade of Topsham.
TORQUAY NATURAL HISTORY SOCIETY MUSEUM, Babacombe Road, Torquay
Collections illustrate Kent's Cavern and other caves. Devon natural history, local folk culture.
UNDERGROUND PASSAGES, entrance in Princesshay, Exeter
The city medieval aqueducts.

DORSET
OUTSTANDING NATURAL BEAUTY

DORSET (whole)

HISTORIC HOUSES AND CASTLES

ATHELHAMPTON, Athelhampton (Robert Cooke Esq, MP)
One of the finest medieval houses in England. 10 acres of formal and landscaped gardens. Chinese deer.

CLOUDS HILL, Nr Wareham (National Trust)
The home of T. E. Lawrence (Lawrence of Arabia) after the First World War.

DEWLISH HOUSE, Dewlish (J. Anthony Boyden, Esq)
Queen Anne house built 1700.

FORDE ABBEY, Nr Chard (Trustees of G. D. Roper, Esq)
12th-century Cistercian monastery. Famous Mortlake tapestries, 25 acres of beautiful gardens.

HARDY'S COTTAGE, Higher Bockhampton (National Trust)
Birthplace of Thomas Hardy (1840–1928).

THE MANOR HOUSE, Sandford Orcas (Col F. Claridge)
Tudor mansion furnished with antiques, period furniture, pictures, silver, glass, maps, china.

MILTON ABBEY, Nr Blandford (Governors of Milton Abbey School)
Georgian Gothic house built 1771, on the site of 15th-century abbey. Fine hall and ceilings. Abbots hall completed 1498. The ceilings in the house were designed by James Wyatt.

PURSE CAUNDLE MANOR, Purse Caundle (R. E. Winckelmann, Esq)
Medieval manor house. Period furniture. Lawns, roses.

SHERBORNE CASTLE, Sherborne (Simon Wingfield Digby, Esq)
16th-century mansion in continuous occupation of the Digby family since 1617.

SMEDMORE, Kimmeridge (Major J. C. Mansel)
18th-century manor house. Dutch marquetry furniture. Antique dolls. Views.

No 3 TRINITY STREET, Weymouth (E. Wamsley Lewis, Esq, FRIBA)
Converted Tudor cottages, now one house. Completely furnished with 17th-century objects.

WOLFETON HOUSE, Dorchester (Capt N. T. L. Thimbleby)
Fine medieval and Elizabethan manor house with magnificent stonework, great stairs, Jacobean fireplaces and ceilings. 17th-century furniture.

GARDENS

ABBOTSBURY SWANNERY, Abbotsbury (Strangways Estates)
An unspoilt natural breeding place for swans.

ABBOTSBURY SUB-TROPICAL GARDENS, Abbotsbury (Strangeways Estates)
Trees and shrubs from various parts of the world.

COMPTON ACRES GARDENS (J. R. Brady, Esq)
Gardens with valuable bronze and marble statuary and ornaments. 7 separate secluded gardens.

CRANBORNE MANOR GARDENS (Marquess of Salisbury)
Walled gardens, yew hedges and lawns, wild garden with spring bulbs, herb garden, Jacobean mount garden, flowering cherries and collection of old-fashioned and specie roses.

HYDE CROOK, Dorchester (Major P. R. A. Birley)
Flowering trees and shrubs, Japanese cherries, magnolias, camillias, azaleas, daffodils, orchids, narcissi.

MAPPERTON, Beaminster (Victor Montague, Esq)
Terraced and hillside gardens. Modern orangery in classical style. 18th-century stone fish-ponds and summerhouse. Tudor manor house, enlarged

by Charles II. Wing forming courtyard with stables, coach house and small parish church.

MELBURY HOUSE, Nr Yeovil (Lady Teresa Agnew)
Large garden, very fine arboretum, shrubs and lakeside walk; beautiful deer park.

MINTERNE, Dorchester (Lord Digby)
Important collection of rhododendrons, azaleas, and trees set in a beautiful valley.

MUSEUMS AND GALLERIES

ABBEY RUINS MUSEUM, Park Walk, Shaftesbury
Objects from the excavations of the Church of the Benedictine Nunnery founded by Alfred the Great.

BOURNEMOUTH NATURAL SCIENCE SOCIETY'S MUSEUM, 39 Christchurch Road, Bournemouth
Local natural history and archaeology.

BREWERY FARM MUSEUM, Milton Abbas
Brewing, farming and village bygones, from the Dorset countryside.

BRIDPORT MUSEUM AND ART GALLERY, South Street, Bridport (West Dorset District Council)
Collection of local interest. Antiquities and natural history. Collection of paintings, drawings and sketches.

DORSET COUNTY MUSEUM, Dorchester (Dorset Natural History and Archaeological Society)
A regional museum whose collections cover Dorset geology, natural history and prehistory, bygones and history with Thomas Hardy Memorial Room. Temporary exhibitions each month.

DORSET MILITARY MUSEUM, The Keep, Dorchester
Exhibits of Dorset Regiment, Dorset Militia and Volunteers, Queen's Own Dorset Yeomanry and Devonshire and Dorset Regiment (from 1958).

GALLERY 24, Bimport, Shaftesbury
Art gallery with changing exhibitions of paintings by new and internationally known artists. Also the work of over 30 potters and unusual crafts.

GUILDHALL MUSEUM, Market Street, Poole (Poole Borough Council)
18th-century ceramics and glassware. Curiosities, changing exhibitions on wide variety of local themes.

LOCAL HISTORY MUSEUM, Gold Hill, Shaftesbury

MARITIME MUSEUM, Paradise Street (Poole Borough Council)
14th-century town cellars portraying the wealth of Pool's medieval maritime trade and commerce.

THE PHILPOT MUSEUM, Bridge Street, Lyme Regis
Old prints and documents, fossils and coins, an old Sun fire engine of 1710.

PORTLAND ISLAND MUSEUM, Avice's Cottage, Wakeham, Nr Easton
Objects of local, historical and folk interest, natural history.

PRIEST'S HOUSE MUSEUM, High Street, Wimborne Minster
Local archaeology and general history. Tudor building with garden.

RED HOUSE MUSEUM AND ART GALLERY, Quay Road, Christchurch (Hampshire County Museums Service)
Regional museum with natural history and antiquities. Also 19th-century fashion plates, costume dolls and bygones. Art exhibitions frequently changed. In Georgian house with herb and other gardens.

ROTHESAY MUSEUM, 8 Bath Road, Bournemouth (Bournemouth Corporation)
Lucas collection of early Italian paintings and pottery; English porcelain; 17th-century furniture; Victorian bygones and pictures; ethnography; arms and armour; marine rooms; local and exotic butterflies and moths.
ROYAL ARMOURED CORPS TANK MUSEUM, Bovington Camp
Over 300 examples of armoured fighting vehicles from 1915.
RUSSEL-COTES ART GALLERY AND MUSEUM, East Cliff, Bournemouth (Bournemouth Corporation)
17th–20th-century oil paintings, tempera, watercolours, sculpture, miniatures, ceramics, Japanese, Burmese, Chinese, theatrical (Irving). Collection of 'Pictures You May Borrow' available to resident and non-resident subscribers.
SCALPENS COURT (Old Town House), High Street, Poole (Poole Borough Council)
14th-century merchant's house displaying archaeological and local history of Poole, including industrial archaeology.
SHERBORNE MUSEUM, Abbey Gate House, Sherborne (Trustees)
Local geology and history, including abbey, founded AD 705. Sherborne missal AD 1400, and 18th-century local silk industry.

CO DURHAM
HISTORIC HOUSES AND CASTLES

DURHAM CASTLE, Durham (University of Durham)
The Norman castle of the prince bishops has been used by the University since 1832.
RABY CASTLE, Staindrop, Darlington (Lord Barnard, TD)
Principally 14th century, alterations made in 1765 and mid-19th century. Fine pictures and furniture. 10 acre garden.

MUSEUMS AND GALLERIES

THE BOWES MUSEUM, Barnard Castle (Durham County Council)
The main collections are representative of European art from the late medieval period to the 19th century.
DARLINGTON MUSEUM, Tubwell Row, Darlington
Stockton and Darlington and North Eastern Railway history, local and natural history.
THE DORMITORY MUSEUM, The Cathedral, Durham
The relics of St Cuthbert, Anglo-Saxon sculptured stones, medieval seats, vestments and manuscripts.
DURHAM LIGHT INFANTRY MUSEUM AND ART CENTRE, Nr County Hall, Durham
The history of the regiment and a wide variety of constantly changing exhibitions.
GULBENKIAN MUSEUM OF ORIENTAL ART AND ARCHAEOLOGY, Elvet Hill, Durham (University of Durham)
The Northumberland collection of Egyptian and Mesopotamian antiquities; the Malcolm MacDonald collection of Chinese pottery and porcelain; the Sir Charles Hardinge collection of Chinese jade and other hand stone carvings; part of the Sir Victor Sassoon collection of Chinese ivories. Chinese textiles, ancient Near Eastern pottery, Indian sculpture, Japanese and Tibetan art.
NORTH OF ENGLAND OPEN AIR MUSEUM, Nr Stanley, Beamish
A museum representing the industrial development and social history of the North of England.

EAST SUSSEX
OUTSTANDING NATURAL BEAUTY
SUSSEX DOWNS (part)

HISTORIC HOUSES AND CASTLES

ALFRISTON CLERGY HOUSE, Nr Seaford (National Trust)
A pre-Reformation parish priests' house, circa 1350. Bought in 1896, the first building acquired by the Trust.

BATEMAN'S, Burwash (National Trust)
Built 1634. Rudyard Kipling lived here. Watermill restored by the National Trust. Attractive garden, yew hedges, lawns, daffodils.

BATTLE ABBEY, Battle
Founded by William the Conqueror.

BEECHES FARM, Nr Uckfield (Mrs Vera Thomas)
16th-century tile hung farm house. Lawns, yew trees, borders, sunken gardens, roses, fine views.

BODIAM CASTLE, Nr Hawkhurst (National Trust)
Built 1386–9, one of the best preserved examples of medieval moated military architecture.

BRICKWALL HOUSE, Northiam, Rye (Frewen Educational Trust)
Home of the Frewen family since 1666. 17th-century drawing-room with richly decorated plaster ceiling. Dining-room with collection of family portraits.

CHARLESTON MANOR, Westdean, Seaford (Lady Birley)
Fine example of Norman, Tudor and Georgian architecture in a romantic setting. Famous Romanesque window in Norman wing.

DURBAR HALL, Hastings (Hastings Borough Council)
Indian Palace (Punjab and Bombay) built for the Indian and Colonial Exhibition 1886. Acquired by Lord Brassey. Contains collections of Oriental and Primitive art based on those of Lord and Lady Brassey.

FIRLE PLACE, Nr Lewes (Viscount Gage, KCVO)
Important collection of Italian, Dutch and English pictures. Sèvres China, French and English furniture and objects of American interest.

GLYNDE PLACE, Nr Lewes (Mrs Humphrey Brand)
Beautiful example of 16th-century architecture. Pictures, bronzes, needlework, historical documents, pottery.

GREAT DIXTER, Northiam (Quentin Lloyd, Esq)
15th-century half-timbered manor house in a Lutyens designed garden.

*KIDBROOKE PARK, Forest Row (Council of Michael Hall School)
Sandstone house and stables built in 1730s with later alterations.

LAMB HOUSE, Rye (National Trust)
Georgian house with garden. Home of Henry James from 1898 to his death in 1916.

MICHELHAM PRIORY, Nr Hailsham (Sussex Archaeological Trust)
Founded in 1229 this Augustinian priory is surrounded by one of the largest moats in England. Elizabethan wing and 14th-century gatehouse. Special exhibitions and events. Tudor barn.

THE OLD MINTHOUSE, Pevensey (Mr and Mrs J. C. Nicholson)
Historic mint house circa AD 1342. Occupied by King Edward VI and Andrew Boarde. Coins struck on this site AD 1076. Flowered courtyard.

PRESTON MANOR, Brighton (Borough of Brighton)
Georgian house with Thomas-Stanford: Macquoid bequests of fine furniture, pictures, etc.

ROYAL PAVILION, Brighton (Borough of Brighton)
Unique building by Henry Holland and John Nash, built for the Prince Regent.
SHEFFIELD PARK, Nr Uckfield (Mr and Mrs P. J. Radford)
Tudor house remodelled by James Wyatt, 1775–8. Dickens's letters, rare books, weapons. The property is under restoration.

GARDENS

BENTLEY, Halland, Nr Lewes (Mrs Gerald Askew)
Wildfowl Gardens. There are over 1000 birds of more than 110 different species: swans, geese, duck, flamingos, peacocks and pheasants.
HORSTED PLACE GARDENS, Nr Uckfield (Lord Rupert Nevill, DL JP)
Charming Victorian garden, rose borders, rhododendrons, shaded walks.
SHEFFIELD PARK GARDEN, Nr Uckfield (National Trust)
Large gardens with series of lakes linked by cascades, and great variety of unusual shrubs.
THE SPRING HILL WILDFOWL COLLECTION, Forest Row (R. A. and D. M. Pendry)
15th-century farmhouse (*not* open). Beautiful Ashdown Forest setting. 10 acres, ponds, shrub and terraces. Over 1000 birds, including rare geese, swans, flamingos, cranes, peacocks and pheasants.

MUSEUMS AND GALLERIES

ANNE OF CLEVES' HOUSE, High Street, Southover, Lewes (Sussex Archaeological Society)
A picturesque half-timbered house, containing collection of household equipment, furniture, bygones, the Every collection of Ironwork and Firebacks and the Lewes collection.
BARBICAN HOUSE MUSEUM, High Street, Lewes (Sussex Archaeological Society)
Large collection of prehistoric, Romano-British and medieval antiquities relating to Sussex. Prints and watercolours of Sussex.
BATTLE MUSEUM, Langton House, Battle (Battle and District Historical Society)
Facing the Abbey gateway. Battle of Hastings diorama, Roman-British remains from local sites. Sussex iron industry collection of ores and cinders.
BEXHILL MUSEUM, Egerton Park, Bexhill
Natural history and archaeology of the district.
BODIAM CASTLE MUSEUM (National Trust)
Relics found during excavations of this fine example of medieval architecture.
THE BOOTH MUSEUM OF NATURAL HISTORY, Dyke Road, Brighton (Brighton Borough Council)
A comprehensive display of birds, mounted in their natural habitat, also reference collections of eggs, insects, minerals, palaeontology, osteology, bird and mammal skins and herbaria.
BRIGHTON MUSEUM AND ART GALLERY, Church Street, Brighton (Brighton Borough Council)
The collections include old master paintings, watercolours, furniture and ceramics; the Willitt collection of English pottery and porcelain; the Edward James collection of surrealist paintings; fine and applied art of the Art Nouveau and Art Deco periods; important collections of ethnography and archaeology; musical instruments, Brighton history, special exhibitions.
THE FISHERMAN'S MUSEUM, Rock-a-nore, Hastings
All the exhibits in the museum are donations. Among them is a large picture of

the presentation to Sir Winston Churchill of a golden winkle at The Enterprise on Winkle Island, September 1955.

THE GRANGE ART GALLERY AND MUSEUM, Rottingdean (Brighton Borough Council)
A Georgian house, adjacent to Kipling's home, displays letters, books and illustrations of the author, Sussex folk-life collection, and a large display of toys from the Toy Museum. Frequent temporary displays in the Brighton Art Gallery.

HOVE MUSEUM OF ART, 19 New Church Road, Hove (Hove Borough Council)
English fine and applied art of the 18th and 19th centuries – paintings and prints, English, Continental and Oriental ceramics. Furniture, silver, glass, watches, coins and medals, dolls, local history items, and galleries for special exhibitions.

MANOR LIBRARY COSTUME MUSEUM, Manor House Gardens, Old Town, Bexhill

MUSEUM AND ART GALLERY, Cambridge Road, Hastings (Hastings Borough Council)
Local history, archaeology, zoology and geology; Sussex ironwork and pottery; English, European, Oriental and primitive art, especially ceramics; Durbar Hall; temporary exhibition gallery.

MUSEUM OF LOCAL HISTORY, Old Town Hall, High Street, Hastings (Hastings Borough Council)
Local history, folk-life, topography and archaeology; maritime history.

ROYAL NATIONAL LIFEBOAT INSTITUTION MUSEUM, Grand Parade, Eastbourne
All types of lifeboats from the earliest date to the present time. Various items used in lifeboat service.

RYE MUSEUM, Ypres Tower, Rye
Local history collections housed in a 13th-century tower. Medieval pottery from the Rye kilns, Cinque Ports material, militaria, shipping, dolls, toys and glass.

TOWER 73 (The Wish Tower), Eastbourne
A restored Martello tower. Displays show the historical background, disposition, building and manning of these defence forts built during the Napoleonic War, together with examples of equipment, weapons, uniforms and documents relating to the building.

THE TOWNER ART GALLERY, Manor House, 9 Borough Lane, Eastbourne
British painters of 19th and 20th centuries, contemporary original prints. Frequent temporary exhibitions. Collection of Sussex pictures. Set of Georgian caricatures. Original drawings by British book illustrators. Bell collection of British butterflies.

THE TOY MUSEUM, The Grange, Rottingdean, Brighton
(National Toy Collection.)
This collection has over 20,000 toys and playthings from many lands.

WILMINGTON MUSEUM, Wilmington Priory (Sussex Archaeological Society)
Collection of old agricultural implements and farmhouse utensils.

WINCHELSEA MUSEUM, Court Hall, Winchelsea
Collection illustrating the history of the Cinque Ports. Handcrafts, archaeological specimens, models, maps, documents.

ESSEX

OUTSTANDING NATURAL BEAUTY

DEDHAM VALE (part)

HISTORIC HOUSES AND CASTLES

AUDLEY END HOUSE, Saffron Walden (Department of the Environment)
Palatial Jacobean mansion begun in 1603 on site of a Benedictine abbey. State rooms and hall.

BLUE BRIDGE HOUSE, Halstead (Mr and Mrs B. E. Pleydell-Bouverie)
Enchanting, small Queen Anne house.
BOURNE MILL, Colchester (National Trust)
Fishing lodge built in 1591, later converted into a mill.
CASTLE HOUSE, Dedham
Home of the late Sir Alfred Munnings, KVCO, President of the Royal Academy
(1944–9). Many paintings, drawings, sketches and other works.
GOSFIELD HALL, Halstead (Mutual Households Association Limited)
Very fine Tudor gallery.
HEDINGHAM CASTLE, Castle Hedingham (Miss Musette Majendie, CBE and Dr
Margery Blackie)
Great Norman keep and Tudor bridge.
INGATESTONE HALL, Ingatestone (Lord Petre and Essex County Council)
Tudor gallery exhibition 'Essex at War'.
LAYER MARNEY TOWER, Nr Colchester (Major and Mrs Gerald Charrington)
1520 Tudor brick house with 8-storey gate tower. Terracotta dolphin cresting and
windows. Formal yew hedges, rose bushes and lawns.
PAYCOCKE'S, Coggeshall (National Trust)
Richly ornamented merchant's house dating from about 1500.

MUSEUMS AND GALLERIES

BEECROFT ART GALLERY, Station Road, Westcliff-on-Sea (Borough of Southend-
on-Sea)
Municipal, Thorpe Smith and Beecroft collections. Monthly loan exhibitions.
CHELMSFORD AND ESSEX MUSEUM, Oaklands Park, Moulsham Street, Chelmsford
(Chelmsford District Council) (Incorporating the Essex Regiment Museum)
Collection of archaeological material from Chelmsford and Essex, bygones, coins,
costume, paintings, ceramics, natural history and geology. Temporary exhibition
programme.
COLCHESTER AND ESSEX MUSEUM (Colchester Borough Council)
  THE CASTLE
  A Norman keep standing on the site of a Roman temple. It contains archae-
  ological material of all kinds from Essex, and the finds of Roman Colchester.
  THE HOLLY TREES
  A 1718 house used as a museum of later social history.
  MUSEUM OF NATURAL HISTORY, All Saints Church, High Street
  The natural history of Essex.
  HOLY TRINITY CHURCH, Trinity Street
  Country life and crafts.
THE MINORIES ART GALLERY, High Street, Colchester (Victor Batte-Lay Trust)
Monthly exhibitions – retrospectives, one man, group or theme shows covering
modern and past art in the setting of a Georgian house.
PRITTLEWELL PRIORY MUSEUM, Priory Park, Southend-on-Sea (Borough of
Southend-on-Sea)
Originally a Cluniac monastry, now a museum of local and natural history.
SAFFRON WALDEN MUSEUM, Museum Street, Saffron Walden
Collections of local archaeology, natural history, geology, local building methods,
ceramics, glass, costumes, toys, ethnography.
SOUTHCHURCH HALL, Southchurch Hall Close, Southend-on-Sea (Borough of
Southend-on-Sea)
Moated timber-framed manor house early 14th century with small Tudor wing,

the open hall furnished as a medieval manor. Exhibition room.

THURROCK LOCAL HISTORY MUSEUM, Central Library, Orsett Road, Grays
(Thurrock Borough Council)
Prehistoric, Romano-British and pagan Saxon archaeology. Social, agricultural
and industrial history of the locality.

GLOUCESTER
OUTSTANDING NATURAL BEAUTY

COTSWOLDS (part)
MALVERN HILLS (part)
WYE VALLEY (part)

HISTORIC HOUSES AND CASTLES

ARLINGTON MILL, Bibury (D. C. W. Verey, Esq)
Large 17th-century mill with old mill machinery. Country museum. Staffordshire
china. Furniture by Peter Waals, Victorian costumes and furniture.

ASHLEWORTH TITHE BARN, Nr Hartpury (National Trust)
15th-century tithe barn with 2 projecting porch bays and fine roof timbers with
queenposts.

*BARNSLEY PARK, Cirencester (C. M. Henderson)
Georgian baroque mansion build 1720–31. Early 18th- and 19th-century decoration. Nash conservatory. Fine vistas. 400 acres of parkland.

BERKELEY CASTLE, Nr Bristol (Mr and Mrs R. J. Berkeley)
An historic castle over 800 years old and still lived in by the Berkeleys. Scene of
the murder of Edward II (1327).

BUCKLAND RECTORY, Nr Broadway (The Rev Michael Bland, MA)
England's oldest rectory. 15th-century great hall with contemporary stained glass.
Earlier staircase and house. Associations John Wesley.

CHAVENAGE, Tetbury (David Lowsley-Williams, Esq)
Elizabethan Cotswold manor house with Cromwellian associations. 2 tapestried
rooms. Also medieval Cotswold barn.

CLEARWELL CASTLE, Nr Coleford (Mr B. Yeates)
A 'mock Gothic castle' reputed to be the oldest in Britain. Regency interior restored
from a ruin over past 20 years. 8 acres of formal gardens. Still under restoration.

COURT HOUSE, Painswick (Mrs L. O. Collett)
Cotswold Manor. Original court room and bedchamber of Charles I. Handsome
panelling. Collection of antique furniture.

KELMSCOTT MANOR, Nr Lechdale (Society of Antiquarie of London)
Cotswold style manor of 16th and 17th centuries. Summer home of William
Morris from 1871 until death in 1876. Original Morris possessions and examples
of his designs. Small formal garden.

SNOWSHILL MANOR, Broadway (National Trust)
Tudor manor house with a later façade containing a 'magpie' collection of musical
instruments, clocks, toys, etc. Terraced garden.

SUDELEY CASTLE, Winchcombe (Mrs Elizabeth Dent-Brocklehurst)
12th-century house, home of Katherine Parr. Rich in art treasures. Gardens highlighted by historic Elizabethan garden.

UPPER SLAUGHTER MANOR HOUSE, Cheltenham (Mr E. Turrell)
Elizabethan manor house with typical Edwardian rose and herb gardens.

GARDENS

BARNSLEY HOUSE GARDEN, Barnsley, Nr Cirencester (Mr and Mrs D. C. W. Verey)
Garden laid out in 1770, trees planted 1840. Replanned 1960. Many spring bulbs.
Laburnum avenue (early June). Lime walk, herbaceous and shrub borders. Ground
cover. Knot garden. Gothic summer house 1770. Classic temple 1780. House 1697
(*not* open).

HIDCOTE MANOR GARDEN, Hidcote Bartrim (National Trust)
One of the most beautiful English gardens.

KIFTSGATE COURT, Nr Chipping Campden (Mrs D. H. Binny)
Garden with many rare shrubs and plants including exceptional collection of specie
and old fashioned roses.

MISARDEN PARK, Nr Stroud (Mrs Huntley Sinclair)
Herbaceous borders.

WESTBURY COURT GARDEN, Westbury-on-Severn (National Trust)
Formal water-garden with canals and yew hedges, laid out 1696–1705–the
earliest of its kind remaining in England.

MUSEUMS AND GALLERIES

BISHOP HOOPER'S LODGING, 99–103 Westgate Street, Gloucester (Gloucester
Corporation)
Group of 3 Tudor timber-framed buildings, scheduled as ancient monuments.
Collections illustrate bygone crafts and industries of the country, agriculture,
Severn fishing, local history and history of Gloucestershire Regiment.

CHEDWORTH ROMAN VILLA AND MUSEUM (National Trust)
Exceptionally fine villa AD 150–350 with mosaic pavements.

CHELTENHAM ART GALLERY AND MUSEUM, Clarence Street, Cheltenham (Cheltenham
Borough Council)
Baron de Ferrieres Gallery of Dutch paintings and permanent collection of oils,
watercolours, etchings and local prints. Museum contains large collection of
English pottery and porcelain, Chinese porcelain, furniture, social history material
relating to Cheltenham and the Cotswolds and archaeology. Variety of temporary
exhibitions.

CITY MUSEUM AND ART GALLERY, Brunswick Road, Gloucester (Gloucester
Corporation)
Local archaeology, natural history, geology and numismatics; English period
furniture and barometers, pottery, glass, silver and costume. Temporary art
exhibitions.

CITY WALL AND BASTION, entrance in King's Walk, Gloucester (Gloucester
Corporation)
The Roman and medieval city defences in an underground exhibition chamber.

CORINIUM MUSEUM, Park Street, Cirencester (Cotswold District Council)
A redevelopment museum for the Cotswold region, includes collection of Roman
antiquities from the site of Corinium Dobunnorum.

*FILKINS AND BROUGHTON POGGS MUSEUM, Filkins Nr Lechdale
Domestic articles, folklore, tools.

FOLK MUSEUM, Town Hall, Winchcombe
Small collection of objects of local interest.

HAILES ABBEY MUSEUM, Hailes Abbey, Winchcombe (Department of the
Environment)
Medieval sculpture and other archaeological fragments found in the Abbey ruins.

HOLST BIRTHPLACE MUSEUM, 4 Clarence Street, Cheltenham (Cheltenham Borough Council)
Regency house with period rooms containing Gustav Holst memoralia and reference collections.

STROUD MUSEUM, Lansdown, Stroud (Cowle Trust)
Collections covering geology, archaeology, local crafts and industrial archaeology, farming and household equipment, ceramics, dolls, etc, paintings, photographs and records of local houses and mills.

TEWKESBURY MUSEUM, Barton Street, Tewkesbury (Tewkesbury Borough Council)
Collections of archaeology, costumes, furniture, military and local history.

GREATER MANCHESTER
NATIONAL PARKS

PEAK DISTRICT (part)

HISTORIC HOUSES AND CASTLES

FLETCHER MOSS, Didsbury (Manchester City Art Galleries)
Set in pleasant gardens. An old parsonage of late Georgian and early Victorian character. Houses the best of the City Art Galleries' collection of English water-colours from Paul Sandby to the present.

HALL-I'-TH'-WOOD, Bolton (Bolton Metropolitan Borough)
Half-timbered house (1483); stone wing (1591 and 1648). Now used as folk museum.

HEATON HALL, Prestwich (Manchester City Art Galleries)
Former home of the Earls of Wilton, designed by James Wyatt in 1772. Contains one of the few surviving Etruscan rooms and an organ by Samuel Green, furniture and pictures of the 18th and early 19th century and a display of contemporary ceramics, glass and enamels.

NEWTON HALL, Hyde (William Kenyon and Sons Limited)
Restored Cruck-framed manor hall, built 1380. Original cruck beams and spurs with side wall. 2 acres parkland.

PLATT HALL, Rusholme (Manchester City Art Galleries)
The Gallery of English costume. A Georgian country house of the early 1760s designed by John Carr of York, formerly the seat of the Worsley family. Houses one of the country's finest collections of English clothing from the 17th century to the present day costume.

SMITHILLS HALL, Bolton (Bolton Metropolitan Borough)
14th- and early 16th-century timbered hall. Tudor panelling, 17th-century furniture.

WYTHENSHAWE HALL, Northenden (Manchester City Art Galleries)
A half-timbered manor house set in fine parkland. Seat of the Tatton family for over 500 years. Furniture and pictures of the 17th century. Royal Lancastrian pottery, local history material and modern pottery.

MUSEUMS AND GALLERIES

ART GALLERY, Esplanade, Rochdale (Rochdale Metropolitan District Council)
Important exhibitions of contemporary British art-craft gallery. Large collection of British paintings, Victorian to modern.

ART GALLERY AND MUSEUM, Union Street, Oldham (Oldham Metropolitan Borough)

Frequently changed exhibitions. Early English watercolours, British paintings of 19th and 20th centuries, and contemporary art. British glass. Oriental collection.

THE ASTLEY CHEETHAM ART GALLERY, Trinity Street, Stalybridge (Stalybridge Town Council)

THE ATHENAEUM ANNEXE, Princess Street, Manchester

Museum of Ceramics, this old club, designed by Sir Charles Barry (1837) houses the City Art Gallery's school service centre.

BRAMALL HALL, Bramhall

15th- and 18th-century house with fine timber and plasterwork containing a museum.

BURY ART GALLERY AND MUSEUM, Moss Street, Bury (Metropolitan Borough of Bury)

Museum: local history.

Art Gallery: permanent collection and Wrigley collection of oil and watercolour paintings.

THE CITY ART GALLERY, Moseley Street, Manchester

Designed by Sir Charles Barry (1824). Paintings, sculpture, silver and pottery. The Assheton Bennett collection of silver and Dutch 17th-century pictures, and the Greg collection of English pottery.

FACULTY OF ART AND DESIGN GALLERIES, Cavendish Street, All Saints, Manchester (Manchester Polytechnic)

Temporary exhibitions, chiefly of contemporary art and design.

LOCAL INTEREST CENTRE, Greaves Street, Oldham (Oldham Metropolitan Borough)

Local studies, library, local history museum, small gallery.

MONKS HALL MUSEUM, 42 Wellington Road, Eccles (City of Salford)

Nasmyth machine tools, temporary exhibitions including art, science, bygones.

MUNICIPAL MUSEUM, Vernon Park, Turncroft Lane, Stockport (Metropolitan Borough of Stockport)

Local history, natural history, geology, ceramics, Victoriana. Temporary exhibitions.

MUSEUM, Sparrow Hill, Rochdale

Large collections of local history, natural history (vivarium), furniture, costume.

MUSEUM AND ART GALLERY, Civic Centre, Bolton (Bolton Borough Council)

Museum: Botany, zoology and prehistory, Egyptian collection, aquarium.

Art Gallery: paintings and sculpture of English and European schools, English watercolours, 18th-century English pottery.

MUSEUM AND ART GALLERY, The Crescent, Peel Park, Salford (City of Salford)

Chief features: L. S. Lowry collection of paintings and drawings; 'Lark Hill Place', and 19th-century 'street' of shops and period rooms.

ORDSALL HALL MUSEUM, Taylorson Street, Salford (City of Salford)

Manor house with fine 15th-century spere truss in great hall; collections of furniture, kitchen equipment and local history items.

QUEEN'S PARK ART GALLERY AND MILITARY MUSEUM, Rochdale Road, Manchester

1878 purpose-built Victorian gallery hung with large Academy works. Paintings by the Manchester School and Adolphe Valette. Museum of the military collections of the Manchester Regiment and the 14th/20th Hussars.

ROCHDALE COOPERATIVE MUSEUM, Toad Lane, Rochdale

The original store of the Rochdale Cooperative Pioneers containing documents, pictures and other material of British and international cooperative interest.

SWINTON MEMORIAL ART GALLERY, Central Library, Chorley Road, Swinton, Salford (City of Salford)

Temporary art exhibitions.

TONGE MOOR TEXTILE MACHINERY MUSEUM, Tonge Moor Road, Bolton
Historic textile machines, including Crompton's Mule, Hargreave's Jenny and
Arkwright's water frame.
TURNPIKE GALLERY, Leigh (Metropolitan Borough of Wigan)
Small watercolour collection. Major touring exhibitions.
WAR MEMORIAL ART GALLERY, Wellington Road South, Stockport (Metropolitan
Borough of Stockport)
Permanent collection – British artists, mainly watercolours. Epstein's head of
Yehudi Menuhin.
WHITWORTH ART GALLERY, Oxford Road, Manchester (University of Manchester)
Outstanding collections of English watercolours. Old master drawings, Post-
Impressionist and 20th-century Continental drawings. Contemporary paintings
and sculpture. Prints, ranging from the Renaissance period to the present day,
including Japanese colour wood-cuts. Important textiles collection.
WIGAN MUSEUM, Station Road, Wigan (Wigan Metropolitan Borough)
Local collections of geology, archaeology, history, coal-mining, pewter, bell-
founding, clogging, local art collection, Rimmer collection of musical instruments.

HAMPSHIRE
OUTSTANDING NATURAL BEAUTY
CHICHESTER HARBOUR (part)
EAST HAMPSHIRE
NORTH WESSEX DOWNS (part)
SOUTH HAMPSHIRE COAST (part)

HISTORIC HOUSES AND CASTLES
AVINGTON PARK, Winchester (J. B. Hickson, Esq)
Red brick house in Wren tradition.
BEAULIEU ABBEY AND PALACE HOUSE, NATIONAL MOTOR MUSEUM (Lord Montagu
of Beaulieu)
Cistercian Abbey founded 1204. Palace house originally great gate-house of abbey
converted 1538. Historic car, motor cycle and cycle museum, with over 200 exhibits
and displays. Fine garden.
BREAMORE HOUSE, Nr Fordingbridge (Sir Westrow Hulse, Bt)
Elizabethan manor house (1583) with fine collection of paintings, tapestries,
furniture. Countryside museum. Carriage museum.
GROVE PLACE, Nursling, Southampton (Northcliffe School Trust Limited)
Elizabethan House. Contents for boys' boarding school.
JANE AUSTEN'S HOME, Chawton (Jane Austen Memorial Trust)
Jane Austen's home with many interesting personal relics of herself and her family.
MOTTISFONT ABBEY, Mottisfont (National Trust)
Originally a 12th-century Augustinian priory. South front 18th century. Drawing-
room by Rex Whistler. Fine lawns and trees. Walled gardens with Trust's
collection of old-fashioned roses.
THE PILGRIMS' HALL, Winchester (Dean and Chapter, Winchester Cathedral)
14th-century with fine hammer-beam roof.
SANDHAM MEMORIAL CHAPEL, Nr Newbury (National Trust)
Walls covered with paintings by Stanley Spencer.
STRATFIELD SAYE HOUSE, Reading (Trustees of the Duke of Wellington)
1630 house filled with the Great Duke's possessions and atmosphere of his
personality.

THE VYNE, Basingstoke (National Trust)
Early 16th-century house with classical portico added 1654. Tudor panelling, 18th-century ornamented staircase. Extensive lawns, lake, trees, herbaceous border.
*WEST GREEN HOUSE, Hartley Wintey (National Trust)
Red brick early 18th-century house in walled garden.
*WINCHESTER CITY MILL, High Street (National Trust)
Built over river in 1744. Now leased to Youth Hostels Association.

GARDENS

FURZEY GARDENS, Minstead, Nr Lyndhurst (H. J. Cole, Esq)
8 acres of gardens with heathers, azaleas, rhododendrons, bluebells, peonies, tree peonies, irises and roses and many other plants.
HURST MILL, Petersfield (Mr and Mrs Willoughby Norman)
Waterfall, mill stream and bog garden, flowering shrubs, forest and ornamental trees.
JENKYN PLACE, Bentley (G. E. Coke, Esq)
Large garden of variety – old fashioned and specie roses, herbaceous borders, collection of shrubs.
SPINNERS, Boldre (Mr and Mrs P. G. G. Chappell)
Azaleas, rhododendrons, primulas and woodland plants.

MUSEUMS AND GALLERIES

BARGATE GUILDHALL MUSEUM, High Street, Southampton (Southampton Corporation)
Local historical exhibits and changing exhibitions, housed in the former hall of guilds above the medieval north gate.
CALLEVA MUSEUM, Rectory Grounds, Silchester Common
Roman objects from site of Calleva.
CITY MUSEUM AND ART GALLERY, Museum Road, Portsmouth (City of Portsmouth)
English furniture, pottery and glass; contemporary and topographic paintings and prints. Local history galleries. Temporary exhibitions.
CUMBERLAND HOUSE MUSEUM AND AQUARIUM, Eastern Parade, Southsea, Portsmouth (City of Portsmouth)
Natural history and geology of the Hampshire basin.
THE CURTIS MUSEUM, High Street, Alton (Hampshire County Council)
Local collections of geology, botany, zoology, archaeology and history; craft tools, pottery and dolls, toys and games. The Museum Annexe and the Allen Gallery (10 and 12 Church Street) contain respectively a collection of sporting firearms and selections of paintings from the W. H. Allen collection and loan exhibitions.
DICKENS'S BIRTHPLACE MUSEUM, 393 Commercial Road, Mile End, Portsmouth (City of Portsmouth)
The house where Dickens was born in 1812, furnished in the taste of the period.
EASTNEY NEW BEAM ENGINE HOUSE AND GAS ENGINE HOUSE, Portsmouth
Building and steam pumps of 1887.
FORT WIDLEY, Portsdown Hill, Portsmouth (City of Portsmouth)
Palmerston folly 1868.
GILBERT WHITE MUSEUM AND THE OATES MEMORIAL LIBRARY AND MUSEUM, The Wakes, Selborne
Relics of Gilbert White, pioneer naturalist, Capt L. E. G. Oates, Antarctic explorer and Frank Oates, African explorer.

GOD'S HOUSE TOWER MUSEUM, Town Quay, Southampton (Southampton Corporation)
Early 15th-century fortification, now a museum of archaeology.
GUILDHALL PICTURE GALLERY, High Street, Winchester (Winchester City Council)
Local topographical pictures and loan exhibitions.
MARITIME MUSEUM, Buckler's Hard, Beaulieu
Collection of models and exhibits of ships built at Buckler's Hard for Nelson's fleet.
MARITIME MUSEUM, Wool House, Bugle Street, Southampton (Southampton Corporation)
14th-century wool store, now a museum of shipping.
THE PORTSMOUTH ROYAL NAVAL MUSEUM, HM Naval Base, Portsmouth
Situated adjacent to HMS *Victory* and containing personal items of Nelson, his officers and men. Ships models and figureheads and the 'Panorama of Trafalgar'. The Nelson-McCarthy collection of commemorative material.
SOUTHAMPTON ART GALLERY, Civic Centre, Southampton (Southampton Corporation)
Specialises in British painting, particularly contemporary; some French 19th-century and continental masters.
SOUTHSEA CASTLE, Clarence Esplanade, Portsmouth (City of Portsmouth)
Local and military history of Portsmouth. Permanent exhibition on the *Mary Rose*. Archaeology.
TUDOR HOUSE MUSEUM, St Michael's Square, Southampton (Southampton Corporation)
16th-century Tudor mansion containing historical and antiquarian exhibits.
THE WESTGATE MUSEUM, High Street, Winchester (Winchester City Council)
Medieval west gate of the city. Exhibits illustrate the civic history of Winchester; city moot horn (13th century) and a collection of medieval and later weights and measures.
THE WILLIS MUSEUM AND ART GALLERY, New Street, Basingstoke (Hampshire County Council)
Local collections of archaeology, natural history, geology; Basingstoke canal, horology and watch and clock-makers' tools, pottery. Temporary exhibitions. A new town history gallery to be opened 1976.
WINCHESTER CATHEDRAL TREASURY
Church silver and additional pieces from parishes and other sources in Hampshire.
WINCHESTER CITY MUSEUM, The Square, Winchester (Winchester City Council)
Archaeology of Winchester and central Hampshire.
WINCHESTER COLLEGE MUSEUM, Winchester
Collections of Greek pottery, English watercolours.

HEREFORD AND WORCESTER
OUTSTANDING NATURAL BEAUTY

COTSWOLDS (part)
MALVERN HILLS (part)
WYE VALLEY (part)

HISTORIC HOUSES AND CASTLES

BERRINGTON HALL, Leominster (National Trust)
Built 1778–81 by Henry Holland. Painted and plaster ceilings. Capability Brown laid out the parks.

BREDON TITHE BARN (National Trust)
14th-century barn 132 feet long with fine porches.

BRILLEY, CWMMAU FARMHOUSE, Whitney-on-Wye (National Trust)
Early 17th-century timber-framed and stone-tiled farmhouse.

BURTON COURT, Eardisland (Lt-Cmdr and Mrs R. M. Simpson)
14th-century great hall. European and Oriental costume and curio exhibition.

CROFT CASTLE, Nr Leominster (National Trust)
Welsh border castle mentioned in Domesday. Inhabited by the Croft family for 900 years.

DINMORE MANOR, Nr Hereford (C. Ian Murray, Esq)
14th-century chapel; also cloisters, 'music room' and rock garden.

EASTNOR CASTLE, Nr Ledbury (The Hon Mrs Hervey-Bathurst)
Excellent specimen of 19th-century castellated architecture containing armour, pictures, etc. Arboretum.

EYE MANOR, Leominster (Mr and Mrs Christopher Sandford)
Built 1680. Lovely Renaissance interior with plasterwork, furniture, pictures, period costumes, books, art and crafts, secret passage.

*THE GREYFRIARS, Worcester (National Trust)
A timber-frame house built 1480 for the then adjoining Franciscan friary.

HANBURY HALL, Nr Droitwich (National Trust)
Red brick house, circa 1700. Only Thornhill's painted ceilings and staircase and 2 furnished rooms are shown.

HARVINGTON HALL, Kidderminster (Roman Catholic Archdiocese of Birmingham)
Moated Tudor manor house containing priests' hiding places. Catholic associations.

HAWFORD DOVECOTE, Nr Worcester (National Trust)
16th-century half-timbered dovecote. Access via the entrance drive to the adjoining house.

HELLEN'S, Much Marcle (Pennington-Mellor-Munthe family)
Manorial house lived in since 1292. Visited by Black Prince and Bloody Mary.

*KENTCHURCH COURT, Hereford (Lt Cmdr J. H. S. Lucas-Scudamore)
Fortified border manor house altered by Nash. Gateway and part of the original 14th-century house still survive. Pictures and Grinling Gibbons carving. Owen Glendower tower.

LITTLE MALVERN COURT (T. P. Berington, Esq)
14th-century prior's guest hall.

LOWER BROCKHAMPTON, Bromyard (National Trust)
Small half-timbered manor house circa 1400.

MIDDLE LITTERTON TITHE BARN, Nr Evesham (National Trust)
13th- or 14th-century barn 140 feet long.

MOCCAS COURT, Moccas
House under restoration; designed by Adam and built by Keck in 1775. Park laid out by Capability Brown.

PEMBRIDGE CASTLE, Welsh Newton (R. A. Cooke, Esq)
17th-century moated border castle.

GARDENS

BROADWAY TOWER COUNTRY PARK, Broadway (Batsford Estates Company)
18th-century folly. Exhibitions. Natural history centre. Approximately 35 acres for walking and picnics.

HERGEST CROFT GARDEN AND PARK WOOD (W. L. and R. A. Banks, Esq)
50 acres of trees, shrubs, rhododendrons and azaleas from all over the temperate world.

SPETCHLEY PARK, Worcester (Mr and Mrs R. J. Berkeley)
30 acres of trees, shrubs and plants. Ornamental waterfall. Red and fallow deer in park.

THE WEIR, Swainshill (National Trust)
Spring garden with fine views over the River Wye and the Welsh and Monmouthshire hills from the cliff garden walks.

MUSEUMS AND GALLERIES

ALMONRY MUSEUM, Vine Street, Evesham (Vale of Evesham Historical Society)
Roman-British, Anglo-Saxon, medieval and monastic remains. Agricultural implements and general exhibits of local historic interest.

ART GALLERY, Market Street, Kidderminster
Loan exhibitions, Brangwyn etchings, small permanent collection.

*AVERY HISTORICAL MUSEUM, Smethwick, Warley
Collection of machines, instruments, weights, records, etc, relating to the history of weighing.

THE AVONCROFT MUSEUM OF BUILDINGS LTD, Stoke Heath, Bromsgrove
Open air museum containing buildings of great variety from a reconstructed Iron Age hut to a 15th century Merchant's house.

BEWDLEY MUSEUM, The Shambles, Load Street, Bewdley (Wyre Forest District Council)
The town's 18th-century market recently converted to a folk museum of Bewdley and the Wyre Forest.

CHURCHILL GARDENS MUSEUM, Venn's Lane, Hereford (Hereford District Council)
Costume, fine furniture, watercolours and paintings by local artists. The Brian Hatton Gallery devoted to the work of this local artist.

CITY MUSEUM AND ART GALLERY, Worcester (Worcester City Council)
Local history, archaeology, geology and natural history illustrating man and his environment in the Severn Valley region with particular reference to the City of Worcester.

THE DYSON PERRINS MUSEUM OF WORCESTER PORCELAIN, The Royal Porcelain Works, Severn Street, Worcester (Dyson Perrins Museum Trust)
The finest and most comprehensive collection of old Worcester in the world.

HEREFORD AND WORCESTER COUNTY MUSEUM, Hartlebury Castle, Hartlebury (Hereford and Worcester County Council)
Changing displays including archaeology and geology, crafts and industries of the county, a restored cider mill, furniture, glass and costume and horse-drawn vehicles, including gypsy caravans.

HEREFORD CITY MUSEUM AND ART GALLERY, Broad Street, Hereford (Hereford District Council)
Archaeology and natural history, costumes, toys, embroidery, textiles, military equipment and agricultural bygones. Pictures by local artists and examples of applied art, silver, pottery and porcelain in the Art Gallery.

MUSEUM, Kidderminster
Local studies and archaeology. Official repository for the Kidderminster and District Archaeological and Historical Society.

THE OLD HOUSE, High Town, Hereford (Hereford District Council)

Preserved and furnished as a Jacobean period museum.
PLAYTHINGS PAST MUSEUM, Beaconwood, Beacon Lane, Nr Bromsgrove
Antique and period dolls, dolls' houses, toys and automata.
TUDOR HOUSE MUSEUM, Fair Street, Worcester (Worcester City Council)
Permanent and temporary displays illustrating the domestic and working life of
the City of Worcester.
Also houses the MUSEUM OF THE WORCESTERSHIRE REGIMENT, and the MUSEUM OF
THE WORCESTERSHIRE YEOMANRY CAVALRY.
The Art Gallery contains travelling exhibitions and the permanent collection.

HERTFORDSHIRE
OUTSTANDING NATURAL BEAUTY

CHILTERNS (part)

HISTORIC HOUSES AND CASTLES

ASHRIDGE, Berkhamsted (Governors of Ashridge Management College)
Early Gothic revival. Begun 1808 by James Wyatt for the Earl of Bridgewater.
17th-century crypt. Tudor barn. Gardens landscaped by Repton.
GORHAMBURY HOUSE, St Albans (Earl of Verulam)
Mansion built 1777–84 in modified classical style by Sir Robert Taylor. 16th-
century enamelled glass and historic portraits.
HATFIELD HOUSE, Hatfield (Marquess of Salisbury)
Jacobean house and Tudor palace, childhood home of Elizabeth I. House built
by Robert Cecil, first Earl of Salisbury, in 1611. Fine portraits, furniture and
relics of Elizabeth I. Fine gardens and large park. Exhibition including facsimiles
and transcripts of Tudor papers in the archives and costumes from famous portraits
of Elizabeth I and her courtiers.
KNEBWORTH HOUSE, Knebworth (The Hon David Lytton Cobbold)
Tudor mansion started in 1492. External decoration in the Gothic style by Sir
Edward Bulwer-Lytton in 1843. Gardens.
MOOR PARK MANSION (Three Rivers District Council)
Palladian house reconstructed in 1727 incorporating house built in 1607.
Magnificent interior decorations by Verrio, Thornhill and others. Under
restoration.
PICCOTTS END MEDIEVAL MURALS (A. C. Lindley, Esq)
Remarkable 15th-century wall paintings in a hall house.
SALISBURY HALL, London Colney (W. J. Goldsmith, Esq)
17th-century house surrounded by medieval moat. Fine staircase, panelling.
Beautiful fireplaces. Prototype de Havilland Mosquito, Vampire, Venom.
SHAW'S CORNER, Ayot St Lawrence (National Trust)
Home of George Bernard Shaw, 1906–50.

GARDENS

ARKLEY MANOR, Nr Barnet (Dr W. E. Shewell-Cooper, MBE)
Organic gardens, no digging or chemicals yet totally weedless. Fruit, flowers and
vegetables, weeping garden.

MUSEUMS AND GALLERIES

ASHWELL VILLAGE MUSEUM, Swan Street, Ashwell (Trustees)
Illustrates life and work in the village from Stone Age to the present. A folk museum.

CITY MUSEUM, Hatfield Road, St Albans
County collections in biology and geology. Salaman collection of tools to illustrate local crafts and trades. Collections of 19th-century glass and pottery.

CLOCK TOWER, Market Place, St Albans (St Albans District Council)
Erected 1402–11, restored by Sir Gilbert Scott in 1866, the tower is 77 feet high, with 5 storeys.

HERTFORD MUSEUM, 18 Bull Plain, Hertford (Hertford Town Council)
Local archaeology, history, geology and natural history.

HITCHIN MUSEUM AND ART GALLERY, Paynes Park, Hitchin (North Herts DC)
Archaeology, local and natural history, costume, Hertfordshire Yeomanry room; pictures by Samuel Lucas, special exhibitions.

LETCHWORTH MUSEUM AND ART GALLERY, Town Square, Letchworth (North Herts DC)
North Hertfordshire archaeological material, natural history, history of first garden city. Monthly art exhibitions.

RHODES MEMORIAL MUSEUM, Bishop's Stortford
Collections illustrating life of Cecil Rhodes in house in which he was born. Illustrations of Southern and Central African history.

STEVENAGE MUSEUM, New Town Centre, Stevenage
Local archaeology, local and natural history, live animals, etc.

THE VERULAMIUM MUSEUM, St Michael's, St Albans (St Albans District Council)
Stands on the site of the Roman city of Verulamium and houses material from the Roman and Belgic cities, including several of the first mosaics in Britain, one of which is preserved in situ in the 'Hypocaust annexe'.

WATFORD ART COLLECTION, Central Public Library, Hempstead Road, Watford
Local prints, paintings, fossils, flints, etc. A continuous programme of exhibitions.

ZOOLOGICAL MUSEUM, BRITISH MUSEUM (NATURAL HISTORY), Akeman Street, Tring
Mounted specimens of animals from all parts of the world.

HUMBERSIDE

OUTSTANDING NATURAL BEAUTY

LINCOLNSHIRE WOLDS (part)

HISTORIC·HOUSES AND CASTLES

BURTON AGNES HALL, Bridlington (Marcus Wickham Boynton, Esq, DL)
One of the least altered of Elizabethan country houses. Fine collection of old and French impressionist paintings, carved ceilings and overmantels.

BURTON CONSTABLE, Nr Hull (J. Chichester Constable, Esq)
Elizabethan house, built 1570. Interior by R. Adam, Wyatt, Carr and Lightoler. Beautiful gardens, lakes, park, laid by Capability Brown.

EPWORTH, The Old Rectory (Trustees of the World Methodist Council)
Built 1709, restored 1957. Childhood home of John and Charles Wesley, and oldest Methodist shrine.

MAISTER HOUSE, Hull (National Trust)
Rebuilt 1744 with a superb staircase-hall, designed in the Palladian manner.

NORMANBY HALL, Scunthorpe (Scunthorpe Corporation)
Regency mansion by Sir Robert Smirke, furnished and decorated in period. Costume displays, spacious garden and deer park. Riding school.

SEWERBY HALL, Bridlington (Borough of North Wolds)
Built 1714–20 by John Greame with additions 1803. Gardens of great botanical interest. Also Bridlington art gallery and museum: loan exhibitions of art and permanent Amy Johnson exhibition; local and natural history and archaeology.

SLEDMERE HOUSE, Driffield (Sir Richard Sykes, DL JP)
Georgian house built 1787. Adam ceilings, fine collection of furniture and paintings, famous 100 ft long library. Gardens and park by Capability Brown.

WILBERFORCE HOUSE, 25 High Street, Hull (Hull Corporation)
17th-century mansion, birthplace of William Wilberforce, the slave emancipator. Now a local historical museum and memorial to Wilberforce.

GARDENS

BURNBY HALL GARDENS, Pocklington (Stewart's Burnby Hall Gardens and Museum Trust)
Museum housing Stewart collection of animal heads and native objects.

ELSHAM HALL, COUNTRY PARK AND CREATIVE CENTRE, Brigg (Capt J. Elwes, DL)
The home of the country quiz, bird sanctuary, domestic animals. The Wrawby Moor Art Gallery; country trails and other attractions.

MUSEUMS AND GALLERIES

BEVERLEY ART GALLERY AND MUSEUM, Champney Road, Beverley (Beverley Borough Council)
Museum of local antiquities. Art gallery includes work by the Beverley artist, F. W. Elwell, RA.

BOROUGH MUSEUM AND ART GALLERY, Oswald Road, Scunthorpe (Scunthorpe Corporation)
Important prehistoric collections; Roman and later archaeology, geology, natural history, local industry. Bygones, period rooms. John Wesley collection. Art exhibitions.

CENTRAL LIBRARY, Town Hall Square, Grimsby (Humberside County Council)
Travelling and local exhibitions constantly on display.

DOUGHTY MUSEUM, Town Hall Square, Grimsby (Grimsby Corporation)
Model ships, especially fishing vessels; china constituting the Doughty bequest, with supplementary exhibits.

FERENS ART GALLERY, Queen Victoria Square, Hull (Hull City Council)
Permanent collection of old masters, English 18th and 19th century' portraits, Humberside marines, a modern collection. Frequent visiting exhibitions.

GEORGIAN HOUSES (Museum Headquarters), 23 and 24 High Street, Hull (Hull City Council)

TOWN DOCKS MUSEUM, Queen Victoria Square, Hull (Hull City Council)
First exhibition of Whales and Whaling open from midsummer 1975, further displays devoted to fishing and shipping industries.

TRANSPORT AND ARCHAEOLOGICAL MUSEUM, 36 High Street, Hull (Hull City Council)
Collection of coaches and motor cars. Archaeology of East Yorkshire. Roman mosaics of Humberside.

ISLE OF WIGHT

OUTSTANDING NATURAL BEAUTY

ISLE OF WIGHT (whole)

HISTORIC HOUSES AND CASTLES

ARRETON MANOR, Arreton (Court L. H. Slade De Pomeroy, KCG, KGCE)
17th-century manor house, early and late Stuart furniture. Toys, doll and folk collections, King Charles I relics. Wireless Preservation Society Museum.

BEMBRIDGE WINDMILL (National Trust)
Only remaining windmill on the island with much of original wooden machinery. Last used 1913.

CARISBROOKE CASTLE (Department of the Environment)
Very fine medieval castle with museum illustrating history of the island and relics of Charles I. Museum contains oldest organ in the country still in working order.

NEWTON OLD TOWN HALL, Newton (National Trust)
18th-century brick and stone building; copies of ancient documents of the borough may be seen in the hall.

NUNWELL HOUSE, Brading (D. Oglander, Esq)
Home of the Oglanders since 1522. Paintings, antique furniture and documents dating back to the Middle Ages. Family museum with displays of dolls and children's books. Garden being restored.

OSBORNE HOUSE, East Cowes (Department of the Environment)
Queen Victoria's favourite residence.

MUSEUMS AND GALLERIES

MUSEUM OF ISLE OF WIGHT GEOLOGY, High Street, Sandown (Sandown and Shanklin Urban District Council)
Unique collection of fossils from secondary and tertiary strata of the island.

OSBORNE-SMITH'S WAX MUSEUM, Brading
Cameos of island history with authentic costume, war figures, period furniture and harmonious settings, brought to life with the added realism of sound, light and motion. Displayed in the island's oldest house, AD 1228.

*THE RUSKIN GALLERY, Bembridge School, Bembridge
Large collection of pictures and manuscripts by Ruskin and his contemporaries.

KENT

OUTSTANDING NATURAL BEAUTY

KENT DOWNS

HISTORIC HOUSES AND CASTLES

ALLINGTON CASTLE, Nr Maidstone (Order of the Carmelites)
13th-century castle. Former home of Tudor poet, Thomas Wyatt, restored by Lord Conway in early part of this country. A fine collection of ikons and Renaissance paintings. The castle is now run by the Carmelite friars as a Christian centre.

AYLESFORD–THE FRIARS (The Carmelite Order)
Restored 13th-century friary and shrine of Our Lady. Original 14th-century cloisters. Sculpture and ceramics by contemporary artists. Pottery, Rose garden.

BLACK CHARLES, Nr Sevenoaks (Mr and Mrs William Temple)
14th-century home of John de Blakecherl and his family 1317–1746. Wealth of old oak beams, Elizabethan panelling, Tudor fireplaces and other interesting features, furniture, etc. Old world garden.

BOUGHTON MONCHELSEA PLACE, Nr Maidstone (M. B. Winch, Esq)
Grey stone, battlemented Elizabethan manor house with views over 18th-century landscaped park and fallow deer.

CHARTWELL, Westerham (National Trust)
Home of Sir Winston Churchill for many years.

CHIDDINGSTONE CASTLE, Nr Edenbridge (Denys E. Bower, Esq)
Pictures and furnishings. Royal Stuart and Jacobite collection; ancient Egyptian collection; Japanese lacquer, swords, netsuke.

COBHAM CASTLE (Westwood Educational Trust Limited)
Mixture of Gothic and Renaissance architecture with good examples of the work of James Wyatt. Now open as a girls' public school.

DEAL CASTLE, Deal (Department of the Environment)
16th-century coastal fortification.

DOVER CASTLE, Dover (Department of the Environment)
Keep built by Henry II in 1180–6. Outer curtain built in 15th century.

DOWN HOUSE, Downe (Royal College of Surgeons of England)
Home of Charles Darwin for 40 years.

EYHORNE MANOR, Hollingbourne (Mr and Mrs Derek Simmons)
Early 15th-century timber-framed house. Galleried chimney. Laundry museum. Herbs and old fashioned roses.

FREEMASON'S HALL, Faversham (Lodge of Harmony No 133)
Queen Elizabeth's Grammar School (1576).

GODINGTON PARK, Ashford (Alan Wyndham Green, Esq)
Mainly Jacobean house, interior containing panelling and carving, portraits, furniture and china. Formal gardens.

GREAT MAYTHAM HALL, Rolvenden (Mutual Households Association Limited)
Built in 1910 by Sir Edwin Lutyens.

HEVER CASTLE, Nr Edenbridge (Lord Astor of Hever)
Formal Italian garden with statuary and sculpture, lake and 13th-century moated castle.

*IAN RAMSEY COLLEGE, BRASTED PLACE, Nr Westerham (The Principal)
A clergy training college housed in Brasted Place (Robert Adam 1784).

IGHTHAM MOTE, Ivy Hatch (C. H. Robinson, Esq)
One of the most complete remaining specimens of an ancient moated manor house.

KNOLE, Sevenoaks (National Trust)
One of the largest private houses in England, dating mainly from the 15th century. Splendid Jacobean interior and fine collection of 17th- and 18th-century furnishings.

LEEDS CASTLE, Nr Maidstone (Leeds Castle Foundation)
Castle of the medieval queens of England. Water and woodland gardens, ducks, aviary.

LYMPNE CASTLE, Nr Hythe (Henry Margary, Esq)
14th-century building restored in 1905. Once owned by the archdeacons of Canterbury. Terraced gardens.

OLD SOAR MANOR (National Trust, under guardianship of Department of the Environment)
Solar block of late 13th-century knight's dwelling.

OWLETTS, Cobham (National Trust)

Red brick Carolean house with contemporary staircase and plasterwork ceiling.

*PATTYNDENNE MANOR, Goudhurst (Mr and Mrs D. C. Spearing)
Unspoint Wealden Manor, built 1470. Exceptional timbering. Remains of 13th-century stone prison. Associated with Henry VIII and Catherine of Aragon.

PENSHURST PLACE, Tunbridge Wells (The Rt Hon Viscount De L'Isle, VC KG)
The early house, including the Great Hall, dates from 1340. There are later additions but the whole house conforms to the English Gothic style in which it was begun.

QUEBEC HOUSE, Westerham (National Trust)
Probably early 16th century in origin, now mainly 17th century. Relics of General Wolfe.

SALTWOOD CASTLE, Nr Hythe (The Hon Alan Clark, MP)
Medieval castle, subject of quarrel between Thomas à Becket and Henry II. Grounds and parts of castle, including battlement walk, undercroft, armoury.

SISSINGHURST CASTLE, Sissinghurst (National Trust)
Famous garden created by the late V. Sackville-West and Sir Harold Nicolson. The tower and the long library are also open.

SMALLHYTHE PLACE, Tenterden (National Trust)
Timbered yeoman's house, dating from 1480, containing the Ellen Terry Memorial Museum with relics of Dame Ellen Terry, Mrs Siddons, etc.

SQUERRYES COURT, Westerham (J. St A. Warde, Esq)
William and Mary manor house. Period furniture, paintings, tapestries and china. Objects of interest connected with General Wolfe. Attractive grounds with lake, fine display of spring bulbs, rhododendrons and azaleas.

*STONEACRE, Otham (National Trust)
A yeoman's half-timbered hall house, circa 1480.

SWANTON MILL, Mersham (Mrs G. Christensen)
Working water mill.

TEMPLE MANOR, Rochester (Department of the Environment)
Surviving building comprises 13th-century stone hall with a vaulted undercroft. 17th-century extensions.

TUDOR YEOMAN'S HOUSE, Sole Street (National Trust)
A yeoman's house of timber construction. Main hall only open.

WARDEN MANOR, Isle of Sheppey [Voluntary and Christian Service (Trustees)]
Small manor house built 1468, now used as a guest house for Christian and public-spirited movements.

WALMER CASTLE, Walmer (Department of the Environment)
Built for coastal defence, 1540. The residence of the Lord Warden of the Cinque Ports.

WOOL HOUSE, Loose (National Trust)
15th-century half-timbered house, formerly used for cleaning wool.

MUSEUMS AND ART GALLERIES

AGRICULTURAL MUSEUM, Wye Cottage (University of London) Court Lodge Farm, Brook, Wye
Agricultural implements, machinery, hand tools and other farming equipment.

THE ART CENTRE, New Metropole, The Leas, Folkestone (Kent County Council Education Committee)
Art exhibitions, films, lectures, poetry and music.

THE BUFFS REGIMENTAL MUSEUM, Poor Priests Hospital, Stour Street, Canterbury (Canterbury City Council)

Collections of medals, weapons, uniforms, pictures and trophies.

DARTFORD DISTRICT MUSEUM, Market Street, Dartford
Local geological and Roman, Saxon and natural history.

*DEAL MUSEUM, Town Hall, High Street, Deal
Collection of local prehistoric and historic antiquities. Complete robes of a baron of the Cinque Ports.

DICKENS'S HOUSE MUSEUM, Victoria Parade, Broadstairs (Thanet District Council)
Dickens's letters and personal belongings. Local Dickensian prints, costume and Victoriana.

DOVER MUSEUM, Ladywell, Dover
Local history, Roman pottery, ceramics, lepidoptera, zoology, horology, coins. Victoriana, geology, etc.

FOLKESTONE MUSEUM AND ART GALLERY, Grace Hill, Folkestone (Kent County Council)
Museum: local history, archaeology, and natural science.
Art Gallery: temporary loan exhibitions.

THE GUILDHALL MUSEUM, Sandwich (Sandwich Town Council)
Collection of ancient and interesting items.

HERNE BAY MUSEUM, High Street, Herne Bay
Exhibits of local or Kentish interest – Stone, Bronze and Early Iron Age specimens. Roman material from Reculver. Collection of pictures, maps and bygones.

HYTHE BOROUGH MUSEUM, Oaklands, Stade Street, Hythe (Hythe Corporation)
Local antiquities.

MAISON DIEU, Ospringe, Faversham (Department of the Environment)
13th-century building containing finds from a Roman cemetery discovered at Ospringe.

MUSEUM AND ART GALLERY, St. Faith's Street, Maidstone (Maidstone Borough Council)
A 16th-century manor house containing archaeological, art and natural history collections for Kent. Pacific and Oriental section, William Hazlitt relics, costume gallery, bygones, ceramics and 17th-century Dutch and Italian oil paintings. The Queen's Own Royal West Kent Regiment occupies a gallery in this building.

THE POWELL-COTTON MUSEUM, Quex Park, Birchington
Zoological specimens. African and Indian jungle scenes, native arts, crafts, and household objects.

RICHBOROUGH CASTLE, Richborough (Department of the Environment)
Objects found during excavation of the site, Roman pottery, coins and other small objects.

ROCHESTER PUBLIC MUSEUM, Eastgate House, Rochester (Medway Borough Council)
Charles Dickens's chalet and relics. Local history, archaeology, arms and armour, costumes, Victoriana, furniture, models of ships and aircraft.

THE ROMAN PAVEMENT, Butchery Lane, Canterbury (Canterbury City Council)
Foundations of Roman villa including 2 coloured mosaic floors and hypocaust.

THE ROYAL MUSEUM, The Beaney, High Street, Canterbury (Canterbury City Council)
Local archaeological material, natural history collection, mineralogical exhibits and collection of pottery and porcelain. Local and other prints, engravings and pictures.

ROYAL TUNBRIDGE WELLS MUSEUM AND ART GALLERY, Civic Centre, Tunbridge Wells (Borough Council)
Prints of old Tunbridge Wells, domestic and agricultural bygones, dolls, toys,

natural history, geology, Wealden prehistory, Tunbridge ware, Victorian paintings.
TYRWHITT-DRAKE MUSEUM OF CARRIAGES, Archbishop's Stables, Mill Street, Maidstone (Maidstone Borough Council)
Horse-drawn vehicles, including most types of state, official and private carriages and items such as models, dealing with the history of horse transport and coach building.
THE WESTGATE, Canterbury (Canterbury City Council)
Museum of arms and armour housed in the 14th-century city gate-house.

LANCASHIRE

OUTSTANDING NATURAL BEAUTY

ARNSIDE AND SILVERDALE (part)
FOREST OF BOWLAND (part)

HISTORIC HOUSES AND CASTLES

ASTLEY HALL, Chorley (Corporation of Chorley, 1922)
Elizabethan house reconstructed in 1666. Furniture, pottery, tapestries, pictures.
CHINGLE HALL, Goosnargh, Nr Preston (Mrs Margaret H. Howarth)
Small moated manor house built 1260. Birth place of Saint John Wall, 1620. Described as one of the most haunted houses in Britain. Rose garden and lawns.
GAWTHORPE HALL, Padiham (National Trust)
Early 17th-century manor house restored in 1860s. Fine panelling and moulded ceilings. Houses Kay-Shuttleworth collection of lace and embroidery.
LEIGHTON HALL, Carnforth (Major and Mrs Reynolds)
Early neo-Gothic façade in superb setting. Fine pictures and furniture. Extensive grounds.
*MARTHOLME GATEHOUSE, Great Harwood (Mrs Rose McFarlane)
Tudor gate-house, built 1561, restored 1969.
RUFFORD OLD HALL, Rufford (National Trust)
Outstanding half-timbered hall with rare 15th-century screen. Contains the Philip Ashcroft Collection of relics of Lancashire folk life.

GARDENS

CRANFORD, Aughton (T. J. C. Taylor, Esq)
Modern half-acre garden, unusually planned.
RAVENHURST, Bolton (Mr and Mrs T. J. Arkwright)
Italian-style garden in wooded setting, sunken and water gardens, flowering shrubs and herbaceous borders.
WINDLE HALL, St Helen's (Lord and Lady Pilkington)
3 acre walled garden, surrounded by lawns and woodland, herbaceous borders, rockery, greenhouses and roses.

MUSEUMS AND GALLERIES

BACUP NATURAL HISTORY SOCIETY'S MUSEUM, 24 Yorkshire Street, Bacup
Collection of natural history subjects; a local geology collection and domestic bygones.
BLACKBURN MUSEUM AND ART GALLERY, Library Street, Blackburn
Coins, local history, medieval manuscripts, Japanese prints, ceramics, ethnography

and natural history; also the East Lancashire Regiment Collection.

BRITISH IN INDIA MUSEUM, Sun Street, Colne
Paintings, photographs, coins, stamps, medals, diorama, model railway and other items.

GRUNDY ART GALLERY, Queen Street, Blackpool (Blackpool Corporation)
Collection of paintings and drawings by outstanding 19th- and 20th-century British artists.

HARRIS MUSEUM AND ART GALLERY, Market Square, Preston (Preston Corporation)
Specialist collections covering fine arts, decorative art, archaeology, natural and social history, and includes work by the Devis family, the Newsham Bequest, and the Cedric Houghton Bequest.

HAWORTH ART GALLERY, Haworth Park, Accrington (Accrington Corporation)
Works of the early English watercolour period and large collection of Tiffany glass. Special exhibitions.

LANCASTER MUSEUM, Old Town Hall, Market Square, Lancaster (Lancaster City)
Prehistory, Roman and medieval remains, bygones. Museum of the King's Own Regiment.

LEWIS TEXTILE MUSEUM, Exchange Street, Blackburn
Groups can be shown in action the adventures of Kay, Hargreaves, Arkwright and Crompton, by a member of the Museum staff, Art exhibitions.

*MERCER MUSEUM AND ART GALLERY, Mercer Park, Rishton Road, Clayton-le-Moors
Personal relics of the late John Mercer; collections of coal and coke products, sea-shells and the fine arts.

THE RIBCHESTER MUSEUM OF ROMAN ANTIQUITIES, Ribchester (National Trust)
Remains from the Roman site of Bremetennacum including an excavated area adjoining the Museum revealing part of the granaries, north wall and gateway.

ROSSENDALE MUSEUM, Whitaker Park, Rawtenstall (Rossendale Borough Council)
Fine arts, natural history, Rossendale collection. Summer exhibitions.

TOWNELEY HALL ART GALLERY AND MUSEUM, Burnley (Burnley Borough Council)
Oil paintings and early English watercolours, period furniture, ivories, 18th-century glassware and Chinese ceramics and natural history. Also contains the Museum of Local Crafts and Industries, and the East Lancashire Regiment Room.

TURTON TOWER, Turton, Blackburn
15th-century Pele tower with 16th-century farmhouse attached. Local history, weapons, period furniture.

LEICESTERSHIRE
HISTORIC HOUSES AND CASTLES

BELGRAVE HALL, Leicester (Leicestershire Museums, Art Galleries and Record Service)
A small Queen Anne house built 1709–13 with furniture of 18th and early 19th centuries. Garden.

BELVOIR CASTLE, Nr Grantham (His Grace the Duke of Rutland)
Seat of the Dukes of Rutland since Henry VIII's time, rebuilt by Wyatt 1816. Notable pictures, furniture, objets d'art.

GUILDHALL, Leicester (Leicestershire Museums, Art Galleries and Records Service)
A medieval timber building dating from 14th to 17th centuries. Mayor's parlour, library and old police cells.

LANGTON HALL, Nr Market Harborough (Mrs L. D. Cullings)
Small English country house dating from 15th and 16th centuries set in parkland. Gardens laid out in the French style.

MANOR HOUSE, Donington le Heath (Leicestershire Museums, Art Galleries and Records Service)
13th-century manor house with early English furniture.

OAKHAM CASTLE, Oakham (Leicestershire Museums, Art Galleries and Records Service)
Late 12th-century Norman hall with collection of horseshoes given by peers of the realm.

PRESTWOLD HALL, Loughborough (Mr and Mrs Packe-Drury-Lowe)
Fine early 19th-century house set in large gardens. Home of the Packe family for over 300 years.

QUENBY HALL, Hungarton (The Squire de Lisle)
Unspoilt Jacobean Hall built circa 1620. Fine panelling and ceilings, pictures and furniture. Lawns and majestic cedars.

STANFORD HALL, Lutterworth (Lord and Lady Braye)
William and Mary house dating from 1690. Furniture, pictures, 1898 flying machine. Motor cycle and car museum. Antique kitchen utensils. Walled rose garden leading to old forge and crafts centre. Nature trail.

STAPLEFORD PARK, Nr Melton Mowbray (Lord Gretton, OBE)
Part of the present house dates from 1500, restored 1633. Exterior decoration of exceptional interest. The Thomas Balston collection of Victorian Staffordshire figures (owned by the National Trust). Lion reserve and animal land in the park and other amusements.

WYGSTON'S HOUSE, Leicester (Leicestershire Museums, Art Galleries and Records Service)
Museum of Costume (1769–1924) in a medieval house with Georgian additions. Shop reconstructions.

MUSEUMS AND GALLERIES

JEWRY WALL MUSEUM, St Nicholas Circle, Leicester (Leicestershire County Council)
Museum of archaeology from prehistoric times to 1500. Roman Jewry wall and baths.

THE LEICESTERSHIRE MUSEUM AND ART GALLERY, New Walk, Leicester
(Leicestershire County Council)
Collections 18th-, 19th- and 20th-century English paintings, drawings, and water-colours. Unique collection of German Expressionists, 19th- and 20th-century French paintings and some old master paintings. Also old master and modern prints. English ceramics, from 17th to 20th century, with some Oriental and Near Eastern specimens. English silver including some civic plate, glass. Displays of British mammals, birds, freshwater fish (aquarium). Leicestershire and general geology. Egyptology.

LEICESTERSHIRE MUSEUM OF TECHNOLOGY, Abbey Pumping Station, Corporation Road, Leicester
Power gallery, knitting machines, transport items, steam shovel, Beam engine 1891.

LEICESTERSHIRE RECORD OFFICE, 57 New Walk and New Walk Museum, Leicester
(Leicestershire County Council)
Extensive collection of official and private archives, both rural and urban, relating to the County of Leicestershire.

MARKET HARBOROUGH ARCHAEOLOGICAL AND HISTORICAL SOCIETY MUSEUM, Market Harborough (The County Library)

MUSEUM OF THE ROYAL LEICESTERSHIRE REGIMENT, The Magazine, Oxford Street, Leicester (Leicestershire County Council)
Mementos, battle trophies and relics.

NEWARKE HOUSES MUSEUM, The Newarke, Leicester (Leicester County Council)
Social history of the city and county from 15th century to the present. 19th-century street scene, 17th-century room, local clocks, musical instruments.

RUTLAND COUNTY MUSEUM, Catmos Street, Oakham (Leicestershire County Council)
Anglo-Saxon jewellery, Roman coins, craft tools, local history, Victorian shop. Courtyard contains farm wagons and agricultural implements.

LINCOLNSHIRE
OUTSTANDING NATURAL BEAUTY

LINCOLNSHIRE WOLDS (part)

HISTORIC HOUSES AND CASTLES

AUBORN HALL, Nr Lincoln (H. N. Nevile, Esq)
Interesting 16th-century house. Carved staircase and panelled rooms.

BELTON HOUSE, Grantham (Lord Brownlow)
Built 1685 and attributed to Sir Christopher Wren. Fine furniture. Magnificent Grinling Gibbons carvings; paintings by old masters include a 'Mona Lisa'. Duke of Windsor souvenirs. Park and formal gardens.

DODDINGTON HALL, Doddington (A. G. Jarvis, Esq)
Elizabethan manor house, furniture. Rose gardens.

FYDELL HOUSE, Boston (Boston Preservation Trust)
Built 1726 by William Fydell, three times Mayor of Boston. Now houses Pilgrim College.

GRANTHAM HOUSE, Grantham (National Trust)
House dated from 14th and 15th centuries. Extensively altered in the 18th century. Garden.

*GUNBY HALL, Burgh-le-Marsh (National Trust)
Built by Sir William Massingberd in 1700. Walled gardens full of flowers and roses.

MARSTON HALL, Grantham (Rev Henry Thorold, FSA)
16th-century manor house. Interesting pictures and furniture. Held by Thorolds since 14th century. Ancient garden with notable trees. Gothic gazebo.

THE OLD HALL, Gainsborough (Friends of the Old Hall Association)
15th-century black and white manor house.

TATTERSHALL CASTLE (National Trust)
The keep is one of the finest survivals of fortified brick dwelling.

WOOLSTHORPE MANOR, Nr Grantham (National Trust)
17th-century house, birthplace of Sir Isaac Newton.

MUSEUMS AND GALLERIES

AYSCOUGHFEE HALL, Churchgate, Spalding
The Ashly Maples Collection of British Birds

BOSTON MUSEUM, The Guildhall, South Street, Boston (Boston Corporation)
15th-century building associated with the early Pilgrim Fathers. Items of local historical and archaeological interest; local prints and pictures.

CHURCH FARM MUSEUM, Church Road, Skegness (Lincolnshire County Council)
The Bernard Best Collection of agricultural and domestic equipment.

LINCOLN CATHEDRAL LIBRARY, The Cathedral, Lincoln
Medieval manuscripts, and early printed books. Wren library by appointment only.

LINCOLN CATHEDRAL TREASURY, The Cathedral, Lincoln
Gold and silver plate from the diocese; Magna Carta.

LINCOLN CITY AND COUNTY MUSEUM, Broadgate, Lincoln (Lincolnshire County Council)
Collections are local with emphasis on prehistoric, Roman and medieval antiquities, arms and armour, and natural history.

MUSEUM, St Peter's Hill, Grantham (Lincolnshire County Council)
Local prehistoric, Roman and Saxon archaeology. Grantham local history, trades and industries, and a collection devoted to Sir Isaac Newton.

MUSEUM, High Street, Stamford (Lincolnshire County Council)
Local archaeology and history.

MUSEUM OF LINCOLNSHIRE LIFE, Burton Road, Lincoln (Lincolnshire County Council)
Display of material illustrating life in Lincolnshire during the past 200 years.

SPALDING MUSEUM, Broad Street, Spalding (Spalding Gentlemen's Society)
Bygones, ceramics, glass, coins, metals and prehistoric relics.

USHER GALLERY, Lindum Road, Lincoln (Lincolnshire County Council)
Collections include the Usher collection of fine antique watches, miniature portraits and porcelain. Gallery of works by the famous English watercolourist, Peter de Wint. Tennyson Collection. Topographical collections relating to the county and the city.

(GREATER) LONDON
HISTORIC HOUSES AND CASTLES

ASHBURNHAM HOUSE, Westminster (Westminster School)
Formerly the home of the Earls of Ashburnham.

BOSTON MANOR HOUSE, Brentford (London Borough of Hounslow)
Tudor and Jacobean mansion with very fine examples of period ceilings. Park and gardens.

CHISWICK HOUSE (Department of the Environment)
Villa designed by the Earl of Burlington 1725 and derived from Palladio's Villa Capra. William Kent decorated the rooms.

EASTBURY MANOR HOUSE, Barking (National Trust, administered by London Borough of Barking)
A very fine example of a medium-sized Elizabethan manor house.

HALL PLACE, Bexley (Bexley London Borough Council)
Historic mansion (1540). Rose, rock, water, herb, peat gardens. Conservatories. Parkland. Topiary designed in the form of the Queen's Beasts.

HAMPTON COURT PALACE (Department of the Environment)
Royal palace built in 1514 by Wolsey, additions by Henry VIII, and later by Wren for William III. State rooms, tapestries, pictures. Famous gardens are at their best in mid-May.

KENSINGTON PALACE, Kensington (Department of the Environment)
Bought by William III, 1689. Altered and added to by Wren and later alterations.

KEW PALACE, Kew (Dutch House) (Department of the Environment)
Built 1631, Dutch style. Souvenirs of George III.

LANCASTER HOUSE, Nr St James's (Department of the Environment)
Finest surviving example in London of a great town mansion of the early Victorian period.

MARBLE HILL HOUSE, Twickenham (Greater London Council)
A complete example of an English Palladian villa. Early Georgian paintings and furniture.

*MARLBOROUGH HOUSE, Pall Mall (Foreign and Commonwealth Office)
Built by Wren for Sarah, Duchess of Marlborough, subsequently a royal residence, and now a Commonwealth centre.

THE OLD PALACE, Croydon (Community of the Sisters of the Church)
Seat of Archbishops of Canterbury since 871. 15th-century banqueting hall and guardroom, Tudor chapel, Norman undercroft.

OSTERLEY PARK HOUSE, Osterley (National Trust, administered by the Victoria and Albert Museum)
Splendid state rooms furnished by Robert Adam, including a Gobelins tapestry room. Garden houses and Tudor stable block.

THE QUEEN'S HOUSE, Greenwich (National Maritime Museum)
Designed by Inigo Jones for Anne of Denmark, wife of James I. Completed 1635 for Henrietta Maria, wife of Charles I.

ROYAL NAVAL COLLEGE, Greenwich (The Admiralty)
Begun by Webb, finished by Wren, Hawksmoor and Vanbrugh. Painted hall and chapel.

SYON HOUSE, Brentford (His Grace the Duke of Northumberland, KG)
Noted for its magnificent Adam interior and furnishings, famous picture collections, and historical associations dating back to 1415. Capability Brown landscape.

TOWER OF LONDON, Tower Bridge (Department of the Environment)
Dating from Norman times. Historical relics, armouries, dungeons. Crown jewels.

*WHITE LODGE, Richmond Park (Governors of the Royal Ballet School)
A former royal residence, built early 18th century.

MUSEUMS AND GALLERIES

ARTILLERY MUSEUM, The Rotunda, Woolwich Common
The Rotunda is the tent erected in St James's Park for the visit of the Allied Sovereigns in 1814. Collection of guns, muskets, rifles, etc.

BADEN-POWELL HOUSE, Queen's Gate (The Scout Association)
Mementoes of Baden-Powell and historical records.

BARNET MUSEUM, 31 Wood Street, Barnet, Herts (Barnet and District Local History Society)
Archaeological and historical exhibits relating to the area. Bygones and miscellaneous. Reference library.

BETHNAL GREEN MUSEUM, Museum of Childhood (Victoria and Albert Museum)
The Museum is being developed as a Museum of Childhood and is notable for its collections of toys, games, dolls and dolls' houses. Also Spitalfields silks (once a local industry); sculptures by Rodin; wedding dresses; 19th-century continental decorative arts.

BEXLEY LONDON BOROUGH MUSEUM, Hall Place, Bourne Road, Bexley
Temporary exhibitions, general and local. Local studies centre. Beautiful gardens. Erith Museum Study Centre.

BRITISH MUSEUM, Great Russell Street, London W1

Comprising the National Museum of Antiquities, Ethnography, and Prints and Drawings. The Museum departments are: coins and medals; Egyptian antiquities; Western Asiatic antiquities; Greek and Roman antiquities; prehistoric and Romano-British antiquities; medieval and later antiquities; Oriental antiquities and prints and drawings.

BRITISH MUSEUM (NATURAL HISTORY), Cromwell Road, South Kensington, SW7
The home of the national collections of animals and plants, extinct as well as existing, and of the rocks and minerals which make up the earth's crust. In addition to large selections of these specimens, the galleries have special exhibits illustrating evolution and other biological topics.

BROOMFIELD MUSEUM, Broomfield Park, Palmers Green, N13 (London Borough of Enfield)
An ancient mansion situated in a beautiful park. Collections of local antiquities and bygones, natural history, pottery and paintings.

BRUCE CASTLE MUSEUM, Lordship Lane, Tottenham, N17
Local history. Postal history. Museum of the Middlesex Regiment.

BUCKINGHAM PALACE, THE QUEEN'S GALLERY, Buckingham Palace Road, SW1
Exhibitions from the Royal Collection of paintings, furniture and other works of art.

BUTLER MUSEUM, Harrow School, Harrow-on-the-Hill
Natural history, herbarium, British and tropical lepidoptera, British birds.

CARLYLE'S HOUSE, 24 Cheyne Row, Chelsea, SW3 (National Trust)
Portraits, letters, furniture, prints, manuscripts and a small library of books belonging to Thomas Carlyle.

CHARTERED INSURANCE INSTITUTE'S MUSEUM, 20 Aldermanbury, EC2
Collection of insurance companies' fire marks, fire-fighting equipment, helmets, medals indicating the part played by insurance companies in lessening the dangers of fire.

THE CHURCH FARM HOUSE MUSEUM, Greyhound Hill, Hendon, NW4 (London Borough of Barnet)
Local history, furnished rooms in period style.

COMMONWEALTH INSTITUTE, Kensington High Street, W8
The national centre for spreading knowledge and understanding of the Commonwealth.

COURTAULD INSTITUTE GALLERIES, Woburn Square, WC1
The galleries of the University of London; including the Lee Collection, the Gambier-Parry Collection, the important Courtauld Collection of Impressionist and Post-Impressionist paintings, and the Fry Collection.

THE CRICKET MEMORIAL GALLERY, Lord's Ground, NW8 (Marylebone Cricket Club)
Unique collection of pictures, objets d'art, trophies and bygones illustrating the history of cricket (including the Ashes).

CUMING MUSEUM, Walsworth Road, SE17 (London Borough of Southwark)
History of Southwark and district. Local collection includes: Roman, medieval and post-medieval objects from archaeological excavations, Dickensian Marshalsea prison pump and 'Dog and Pot' shop sign, examples of George Tinworth's modelling. Collection of London superstitions.

THE *CUTTY SARK*, Cutty Sark Gardens, Greenwich Pier, SE10 (The Cutty Sark Society)
Last and most famous of all tea clippers, now permanently in a riverside berth at Greenwich. Refitted and rigged as she would be in harbour for a spell in the heyday of her sea-going career. She also holds two exhibitions – the story of the *Cutty Sark* and figureheads from the 'Long John Silver' Collection.

DARWIN MUSEUM, Down House, Downe, Kent
Home of Charles Darwin: the study, drawing-room and relics of his family and
work. Garden and famous sandwalk.

DICKENS HOUSE, 48 Doughty Street, WC1
House occupied by Dickens and his family 1837–9. Relics displayed include
manuscripts, furniture, autographs, portraits, letters and first editions.

DULWICH COLLEGE PICTURE GALLERY, College Road, SE21
Excellent examples of Rembrandt, Rubens, Claude, Poussin, Gainsborough,
Watteau, Lancret, etc. Collection includes Spanish paintings and some small Dutch
paintings.

EPPING FOREST MUSEUM, Queen Elizabeth's Hunting Lodge, Chingford, E4
(Corporation of London – Conservators of Epping Forest)
Exhibits illustrative of animals, birds and plant life in Epping Forest and man's
association therewith.

FEDERATION OF BRITISH ARTISTS, The Mall Galleries, The Mall, SW1
Changing exhibitions.

FENTON HOUSE, Hampstead Grove, Hampstead, NW3 (National Trust)
The Benton-Fletcher Collection of early musical instruments and the Binning
Collection of porcelain and furniture in a William and Mary House.

GEFFRYE MUSEUM, Kingsland Road, Shoreditch, E2 (Greater London Council,
administered by the Inner London Education Authority)
The permanent display of period rooms shows the development of the middle-
class English home from about 1600. Reference library of books and periodicals
on the decorative arts. Temporary exhibitions, art film shows.

GEOLOGICAL MUSEUM, Exhibition Road, South Kensington (A National museum)
Illustrates earth history and the general principles of geological science; the
regional geology of Great Britain and the economic geology and mineralogy of
the world. Famous collection of gemstones. Special exhibits arranged at intervals.
Programme of talks, demonstrations and films.

GIPSY MOTH IV, Greenwich Pier, SE10 (Maritime Trust)
The yacht in which Sir Francis Chichester made his epic single-handed voyage
round the world in 1966–7.

*GOLDSMITHS' HALL, Foster Lane, Cheapside, EC2 (Worshipful Company of
Goldsmiths)
Fine collection of antique plate, including some pieces with interesting historical
associations. The largest collection of modern silver and jewellery in the country.

GREENWICH BOROUGH MUSEUM, 232 Plumstead High Street, SE18 (London Borough
of Greenwich)
Exhibitions of prehistory, history and natural history relating to the environment
of Greenwich.

GUILDHALL ART GALLERY, King Street, Cheapside, EC2 (Corporation of London)
Exhibitions, at intervals, of selections from the permanent collection, Corporation
sponsored exhibitions, loans of master paintings, and work of art societies.

GUILDHALL MUSEUM, Gillett House, 55 Basinghall Street, EC2 (Corporation of
London)
History and archaeology of the City from Roman Times.

GUNNERSBURY PARK MUSEUM, Gunnersbury Park, London W3 (London Boroughs
of Ealing and Hounslow)
Local archaeology, history, social history and topography, some transport items,
in the Rothschilds' early 19th-century mansion.

HAM HOUSE, Petersham, Richmond (National Trust administered by the Victoria
and Albert Museum)

Built 1610 and altered at various times in the 17th century. Fine collection of late Stuart furniture.

HAYES AND HARLINGTON MUSEUM, Gold Crescent, Hayes (Hayes and Harlington Local History Society and London Borough of Hillingdon)
A small museum of local history.

HAYWARD GALLERY, Belvedere Road, South Bank, SE1 (Arts Council)
Temporary exhibitions of British and foreign art.

HMS *BELFAST*, Symons Wharf, Vine Lane, SE1
The largest cruiser ever constructed for the Royal Navy and is a ship with a fine history. She is on exhibition as a museum and new spaces are being constantly added to those open to the public.

HOGARTH'S HOUSE, Hogarth Lane, Chiswick, W4
The artist's country house for 15 years. Copies of Hogarth's paintings, impressions from engravings and relics.

HORNIMAN MUSEUM, London Road, Forest Hill, SE23 (Greater London Council, administered by the Inner London Education Authority)
An ethnographical museum dealing with the study of man and his environment. Natural history collections and aquarium. There is a large collection of musical instruments from all parts of the world. Extensive library. Education centre for schools and children's leisure activities. Free lecturers and concerts.

IMPERIAL WAR MUSEUM, Lambeth Road, SE1 (A National Museum)
Illustrates and records all aspects of the two world wars and other operations involving Britain and the Commonwealth since 1914.

THE IVEAGH BEQUEST, Kenwood, Hampstead NW3 (Greater London Council)
Works by Rembrandt, Vermeer, Van Dyck, Reynolds, Gainsborough etc.

THE JEWISH MUSEUM, Woburn House, Upper Woburn Place, WC1 (Jewish Memorial Council)
A comprehensive collection of Jewish antiquities illustrating the public and private worship of the Jews.

JOHN EVELYN SOCIETY'S MUSEUM, Village Club, Ridgway, Wimbledon, SW19
Watercolours, prints and photographs of Wimbledon's historic buildings and worthies.

DR JOHNSON'S HOUSE, 17 Gough Square, EC4
Where he lived from 1748–59. Relics and small library.

KEAT'S HOUSE (Wentworth Place), Keats Grove, Hampstead, NW3 (Camden Borough Council)
Keats's Regency home where he spent the greater part of his 5 creative years. Relics and manuscripts.

KINGSTON-UPON-THAMES MUSEUM AND ART GALLERY, Fairfield West, Kingston-upon-Thames
Local archaeology (especially Bronze Age and Anglo Saxon), history and natural history. Also 'Zoopraxiscope' of Eadweard Muybridge. Art Gallery: circulating and local artists' exhibitions.

THE KODAK MUSEUM, Wealdstone, Harrow, Middlesex (Kodak Limited)
Extensive collection covering the history of photography and cinematography.

LEIGHTON HOUSE ART GALLERY AND MUSEUM, 12 Holland Park Road, W14 (Kensington and Chelsea Borough Council)
Designed by George Aitchison RA in collaboration with Frederic, Lord Leighton, PRA, who lived there from 1866 until his death in 1896. Contains an Arab Hall with applied tiles from Rhodes, Damascus, Cairo and elsewhere. A permanent exhibition of high Victorian art, includes paintings, drawings and sculpture by Leighton, Burne-Jones, Alma-Tadema, Millais, Poynter, Stevens, Watts and other

contemporaries and friends. Rooms in period decoration, also house Victorian furniture. Includes loan collections from the Tate Gallery, Victoria and Albert Museum and York Art Gallery.

LIVESEY MUSEUM, 682 Old Kent Road, SE15 (London Borough of Southwark)
Changing exhibitions of local interest.

LONDON TRANSPORT COLLECTION, Syon Park, Brentford (London Transport Executive)
Transport relics, buses, trains, trolleybuses, tramcars, horse-drawn vehicles, posters, signs and models.

MARTINWARE POTTERY COLLECTION, Public Library, Osterley Park Road, Southall (London Borough of Ealing)
A large collection of Martinware, including birds, face mugs, grotesques and other delightful pieces.

MUSEUM OF LONDON, London Wall, EC2
Due to open at the end of 1976. Formed from the collections of the former London and Guildhall museums. The new permanent exhibition will illustrate the social history of London, in chronological sequence, from prehistoric times to the present day.

MUSEUM OF MANKIND, 6 Burlington Gardens, London W1
(Ethnography Department of the British Museum)

THE MUSICAL MUSEUM, by the gasholder, Kew Bridge
A unique collection of automatic pianos, organs, orchestrations and music boxes that all work.

NATIONAL ARMY MUSEUM, Royal Hospital Road, SW3 (A National Museum)
Paintings, uniforms, weapons, equipment, regimental and personal mementoes and colours illustrating the history of the British, Indian and Colonial forces from 1485 to 1914.

NATIONAL FILM ARCHIVE, 81 Dean Street, W1 (British Film Institute)
Collection of cinematograph films and recorded television programmes, both fiction and non-fiction, illustrating history of cinema and television as art and entertainment, and contemporary life and people, ethnography, transport, exploration, etc. Also a large collection of film stills and posters.

NATIONAL GALLERY, Trafalgar Square, WC2 (The Nation's collection of master-pieces)
Founded 1824 as the National Collection of European Painting. Representative collection of Italian, Dutch, Flemish, Spanish, German schools; French painting up to 1900; a selection of British painters from Hogarth to Turner.

NATIONAL MARITIME MUSEUM, Romney Road, Greenwich, SE10 (A National Museum)
Galleries here and in the Old Royal Observatory in Greenwich Park, now part of the Museum, show many aspects of maritime history in paintings and prints, ship models, relics of distinguished sailors and events, navigational instruments and charts, history of astronomy, medals, a large library with a reference section and information service, and a fine collection of manuscripts. See the New Neptune Hall with the paddle tug. *Reliant*, boat-building shed, Barge House and collection of boats. Also east wing new galleries and Convoy Room. The Planetarium gives educational and public performances at stated times.

NATIONAL MONUMENTS RECORD, Fortress House, 23 Savile Row, London W1
(Royal Commission on Historical Monuments)
Includes National Buildings Record. Library of over 800,000 photographs, measured drawings of the historic architecture of England.

NATIONAL PORTRAIT GALLERY, St Martin's Place, Trafalgar Square, WC2 (A

National Collection)
A collection of portraits of the famous and infamous in British history, including paintings, sculpture, miniatures, engravings and photographs. Exhibition annexe at 15 Carlton House Terrace, SW1.

NATIONAL POSTAL MUSEUM, King Edward Building, King Edward Street, EC1
Reginald M. Phillips and Post Office Collections of British postage stamps. UPU Collection of the whole world since 1878. Philatelic archives of Thos De La Rue and Co, covering postage stamps of 200 countries 1855–1965.

ORLEANS HOUSE GALLERY, Riverside, Twickenham (London Borough of Richmond-upon-Thames)
James Gibbs's baroque Octagon Room, 1720. Ionides collection of 18th- and 19th-century paintings, watercolours and engravings of Richmond and Twickenham. Some special exhibitions.

PASSMORE EDWARDS MUSEUM, Romford Road, Stratford, E15 (London Borough of Newham)
Collection of Essex archaeology, local history, geology, and natural history.

PERCIVAL DAVID FOUNDATION OF CHINESE ART, 53 Gordon Square, WC1
(University of London School of Oriental and African Studies)
The Foundation comprises the collection of Chinese ceramics and a library of Chinese and other books dealing with Chinese art and culture presented by Sir Percival David to the University of London in 1950.

*PHARMACEUTICAL SOCIETY'S MUSEUM, 17 Bloomsbury Square, WC1
Collection of crude drugs of vegetables and animal origin used in the 17th century; early printed works, manuscripts and prints relating to pharmacy; English delft drug jars, leech jars, bell-metal mortars, medicine chests, dispensing apparatus, etc.

PUBLIC RECORD OFFICE AND MUSEUM, Chancery Lane, WC2
Contains the national archives. The Museum is rich in fascinating possessions. William the Conqueror's Domesday Book. Signatures of the Kings and Queens of England, Shakespeare, Milton and Guy Fawkes; Wellington's despatch from Waterloo. The log of Nelson's *Victory* and several Churchill documents.

RANGER'S HOUSE, Chesterfield Walk, Blackheath, SE10 (Greater London Council)
A new gallery of English portraits from the Elizabethan to the Georgian period in the famous 4th Earl of Chesterfield's house at Blackheath.

RIBA HEINZ GALLERY, RIBA Drawings Collection, 21 Portman Square, W1
Regular exhibitions of architectural drawings.

ROYAL ACADEMY OF ARTS, Piccadilly, W1
Annual summer exhibition of painting, sculpture, architecture and engraving by living artists (May to July). Major loan exhibitions and other special exhibitions.

ROYAL AIR FORCE MUSEUM, Aerodrome Road, Hendon, NW9 (A National Museum)
The only national museum to be devoted solely to aviation and to telling the complete story of a service, including its predecessors, from its start to the present.

ROYAL ARTILLERY REGIMENTAL MUSEUM, Royal Military Academy, Academy Road, Woolwich.

ROYAL BOTANIC GARDENS (KEW GARDENS)
The most famous botanical gardens in the world with general botanical and wood museums, orangery and Marianne North gallery.

ROYAL COLLEGE OF MUSIC, Prince Consort Road, South Kensington, SW7
Museum of historical musical instruments.

*ROYAL COLLEGE OF SURGEONS' MUSEUM, Lincoln's Inn Fields, WC2
The Hunterian Collection and other items of interest in medical history.

ROYAL HOSPITAL MUSEUM, Royal Hospital, Royal Hospital Road, SW3
(Commissioners Royal Hospital)

Pictures, plans and maps, medals and uniforms, connected with Royal Hospital.
ROYAL MEWS, Buckingham Palace Road, SW1 (Her Majesty the Queen)
Royal horses and equipages.
ROYAL SOCIETY OF PAINTER-ETCHERS, 26 Conduit Street, W1
Contemporary print exhibition.
ST BRIDE'S CRYPT MUSEUM, St Bride's Church, Fleet Street, EC4 (Rector and Churchwardens of St Bride's Church)
During excavations made prior to rebuilding over 1000 years of unrecorded history were revealed. Roman pavement and remains of 7 previous churches (dating from 6th century) on site can be seen together with permanent display of history of print, etc.
*ST JOHN'S GATE, St John's Square, Clerkenwell, EC1
The Headquarters of the Most Venerable Order of St John of Jerusalem. Early 16th-century gate-house containing silver, furniture, pictures and other treasures of the Knights of St John.
SCIENCE MUSEUM, Exhibition Road, South Kensington (Department of Education and Science)
Historical collection portraying the sciences of mathematics, physics and chemistry and their applications, and the development of engineering, transport and communications, mining and industries generally from early times to the present day.
SERPENTINE GALLERY, South Carriageway, Kensington Gardens, W2 (Arts Council)
Exhibitions of contemporary art.
SIR JOHN SOANE'S MUSEUM, 13 Lincoln's Inn Fields, WC2
The Museum was built by Sir John Soane, RA, in 1812–13 as his private residence and contains his collection of antiquities and works of art.
SOUTH LONDON ART GALLERY, Peckham Road, SE5 (London Borough of Southwark)
Reference collection of original 20th-century prints. Changing exhibitions.
TATE GALLERY, Millbank, SW1
The national collections of British painting up to about 1900 and modern painting and sculpture, British and foreign, from Impressionism to the present day. Special collections of Turner, Blake and the Pre-Raphaelites.
THOMAS CORAM FOUNDATION FOR CHILDREN, 40 Brunswick Square, WC1
Pictures by Hogarth, Gainsborough, Reynolds, sculpture by Roubiliac and Rysbrack. Relics of Handel. Mementoes of the Foundling Hospital.
TUDOR BARN ART GALLERY, Well Hall Pleasaunce, SE9 (London Borough of Greenwich)
Restored 16th-century building housing art gallery on first floor. Temporary exhibitions, mostly by local amateur societies.
*UNIVERSITY COLLEGE DEPARTMENT OF EGYPTOLOGY MUSEUM, Gower Street, WC1
Contains the collections of the late Miss Amelia Edwards and of the late Professor Sir Flinder Petrie.
UNIVERSITY COLLEGE MUSEUM OF ZOOLOGY AND COMPARATIVE ANATOMY, Gower Street, WC1
Specialised teaching collection of zoological material. By arrangement for university students only.
VALENCE HOUSE MUSEUM, Becontree Avenue, Dagenham, Essex (London Borough of Barking)
A 17th-century manor house still partly moated, devoted exclusively to local history, including Fanshawe portraits.
VICTORIA AND ALBERT MUSEUM, Cromwell Road, South Kensington, SW7 (Department of Education and Science)

An outstanding art museum comprising collections of fine and applied arts of all countries, periods and styles. The European collections are mostly of art from early Christian times to the 19th century. Series of special rooms display masterpieces from all periods.

WALLACE COLLECTION, Hertford House, Manchester Square, W1 (A National Museum)
The collection consists of paintings of the French, Spanish, Italian, Flemish, Dutch and British schools. Miniatures, sculpture, furniture, armour, goldsmiths' work, ceramics, and other works of art bequeathed to the nation by the late Lady Wallace in 1897.

WALTHAMSTOW MUSEUM, Old Vestry House, Vestry Road, Walthamstow, E1 (London Borough of Waltham Forest)
An early 18th-century workhouse containing local relics and objects of historical interest. Local archives.

WELLCOME INSTITUTE FOR THE HISTORY OF MEDICINE, The Wellcome Building, Euston Road, London, NW1 (The Wellcome Trustees)
The collections illustrate the history of medicine and allied sciences from the earliest times to the present century. Selected material and special exhibitions are open to the public.

WELLINGTON MUSEUM (Apsley House), Hyde Park Corner, W1 (Victoria and Albert Museum)
The Duke of Wellington's London home, containing many of his trophies, uniforms, decorations, batons and presentations made by grateful royalty; also fine paintings from the Duke's collection.

WESLEY'S HOUSE AND MUSEUM, 47 City Road, EC1
The house in which John Wesley lived and died is now a museum, containing a large collection of his personal possessions, etc.

WHITECHAPEL ART GALLERY, Whitechapel High Street, E1
Exhibition gallery principally for modern and contemporary art. No permanent collection.

WILLIAM MORRIS GALLERY, Water house, Lloyd Park, Forest Road, Walthamstow, E17 (London Borough of Waltham Forest)
18th-century house, the boyhood home of William Morris. Collections include textiles, wallpapers, designs, etc, by Morris, the Pre-Raphaelites and contemporaries. The Frank Brangwyn collection of pictures and sculpture by 19th-century and other artists and by the donor.

'WOODLANDS' LOCAL HISTORY CENTRE AND ART GALLERY, 90 Mycenae Road, SE3 (London Borough of Greenwich)
Built in 1774 for John Julius Angerstein, founder of Lloyd's and patron of the arts. Permanent collection of material relating to Greenwich. Temporary exhibitions.

MERSEYSIDE
HISTORIC HOUSES AND CASTLES

SPEKE HALL, Liverpool (National Trust, administered by Merseyside County Museums Department)
Richly half-timbered house dating from circa 1490–1612. Great hall. Elaborate plasterwork.

MUSEUMS AND GALLERIES

ATKINSON ART GALLERY, Lord Street, Southport
Paintings, watercolours and sculpture. Exhibitions of art.

BIRKENHEAD PRIOR, Priory Street, Birkenhead (Wirral Metropolitan Borough Council)
Remains of Benedictine monastery, established 1150. Site museum.

BOTANIC GARDENS MUSEUM, Churchtown, Southport (Merseyside-Sefton Borough)
Collections of local and natural history. Victorian period room.

BOOTLE MUSEUM AND ART GALLERY, Oriel Road, Bootle (Sefton Metropolitan Borough)
Museum: Lancaster Collection of English figure pottery and Bishop Collection of Liverpool pottery. Art exhibitions changed monthly.

HORNBY LIBRARY, William Brown Street, Liverpool (Merseyside County Council)
Prints, manuscripts, fine bindings, and illustrated and rare books illustrating the art of the print, manuscript and book through the ages.

THE LADY LEVER ART GALLERY, Port Sunlight
Paintings, watercolours, engravings and miniatures, mainly of the British school; antique, Renaissance and British sculpture; Chinese pottery and porcelain; Wedgwood wares; English furniture.

MERSEYSIDE COUNTY MUSEUMS, William Brown Street, Liverpool (Merseyside County Council)
A selection from the Joseph Mayer Collections is on display. The Rushworth and Dreaper Collection of historic musical instruments. Land transport, natural history, shipping, history of the Kings Regiment, are among the exhibitions. Also a planetarium.

MUSEUM AND ART GALLERY, Gamble Institute, St Helens (St Helens Borough Council)
Local history and industries, clay pipe-making, glass containers. Natural history, geology, archaeology, egyptology, ceramics. Pilkington collection of watercolours. Local society exhibitions.

MUSEUM OF THE UNIVERSITY OF HYGIENE, 126 Mount Pleasant, Liverpool
Public health exhibits mainly of interest to students.

PILKINGTON GLASS MUSEUM, Prescot Road, St Helens (Pilkington Brothers Limited)
The museum shows the evolution of glass-making techniques.

SUDLEY ART GALLERY, Mossley Hill Road, Liverpool (Merseyside County Council)
The Emma Holt Bequest of 18th- and 19th-century paintings, mainly English.

WALKER ART GALLERY, William Brown Street, Liverpool (Merseyside County Council)
Notable collection of European paintings, famous for the early Italian and Flemish pictures. The later Italians, Dutch and Germans and the English schools from Holbein onwards are well represented. Also paintings by the Liverpool school, the Pre-Raphaelites, late Victorian academic paintings, and 20th-century paintings and sculpture.

WILLIAMSON ART GALLERY AND MUSEUM, Slatey Road, Birkenhead (Wirral Metropolitan Borough Council)
Valuable art collection including comprehensive watercolour section. Applied arts include Della Robbia (Birkenhead) pottery and collection of Liverpool porcelain. Shipping gallery. Local exhibits. Frequent art exhibitions.

NORFOLK
OUTSTANDING NATURAL BEAUTY
NORFOLK COAST (part)

HISTORIC HOUSES AND CASTLES

BLICKLING HALL, Aylsham (National Trust)
Great Jacobean house, altered 1765–70. State rooms include Peter the Great Room with fine Russian tapestry. Long gallery with exceptional ceiling and state bedroom. The formal garden design dates from 1729. Temple and orangery, park and lake.

CAISTER CASTLE, Great Yarmouth (Dr P. R. Hill, JP)
Large private collection of early motor cars. Moated castle, circa 1432. 100 ft tower with magnificent views. Home of Shakespeare's Sir John Falstaff and Paston letters.

FELBRIGG HALL, Nr Cromer (National Trust)
17th-century country house with Georgian interiors set in a fine wooded park. Important 18th-century library and orangery. Traditional walled garden. Woodland walk.

HOLKHAM HALL, Wells (The Earl of Leicester, MVO DL)
Fine Palladian mansion (1734). Pictures, tapestries, statuary, furnishings. Sir Charles Berry laid out the formal garden.

HOUGHTON HALL, King's Lynn (Marquess of Cholmondeley)
18th-century mansion built for Sir Robert Walpole. State rooms, pictures and china. Pleasure grounds.

OXBURGH HALL, Swaffham (National Trust)
Late 15th-century moated house. Outstanding gate-house tower. Needlework by Mary Queen of Scots. Unique French parterre laid out circa 1845.

ST GEORGE'S GUILDHALL, King's Lynn (National Trust)
Largest medieval guildhall in England.

TRINITY HOSPITAL, Castle Rising (Trustees)
Nine 17th-century brick and tile almshouses with court, chapel and treasury.

WALSINGHAM ABBEY, Walsingham (Walsingham Estate Company)
Augustinian priory and crypt.

WOLTERTON HALL, near Norwich (Lord and Lady Walpole)
Built by Horatio Walpole (1727–41). Tapestries, porcelain, furniture.

GARDENS

FRITTON LAKE AND GARDENS (Lord and Lady Somerleyton)
Beautiful 2 mile long lake and gardens with spring bulbs, herbaceous borders and ornamental trees. Wooded walks, fishing, boating.

SANDRINGHAM GROUNDS, Sandringham (Her Majesty the Queen)
Grounds and museum only open.

MUSEUMS AND GALLERIES

THE ANCIENT HOUSE MUSEUM, White Hart Street, Thetford (Norfolk Museums Service)
15th-century timbered house with collections illustrating Thetford and Breckland life, history and natural history.

BRIDEWELL MUSEUM OF LOCAL INDUSTRIES AND RURAL CRAFTS, Bridewell Alley, Norwich (Norfolk Museums Service)

Exhibits illustrating industries and rural crafts of Norwich, Norfolk and North Suffolk.

DULEEP SINGH COLLECTION, The Guildhall, Thetford (Thetford Town Council)
Gallery of Norfolk and Suffolk portraits.

ELIZABETHAN HOUSE MUSEUM, South Quay, Great Yarmouth
Merchant's house displaying Victorian domestic life.

EXHIBITION GALLERIES, CENTRAL LIBRARY, Great Yarmouth
Travelling and local art exhibitions.

THE LYNN MUSEUM, On the Bus Station, King's Lynn (Norfolk Museum Service)
Natural history, archaeology, local history, folk history relating to North-West Norfolk.

MUSEUM OF SOCIAL HISTORY, 27 King Street, next to St George's Guildhall, King's Lynn
Domestic life and dress, toys, dolls, notable local glass collection.

NORWICH CASTLE MUSEUM, Norwich (Norfolk Museums Service)
Large collections of art (particularly of the Norwich school), local archaeology and natural history (Norfolk room dioramas) and social history. Important loan exhibitions.

OLD MERCHANT'S HOUSE, Row 117, Great Yarmouth (Department of the Environment)
Collection of domestic ironwork from the 17th to the 19th century in an early 17th-century house.

ST PETER HUNGATE CHURCH MUSEUM, Princes Street, Norwich (Norfolk Museums Service)
15th-century church used for display of ecclesiastical art and East Anglian antiquities.

THE STEAM DRIFTER, South Quay, Great Yarmouth
The last steam drifter: *Lydia Eva*.

STRANGER'S HALL, Charing Cross, Norwich (Norfolk Museums Service)
Late medieval mansion furnished as a museum of urban domestic life 16th-19th centuries.

TOLHOUSE, Tolhouse Street, Great Yarmouth
Medieval building housing local history museum.

NORTHAMPTONSHIRE
HISTORIC HOUSES AND CASTLES

ALTHORP, Northampton (The Earl Spencer)
Dates from 16th century, with alterations 1670, 1790 and 1877. Splendid interior containing pictures of many European schools; historic portraits; large collection of porcelain, both Oriental and European, and 18th-century furniture.

AYNHOE PARK, Aynho (Mutual Households Association Limited)
17th-century mansion. Alterations by Soane.

BOUGHTON HOUSE, Kettering (Buccleuch Estates)
15th-century monastery added to between 1530–1695. Collection of early French and English furniture, tapestries, carpets, porcelain. Parkland with lakes. Picnic area.

BURGHLEY HOUSE, Stamford (The Marquess of Exeter, KCMG LLD)
Finest example of later Elizabethan architecture. State apartments, pictures, furniture, silver fireplaces, painted ceilings, tapestries.

CASTLE ASHBY, Northampton (The Earl of Compton)

Elizabethan with Inigo Jones (1635) front. 17th-century ceilings, staircases and panelling. Valuable collection of pictures, garden.

*COTTERSTOCK HALL, nr Peterborough (Mr and Mrs Lewis F. Sturge)
17th-century grey stone manor house having associations with the poet Dryden. Herbaceous borders, yews and shrubs.

DEENE PARK, Nr Corby (Edmund Brudenell, Esq)
Home of the Brudenells since 1514. House of great architectural importance and historical interest. Large lake and well-wooded park. Long border. Rare trees and shrubs.

DELAPRE ABBEY, Nr Northampton (Northamptonshire County Council)
House rebuilt or added to 16th–19th centuries. Converted for use as offices and storerooms.

HINWICK HOUSE, nr Wellingborough (Capt. R. A. B. Orlebar)
A Queen Anne house of excellent architecture. Pictures by Van Dyck, Lely, Kneller, etc. Tapestries and needlework. Furniture.

KIRBY HALL, Gretton (Department of the Environment)
Built 1570 (partly roofed). 17th-century gardens.

LAMPORT HALL, Northampton (Sir Gyles Isham, Bt)
The home of the Isham family since 1560. Present house dates mainly from 17th and 18th centuries.

LYVEDEN NEW BIELD, Oundle (National Trust)
An unusual Renaissance building erected about 1600 by Sir Thomas Tresham to symbolise the Passion. It was never finished as he became involved in the Gunpowder Plot.

*PRIEST'S HOUSE, Easton-on-the-Hill (National Trust)
Pre-Reformation priest's house given to the National Trust by the Peterborough Society.

ROCKINGHAM CASTLE, Nr Corby (Commander Michael Watson)
Royal castle till 1530, since then home of the Watson family. Spans 900 years of English life and culture set amid lovely gardens and fine views.

SOUTHWICK HALL, Nr Oundle (G. C. Capron, Esq)
Manor house, retaining medieval building, dating from 1300, with Tudor rebuilding and 18th-century additions. Exhibition of Victorian dresses, etc.

STOKE PARK PAVILIONS, Towcester (R. D. Chancellor Esq)
Two pavilions and colonnade. Built 1630 by Inigo Jones.

SULGRAVE MANOR, Banbury (Sulgrave Manor Board)
Early English home of ancestors of George Washington. A good example of a small manor house and garden of Shakespeare's time.

GARDENS

COTON MANOR WILDLIFE GARDEN (Commander and Mrs H. Pasley-Tyler)
An outstanding old English garden of exceptional charm and beauty. Enhanced by flamingoes, wildfowl and tropical birds at large in the water gardens.

GUILSBOROUGH GRANGE BIRD AND PET PARK, Guilsborough (Major and Mrs S. J. Symington)
Birds and wildlife in country house and garden setting in beautiful natural surroundings with fine views.

MUSEUMS AND GALLERIES

ABINGTON MUSEUM, Abington Park, Northampton (Northampton Borough Council)
15th-century manor house, rebuilt in part in 1745. Period rooms, folk material, Chinese ceramics. Ethnographic and natural history material.

ALFRED EAST ART GALLERY, Sheep Street, Kettering
Permanent collection including oils, watercolours and etchings by Sir Alfred East, RA. Loan exhibitions.

CENTRAL MUSEUM AND ART GALLERY, Guildhall Road, Northampton (Northampton Borough Council)
Collections of footwear through the ages; cobbler's shop. Local archaeology and English ceramics. Old master and modern oil and water-colour paintings.

WESTFIELD MUSEUM, West Street, Kettering
Archaeological and social history material from the area. Collections of footwear, shoe-making tools and machinery. Exhibition of the geology of North Northamptonshire.

NORTHUMBERLAND

NATIONAL PARKS

NORTHUMBERLAND

OUTSTANDING NATURAL BEAUTY

NORTHUMBERLAND COAST

HISTORIC HOUSES AND CASTLES

ALNWICK CASTLE, Alnwick (His Grace the Duke of Northumberland, KG)
Important example of medieval fortification restored by Salvin, dating to 12th century.

BAMBURGH CASTLE, Bamburgh (Lord Armstrong)
Fine 12th-century Norman keep. Remainder of castle considerably restored.

CALLALY CASTLE, Whittingham (Major A. S. C. Browne, DL)
17th-century mansion incorporating 13th-century Pele tower with Georgian and Victorian additions.

DUNSTANBURGH CASTLE, Nr Alnwick (National Trust)
Dundand and Foreshore, site of the ruined castle begun in 1316.

LINDISFARNE CASTLE, Holy Island (National Trust)
Built about 1550. Made habitable by Lutyens.

SEATON DELAVAL HALL, Nr Newcastle-upon-Tyne (Lord Hastings)
Masterpiece of Sir John Vanbrugh.

WALLINGTON HALL, Cambo (National Trust)
Built 1688, altered 18th century. Central hall added in 19th century and decorated by Ruskin and others.

GARDENS

HOWICK GARDENS, Alnwick (Lord Howick of Glendale)
Lovely flower, shrub and rhododendron gardens.

MUSEUMS AND GALLERIES

BERWICK-ON-TWEED MUSEUM AND ART GALLERY, Marygate, Berwick-on-Tweed
(Borough of Berwick-on-Tweed)
Museum: general collection including ceramics and brassware. Special exhibition
of local antiquities.
Art Gallery: artists include Degas, Daubigny, Boudin and Opie.
THE CLAYTON COLLECTION, Hadrian's Wall, Nr Chollerford, Chesters (Department
of the Environment)
Roman inscriptions, sculpture, weapons, tools and ornaments from the forts at
Chesters, Carrawburgh, Housesteads, Greatchesters and Carvoran.
CORBRIDGE ROMAN STATION, Corbridge (Department of the Environment)
Roman pottery, sculpture, inscribed stones, and small objects
THE GRACE DARLING MUSEUM, Bamburgh (Royal National Lifeboat Institution)
Grace Darling relics.
HADRIAN'S WALL (National Trust): HOUSESTEADS MUSEUM AND FORT
Barton Mill, Hexham, Housesteads (Department of the Environment)
3½ miles of the wall itself, and several castles; also Housesteads, the best preserved
of the forts. The museum contains Roman pottery, sculpture, inscribed stones and
small objects.
LINDISFARNE PRIORY, Holy Island, Lindisfarne (Department of the Environment)
Anglo-Saxon sculpture, and a reproduction of the Lindisfarne gospels; medieval
pottery.

NORTH YORKSHIRE

NATIONAL PARKS

NORTH YORKSHIRE MOORS (part)
YORKSHIRE DALES (part)

OUTSTANDING NATURAL BEAUTY

FOREST OF BOWLAND (part)

HISTORIC HOUSES AND CASTLES

BEDALE HALL, Bedale (Hambleton District Council)
Georgian mansion with fine ballroom wing and museum room. Domestic and craft
exhibits.
BENINGBROUGH HALL, Nr Shipton (National Trust)
Early 18th-century house, possibly by Thomas Archer. Fine hall, staircase, friezes
and panelling.
BRAITHWAITE HALL, Nr Middleham (National Trust)
17th-century hall, now a working farmhouse.
*BROUGHTON HALL, Skipton (H. R. Tempest, Esq)
Georgian front. Built 1598 and altered in 1810 and 1840. Private Chapel.
Extensive grounds with Italian garden laid out by W. A. Nesfield.
CASTLE HOWARD, York (George Howard, Esq)
Designed by Vanbrugh 1699–1726 for the 3rd Earl of Carlisle, assisted by
Hawksmoor, who designed the mausoleum. Fine collection of pictures, statuary
and furniture. Beautiful park and grounds. Costume Galleries covering 18th to
20th centuries in the stable court. Displays changed every year.

DUNCOMBE PARK, Helmsley (Trustees of Duncombe Park)
Two 18th-century temples. Formal gardens.

FOUNTAINS ABBEY, Ripon (Department of the Environment)
Ruins of Cistercian monastery. Ornamental gardens laid out by John Aislabie, 1720.

GEORGIAN THEATRE, Richmond (The Georgian Theatre (Richmond) Trust Limited)
Built by Samuel Butler. Opened in 1788 'as a proper theatre... to accommodate the town and country in a more commodious manner'.

GILLING CASTLE, Helmsley (Ampleforth Abbey Trustees)
Original Norman keep with 16th- and 18th-century additions.

JERVAULX ABBEY, Nr Masham (Major V. Burdon)
Ruins of Cistercian monastery in incomparable setting.

MARKENFIELD HALL, Ripon (The Lord Grantley, MC)
Fine example of English manor house. 14th-, 15th- and 16th-century buildings surrounded by moat.

MERCHANT ADVENTURERS' HALL, Fossgate, York (The Company of Merchant Adventurers of the City of York)
The hall is an amalgam of buildings, dating from the 14th century or earlier. The major structure is apparently 15th century.

MOULTON HALL, Nr Richmond (National Trust)
Built about 1650 with fine carved wood staircase.

MOUNT GRACE PRIORY, Nr Northallerton (National Trust)
Most important Carthusian ruin in England.

NEWBURGH PRIORY, Coxwold (Capt. V. M. Wombwell)
Originally 12th-century Augustinian priory with 16th-, 17th- and 18th-century alternations and additions. Wild water garden and collection of rock plants. Walled garden.

NEWBY HALL, Ripon (R. E. J. Compton)
One of the most famous Adam houses, containing superb tapestries and fine collection of sculpture. 25 acres of gardens.

NUNNINGTON HALL, Ryedale (National Trust)
A large manor house, mainly of late 17th century.

THE OLD RECTORY – FOSTON (Major R. F. Wormald)
Designed and built by Sydney Smith, 1813–14. Pink brick, largely in Flemish Bond. Walled garden – roses.

RIEVAULX TERRACE, Helmsley (National Trust)
Two 18th-century temples. Grass terrace with views of the abbey.

RIPLEY CASTLE, Ripley (Sir Thomas Ingilby, Bart)
Has been home of the Ingilby family since early 14th century. Main gateway dates from reign of Edward IV. Extensive gardens.

RUDDING PARK, Harrogate (The Mackaness Organisation)
Distinguished Regency house set in a park designed by Repton. Rose gardens and rhododendron walks, beautiful parkland and woods.

SHANDY HALL, Coxwold (The Laurence Sterne Trust)
Unusual medieval house. Altered in 17th and 18th centuries but has changed little since. Laurence Sterne wrote *A Sentimental Journey* and most of *Tristram Shandy* there.

SKIPTON CASTLE, Skipton
Fully roofed massive medieval fortress. Attractive 15th-century courtyard. Tudor gate-house.

SUTTON PARK, Sutton-on-the-Forest (Major E. C. R. Sheffield, DL, TD, JP and Mrs Sheffield)

Early 18th-century house. Landscaped setting by Capability Brown. 18th-century furniture, pictures and porcelain. Terraced gardens, herbaceous borders and woodland walks. All rooms shown are the private rooms of the family.

TREASURER'S HOUSE, York (National Trust)
Large 17th-century house of great interest. Fine furniture and paintings.

MUSEUMS AND GALLERIES

THE ALDBOROUGH ROMAN MUSEUM, Boroughbridge, Aldborough (Department of the Environment)
The museum contains Roman finds, including pottery, glass, metalwork and coins, from the Roman town.

ART GALLERY, Library Buildings, Victoria Avenue, Harrogate
Permanent collection of oils and watercolours. Many temporary exhibitions.

CITY OF YORK ART GALLERY, Exhibition Square, York (York District Council)
Collection of old master, modern English and European paintings; ceramics, topographical watercolours and prints.

CRAVEN MUSEUM, Town Hall, High Street, Skipton
Craven antiquities, social history, geological specimens.

CRESCENT ART GALLERY, The Crescent, Scarborough (Scarborough Corporation)
Local artists. Laughton Collection (English school). Frequent loan exhibitions.

THE GREEN HOWARDS MUSEUM, Trinity Church Square, Richmond
Uniform, medals, campaign relics, contemporary manuscripts, pictures and prints, head-dresses, buttons, badges and embellishments from 17th century onwards.

LONDESBOROUGH LODGE, Scarborough
Museum of Scarborough history.

NATIONAL RAILWAY MUSEUM, Leeman Road, York (Department of Education and Science)
Collections illustrating the history and development of British railway engineering including the social and economic aspects.

ROMAN MALTON MUSEUM, Milton Rooms, Market Place, Malton
Extensive Romano-British collections from the Malton District and the Roman Derventio Fortress. Also prehistoric and medieval material.

ROTUNDA MUSEUM, Vernon Road, Scarborough (Scarborough Corporation)
Archaeological collections of all periods represented in North-East Yorkshire. Scarborough bygones.

ROYAL PUMP ROOM MUSEUM, opp Valley Gardens, Harrogate
Original sulphur well of the Victorian spa. Costume, pottery, local history and prehistory.

RYEDALE FOLD MUSEUM, Hutton-le-hole (Crossland Foundation)
Prehistoric and Roman antiquities; extensive collections of tools of many 19th-century crafts. Furniture and domestic equipment covering 300 years of history. Folk park in museum grounds housing blacksmith's shop, wagon park, unique Elizabethan glass furnace, 16th-century manor house and medieval longhouse.

WAKEMAN'S HOUSE MUSEUM, Market Place, Ripon (Ripon Corporation)
A small folk museum.

WHITBY ART GALLERY, Pannett Park, Whitby (Whitby Urban District Council)
Early and contemporary English watercolours and oil paintings.

WHITBY MUSEUM OF WHITBY LITERARY AND PHILOSOPHICAL SOCIETY, Whitby
Fossils, relics of prehistoric man and of Roman occupation. Local history and bygones. Shipping gallery. Captain Cook relics. Natural history.

WOODEND MUSEUM, The Crescent, Scarborough (Scarborough Corporation)

Formerly the home of the Sitwell family; two rooms are devoted to paintings and first editions of this famous literary family. Permanent exhibitions of British and foreign natural history. Yorkshire geological material and an aquarium.

YORK CASTLE MUSEUM, Tower Street, York (York City Council)
An outstanding folk museum of Yorkshire life based on the Kirk Collection of bygones and including period rooms, a cobbled street, domestic and agricultural equipment, early crafts, costumes, toys. Yorkshire militaria, an Edwardian Street and a water-driven corn mill.

THE YORKSHIRE MUSEUM, Museum Gardens, York (North Yorkshire County Council)
Contains extensive natural history collections, archaeological galleries, geology, pottery and coins and the Medieval Architectural Museum. The gardens contain Roman and medieval ruins and the Hospitium housing a large Roman collection.

NOTTINGHAMSHIRE
HISTORIC HOUSES AND CASTLES

HOLME PIERREPONT HALL, Nr Nottingham (Mr and Mrs Robin Brackenbury)
Medieval brick manor house. Formal 19th-century courtyard garden. Oak furniture.

NEWSTEAD ABBEY, Linby (Nottingham City Council)
Part of original priory survives bought by Sir John Byron, 1540, and converted to a house. Byron relics, pictures, furniture. Extensive and beautiful gardens.

THORESBY HALL, Ollerton (Countess Manvers)
Built by Salvin in 1864. The only mansion in the Dukeries still occupied as the home of the original owners. State apartments. Great hall. Frank Bradley exhibition of toy and model theatres.

THRUMPTON HALL, Nottingham (George FitzRoy Seymour, Esq)
Jacobean. Magnificent carved staircase. Fine pictures and furniture. Owner occupied.

WOLLATON HALL, Nottingham (City of Nottingham)
Fine example of late Elizabethan Renaissance architecture. Natural history museum.

MUSEUMS AND GALLERIES

BREWHOUSE YARD MUSEUM, Nottingham (Nottingham City Council)
Four 17th- and 18th-century cottages at the foot of the Castle Rock are being restored in open in 1976 to present an interpretation of domestic life in Nottingham.

CASTLEGATE MUSEUM, Nottingham (Nottingham City Council)
An elegant row of Georgian terraced houses containing the City's costume and textile collections. Women's costume from the 17th century to the present day. Smaller collections of men's and children's wear. The Middleton Collection of 17th century and later embroideries. Foreign textiles. Dolls in fashionable dress. Very fine collection of lace, especially machine made. Lace-making equipment.

FRAMEWORK KNITTER'S MUSEUM, Chapel Street, Ruddington
Unique complex of frameshops and cottages: reconstructed stockingers' shop, handframes, etc.

INDUSTRIAL MUSEUM, Wollaton Park, Nottingham (Nottingham City Council)
18th-century stables presenting a history of Nottingham's industry: printing,

pharmacy, hosiery and lace-making. Victorian beam engine, horse gin, agricultural machinery, transport and craft workshops.

MANSFIELD MUSEUM AND ART GALLERY, Leeming Street, Mansfield (Mansfield District Council)
Collection: zoological specimens, Wedgwood, Rockingham, Derby, Pinxton and lustre ware, watercolours of Old Mansfield, bygones. Regular loan exhibitions.

MUSEUM AND ART GALLERY, Appleton Gate, Newark-on-Trent (Newark District Council)
Collections of local archaeology and history, some natural history and art, and temporary exhibitions in the 'Tudor Hall'.

NOTTINGHAM CASTLE MUSEUM, Nottingham (Nottingham City Council)
A 17th-century residence built by the dukes of Newcastle on the site of the medieval royal castle and converted to a museum in 1878. Fine collections of ceramics, silver and glass, medieval Nottingham alabaster carvings, local historical and archaeological displays, classical, oriental and ethnographical antiquities. First floor art gallery including works by Nottingham born artists R. P. Bonington and Thomas and Paul Sandby. Two temporary exhibition galleries. The Sherwood Foresters' Regimental Museum is also in the Castle.

UNIVERSITY ART GALLERY, Portland Building, University Park, Nottingham
Exhibitions changed 3 to 4 times each term.

WORKSHOP MUSEUM, Memorial Avenue, Worksop (Bassetlaw District Council)
Local archaeological and historical display. Bygones and Victoriana. Local birds, butterflies and moths.

OXFORDSHIRE
OUTSTANDING NATURAL BEAUTY

CHILTERNS (part)
COTSWOLDS (part)
NORTH WESSEX DOWNS (part)

HISTORIC HOUSES AND CASTLES

ABBEY BUILDINGS, Abingdon (Friends of Abingdon)
Long gallery, granary and checker hall of the former Abbey of Abingdon (AD 675–1538). The buildings contain an Elizabethan-style theatre. Exhibitions, lectures, music and drama events.

ASHDOWN HOUSE, Nr Lambourn (National Trust)
Built late 17th century by first Lord Craven for Elizabeth of Bohemia. Mansard roof crowned by a cupola with a golden ball. Contains the Craven family portraits associated with Elizabeth of Bohemia. Box parterre.

BLENHEIM PALACE, Woodstock (His Grace the Duke of Marlborough)
Masterpiece of Sir John Vanbrugh in the classical style. Fine collection of pictures and tapestries. Gardens and park designed by Vanbrugh and Queen Anne's gardener, Henry Wise. Later construction was carried out by Capability Brown, who also created the famous Blenheim lake.

BROUGHTON CASTLE, Banbury (Lord Saye and Sele)
Romantic moated Elizabethan mansion with early 14th-century nucleus. Fine fireplaces, ceilings and panelling.

BUSCOT OLD PARSONAGE, Nr Lechlade (National Trust)
Built in 1703 of Cotswold stone and stone tiles. On the banks of the Thames.

BUSCOT PARK, Nr Faringdon (National Trust)
Built in 1780. Fine paintings and furniture. Briar Rose room. Attractive garden walks, lake.

CHASTLETON HOUSE, Moreton-in-Marsh (Alan Clutton Brock, Esq)
Built 1603. Fine plasterwork and panelling. Original furniture and tapestries. Topiary garden designed 1700.

DITCHLEY PARK, Enstone (Ditchley Foundation)
Third in size and date amongst the great 18th-century mansions of Oxfordshire. Designed by Gibbs, decoration of Great Hall by Kent.

EDGCOTE, Chipping Warden (E. R. Courage, Esq)
Stone-built mid-18th-century house. Good Palladian and rococo interior features.

THE GREAT BARN, Great Coxwell (National Trust)
13th-century stone-built, stone-tiled roof, exceptionally interesting timber roof construction. Magnificent proportions.

GREYS COURT, Henley-on-Thames (National Trust)
Beautiful gardens, medieval ruins, a Tudor donkey wheel for raising well water and a 16th-century house containing interesting 18th-century plasterwork and furniture.

MAPLEDURHAM HOUSE, Mapledurham (J. J. Eyston, Esq)
Late 16th-century Elizabethan home of the Blount family. Original moulded ceilings; great oak staircase; fine collection of paintings and private chapel.

MILTON MANOR HOUSE, Nr Abingdon (Surgeon Capt and Mrs E. J. Mockler)
17th-century house with Georgian wings. Traditionally designed by Inigo Jones. Walled garden and pleasure grounds.

NUNEHAM, Nr Oxford (University of Oxford, leased to Culham College of Education)
Thames-side Palladian villa (additions by Brown and Smirke) in a picturesque setting created by William Mason and Capability Brown. Temple church by 'Athenian' Stuart. No contents.

PRIORY COTTAGES, Steventon (National Trust)
Formerly monastic buildings, converted into three houses, one containing the great hall of the original priory.

UNIVERSITY OF OXFORD (In most Colleges, only the Chapels and Halls are open)
ALL SOUL'S COLLEGE, High Street (1438)
BALLIOL COLLEGE, Broad Street (1263)
BRASENOSE COLLEGE, Radcliffe Square (1509)
CHRIST CHURCH, St Aldate's (1546)
CORPUS CHRISTI COLLEGE, Merton Street (1516)
EXETER COLLEGE, Turl Street (1314)
HERTFORD COLLEGE, Catte Street (1284, 1740 and 1874)
JESUS COLLEGE, Turl Street (1571)
KEBLE COLLEGE, Parks Road (1868)
LINCOLN COLLEGE, Turl Street (1427)
MAGDALEN COLLEGE, High Street (1458)
MERTON COLLEGE, Merton Street (1264)
NEW COLLEGE (admission at New College Lane and Holywell Street) (1379)
NUFFIELD COLLEGE, New Road (1937)
ORIEL COLLEGE, Oriel Square (1326)
PEMBROKE COLLEGE, St Aldate's (1624)
THE QUEEN'S COLLEGE, High Street (1340)
ST EDMUND HALL, Queen's Lane (1270)
ST JOHN'S COLLEGE, St Giles' (1555)

TRINITY COLLEGE, Broad Street (1554)
UNIVERSITY COLLEGE, High Street (1249)
WADHAM COLLEGE, Parks Road (1610)
WORCESTER COLLEGE, Worcester Street (1714)

GARDENS

BOTANIC GARDENS, Oxford (University of Oxford)
Oldest botanic garden in Britain, founded 1621.
KINGSTON HOUSE, Kingston Bagpuize (Miss Raphael)
Bulbs, flowering shrubs, roses, herbaceous borders.
PUSEY HOUSE GARDENS, Nr Faringdon (Michael Hornby, Esq)
Herbaceous borders, walled gardens, water garden, large collection of shrubs and roses. Many fine trees.

MUSEUMS AND GALLERIES

THE ASHMOLEAN MUSEUM OF ART AND ARCHAEOLOGY, Beaumont Street, Oxford
British, European, Mediterranean, Egyptian and Near-Eastern archaeology. European oil paintings, old masters and modern drawings, watercolours, and prints; miniatures; European ceramics; sculpture and bronzes; English silver; objects of applied art. Hope collection of engraved portraits. Other Chinese, Japanese, Tibetan and Islamic collections.
BANBURY MUSEUM, Marlborough Road, Banbury (Oxfordshire County Council with Cherwell District Council)
'Scrapbook of Victorian Banbury' exhibition. Many items and displays of local interest. Globe Room: fine 17th-century panelling from local inn. Temporary exhibitions.
CHRIST CHURCH LIBRARY, Peckwater Quadrangle, Oxford
Statuary, music, Carrolliana, manuscripts and printed books.
CHRIST CHURCH PICTURE GALLERY, Canterbury Quadrangle, Oxford
Old master paintings and drawings.
MUSEUM OF THE HISTORY OF SCIENCE, Broad Street, Oxford
Early scientific instruments, photographic apparatus, clocks and watches. Also library, manuscripts and photographic records.
MUSEUM OF MODERN ART, Pembroke Street, Oxford
Temporary exhibitions of contemporary British and international art.
MUSEUM OF OXFORD, St Aldate's Oxford (Oxfordshire County Council)
Large, permanent exhibition of 'The Story of Oxford' including many treasures on loan from colleges, etc. Also temporary exhibitions.
OXFORDSHIRE COUNTY MUSEUM, Fletcher's House, Woodstock (Oxfordshire County Council, Department of Museum Services)
Archaeology, crafts, industry and domestic life of the region. Temporary exhibitions.
OXFORD UNIVERSITY MUSEUM, Parks Road, Oxford
Zoological, entomological, geological and mineralogical collections of the University.
PENDON MUSEUM OF MINIATURE LANDSCAPE AND TRANSPORT, Long Wittenham, Abingdon
Scenes in miniature showing the countryside and its transport in the thirties, including historically accurate trains and parts of a thatched village in fine detail. Also railway relics from 1812 to the present day.

THE PITT RIVERS MUSEUM, Parks Road, Oxford
Ethnology and prehistoric archaeology of the peoples of the world. Musical instruments.

THE ROTUNDA, Grove House, 44 Iffley Turn, Oxford
Early dolls' houses, 1700–1885, and contents.

TOLSEY MUSEUM, High Street, Burford (Tolsey Museum Committee)
Historical collection of charters, maces, seals, bygones and Burford craftsmen's dolls' house in a replica Regency room with period furnishings and costumes.

TOWN MUSEUM, The County Hall, Abingdon (Abingdon Town Council)
Fine 17th-century building containing local fossil remains, archaeological material (including finds from Anglo-Saxon cemetery) and history. Collection, prints, charters and documents.

SHROPSHIRE
OUTSTANDING NATURAL BEAUTY

SHROPSHIRE HILLS

HISTORIC HOUSES AND CASTLES

ACTION ROUND HALL, Bridgnorth (Mr H. L. Kennedy)
Built circa 1695 as a dower house for Aldenham Park. Retains much original panelling.

ATTINGHAM PARK, Nr Shrewsbury (National Trust)
Designed in 1785 by George Stuart for 1st Lord Berwick. Remarkable for its interior decoration. Famous painted boudoir.

BENTHALL, HALL, Much Wenlock (National Trust)
16th-century stone house with mullion windows, interior improved in the 17th century. Fine oak staircase and plaster ceilings. Interesting small garden.

BOSCOBEL HOUSE, Shifnal (Department of the Environment)
17th-century house. Charles II took refuge here after the Battle of Worcester.

*MAWLEY HALL, Cleobury Mortimer (A. M. G. Galliers-Pratt, Esq)
18th-century house attributed to Smith of Warwick. Notable contemporary plasterwork and panelling.

*MORVILLE HALL, Nr Bridgnorth (National Trust)
Modest Elizabethan house converted in the 18th century.

SHIPTON HALL, Much Wenlock (C. R. N. Bishop, Esq)
Elizabethan manor house, with interior designs and stable block by Pritchard. Stone walled garden, medieval dovecote.

*TYN-Y-RHOS HALL, Nr Oswestry (Chevalier M. Thompson-Butler-Lloyd)
Small ancient seat of the Phillips family. Contains fine oak staircase, 2 beautiful carved oak fireplaces with early Delph tiles. Furnished in the Victorian style.

UPTON CRESSETT HALL, Bridgnorth (William Cash, Esq)
Elizabethan manor house with fine brick and plasterwork and 14th-century aisled hall and gate-house.

WENLOCK PRIORY, Much Wenlock (Department of the Environment)
7th-century Saxon foundation refounded in the 12th century as Cluniac priory.

WESTON PARK, Nr Shifnal (Earl of Bradford)
Built 1671 by Lady Wilbraham, one of the finest examples of the Restoration period. Magnificent gardens and vast parklands designed by Capability Brown.

THE WHITE HOUSE, Aston Munslow (Miss J. C. Purser)
Medieval site comprising a Norman dovecote, 13th-century. Undercroft, 14th-century. Cruck hall, 1570 half-timbered cross-wing, 18th-century addition. Implements and tools, domestic and dairy utensils in their natural environment.

WILDERHOPE MANOR, Wenlock Edge (National Trust)
Built in 1586. 17th-century plaster ceilings.

GARDENS

BURFORD HOUSE GARDENS, Nr Tenbury Wells (J. Treasure, Esq)
Gardens containing many interesting trees, shrubs, clematis and plants, ornamental pools and streams in beautiful setting by River Teme.

HODNET HALL GARDENS, Nr Market Drayton (Mr and the Hon Mrs Heber Percy)
Garden extends over 60 acres.

MUSEUMS AND GALLERIES

CLIVE HOUSE, College Hill, Shrewsbury
Fine Georgian house containing outstanding collection of Shropshire ceramics together with art, furniture and the Regimental Museum of 1st Queen's Dragoon Guards.

CLUN TOWN TRUST MUSEUM, Clun
Local geology, pre-history earthworks, footpaths, commons, rights of way, etc, local history, early photographs, etc.

COLEHAM PUMPING STATION, Old Coleham, Shrewsbury
Preserved beam engines.

IRONBRIDGE GORGE MUSEUM, Telford (Ironbridge Gorge Museum Trust)
A major open-air museum based on a unique series of industrial monuments in the Severn Gorge:

BLISTS HILL OPEN AIR MUSEUM
A 42 acre woodland site with steam blowing engines, pitheads, restored canal and Hay Inclined Plane. Telford road and working potter.

COALBROOKDALE MUSEUM AND FURNACE SITE
Abraham Darby's blast furnace history of the Coalbrookdale Company and collection of art castings.

IRON BRIDGE INFORMATION CENTRE
In the tollhouse, next to the world's first iron bridge.

LUDLOW MUSEUM, Butter. Cross, Ludlow
Fine collection of fossils; local collections of prehistoric, Roman and medieval material, including local arms and armour.

READER'S HOUSE, Ludlow (King Edward VI Ludlow Charities)
Extensive restoration work is being carried out.

ROWLEY'S HOUSE MUSEUM, Barker Street, Shrewsbury (Borough of Shrewsbury and Atcham)
Fine collection of Roman material from Viroconium (Wroxeter), medieval, prehistoric.

SHREWSBURY ART GALLERY, Castle Gates, Shrewsbury (Borough of Shrewsbury and Atcham)

VIROCONIUM MUSEUM, Wroxeter (Department of the Environment)
Objects found during the excavation of the site, Roman inscription, pottery, coins and other small objects.

THE WHITEHOUSE MUSEUM OF BUILDINGS AND COUNTRY LIFE, Aston Munslow
The Stedman Homestead, 4 houses in one, 13th, 14th, 16th and 18th century, dovecote 13th century; another 16th-century house; cider house 17th century;

stable 1680 AD; other buildings of 17th, 18th century in original positions in functional relation to each other. Farming implements, tools, domestic utensils, dairy equipment in functional positions. Horsedrawn wagons, carts, etc.

SOMERSET

NATIONAL PARKS

EXMOOR (part)

OUTSTANDING NATURAL BEAUTY

MENDIP HILLS (part)
QUANTOCK HILLS

HISTORIC HOUSES AND CASTLES

BARFORD PARK, Enmore (Mr and Mrs Michael Stancomb)
Georgian mansion in miniature.
BARRINGTON COURT, Ilminster (National Trust)
16th-century house and extensive garden.
BRYMPTON D'EVERCY, Nr Yeovil (Charles E. B. Clive-Ponsonby-Fane, Esq)
Mansion house with late 17th-century south front and Tudor west front. 13th-century priest house and church adjacent. Longest straight staircase in England. Vineyard and formal gardens. Agricultural museum.
COLERIDGE COTTAGE, Nether Stowey (National Trust)
Home of S. T. Coleridge, 1797–1800.
DODINGTON HALL, Nether Stowey (Lady Michael Gass)
Historic hall dating from 14th and 15th century. Timbered minstrel's gallery.
DUNSTER CASTLE, Dunster (National Trust)
Castle dating from 13th century, remodelled by Anthony Salvin in 19th century. Fine 17th-century staircase and plaster ceilings.
EAST LAMBROOK MANOR, South Pether (Mr and Mrs F. H. Boyd-Carpenter)
15th-century house with 16th-century additions and panelling. Interesting cottage style garden with rare plants. A memorial to the late Margery Fish.
GAULDEN MANOR, Tolland, Nr Taunton (Mr and Mrs James LeGendre Starkie)
Small historic manor of great charm originating from 12th century. Past home of the Turberville family. Great hall has unique plaster ceiling and oak screen to former chapel. Fine antique furniture. Interesting grounds include bog garden with many varieties of primula. Herb garden.
KING JOHN'S HUNTING LODGE, Axbridge (National Trust)
Early Tudor merchant's house extensively restored in 1971. Museum of local history.
LYTES CARY, Somerton (National Trust)
14th-and 15th-century manor house with chapel; formal garden.
*THE MILL, Hightham (National Trust)
A thatched windmill dating from 1820; in use until 1910.
MONTACUTE HOUSE, Yeovil (National Trust)
Magnificent Elizabethan house of Ham Hill stone begun in 1588 by Edward Phelips. Fine heraldic glass, tapestries, panelling and furniture. National Portrait Gallery exhibitions of Elizabethan and Jacobean portraits. Very fine formal garden and topiary.

NETTLECOMBE COURT, Nr Williton (Leonard Wills Field Centre)
Ancestral home of the Raleigh and Trevelyans. Elizabethan and Georgian manor house.
*PRIEST'S HOUSE, Muchelney (National Trust)
Late medieval house, originally the residence of the secular priests who served the parish church.
TREASURER'S HOUSE, Mortlock (National Trust)
Small house dating from 13th and 14th centuries with medieval kitchen and hall.
STOKE-SUB-HAMDON PRIORY (National Trust)
Complex of buildings begun in 14th century for the priests of the chantry chapel of St Nicholas (destroyed). Only the great hall is left open to the public.
TINTINHULL HOUSE, Yeovil (National Trust)
17th-century house with a beautiful garden.

GARDENS

STOWELL HILL, Templecombe (Lady McCreefy)
Spring bulbs; collection of flowering shrubs, including rhododendrons, azaleas, magnolias, and Japanese cherries.

MUSEUMS AND GALLERIES

ADMIRAL BLAKE MUSEUM, Blake Street, Bridgwater (Sedgemoor District Council)
Reputed birthplace of Admiral Blake, containing Blake relics, exhibits relating to Battle of Sedgemoor. Archaeology and local history.
AXBRIDGE CAVING GROUP AND ARCHAEOLOGY, The Museum, Town Hall, Axbridge
History and prehistory of the Axbridge-Banwell-Cheddar area.
BOROUGH MUSEUM, Hendford Manor Hall, Yeovil (Yeovil Corporation)
Local history and archaeology, containing the Henry Stiby Firearm Collection and the Bailward Costume Collection.
CHEDDAR MOTOR AND TRANSPORT MUSEUM, The Cliffs, Cheddar (Cheddar Veteran and Vintage Car Museum Limited)
Cars, motor cycles, cycles and motoring accessories and Cheddar section on discovery of caves, etc.
FARLEIGH CASTLE, Farleigh Hungerford (Department of the Environment)
Arms and armour, largely from Civil War period, fragments of medieval stained glass, housed in castle's chapel.
FLEET AIR ARM MUSEUM, Royal Naval Air Station, Yeovilton
Development of Naval aviation from origins in 1910, through the Royal Naval Air Service of World War I, to the Fleet Air Arm of today.
GLASTONBURY LAKE VILLAGE MUSEUM, The Tribunal, High Street, Glastonbury
Collections of late prehistoric antiquities from Glastonbury Lake Village and items of local interest.
GOUGH'S CAVE MUSEUM, Cheddar
Upper Paleolithic remains: almost complete skeleton, flints, amber and engraved stones.
SHEPTON MALLET MUSEUM, Market Place, Shepton Mallet (Shepton Mallet Urban District Council)
SOMERSET COUNTY MUSEUM, Taunton Castle, Taunton
Collections relevant to the County of Somerset, including archaeology, geology and palaeontology, natural history, ceramics, folk-life, costume and military gallery.

STREET SHOE MUSEUM, High Street, Street (C. and J. Clark Limited)
Shoes from Roman times to present; shoe machinery from 1860s to 1920; 19th-century documents and photographs illustrating the early history of C. and J. Clark.

WELLS MUSEUM, Cathedral Green, Wells
Local bygones, prehistoric cave finds, coins, natural history, Mendip rocks, fossils and minerals.

WOOKEY HOLE, The caves, Wookey Hole
Caves Museum – animal remains of the newer Pliocene period. Relics of the late Celtic and Romano-British civilisation. Madame Tussaud's store room. Lady Bangor's collection of fairground carvings. The paper mill – an exhibition about handmade paper-making.

SOUTH YORKSHIRE
NATIONAL PARKS

PEAK DISTRICT (part)

HISTORIC HOUSES AND CASTLES

CANNON HALL, Cawthorne (Barnsley Metropolitan Borough Council)
18th-century house by Carr of York. Collections of fine furniture, paintings and glassware. The William Harvey Bequest of Dutch and Flemish paintings now on permanent display. Also the Regimental Museum of the 13th/18th Royal Hussars. 70 acres of parkland.

OAKES PARK, Nr Sheffield (Major and Mrs T. Bagshawe)
Georgian house with an abundance of old oak furniture, tapestries, paintings and a collection of dolls, etc. Attractive gardens with long lake.

MUSEUMS AND GALLERIES

ABBEYDALE INDUSTRIAL HAMLET, Abbeydale Road South, Sheffield (Sheffield Corporation)
An 18th-century scytheworks comprising a Huntsman's type crucible steel furnace, tilt-hammers, grinding hull, hand-forges and workman's cottage.

BENTLEY MUSEUM, Bentley Public Library, Doncaster
Local historical and environmental exhibits.

BISHOP'S HOUSE, Meersbrook Park, Sheffield (Sheffield Corporation)
A late 15th-century timbered building with 16th- and 17th-century additions.

COOPER ART GALLERY, Church Street, Barnsley (Trustees)
17th-, 18th- and 19th-century paintings; English drawings, Sir Michael Sadler Collection; temporary loan exhibitions.

CUSWORTH HALL MUSEUM, Cusworth Lane, Doncaster
Folk-life exhibits, particularly relating to South Yorkshire.

DONCASTER MUSEUM AND ART GALLERY, Chequer Road
Natural history, prehistoric and Romano-British exhibits, local history and costumes. Art collection and frequent temporary loans.

GRAVES ART GALLERY, Surrey Street, Sheffield (Sheffield Corporation)
An introduction to British portraiture and important examples of European painting. Also important collections of Chinese, Indian, Islamic and African art. Frequent loan exhibitions.

INDUSTRIAL STORE, Kelham Island, Sheffield (Sheffield Corporation)

A palletised warehouse where material for the projected industrial museum is being collected.

MAPPIN ART GALLERY, Weston Park, Sheffield (Sheffield Corporation)
Paintings and sculpture mainly representative of the British School of the 18th, 19th and 20th centuries. Frequent loan exhibitions of contemporary painting, sculpture and graphic art.

ROTHERHAM MUSEUM AND ART GALLERY, Clifton Park, Rotherham (Rotherham Metropolitan Borough Council)
Antiquities from Roman forts at Templebrough; gem stones and jewellery; English glass, church silver. Rockingham porcelain and natural history.

SHEFFIELD CITY MUSEUM, Weston Park, Sheffield (Sheffield Corporation)
General collections of natural history, geology, ceramics, coins and bygones; specialised collections of cutlery, Old Sheffield plate, local archaeology and local history. Temporary exhibition gallery.

SHEPHERD WHEEL, Whiteley Wood, Hangingwater Road, Sheffield (Sheffield Corporation)
A Sheffield 'Little Mesters' water-powered grinding shop.

VICTORIA JUBILEE MUSEUM, Cawthorne
Natural history, geology and objects of local interest.

STAFFORDSHIRE

NATIONAL PARKS
PEAK DISTRICT (part)

OUTSTANDING NATURAL BEAUTY
CANNOCK CHASE

HISTORIC HOUSES AND CASTLES

BLITHFIELD HALL, Nr Rugeley (Lady Bagot)
Elizabethan House with Georgian and Regency Gothic additions. Landscape gardens, orangery and formal rose garden. 14th-century church. Children's toy museum.

CHILLINGTON HALL, Nr Wolverhampton (P. R. de L. Giffard)
Georgian house, Part 1724 (Francis Smith) part 1785 (Sir John Soane). Fine saloon. Grounds by Capability Brown.

HOAR CROSS HALL, Nr Burton-on-Trent (W. A. Bickerton-Jones, Esq)
Elizabethan-style mansion. Varied collection of arms and armour. 17th-, 18th- and 19th-century furniture and paintings. Plasterwork in the hall and private chapel by G. F. Bodley. Landscaped and terraced gardens, yew tree walks and lily ponds.

SHUGBOROUGH, Great Haywood (National Trust, administered by Staffordshire County Council)
Seat of the Earls of Lichfield. Architecture by James Stuart and Samuel Wyatt. Chinese garden house, classical temple, extensive grounds in area of river, beautiful trees and shrubs.

GARDENS

ELDS WOOD, Willoughbridge (Willoughbridge Garden Trust)

200-year-old gravel quarry converted into unique woodland garden.
TRENTHAM GARDENS, Trentham (Countess of Sutherland)
Covers some 600 acres of formal gardens, woodland and parkland.

MUSEUMS AND GALLERIES

ARNOLD BENNETT MUSEUM, 205 Waterloo Road, Cobridge, Stoke-on-Trent
(Stoke District Council)
Arnold Bennett's early home with two rooms devoted to drawings and personal
relics.
BOROUGH MUSEUM AND HOBBERGATE ART GALLERY, Brampton Park, Newcastle-
under-Lyme
Museum: ceramics, weapons, clocks, textiles, natural and local history.
Art Gallery: permanent collections of English oil and watercolour paintings,
17th to 20th centuries, and changing exhibitions of contemporary art and
sculpture.
CHEDDLETON FLINT MILL, Nr Leek (Cheddleton Flint Mill Industrial Heritage Trust)
Twin water wheels on River Churnet operate flint grinding pans. Museum collec-
tion of machinery used in pottery milling. Narrow boat *Vienna* moored on Caldon
Canal.
CITY MUSEUM AND ART GALLERY, Broad Street, Hanley, Stoke-on-Trent
(Stoke District Council)
DR JOHNSON'S BIRTHPLACE, Breadmarket Street, Lichfield
Relics and pictures of Dr Johnson and his contemporaries.
FORD GREEN HALL, Smallthorne, Stoke-on-Trent (Stoke District Council)
16th-century timbered-frame manor house containing furniture and domestic
utensils. Associations with Izaak Walton and the early Quakers.
GLADSTONE POTTERY MUSEUM, Uttoxeter Road, Longton, Stoke-on-Trent
(Staffordshire Pottery Industry Preservation Trust)
The living and working museum of British Pottery. Early Victorian 'potbank'
complete with original bottle ovens and restored old workshops in which pottery
is seen being made by craftsmen. Galleries relate the development of Staffordshire
potteries, ceramic tiles, sanitary ware and decorating techniques.
IZAAK WALTON COTTAGE, Shallowfield, Stafford (Staffordshire County Council)
The angler Izaak Walton's restored country cottage.
LEEK ART GALLERY, Nicholson Institute, Leek
Small permanent collection supplemented by travelling exhibitions.
LETOCETUM MUSEUM, Wall (Department of the Environment)
Finds from the excavated Roman Station Letocetum.
LICHFIELD ART GALLERY AND MUSEUM, Bird Street, Lichfield (Lichfield Corporation)
Local history museum. Art Gallery shows loan and local exhibitions and has
picture loan service.
MUSEUM AND ART GALLERY, Guild Street, Burton upon Trent
Museum of local history and British birds. Art Gallery sponsors travelling art
exhibitions.
SPITFIRE MUSEUM, Bethesda Street, Hanley, Stoke-on-Trent
Houses a Spitfire RW388 Mk LF 16E built in 1944, together with a number of
other items of aeronautical interest.
STAFFORD MUSEUM AND ART GALLERY, The Green, Stafford (Staffordshire County
Council)
Museum of history, social life, art and industry of the locality. Art Gallery

shows loan and local art exhibitions.

TAMWORTH CASTLE MUSEUM, The Holloway, Tamworth
The Norman castle with medieval banqueting hall and Jacobean state apartments; houses a local history museum.

THE WEDGWOOD MUSEUM, Barlaston, Stoke-on-trent (Josiah Wedgwood and Sons Ltd)
An extensive collection of early Wedgwood ware.

SUFFOLK
OUTSTANDING NATURAL BEAUTY

DEDHAM VALE (part)
SUFFOLK COAST AND HEATHS

HISTORIC HOUSES AND CASTLES

CHRISTCHURCH MANSION, Ipswich (Borough of Ipswich)
Tudor house, furnished as period house.

EUSTON HALL, Thetford (Duke of Grafton)
18th-century house. Fine collection of paintings. Pleasure grounds by John Evelyn and William Kent Gardens and 17th-century parish church in Wren style.

GAINSBOROUGH'S HOUSE, Sudbury (Gainsborough's House Society)
Gainsborough's birthplace. Pictures, etc.

GLEMHAM HALL, Nr Woodbridge (Lady Blanche Cobbold)
Red brick Elizabethan house. Altered early 1700. Panelled rooms, fine staircase, Queen Anne furniture. Red brick-walled garden.

THE GUILDHALL, Hadleigh (Hadleigh Market Feoffment Charity)
Dating from the 15th century.

HAUGHLEY PARK, Nr Stowmarket (Mr and Mrs A. J. Williams)
Jacobean manor house. Gardens and park.

HEVENINGHAM HALL, Nr Halesworth (Department of the Environment)
Georgian mansion in English Palladian tradition. Interior design and decoration by James Wyatt of outstanding quality and beauty in Neo-classical style. Park and gardens by Capability Brown.

ICKWORTH, Nr Bury St Edmunds (National Trust)
The house, begun circa 1794, was not completed until 1830. Contents of this architectural curiosity include late Regency and 18th-century French furniture, magnificent silver, pictures. Formal gardens, herbaceous borders, orangery. Albana woodland walk.

KENTWELL HALL, Long Melford (J. Patrick Phillips, Esq)
Red brick Elizabethan E-plan mansion surrounded by a broad moat. Exterior little altered. Interior recently refurbished. Inter-connecting gardens with specimen trees and magnificent avenue of ancient limes.

LITTLE HALL, Lavenham (Suffolk Preservation Society)
15th-century high hall house, rooms furnished with Gayer Anderson Collection of furniture, pictures, china, books, etc.

MELFORD HALL, Nr Sudbury (National Trust)
Built between 1554 and 1578 by Sir William Cordell, contains fine pictures, furniture and Chinese porcelain. Interesting garden and gazebo.

SOMERLEYTON HALL, Nr Lowestoft (Lord and Lady Somerleyton)
Present building dates from 16th century, added to in 1844. Grinling Gibbons

carving, library, tapestries, pictures. Beautiful garden. Children's farm. Heritage display.

THEATRE ROYAL, Bury St Edmunds (National Trust)
Built by William Wilkins in 1819. A rare example of a late Georgian playhouse with finepit, boxes and gallery. Working theatre.

GARDENS

HELMINGHAM HALL GARDENS, Ipswich (Lord and Lady Tollemache)
Moated gardens in ancient deer park, ornamental waterfowl, safari rides.

MUSEUMS AND GALLERIES

THE ABBOT'S HALL MUSEUM OF RURAL LIFE OF EAST ANGLIA, Stowmarket
Rural life of the area, agriculture, crafts, and domestic utensils. A 70 acre open air museum is being established.

THE GERSHOM-PARKINGTON MEMORIAL COLLECTION OF CLOCKS AND WATCHES, 8 Angel Hill, Bury St Edmonds (National Trust and Bury St Edmonds Borough Council)
A collection of clocks and watches in a Queen Anne House.

IPSWICH MUSEUM, High Street, Ipswich
Geology, prehistory, archaeology of Suffolk from earliest times to the medieval period; natural history; ethnography.

MOYSE'S HALL MUSEUM, Cornhill, Bury St Edmunds (Bury St Edmunds Borough Council)
12th-century dwellinghouse containing local antiquities and natural history.

SOUTHWOLD MUSEUM, St Bartholomew's Green, Southwold
Local archaeology, natural history and bygones.

SURREY
OUTSTANDING NATURAL BEAUTY

SURREY HILLS

HISTORIC HOUSES AND CASTLES

ALBURY PARK, Albury, Guildford (Mutual Households Association Limited)
Country mansion by Pugin.

CLANDON PARK, Nr Guildford (National Trust)
A Palladian house built 1731–5 by Giacomo Leoni. Fine plasterwork. Collection of furniture and pictures.

CLAREMONT, Esher (Claremont School Trust Limited)
Excellent example of Palladian style, was built 1772 by Capability Brown for Clive of India. Henry Holland and John Soane responsible for the interior decoration. It is now a girls' school run by Christian Scientists.

DETILLENS, Limpsfield (D. G. Neville)
Mid-15th-century Wealden House. Fine inglenooks and firebacks, medieval furniture. $1\frac{1}{2}$ acres of mixed garden.

FARNHAM CASTLE, Farnham (Centre for International Briefing)
A seat of the Bishops of Winchester from the 12th century until 1927. Then the seat of the Bishop of Guildford until 1956. The keep is in the care of the Department of the Environment.

GREATHED MANOR, Lingfield (Mutual Households Association Ltd)
Victorian Manor House.

HATCHLANDS, East Clandon (National Trust)
Built by Admiral Boscawen in the 18th century. Interior by Robert Adams with later modifications.

LOSELEY HOUSE, Guildford (J. R. More-Molyneux, Esq)
Elizabethan mansion built 1562. Panelling, furniture, paintings, ceilings.

POLESDEN LACEY, Nr Dorking (National Trust, 1946)
Original Regency villa altered in Edwardian period. Greville collection of pictures, tapestries, furniture. 18th-century garden extended 1906, with herbaceous borders, rose garden, clipped hedges, lawns, beeches. Views.

PUTTENDEN MANOR, Nr Lingfield (Brian D. Thompson, Esq)
Pre-Tudor manor house with superb collection of interesting antique furniture. 14 acres of gardens with small lakes and interesting trees.

GARDENS

CHILWORTH MANOR, Nr Guildford (Sir Lionel Heald, QC)
Garden laid out in 17th century on site of 11th-century monastery: 18th-century walled garden; spring flowers, flowering shrubs, herbaceous border; 11th-century stewponds.

FEATHERCOMBE GARDENS, Hambledon (Mrs Wieler and Miss Parker)
Wide views, flowering shrubs, heathers.

HASCOMBE COURT, Nr Godalming (Mrs C. C. Jacobs)
Massed spring bulbs, rhododendrons, azaleas, camellias, magnolias; herbaceous borders.

RAMSTER, Chiddingfold (Sir Aubrey and Lady Burke)
Large woodland garden, fine rhododendrons, azaleas, camellias, magnolias, trees and shrubs.

WINKWORTH ARBORETUM, Nr Godalming (National Trust)
95 acres of trees and shrubs planted mainly for autumn colour.

WISLEY GARDEN, Wisley, Ripley (Royal Horticultural Society)
British gardening at its best in all aspects.

MUSEUMS AND GALLERIES

CAMBERLEY MUSEUM, Knoll Road, Camberley (Surrey Heath Borough Council)
Local natural history, history and archaeology.

CHARTERHOUSE SCHOOL MUSEUM, Godalming
Carthusiana, archaeology. Greek pottery, medals, old English household equipment, ethnography, natural history. Peruvian pottery.

CHERTSEY MUSEUM, The Cedars, Windsor Street, Chertsey (Runnymede District Council)
18th- and 19th-century costume and furniture, ceramics, local history and archaeology.

THE EGHAM MUSEUM, The Literary Institute, Egham (Runnymede Historical Society)
Archaeology and local history.

FARNHAM MUSEUM, Willmer House, 38 West Street, Farnham (Waverley District Council)
Early Georgian front of cut and moulded brick; fine carving and panelling; walled garden.

GUILDFORD HOUSE, 155 High Street, Guildford (Guildford Borough Council)

Monthly art exhibitions and picture loan service. 17th-century house of architectural interest.

GUILDFORD MUSEUM, Castle Arch, Guildford (Guildford Borough Council)
Archaeological and historical museum for the county, especially West Surrey and Guildford Borough. Needlework collection.

HASLEMERE EDUCATIONAL MUSEUM, High Street, Haslemere
Fine collection of British birds, geology, zoology, botany, local industries, etc.

NATIONAL ARMY MUSEUM DETACHMENT RMA, Sandhurst, Camberley
The Indian Army Memorial Room. The Blenheim Basement includes the museums of the six Irish Regiments disbanded in 1922.

*THE PICTURE GALLERY, Royal Holloway College, Egham (University of London)
Pictures are mainly by British artists of the late 18th and early 19th centuries.

*ROYAL EARLSWOOD HOSPITAL MUSEUM, Redhill
Eight sections dealing with finance, medical and nursing matters, elections, early history and development, education, training and occupation, entertainment, building, farming and engineering.

THE WATTS GALLERY, Compton, Guildford
Paintings by G. F. Watts, OM, RA.

WEYBRIDGE MUSEUM, Church Street, Weybridge
Local exhibits of archaeology, costume and local history.

TYNE AND WEAR

HISTORIC HOUSES AND CASTLES

GIBSIDE CHAPEL AND AVENUE, Gibside (National Trust)
Built to James Paine's design soon after 1760. Outstanding example of Georgian architecture.

WASHINGTON OLD HALL, Washington (National Trust, administered by Washington Urban District Council)
Jacobean manor house incorporating portions of 12th-century house of the Washington family.

MUSEUMS AND GALLERIES

ARBIEA ROMAN FORT, Baring Street, South Shields (Tyne and Wear County Council)
Unique collection of memorial stones and small objects found on the site of the Roman fort.

THE BAGPIPE MUSEUM, The Black Gate, St. Nicholas Street, Newcastle-upon-Tyne
The gate-house added to the 'New Castle' in 1247 now contains a collection of bagpipes.

GRINDON MUSEUM OF LOCAL HISTORY, Grindon Lane, Sunderland (Tyne and Wear County Council)
Period rooms and shop interiors.

JARROW HALL, Church Bank, Jarrow (St Paul's Jarrow Development Trust)
Archaeological finds from excavations of Saxon and medieval monastery of St Paul's, Jarrow. Information room of early Christian sites in the North. Temporary exhibitions of photographs and artists' work. Period furniture.

JOHN G. JOICEY MUSEUM OF LOCAL HISTORY, City Road, Newcastle-upon-Tyne (Tyne and Wear County Council)
Local historical exhibits, furniture and armour.

THE KEEP MUSEUM, St Nicholas Street, Newcastle-upon-Tyne
The keep of the 'New Castle' built by Henry II in 1170. Collections of medieval material.

LAING ART GALLERY, Higham Place, Newcastle-upon-Tyne (Tyne and Wear County Council)
Masterpiece of British art in oils and watercolours from the 17th century onwards. The museum contains collections of pottery and porcelain, glass, silver and metal work.

MONKWEARMOUTH MUSEUM OF LAND TRANSPORT, North Bridge Street, Sunderland (Tyne and Wear County Council)
Neo-classical station of 1848. Restored North Eastern Railway booking office. Exhibits show the history of local land transport and of St Peter's Church.

MUSEUM AND ART GALLERY, Borough Road, Sunderland (Tyne and Wear County Council)
Museum contains collections covering zoology, botany, geology, archaeology, local history, ship models, pottery and English silver. Period rooms. Collection of paintings by British artists in the Art Gallery. Frequent loan exhibitions.

NATIONAL MUSIC HALL MUSEUM, 2 Garden Row, Sunderland (Tyne and Wear County Council)
Illustrating the history and developments of the music hall in England. Late 19th- and 20th-century collection of costume and associated artefacts.

PLUMMER TOWER, Croft Street, Newcastle-upon-Tyne (Tyne and Wear County Council)
18th-century period rooms, also the Thomas Bewick Room, principally a collection of his prints and drawings.

RYHOPE ENGINES MUSEUM, Sunderland
Victorian water pumping station with pair of restored beam engines and small museum.

SCIENCE MUSEUM, Exhibition Park, Great North Road, Newcastle-upon-Tyne (Tyne and Wear County Council)
Engineering, shipbuilding, mining, transport, electrical and other industries, with special reference to the North East.

SHIPLEY ART GALLERY, Prince Consort Road South, Gateshead (Tyne and Wear County Council)
Collection of Dutch and Flemish schools of painting. Modern crafts. Loan exhibitions.

THE UNIVERSITY OF NEWCASTLE-UPON-TYNE
    THE GREEK MUSEUM, Percy Building, The Quadrangle
    Greek and Etruscan art ranging from Minoan to Hellenistic times; vases, terra-cottas, bronzes, gems and armour.

    HANCOCK MUSEUM, Barras Bridge (Jointly with the Natural History Society of of Northumbria)
    Comprehensive collections of natural history. Ethnographical section. Original drawings by Thomas Bewick the Tyneside engraver. Recently completed displays of British Mammals and 'A Picture of Northumberland'. Also Border Forest Museum at Lewisburn, Kielder, Northumberland, organised jointly with the Forestry Commission, dealing with all aspects of natural history, geology and human history in the area.

    THE HATTON GALLERY, The Quadrangle
    A permanent collection of Italian and other paintings. Regular loan exhibitions.

    MUSEUM OF ANTIQUITIES, The Quadrangle (Jointly with the Society of Antiquaries)
Prehistoric, Roman and Anglo-Saxon antiquities, chiefly from Northumberland. Scale models of Hadrian's Wall and reconstructions of Roman arms and armour and a temple of Mithras.

MUSEUM OF THE DEPARTMENT OF MINING ENGINEERING, Queen Victoria Road

Large collection of mine safety lamps and other exhibits illustrating history of mining. Also unique collection of watercolours of Northumberland and Durham mines, 1838–42, by T. H. Hair.

WARWICKSHIRE

HISTORIC HOUSES AND CASTLES

ARBURY HALL, Nuneaton (F. H. FitzRoy Newdegate, Esq)
George Eliot's 'Cheverel Manor'. 18th-century Gothic mansion, pictures, period furniture, etc. Park and landscape gardens.

CHARLECOTE PARK, Warwick (National Trust)
Originally built by the Lucy family 1558. Deer park.

COMPTON WYNYATES, Tysoe (Earl Compton)
Dates from 1480, a picturesque example of Tudor domestic architecture. Topiary garden.

COUGHTON COURT, Alcester (National Trust)
Central gate-house 1509. Two mid-Elizabethan half-timbered wings. Jacobite relics. The home of the Throckmorton family since 1409.

FARNBOROUGH HALL, Nr Banbury (National Trust)
Dates from 17th and 18th centuries. Terrace walk with garden temples and splendid views.

HARVARD HOUSE, Stratford-upon-Avon (Harvard House Memorial Trust)
Built 1596. Home of the mother of John Harvard, founder of the American University.

KENILWORTH CASTLE, Kenilworth (Department of the Environment)
Massive late 12th-century keep. Gate-house.

LORD LEYCESTER HOSPITAL (The Governors of Lord Leycester Hospital)
Group of halls and residences 1383. Chapel 1123. Various historic exhibits.

PACKWOOD HOUSE, Hockley Heath (National Trust)
Timber-framed Tudor house with mid-17th-century additions. Tapestry, needlework, Carolean formal garden, and yew garden of circa 1650 representing the Sermon on the Mount.

RAGLEY HALL, Alcester (Marquess of Hertford)
Built in 1680. Fine paintings, china and furniture and works of art, and a valuable library. Gardens, park and lake. New adventure wood, country trails and picnic areas.

SHAKESPEARE'S BIRTHPLACE TRUST PROPERTIES, Stratford-upon-Avon

ANNE HATHAWAY'S COTTAGE, Shottery
The picturesque thatched home of Anne Hathaway before her marriage to Shakespeare.

HALL'S CROFT, in Old Town
A fine Tudor house complete with period furniture and walled garden where Shakespeare's daughter Susanna and Dr John Hall lived.

MARY ARDEN'S HOUSE, Wilmcote
The Tudor farmhouse where Shakespeare's mother lived, with a farming museum in the barns. Interesting dovecote.

NEW PLACE, Chapel Street
Foundations of Shakespeare's last home, preserved in an Elizabethan garden setting with Nash's House adjoining.

SHAKESPEARE'S BIRTHPLACE, Henley Street
The half-timbered house where Shakespeare was born containing many rare Shakespearian exhibits.

UPTON HOUSE, Edgehill (National Trust)
Tapestries. Fine collection paintings, porcelain. Beautiful terraced gardens.
WARWICK CASTLE, Warwick (Lord Brooke)
One of the finest inhabited medieval castles. The present castle is a fine example
of 14th-century fortification. The state apartments contain a magnificent collection
of pictures. Grounds and gardens landscaped by Capability Brown.

MUSEUMS AND GALLERIES

DOLL MUSEUM, Oken's House, Castle Street, Warwick
The Joy Robinson Collection of antique and period dolls and toys.
LEAMINGTON SPA ART GALLERY AND MUSEUM, Avenue Road, Leamington Spa
(Warwick District Council)
Paintings by Dutch and Flemish masters; mainly English 20th-century oils and
watercolours. 16th-19th century pottery and porcelain. 18th-century and modern
English glass.
NUNEATON MUSEUM AND ART GALLERY, Riversley Park, Nuneaton
Prehistory, archaeology, geology, mining, ethnography and anthropology, paint-
ings and engravings, coins and medals. George Eliot personalia, artistic
exhibitions, etc.
THE ROYAL SHAKESPEARE THEATRE PICTURE GALLERY, Stratford-upon-Avon
Original paintings and designs, portraits of famous actors and actresses. Exhibition
of Shakespeare portraits, and the X-ray radiographs of the 'Flower' and the
'Venice' portraits.
RUGBY LIBRARY, EXHIBITION GALLERY AND MUSEUM, St. Matthew Street, Rugby
Regular loan exhibitions by local societies.
ST JOHN'S HOUSE, Coten End, Warwick (Warwickshire County Council)
Warwickshire bygones, period costume and furniture. Changing exhibitions. The
Museum of the Royal Warwickshire Regiment is also shown. Also houses the
Museum Education Service.
WARWICKSHIRE MUSEUM, Market Place, Warwick (Warwickshire County Council)
Headquarters of the Museum Service. Collection illustrates wild life, geology,
archaeology and history of Warwickshire. Frequent changing exhibitions.

WEST MIDLANDS
HISTORIC HOUSES AND CASTLES

ASTON HALL, Trinity Road, Birmingham (Corporation of Birmingham)
A fine Jacobean house built 1618–35 with many rooms furnished as period settings
MOSELEY OLD HALL, Wolverhampton (National Trust)
An Elizabethan house, formerly half-timbered, a refuge of Charles II after the
battle of Worcester. Reproduction 17th-century box parterre; period plants.
OAK HOUSE, West Bromwich (Metropolitan Borough of Sandwell)
Example of Tudor domestic architecture with Jacobean additions, fine oak
panelling and carving and an excellent collection of period furniture and
furnishings. The house is set in a public park with Elizabethan-style garden at
the front.
WIGHTWICK MANOR, Wolverhampton (National Trust)
William Morris period house. Garden of varied interest.

MUSEUMS AND GALLERIES

ART GALLERY AND MUSEUM, Holyhead Road, Wednesbury (Sandwell Corporation)
Edwin Richards collection of Victorian paintings and watercolours, local history, frequent temporary exhibitions.

*THE ASSAY OFFICE, Newhall Street, Birmingham
Collection of old Birmingham and other silverware, coins, tokens and medals. Library dealing with all aspects of gold and silversmithing. Collection of correspondence of Matthew Boulton comprising some thousands of letters, circa 1760–1810.

BANTOCK HOUSE, Bantock Park, Wolverhampton (Wolverhampton Corporation)
Fine collections of English painted enamels and Japanned ware. Worcester porcelain and Staffordshire and Wedgwood pottery. Dolls and local collections.

BARBER INSTITUTE OF FINE ARTS, The University, Birmingham
Galleries of the Institute contain the art collection belonging to the Trustees.

BILSTON MUSEUM AND ART GALLERY, Mount Pleasant, Wolverhampton
(Wolverhampton Corporation)
Fine examples of English painted enamels and 18th- and 19th-century Local trades.

BIRMINGHAM CITY MUSEUM AND ART GALLERY, Congreve Street, Birmingham

THE DEPARTMENT OF ARCHAEOLOGY, ETHNOLOGY, AND BIRMINGHAM HISTORY
Archaeological objects from West Midlands and other parts of Britain, the Near East, Mediterranean area, India, South and Central America, Ethnographic material from North America and the Pacific. Also the Pinto Collection of Wooden Bygones, a collection of Birmingham-made coins and medals and other items of local interest.

THE DEPARTMENT OF ART
Old master paintings, Italian 17-century paintings and English watercolours. Sculpture, costume and silver.

DEPARTMENT OF CONSERVATION
Undertakes conservation work on collections of the Birmingham City Museum and Art Gallery and, under agreement, for other museums and galleries in the Midlands.

THE DEPARTMENT OF NATURAL HISTORY
Collections include the Beale, Chase and Lysaght Collections of British Birds; the Bagnall and Whitwell Herbaria; the Kenrick Lepidoptera and the Bragge and Ansell Collections of gemstones.

MUSEUM EDUCATION DEPARTMENT
Assists teachers wishing to use the Museum Collections in their work.

THE MUSEUM OF SCIENCE AND INDUSTRY, Newhall Street
A wide range of items of general and scientific interest. Also temporary exhibitions, films and lectures.

BLAKESLEY HALL, Blakesley Road, Yardley, Birmingham
Timber-framed yeoman's farmhouse of about 1600 partly furnished as a period house with displays of the history and crafts of Yardley.

BRIERLEY HILL GLASS MUSEUM AND ART GALLERY, Moor Street, Dudley
A superb and unique collection of international glass, plus reference library. Occasional temporary exhibitions of glass and fine art.

CANNON HILL NATURE CENTRE AND MUSEUM, south-west entrance to Cannon Hill Park, Birmingham
6 acres showing a variety of natural history and conservation subjects, including the animals and plants. It is designed primarily to satisfy the needs of children.

CENTRAL ART GALLERY, Lichfield Street, Wolverhampton (Wolverhampton Corporation)
18th- and 19th-century English watercolours and oil paintings including works by Bonington, Fuseli, Gainsborough and Wilson. Modern prints, painting and drawings. Oriental collections.

DUDLEY MUSEUM AND ART GALLERY, St James's Road, Dudley
Permanent collection of fine art; temporary exhibitions. Geological gallery; reconstructed Black Country nail forge. Adjacent Brooke Robinson museum shows benefactor's personal collection of fine art, Greek pottery, Japanese inro and netsuke and English enamels (open occasionally as advertised). Black Country Museum in course of development.

*GEOLOGICAL DEPARTMENT MUSEUM, The University, Edgbaston, Birmingham
Collections in palaeontology, stratigraphy, petrology, mineralogy and physical geology, including the Holcroft Collection of fossils and the Lapworth Collection of graptolites.

HERBERT ART GALLERY AND MUSEUM, Jordan Well, Coventry
The museum collections are primarily local and include Natural History and Industry. The Art Gallery displays frequent loan exhibitions and has built up collections of British Landscape watercolours, watercolours of Warwickshire, topography, British Domestic Life, figure drawings by British artists of the twentieth century and it also houses the Iliffe collection of Sutherland sketches for the great Cathedral tapestry.

LUNT ROMAN FORT, Coventry

MUSEUM AND ART GALLERY, Lichfield Street, Walsall (Walsall Metropolitan Borough Council)
Garman-Ryan collection of fine art, antiquities and ethnographical material. Local history material including Sister Dora, Loriners and Jerome K. Jerome collections. Museum of Leathercraft. Lock collections (at Willenhall). Regular loan exhibitions from national, regional and local sources.

THE MUSEUM OF LEATHERCRAFT, Central Library and Art Gallery, Lichfield Street, Walsall
'Leather in Life' permanent exhibition.

SAREHOLE MILL, Cole Bank Road, Hall Green, Birmingham
An 18th-century water-powered corn mill also used by Matthew Boulton for metal working. The mill was also used for blade grinding and has now been restored to working order.

STOURBRIDGE GLASS COLLECTION, Mary Stevens Park, Stourbridge
Superb collection of local glass. John Northwood II and Benjamin Richardson II Collections.

WEOLEY CASTLE, Alwold Road, Birmingham
Ruins of a fortified manor house dating from the late 13th century. A small museum exhibits finds showing evidence of earlier occupation.

WHITEFRIARS MUSEUM OF LOCAL HISTORY, Coventry

WEST SUSSEX
OUTSTANDING NATURAL BEAUTY
CHICHESTER HARBOUR (part)
SUSSEX DOWNS (part)

HISTORIC HOUSES AND CASTLES
ARUNDEL CASTLE, Arundel (His Grace the Duke of Norfolk)

Ancient castle rebuilt 18th century and altered 1890. Fine portraits and furniture dating from the 15th century.

*CHRIST'S HOSPITAL, Horsham (The Governors of Christ's Hospital)
Painting by Antonio Verrio (circa 1639–1707) 'The Foundation of the Royal Mathematical School of Christ's Hospital'. The canvas (85 ft by 14 ft) hangs in the school dining-hall.

CUCKFIELD PARK, Cuckfield (M. J. Holt Esq)
Elizabethan manor house and gate-house, outstanding screen, fine panelling and ceilings. Large garden, shrubs, rhododendrons.

DANNY, Hurstpierpoint (Mutual Household Association Limited)
Elizabethan E-shaped house, dating from 1593.

GOODWOOD HOUSE, Chichester (1780–1800) (Goodwood Estate Company Limited)
Jacobean House added to by Chambers and Wyatt – stables by Chambers. Excellent Sussex flintwork. Fine collection of pictures. Tapestries. French and English furniture and porcelain. Superb specimen trees in Park and 'High Wood'.

NEWTIMBER PLACE, Newtimber, Nr Hassocks (Mr and Mrs John Clay)
Moated house – Etruscan wall paintings.

PARHAM, Pulborough (Mr and Mrs P. A. Tritton)
Elizabethan house. Important collection Elizabethan, Jacobean and Georgian portraits. Fine furniture and needlework.

PETWORTH HOUSE, Petworth (National Trust)
Rebuilt 1688–96 by the 6th Duke of Somerset. Later reconstruction by Salvin, in large and beautiful deer park, landscaped by Capability Brown and painted by Turner. 13th-century chapel. Important collection of paintings.

ST MARY'S, Bramber (Miss D. H. Ellis)
Fine example of 15th-century timber-framed house. Rare panelling. Collection of handicraft.

TANYARD, Sharpthorne (M. R. Lewinsohn, Esq)
Medieval tannery with 16th- and 17th-century additions. Great oak beams with open fireplaces with bric-a-brac typical of the period. Walled garden in 12 acre grounds.

*'THE THATCHED COTTAGE', Lindfield (Mrs Margaret G. Aldridge)
Close-studded Wealden house perfectly preserved – reputed Henry VII shooting lodge. Small cottage garden.

UPPARK, South Harting, Nr Petersfield (National Trust)
Built by Lord Tankerville 1690. Interior decoration and furnishings unaltered since 18th century. Victorian kitchen with original fittings. Small garden landscaped by Humphrey Repton.

GARDENS

BORDE HILL GARDEN, Haywards Heath
Large garden of great botanical interest and beauty. Rare trees and shrubs; views; borders; woodland walks.

HEASELANDS, Haywards Heath (Ernest Kleinwort, Esq)
Over 20 acres of garden with flowering shrubs and trees; water gardens; woodland; aviary and small collection of waterfowl.

LEONARDSLEE, Horsham (Sir Giles Loder, Bart, VMH)
Extensive spring flowering shrub garden, valley filled with camellias, rhododendrons, lakes.

NYMANS GARDENS, Handcross (National Trust)
Extensive garden, partly enclosed by walls, with exceptional collection of rare trees, shrubs and plants, herbaceous borders, bulbs.

SOUTH LODGE, Lower Beeding (Miss E. Godman)
Flowering trees, shrubs, rhododendrons, and rock garden.
WAKEHURST PLACE GARDEN, Nr Ardingly (National Trust, administered by Royal Botanic Gardens, Kew)
A wealth of exotic plant species including many fine specimens of trees and shrubs. Watercourse linking several ponds and lakes.

MUSEUMS AND GALLERIES

BINGOR ROMAN VILLA COLLECTION, Bingor
4th-century mosaics, Samian and other pottery, jewellery, plaster, hypocaust, etc
CHICHESTER DISTRICT MUSEUM, 29 Little London, Chichester
Local history and archaeology, collections of the Royal Sussex Regiment, special exhibitions.
GUILDHALL MUSEUM, Priory Park, Chichester
Displays illustrating the archaeology of Chichester and the surrounding area.
HORSHAM MUSEUM, Causeway House, Horsham
Housed in a 16th-century gabled building and shows collections of local history, costumes, toys, early bicycles, domestic and rural life, crafts and industries of Sussex.
LITTLEHAMPTON MUSEUM, 12A River Road, Littlehampton (Arun District Council)
Collections of sailing and marine material and objects of local interest including paintings.
THE MARLIPINS MUSEUM, High Street, Shoreham (Sussex Archaeological Trust)
A building dating from the 12th-century, housing collections of ship models, paintings and photographs of the locality, geological specimens, old maps, household articles and coins.
POTTERS MUSEUM OF CURIOSITY, 6 High Street, Arundel (James Cartland, Esq)
Life and works of Victorian naturalist and taxidermist, Walter Potter, and other curiosities.
PRIEST HOUSE, West Hoathly (Sussex Archaeological Society)
15th-century monks' hall converted into a dwellinghouse containing a suitable collection of old furniture, bygones, dolls and embroideries.
*RICHARD COBDEN COLLECTION, Dunford, Midhurst (National Council of YMCAs)
Portraits and library of Richard Cobden and family.
THE ROMAN PALACE, Salthill Road, Fishbourne, Chichester (Sussex Archaeological Trust)
The largest Roman residence yet found in Britain, the only one in true Italian style. Thought to be the palace of the local King Tiberius Claudius Cogidubnus.
WEALD AND DOWNLAND OPEN AIR MUSEUM, Singleton, Chichester
A magnificent 35 acre site used for re-erecting historic buildings from S E England. The museum is also a country park.
WORTHING MUSEUM AND ART GALLERY, Chapel Road, Worthing (Worthing Borough Council)
Archaeology, geology, costume, Sussex bygones and pottery, works of art including early English watercolours, dolls and jewellery.

WEST YORKSHIRE
NATIONAL PARKS PEAK DISTRICT (part)
HISTORIC HOUSES AND CASTLES
*ACKWORTH SCHOOL, Pontefract (Co-educational Boarding School Society of Friends)

Georgian building (1750)—only remaining building of London Foundling Hospital.

BOLLING HALL, Bradford (Bradford Metropolitan Council)
Interesting example of domestic architecture dating from 15th to late 18th century.

BRAMHAM PARK, Wetherby (Mr and Mrs George Lane Fox)
Queen Anne mansion – containing fine furniture, pictures and porcelain – set in magnificent grounds landscaped in the style of Le Nôtre. Still the home of descendants of the original builder Robert Benson, 1st Lord Bingley.

EAST RIDDLESDEN HALL, Keighley (National Trust)
17th-century manor house. Magnificent tithe barn. Small formal garden.

HAREWOOD HOUSE AND BIRD GARDEN (The Earl of Harewood, Leeds)
18th-century house with decoration and furniture by Robert Adam and Thomas Chippendale. Valuable pictures. Park and garden designed by Capability Brown.

HEATH HALL, Nr Wakefield (Mr and Mrs Muir M. Oddie)
18th-century house by Carr of York. Fine carved woodwork and plasterwork by York stuccodors.

LOTHERTON HALL, Abeford (Leeds Metropolitan District Council)
Edwardian house with attractive gardens. Gascoigne collection of pictures and furniture.

MANOR HOUSE, Ilkley (Bradford Metropolitan Council)
Small Tudor manor built on the site of a Roman fort. Exposed Roman wall in grounds.

NOSTELL PRIORY, Wakefield (National Trust)
Built for Sir Rowland Winn by Paine; a wing added in 1766 by Robert Adam. State rooms contain pictures and Chippendale furniture belonging to Lord St Oswald, who gave the house and whose home it remains. Motor cycle museum. Boating on the lake.

OAKWELL HALL, Batley (Kirklees Metropolitan Council)
16th-century period house. Brontë association. Wall earth closet or 'secret passage'. Permanent and loan collections of period furniture. A park and rural museum is being developed.

REDHOUSE, Cleckheaton (Kirklees Metropolitan Council)
Built in 1660 of red brick. Associations with Charlotte Brontë.

SHIBDEN HALL, Halifax (Corporation of Calderdale)
15th-century timber-framed house with 17th-century furniture; 17th-century barn; early argicultural implements; coaches and harnesses.

TEMPLE NEWSAM. Leeds, (Leeds Metropolitan District Council)
Tudor-Jacobean house, birthplace of Lord Darnley, with collection of pictures and furniture.

GARDENS

HARLOW CAR GARDENS, Harrogate (The Northern Horticultural Society)
45 acres of ornamental gardens and woodlands.

PARCEVALL HALL, Wharfdale (Walsingham College Trust)
17th-century farmhouse not open to the general public. Attractive terraces with outstanding views. Natural rock and water gardens, herbaceous borders.

MUSEUMS AND GALLERIES

ABBEY HOUSE MUSEUM, Kirkstall, Leeds (City of Leeds)
A folk museum illustrating the life and work of the people of Yorkshire over

the last 300 years; it houses three full-sized 19th-century streets of houses, shops and workplaces.

ART GALLERY, Market Place, Bately (Kirklees Metropolitan Borough Council)
Permanent collection of paintings and drawings, etc. Temporary loan exhibitions.

ART GALLERY AND MUSEUM, Cartwright Hall, Bradford (Bradford Metropolitan Council)
The permanent collection covers paintings, watercolours, drawings and prints from 17th century onwards, together with a small collection of antique and modern ceramics and sculpture. The collections are particularly strong in early 20th-century British paintings and modern print.

BAGSHAW MUSEUM, Wilton Park,Bately (Kirklees Metropolitan Borough Council)
Local history, archaeology, geology, ethnography and oriental arts, natural history and bygones.

BANKFIELD MUSEUM AND ART GALLERY, Akroyd Park, Halifax, Calderdale (Calderdale Borough Council)
Textile machinery, textiles, costume, archaeology, local history and natural history of the area. The Duke of Wellington's Regimental Museum and the 4th/7th Royal Dragoon Guards Regimental Museum are also at Bankfield.

BRONTË PARSONAGE MUSEUM, Haworth
Bronteana and Bonnell Collection of manuscripts, etc.

CITY ART GALLERY, Leeds (City of Leeds)
Old masters, English watercolours; 19th- and 20th-century British and French paintings; representative modern painting and sculpture. Leeds and Staffordshire pottery. English silver. Study collections and public picture lending scheme.

CITY ART GALLERY, Wendworth Terrace, Wakefield (Wakefield Metropolitan District Council)
Paintings, sculpture, drawings and prints; some old masters; 18th-century English watercolours and drawings. Emphasis on modern school.

CITY MUSEUM, Municipal Buildings, Leeds (City of Leeds)
Collections illustrating nearly every aspect of natural history, ethnography and archaeology. Although their scope is world-wide they particularly concern the Yorkshire region.

CITY MUSEUM, Wood Street, Wakefield (Wakefield Metropolitan District Council)
British 20th-century art and a small collection of 17th- and 18th-century British and Continental paintings and watercolours.

CLIFFE CASTLE ART GALLERY AND MUSEUM, Keighley
Collection of fine and applied art, natural history, archaeology and folk-life material, including reconstructed craft workshops. Frequent temporary exhibitions.

COLNE VALLEY MUSEUM, Cliffe Ash, Golcar, Huddersfield (Colne Valley Museum Trust)
Local history, weaving workshop in a weaver's cottage with living-room of about 1860. A clog-maker's shop lit by gas. Collections of folk-life and industrial history.

DEWSBURY MUSEUM AND ART GALLERY, Crow Nest Park, Dewsbury
History of Dewsbury. British natural history. Travelling art exhibitions and local art.

HEPONSTALL OLD GRAMMAR CHOOL MUSEUM, Hebden Bridge, Calderdale (Hepton Rural District Council)
17th-century stone.

HUDDERSFIELD ART GALLERY, Princess Alexandria Walk, Huddersfield (Kirklees Metropolitan Borough Council)

Oil paintings, watercolours, drawing, prints, sculpture, dating from the mid-19th century.

INDUSTRIAL MUSEUM, Moorside Mills, Moorside Road, Eccleshill, Bradford (Bradford Metropolitan Council)
The complex includes a mill manager's house which will be converted into a Victorian/Edwardian dwelling and a four-storey mill whose collections will have the emphasis on the woollen and worsted industry, but will also include other local industries, transport, etc.

LIBRARY AND MUSEUM, Carlton Street, Castleford (Wakefield Metropolitan District)
Roman objects and artefacts found in Castleford and Castleford pottery and glass.

LIBRARY OF THE THORESBY SOCIETY, 23 Clarendon Road, Leeds
Collection of books, mauscripts, pictures, medals, coins, maps and relics of old Leeds.

SMITH ART GALLERY, Halifax Road, Brighouse, Calderdale (Calderdale Borough Council)
Permanent collection of oil paintings and watercolours, mainly 19th century.

TOLSON MEMORIAL MUSEUM, Wakefield Road, Huddersfield (Kirklees Metropolitan Borough Council)
Geology, natural history, archaeology, folk-life, toys, development of the cloth industry, horsedrawn vehicles.

TONG HALL, Bradford (Bradford Metropolitan Council)
This 18th-century brick hall is situated in Tong Village (south-east of Bradford).

WILTSHIRE

OUTSTANDING NATURAL BEAUTY
COTSWOLDS (part) NORTH WESSEX DOWNS (part)

HISTORIC HOUSES AND CASTLES

AVEBURY MANOR, Nr Marlborough (Lady Knowles)
Mainly 16th century. Fine example of Elizabethan manor. Beautiful decorative ceilings. Formal gardens with topiary work. Rare and unusual animals.

CORSHAM COURT, Chippenham (Lord Methuen ARICS)
Elizabethan (1582) and Georgian (1760-70) house, fine 18th-century furniture. British, Italian and Flemish old masters. Park and gardens laid out by Capability Brown and Humphrey Repton.

GREAT CHALFIELD MANOR, Melksham (National Trust)
15th-century moated manor house.

LACOCK ABBEY, Nr Chippenham (National Trust)
13th-century abbey converted into a house in 1540 with 18th-century 'Gothick' alterations. The medieval cloisters, the brewery and the house are open to the public. Fine trees.

LITTLECOTE, Nr Hungerford (D. S. Wills, Esq)
Historic Tudor manor circa 1490-1520. Moulded plaster ceilings, panelled rooms. Magnificent great hall with unique Cromwellian armoury.

LONGLEAT HOUSE, Warminster (Marquess of Bath)
Important early Renaissance house built 1566–80 with later alterations early 1800s. Lavishly decorated in the Italian Renaissance fashion during the 19th century—the decorated ceilings being a feature of the property. Fine state rooms, furnishings, paintings and books. Restored Victorian kitchens open during summer.

LUCKINGTON COURT, Luckington (Hon Mrs Tevor Horn)
Mainly Queen Anne with magnificent group of ancient buildings. Beautiful mainly formal garden with fine collection of ornamental trees and shrubs.

LYDIARD MANSION, Purton (Borough of Thamesdown)
Dating from medieval times, reconstructed 1743–9. Outstanding mid-Georgian decoration.

MALMESBURY HOUSE, Salisbury (John H. Cordle, MP)
Queen Anne house dating in part from 14th century. Famous for its baroque and rococo plasterwork.

MOMPESSON HOUSE, Salisbury (National Trust)
Fine Queen Anne town house in Salisbury Close. Georgian plasterwork.

THE OLD DEANERY, Salisbury (Trustees of College of Sarum St Michael)
13th-century domestic building.

PHILLIPS HOUSE, Dinton (National Trust)
Classical house built in 1816 by Sir Jeffry Wyatville for the Wyndham family.

PYTHOUSE, Tisbury (Mutual Households Association Limited)
Palladian style Georgian mansion.

STOURHEAD, Stourton, Nr Mere (National Trust)
Celebrated mid-18th century, landscape gardens; fine trees. Palladian house designed in 1722 by Colen Campbell. Thomas Chippendale the Younger furniture.

WARDOUR CASTLE, Tisbury (Governors of Cranborne Chase School)
Magnificent house designed in the Palladian manner by James Paine in 1768. Fine rooms.

WESTWOOD MANOR, Bradford-on-Avon (National Trust)
15th-century manor house altered in the 16th and 17th centuries.

WILTON HOUSE, Salisbury (Earl of Pembroke)
In present form work of Inigo Jones (circa 1650) and later James Wyatt (1810). Notable 'Double Cube'room. Fine paintings. Kent and Chippendale furniture. Spacious lawns, fine cedar trees. Palladian bridge. Exhibition of model soldiers.

GARDENS

BOWOOD GARDENS, Calne (Earl of Shelburne)
100 acre garden containing many exotic trees, 40 acre lake, waterfalls, caves, and Doric temple. Arboretum. Pinetum, rose garden and Italian garden. 60 acres of rhododendrons separate to the gardens.

BROADLEAS, Devizes (Lady Anne Cowdray)
A garden full of rare and interesting plants.

THE COURTS, Holt (National Trust)
Topiary garden with lily pond and arboretum.

MUSEUMS AND GALLERIES

ALEXANDER KEILLER MUSEUM, Avebury (Department of Environment)
Pottery and other objects of the Neolithic and Bronze Ages and later dates from the excavations of Avebury and Windmill Hill.

ATHELSTAN MUSEUM, Cross Hayes, Malmesbury
Articles concerned with the town; coins, household articles and an old fire engine.

BOROUGH OF THAMESDOWN MUSEUMS AND ART GALLERY, Swindon
GREAT WESTERN RAILWAY MUSEUM, Faringdon Road
Historic GWR locomotives, wide range of nameplates, models, illustrations, posters, tickets, etc.

LYDIARD PARK, Lydiard Tregoze
Fine Georgian mansion set in a pleasant park, together with the adjoining parish church of St Mary, which contains fascinating memorials to the St John family. Permanent and travelling exhibitions.

MUSEUM AND ART GALLERY, Bath Road
Archaeology, natural history and geology of Wiltshire; local bygones, coins and tokens; the Manners Collection of pot lids and ware. Permanent 20th-century British art collection and travelling exhibitions.

RICHARD JEFFERIES MUSEUM, Coate
Personal items, manuscripts, first editions, etc, relating to Richard Jefferies and Alfred Williams.

DEVIZES MUSEUM, 41 Long Street, Devizes (Wiltshire Archaeological and Natural History Society)
Unique archaeological and geological collections, all concerned with Wiltshire, including Sir Richard Colt-Hoare's Stourhead Collection of prehistoric material.

*LACKHAM COLLEGE OF AGRICULTURE, Lacock
Agricultural implements and tools.

SALISBURY AND SOUTH WILTSHIRE MUSEUM, St Ann Street, Salisbury
Collection illustrate the natural and social history of Salisbury and South Wiltshire in all periods. Models of Stonehenge and Old Sarum. Local guild and craft relics, pottery and costumes.

SCOTLAND

There are no national parks or officially designated areas of outstanding national beauty in Scotland, though many areas, including almost the whole of the Highlands, are regarded as such.

BORDER REGION
HISTORIC HOUSES AND CASTLES

ABBOTSFORD HOUSE, Melrose (Mrs P. Maxwell-Scott)
The home of Sir Walter Scott, containing many historical relics collected by him.
BOWHILL HOUSE, Nr Selkirk (His Grace the Duke of Buccleuch)
For many generations the Border home of the Scotts of Buccleuch. The house contains an outstanding collection of pictures, porcelain and furniture.
MELLERSTAIN, Gordon (Lord Binning)
Scotland's famous Adam mansion. Beautifully decorated and furnished interiors. Italian gardens and lake.
TRAQUAIR HOUSE, Innerleithen (P. Maxwell Stuart, Esq)
Historic mansion. Oldest inhabited house in Scotland. Rich in associations with Mary, Queen of Scots and the Jacobite risings.

GARDENS

DAWYCK HOUSE GARDENS, Stobo (Lt-Col A. N. Balfour of Dawyck)
Woodland garden with rare trees and shrubs in beautiful country by river Tweed. Narcissus in season – arboretum.

MUSEUMS AND GALLERIES

HAWICK MUSEUM AND ART GALLERY, Wilton Lodge Park, Hawick
Geological sections, natural history, coins, medals and church tokens. Local history and a hosiery machinery section.
CHAMBERS INSTITUTION, High Street, Peebles
Flora, fauna, geological specimens and exhibits connected with local history.
MARY, QUEEN OF SCOTS' HOUSE, Queen Street, Jedburgh (Roxburgh District Council)
Contains articles dealing with the life of Mary, Queen of Scots; paintings and engravings.
MELROSE ABBEY MUSEUM, Melrose (Secretary of State for Scotland)
The Commendator's house has been fitted up to form an attractive Museum containing architectural and sculptural detail and other items associated with the abbey.
SELKIRK MUSEUM, Ettrick Terrace, Selkirk
Collection of items relating to Mungo Park, Explorer; James Hogg, Ettrick Shepherd, J. B. Selkirk; and of local crafts.

CENTRAL REGION
HISTORIC HOUSES AND CASTLES

THE HOUSE OF THE BINNS, By Linlithgow (National Trust for Scotland (1944) and Mrs Dalyell of the Binns)
Fine plaster ceilings. Interesting pictures. Panoramic viewpoint.
DOUNE CASTLE, Doune (Earl of Moray)
Built 14th century and used as a royal palace. Restored in 1883 and is now one of the best preserved medieval castles in Scotland.
LINLITHGOW PALACE, Linlithgow (Secretary of State for Scotland)
Birthplace of Mary, Queen of Scots.
MENSTRIE CASTLE (Clackmannan District Council (Central) and the National Trust for Scotland)
Birthplace of Sir William Alexander who became James VI's lieutenant for the Plantation of Nova Scotia. Commemoration rooms only open to the public.
STIRLING CASTLE, Stirling (Secretary of State for Scotland)
Royal castle on a great basalt rock.

GARDENS

DOUNE PARK GARDENS, Doune (Earl of Moray)
Garden originally laid out early 19th century by the Earl of Moray. Walled garden, herbaceous borders, rose garden, flowering shrubs, rhododendrons, azaleas and rare exotic conifers. Woodland walks.

MUSEUMS AND GALLERIES

FALKIRK MUSEUM, 15 Orchard Street, Falkirk
Local and natural history
SMITH ART GALLERY AND MUSEUM, Albert Place, Stirling.

DUMFRIES AND GALLOWAY REGION
HISTORIC HOUSES AND CASTLES

CARLYLE'S BIRTHPLACE, Ecclefechan (National Trust for Scotland)
Thomas Carlyle was born here in 1795. Mementoes and manuscripts.
DRUMLANRIG CASTLE, Nr Thornhill (Buccleuch Estates)
Late 17th-century Scottish architecture in local pink sandstone set in parkland. Lous XIV furniture and fine paintings.
RAMMERSCALES, Lockerbie (A. M. Bell Macdonald)
Georgian manor house dated 1760 set on high ground with fine views over Annandale.

GARDENS

KINMOUNT GARDENS, Kinmount, Annan (Hoddom and Kinmount Estates)
Rock garden and woodland walks. Signed walks.
THREAVE GARDENS, Dumfries and Galloway (National Trust for Scotland)
The Trust's school of practical gardening.

MUSEUMS AND GALLERIES

ANNAN MUSEUM, Moat House, Annan (Burgh of Annan)
Natural history, archaeological, historical. Local shipping section. Thomas Carlyle and Dr Arnott material. Original Bruce Motte of 1124 in the garden.

CASTLE DOUGLAS ART GALLERY, Castle Douglas
Permanent collection of paintings by Ethel S. G. Paterson. Temporary exhibitions.

DUMFRIES MUSEUM, The Observatory, Corberry Hill, Dumfries
Natural history, archaeological and folk collections. Branch: Old Bridge House Museum, Old Bridge Street. A 17th-century house with 6 period and historic rooms.

WIGTOWN COUNTY MUSEUM, The County Library, London Road, Stranraer
Collection of local interest.

WHITHORN PRIORY MUSEUM, Whithorn Priory, Whithorn (Secretary of State for Scotland)
Early Christian monuments including the Latinus stone, dating from 5th century and the St. Peter stone, showing a late form of the Christogram or Chi-Rho monogram.

FIFE REGION

HISTORIC HOUSES AND CASTLES

CULROSS, Fife (National Trust for Scotland)
Outstanding survival Scottish 17th-century burgh architecture. carefully restored to 20th-century living standards.

CULROSS PALACE, Fife (Secretary of State for Scotland)
Built between 1597 and 1611. Contains very fine series of paintings on wooden walls and ceilings.

FALKLAND PALACE, Fife (Her Majesty the Queen, Hereditary Constable, Capt & Keeper; Major M. Crichton Stuart, MC, JP, DL, Deputy Keeper; National Trust for Scotland)
Attractive 16th-century royal pleasance, gardens now laid out to the original royal plans.

HILL OF TARVIT, Fife (National Trust for Scotland)
Mansion house built 1696, remodelled 1906. Collection of furniture, tapestries, porcelain and paintings. Part let as convalescent home.

KELLIE CASTLE, Fife (National Trust for Scotland)
Fine example of 16th to 17th-century domestic architecture of lowland counties of Scotland.

MUSEUMS AND GALLERIES

ANDREW CARNEGIE BIRTHPLACE, Junction of Moodie Street and Priory Lane, Dunfermline
The weaver's cottage where the great philanthropist was born and the memorial hall with new displays covering the life of Andrew Carnegie and the work of the trusts he established.

BROUGHTON HOUSE, Kirkcudbright (Trustees of the late E. A. Hornel)
A large reference library with a valuable Burns collection. Pictures by Hornel and other artists. Valuable furniture and other works of art. Magnificent garden.

DUNFERMLINE MUSEUM, Viewfield, Dunfermline
Local history and natural history of the region: occasional art and travelling exhibitions.

DUNIMARLE MUSEUM, Culross
Napoleonic furniture, oil paintings, library, ceramics, glass, silver and objects d'art.

INDUSTRIAL AND SOCIAL HISTORY MUSEUM, Forth House, Kirkcaldy
Display relative to Fife industries, including linoleum, coal. Collection of house-drawn vehicles.

MUSEUM AND ART GALLERY, War Memorial Grounds, Kirkcaldy
Archaeological, historical, maritime, earth and natural sciences, and decorative art collections. Art gallery contains important collection of 19th- and 20th-century Scottish and English paintings.

PITTENCRIEFF HOUSE, Pittencrieff Park, Dunfermline
Costume collection, circa 1800 to present day; travelling and temporary art exhibitions etc; visitor centre and craft shop.

ST ANDREWS CATHEDRAL MUSEUM, St Andrews Cathedral and Priory, St Andrews (Secretary of State for Scotland)
Collection of early Christian and medieval monuments, also pottery, glass work and other relics discovered on the site.

THE SCOTTISH FISHERIES MUSEUM, St Ayles, Harbourhead, Anstruther (Scottish Fisheries Museum Trust Limited)
Architectural Heritage Year Award winner housing marine aquarium, fishing and ships' gear, model fishing boats, period fisher-home interiors, reference library.

THE STEWARTRY MUSEUM, Kirkcudbright
Regional museum depicting the history and culture of Galloway.

GRAMPIAN REGION
HISTORIC HOUSES AND CASTLES

BRAEMAR CASTLE, Braemar (Captain A. A. Farquharson of Invercauld)
Romantic 17th-century castle, originally of the Earls of Mar of architectural and historical interest.

CRAIGIEVAR CASTLE, Lumphanan (National Trust for Scotland)
Exceptional tower house, structurally unchanged since its completion in 1626.

CRATHES CASTLE, Banchory (National Trust for Scotland)
Fine 16th-century baronial castle. Remarkable early painted ceilings. Beautiful gardens.

DRUMINNOR CASTLE, Rhynie (Miss Joan Wright)
15th-century castle and museum. Stronghold of the Clan Forbes. Built 1440, restored in 1966.

DUNNOTTAR CASTLE, Nr Stonehaven (Dunnottar Trust)
An impressive ruined fortress 160ft above sea. Stronghold of Earls Marischal of Scotland.

HADDO HOUSE, Nr Methlick (Marchioness of Aberdeen)
Georgian house built in 1732 by William Adam. Home of the Gordons of Haddo for over 500 years. Terraced gardens.

LEITH HALL, Kennethmont (National Trust for Scotland)
Home of the Leith family since 1650. Jacobite relics. Charming gardens.

MUCHALLS CASTLE, Stonehaven (Mr and Mrs Maurice A. Simpson)
Early 17th century. Elaborate plasterwork ceilings and fireplaces. Built by Burnetts of Leys, 1619.

PROVOST ROSS'S HOUSE, Aberdeen (National Trust for Scotland)
One of the oldest surviving houses in Aberdeen.

TOWIE BARCLAY CASTLE, Nr Auchterless (Marc Ellington, Esq)
Recently restored, the rib and grain vaulted great hall and gallery provide the finest

example in Scotland. In 1639 the first shot of the Civil War was fired here. Stronghold of the Barclay Clan from 1136.

GARDENS

BALMORAL CASTLE, Nr Ballater (Her Majesty the Queen)
Grounds only open.

KILDRUMMY CASTLE GARDEN, Donside (Kildrummy Castle Garden Trust)
10 acre garden with shrubs, heaths, gentians, rhododendrons, lilies, etc. Alpine and water garden dominated by ruins of 13th-century castle.

PITMEDDEN, Udny (National Trust for Scotland 1952)
Reconstructed 17th-century garden. Fountains.

MUSEUMS AND GALLERIES

ABERDEEN ART GALLERY & MUSEUM, Schoolhill, Aberdeen (Aberdeen District Council)
Permanent collection of oil paintings, watercolours, drawings, prints and sculpture. Collection of applied arts. Special exhibitions. Museum of North-East of Scotland (Maritime).

ARBUTHNOT MUSEUM, St Peter Street, Peterhead (Peterhead Town Council)
Collection illustrating local history; whaling and Arctic section; coins.

ABERDEEN UNIVERSITY ANTHROPOLOGICAL MUSEUM. Aberdeen
General archaeological and ethnographical museum with classical, Oriental, Egyptian, American and Pacific collections. Local antiquities and skeletal remains of the Short Stone Cist (Beaker) people.

ABERDEEN UNIVERSITY, NATURAL HISTORY MUSEUM, Tillydrone Avenue, Aberdeen
Zoology Department—teaching and study collections of natural history.

INVERURIE MUSEUM, Public Library Building, Inverurie
Collection of prehistoric material from locality. Small geological and natural history collections. Bygones.

JAMES DUN'S HOUSE, 61 Schoolhill, Aberdeen (Aberdeen District Council)
18th-century house renovated for use as a children's museum with permanent display and changing exhibitions.

PROVOST SKENE'S HOUSE, Guestrow, City Centre, Aberdeen (Aberdeen District Council)
17th-century house, restored and maintained as a museum of local history and domestic life.

SCHOOLS MUSEUM SERVICE CENTRE, Banff (Banff-Buchan District Council)
Antiquities, local and natural history. James Ferguson relics.

HIGHLAND REGION
HISTORIC CASTLES AND GARDENS

DUNROBIN CASTLE, Golspie (Countess of Sutherland)
Wide variety of furniture, paintings, plate and other exhibits. Museum: unique exhibits of local and general interest. Trophies of the chase. Gardens by Barry.

DUNVEGAN CASTLE, Isle of Skye (John MacLeod of MacLeod)
Dating from the 13th century and continuously inhabited by the Chiefs of MacLeod. Fairy flag.

EILEAN DONAN CASTLE, Wester Ross (J. D. H. MacRae, Esq)
13th-century castle. Jacobite relics—mostly with Clan connections.

HUGH MILLER'S COTTAGE, Cromarty (National Trust for Scotland)

Birthplace (10 October 1802) of Hugh Miller, stonemason, who became eminent geologist, editor and writer. Thatched cottage dates from 1650, contains small museum.

GARDENS

INVEREWE, Poolewe, Wester Ross (National Trust for Scotland)
Remarkable garden created by the late Osgood Mackenzie. Rare and sub-tropical plants.

MUSEUMS AND GALLERIES

CARNEGIE LIBRARY AND MUSEUM, Wick
Collection comprise local antiquities and natural history specimens.

CLAN MACPHERSON HOUSE AND MUSEUM, South end of village, Newtonmore (Clan Macpherson Association)
Clan relics and memorials, including Black Chanter, Green Banner, Charmed Sword, etc.

ELGIN MUSEUM, 1 High Street, Elgin (The Elgin Society)
Varied collection including unique fossils, Pictish stones, local bygones.

THE FALCONER MUSEUM
Fossils, arrowheads, etc, from Culbin sands. Foreign articles.

THE HIGHLAND FOLK MUSEUM, Kingussie
A comprehensive collection of old Highland things including examples of craft work and tools, household plenishings, tartan, etc. In the grounds there is a furnished cottage with a mill and a farming shed.

INVERNESS MUSEUM AND ART GALLERY, Castle Wynd, Inverness
Highland and Jacobite collection.

THURSO MUSEUM, The library, Thurso
Zoological, geological and botanical collections. The Dick Collection of plants and mosses.

THE WEST HIGHLAND MUSEUM, Cameron Square, Fort William
Historical, natural history and folk exhibits. Local relics and large Jacobite and Tartan section. Processing of Aluminium. Exhibition—'Prince Charles Edward and the '45 Rising'.

LOTHIAN REGION

HISTORIC HOUSES AND CASTLES

No 7 CHARLOTTE SQUARE, Edinburgh (National Trust for Scotland)
The north side of Charlotte Square is classed as Robert Adam's masterpiece of urban architecture. The main floors of No 7 are open as a typical Georgian house and as a centre for cultural and conservation activities.

DIRLETON CASTLE AND GARDEN, Dirleton (Secretary of State for Scotland)
Well preserved 13th-century castle, attractive gardens.

EDINBURGH CASTLE (Crown Property)
Ancient fortress of great importance. St Margaret's Chapel has Norman features.

GLADSTONE'S LAND, Edinburgh (National Trust for Scotland)
Built 1620, later occupied by Thomas Gladstone. Remarkable painted wooden ceilings.

*HAMILTON HOUSE, Prestonpans (National Trust for Scotland)
Built in 1628 by John Hamilton, a prosperous Edinburgh burgess.

HOPETOUN HOUSE, South Queensferry (The Marquess of Linlithgow)
Fine example of 18th-century Adam architecture. Magnificent reception rooms,

pictures. Deer parks. Grounds laid out on the lines of Versailles.
LAMB'S HOUSE, Leith (National Trust for Scotland)
Residence and warehouse of prosperous merchant of late 16th or early 17th
century. Renovated 18th century. Now old peoples' day centre.
LAURISTON CASTLE, Edinburgh (City of Edinburgh District Council)
Associated with John Law (1671–1729) founder of the first bank in France.
*LUFFNESS CASTLE, Aberlady (Col and Mrs Hope of Luffness)
16th-century castle with 13th-century keep – dry moat and old fortifications. Built
on the site of a Norse raiders camp.
PALACE OF HOLYROOD HOUSE (Royal Palace)
Official residence of Her Majesty the Queen when in Scotland. Largely recon-
structed by Charles II. Relics of Mary, Queen of Scots.
PRESTON MILL, Lothian Region (National Trust for Scotland)
One of the few of its kind still working, and only survivor of many on the banks
of the Tyne. Popular with artists. Renovated machinery.
WINTON HOUSE, Pencaitland (Sir David Ogilvy, Bart)
Rebuilt 1620 – famous twisted stone chimneys and beautiful plaster ceilings in
honour of Charles I's visit. Enlarged 1800. Fine pictures and furniture. Terraced
gardens.

GARDENS

DALKEITH PARK, Nr Edinburgh (Buccleuch Estates)
Woodland walks beside river in extensive grounds of Dalkeith Palace. Tunnel
walk, 18th-century bridge and orangery. Nature trail.
INVERESK LODGE, Inveresk (National Trust for Scotland)
New garden, with large selection of plants.
MALLENY GARDEN, Balerno (National Trust for Scotland)
A delightfully personal garden with a particularly good collection of shrub roses.
ROYAL BOTANIC GARDEN, Edinburgh (Department of Agriculture and Fisheries for
Scotland)
Founded 17th century. Beautiful rock garden. Exhibition plant houses.

MUSEUMS AND GALLERIES

ART CENTRE, Regent Road, Edinburgh (City of Edinburgh)
The historic building by Thomas Hamilton houses the City's permanent collection
of Scottish painting and sculpture. Frequent temporary exhibitions.
BURGH MUSEUM, Burgh Chambers, High Street, South Queensferry (Town Council)
Manuscripts, prints, photographs, exhibits illustrative of local social history.
CANONGATE TOLBOOTH, Canongate, Edinburgh (City of Edinburgh)
Was burgh courthouse and prison for more than 300 years. Collection of
Highland dress and tartan, with occasional exhibitions.
FRUIT MARKET GALLERY, 29 Market Street, Edinburgh
Changing programme of exhibitions of contemporary artists.
HUNTLY HOUSE, 142 Canongate, Edinburgh (City of Edinburgh)
Local history and topography; important collection of Edinburgh silver, glass and
Scottish pottery. Reconstruction of an old Scots kitchen. Original copy of the
'National Covenant' of 1638. Also personal collection of Field Marshal Earl Haig.
LADY STAIR'S HOUSE, Lady Stair's Close, Lawnmarket, Edinburgh (City of
Edinburgh)
A reconstructed town house, dating from 1622. Relics connected with Robert

Burns, Sir Walter Scott and R. L. Stevenson.

LAURISTON CASTLE, Cramond Road South, Edinburgh (Trust–City of Edinburgh) 16th-century with 19th-century additions. Period furniture, tapestries, Blue-John Wool Mosaics.

MUSEUM OF CHILDHOOD, 38 High Street, Edinburgh (City of Edinburgh) Covers all aspects of childhood; games, toys, books, costume, health and education.

NATIONAL GALLERY OF SCOTLAND, The Mound, Edinburgh Comprising both Scotland's national collection of European paintings, sculpture, drawings and prints from the 14th to the 19th century and the national collection of Scottish art up to 1900.

NATIONAL MUSEUM OF ANTIQUITIES OF SCOTLAND, Queen Street, Edinburgh Collections cover the whole of Scotland from the Stone Age to recent times; notably those of prehistoric and Roman objects, sculptured stones, relics of the Celtic Church, Scottish coins and medals, Stuart relics, Highland weapons, domestic life; also reference library; agricultural and crafts section and costume inaccessible except by appointment.

NORTH BERWICK MUSEUM, School Road, North Berwick Archaeology, history and natural history.

QUEENSFERRY MUSEUM, Edinburgh (City of Edinburgh) Situated between the two Forth bridges in the Council Chambers of the former Royal Burgh of Queensferry. Local history collection.

ROYAL SCOTTISH ACADEMY, Junction of The Mound with Princes Street, Edinburgh Changing exhibitions.

ROYAL SCOTTISH MUSEUM, Chambers Street, Edinburgh (National Institution administered by the Scottish Education Department) Houses the national collections of decorative arts of the world, archaeology, ethnography, natural history, geology, technology and science. Displays range from primitive art to space material, from ceramics to fossils, from birds to working models in the Hall of Power. Items of importance in all fields. Main hall of architectural interest. Temporary exhibitions. Lectures, gallery talks, films.

RUSSELL COLLECTION OF HARPSICHORDS AND CLAVICHORDS, St Cecilia's Hall, Niddry Street, Cowgate, Edinburgh (University of Edinburgh) 36 keyboard instruments, including harpsichords, clavichords, fortepianos, regals, spinets, virginals and chamber organs. Pictures. Tapestries and textiles.

SCOTTISH ARTS COUNCIL, 19 Charlotte Square, Edinburgh Changing programme of exhibitions.

SCOTTISH NATIONAL GALLERY OF MODERN ART, Royal Botanic Garden, Edinburgh The Gallery houses the 20th-century collection of the National Galleries of Scotland.

SCOTTISH NATIONAL PORTRAIT GALLERY, Queen Street, Edinburgh Portraits of famous Scottish men and women from the 16th century to modern times; a reference section of over 20,000 engraved portraits and a large collection of photographs of Scottish portraits.

SCOTTISH UNITED SERVICES MUSEUM, Crown Square, Edinburgh Castle (Secretary of State for Scotland) Illustrates by its display of uniforms, headdress, arms and equipment, medals, portraits and models, the history of the armed forces of Scotland. Extensive library and comprehensive collection of prints and uniforms.

STRATHCLYDE REGION

HISTORIC HOUSES AND CASTLES

*BACHELORS' CLUB, Tarbolton (National Trust for Scotland)
17th-century thatched house where Burns and his friends formed their club in 1780.
Period furnishings.

BRODICK CASTLE, Isle of Arran (National Trust for Scotland)
Historic home of the Dukes of Hamilton. The castle dates in part from the 14th
century, furniture, objects d'art.

BURNS COTTAGE, Alloway (Trustees of Burns Monument)
Thatched cottage in which Robert Burns was born, 1759. Museum with Burns'
relics.

CAMERON HOUSE, Alexandria (Patrick Telfer Smollett)
Includes the family literary Museum devoted to the celebrated 18th-century
novelist and historian, Tobias Smollett. Also has fine furniture, porcelain, glass, a
unique 'Whisky Galore' room, model aircraft display. Victorian nursery, etc.
Extensive gardens landscaped by Lanning Roper.

CULZEAN CASTLE, Maybole (National Trust for Scotland)
One of the finest Adam houses in Scotland. Spacious policies and gardens.

INVERARAY CASTLE, Inveraray (His Grace the Duke of Argyll)
Since the 15th century the headquarters of the Clan Campbell. Present castle built
18th century by Robert Morris and Robert Mylne.

POLLOK HOUSE AND PARK, Glasgow (City of Glasgow and District Council)
Designed by William Adam, built 1747–52. Contains Stirling Maxwell collection
of Spanish and other paintings and displays of European decorative arts especially
Spanish glass. Special features of the park include rhododendron walk and the
Royal National Rose Society trial garden. Extensive woodland and walks.

PROVAN HALL, Glasgow (National Trust for Scotland)
Fine 15th-century mansion.

PROVAND'S LORDSHIP, Glasgow (Provand's Lordship Society)
Oldest house in Glasgow, built 1471.

ROSSDHU, Luss (Sir Ivar Colquhoun of Luss Bart, DL JP)
The historic home of the Chiefs of Clan Colquhoun, built in the 18th century
near the site of the original 15th-century castle on the banks of Loch Lomond.

SOUTER JOHNNIE'S COTTAGE, Kirkoswald (National Trust for Scotland)
Thatched home of the original Souter in Burns' 'Tam o' Shanter'. Burns' relics.

WEAVER'S COTTAGE, Kilbarchan (National Trust for Scotland)
Typical cottage of the 18th-century handloom weaver; looms, weaving equipment,
domestic utensils.

GARDENS

ACHAMORE, Isle of Gigha (D. W. N. Landale Esq)
Extensive gardens. Roses, hydrangeas, rhododendrons, azaleas, camellias and
other shrubs.

BELLAHOUSTON PARK (City of Glasgow District Council)
175 acres. Sunk, wall and rock gardens. Wildlife. Dry ski-slope. Athletic and
indoor sports centre.

BENMORE (Younger Botanic Garden) (Secretary of State for Scotland)
A woodland garden on a grand scale.

BOTANIC GARDENS, Glasgow (City of Glasgow District Council)
Covering 43 acres. Plants of unusual species.

GLENAPP CASTLE GARDENS. Ballantrae (Rt Hon The Earl and Countess of Inchcape) Beautiful gardens and grounds with daffodils, rhododendrons, azaleas, flowering shrubs, terraces, lily ponds, herbaceous borders. Woodland walks.

LINN PARK, Glasgow (City of Glasgow District Council) 212 acres pine and deciduous woodlands with enchanting riverside walks. Nature centre. Nature trail and Children's Zoo.

LOCH LOMOND PARK (Dumbarton District Council) 200 acres situated beside Loch Lomond containing many conifers, azaleas and other shrubs. Walled garden. Fairy Glen. Castle, site of old castle and moat. Wildlife, including deer in winter. Natural trail.

ROSS HALL PARK (City of Glasgow District Council) 33 acres. Majestic trees by River Cart. Extensive heather and rock gardens, with water features; nature trails.

ROUKEN GLEN PARK, Glasgow (City of Glasgow District Council) 156 acres. Magnificent trees. Waterfall. Walled garden, alpines and boating pond.

VICTORIA PARK, Glasgow (City of Glasgow District Council) Fossilised tree stumps 300 million years old. 58 acres. Extensive carpet bedding depicting centennial events.

MUSEUMS AND GALLERIES

AIRDRIE PUBLIC MUSEUM, Wellwynd, Airdrie (Burgh of Airdrie) Local historical material; regular programme of exhibitions.

AYR MUSEUM AND ART GALLERY, 12 Main Street, Ayr (Kyle and Carrick District Council) Museum illustrates local history. Art Gallery exhibitions changed monthly.

BURNS' MONUMENT AND MUSEUM, Kay Park, Kilmarnock (Kilmarnock Corporation) Holograph manuscripts dealing with the poet Robert Burns. Burns original first edition McKie Burnsiana.

BUTESHIRE NATURAL HISTORY SOCIETY MUSEUM, Stuart Street, Rothesay Collections of the natural history, archaeology, geology and history of the County of Bute.

CAMPBELTOWN MUSEUM, Campbeltown (Burgh of Campbeltown) Archaeological, geological and natural history of Kintyre.

DICK INSTITUTE MUSEUM, Elmbank Avenue, Kilmarnock Geological ornithological, archaeological and ethnological collections. Walker collection of Scottish basket-hilted swords: Cater collection of small arms; documents of the Boyd family; Incunabula, early Bibles and bibliographical works of Elizabethan period: Children's Museum. Paintings.

GLADSTONE COURT, Biggar Small indoor street of ten shops and workshops, a bank, telephone exchange, school room, and library. Bed used by Cargill the Covenanter in 1861.

GLENCOE AND NORTH LORN FOLK MUSEUM, Glencoe Thatched restored 'Cruck' cottage in Glencoe village. Exhibits include domestic bygones, costume, weapons, Jacobite relics and photographs of local wild flowers.

JOHN HASTIE MUSEUM, Strathaven A local history collection.

THE MCLEAN MUSEUM, 9 Union Street, West End, Greenock Picture gallery and comprehensive natural history, geology and shipping exhibits. Relics of James Watt.

NORTH AYRSHIRE MUSEUM, Kirkgate, Saltcoats

History, industry and life in North Ayrshire.

PAISLEY MUSEUM AND ART GALLERIES, High Street, Paisley (Paisley Corporation)
Paisley shawls; Renfrewshire history, geology and natural history. Arbuthnot
manuscripts; general collections. Gallery of Scottish painters; large collection of
ceramics.

ROBERTSON MUSEUM AND THE AQUARIUM, Marine Station, Millport
The museum and aquarium exhibit marine life found in the Clyde Sea area.

SCOTTISH NATIONAL MEMORIAL TO DAVID LIVINGSTONE, Blantyre
Unique collection of personal relics, tableaux and working models in the house
where the great missionary explorer was born.

TAYSIDE REGION
HISTORIC HOUSES AND CASTLES

BARRIE'S BIRTHPLACE, Kirriemuir (National Trust for Scotland (1937))
Contains mementoes of Sir James Barrie.

BLAIR CASTLE, Blair Atholl (His Grace the Duke of Atholl)
Comyn's Tower built circa 1269. Mansion in Scottish baronial style. Jacobite
relics in Atholl museum.

EDZELL CASTLE AND GARDENS, Edzell (Secretary of State for Scotland)
16th-century castle. Unique renaissance garden.

GLAMIS CASTLE, Glamis (Earl of Strathmore and Kinghorne)
Owes present aspect to 3rd Earl of Strathmore and Kinghorne (1630–95) with
portions much older. Celebrated for legend of secret chamber. Grounds laid out by
Capability Brown.

KELLIE CASTLE, Arbroath (A. Kerr Boyle, Esq)
Built 1170 by William de Mowbray. Restored 1679. Built from pink sandstone
quarried within the 60 acre estate.

SCONE PALACE, Perth (Rt Hon the Earl of Mansfield)
Largely rebuilt in 1803 for the 3rd Earl of Mansfield incorporating parts of the old
1580 palace. Fine collection of French furniture, china, ivories and Vernis Martin
vases and objects d'art.

GARDENS

BRANKLYN GARDEN, Perth (National Trust for Scotland)
One of the finest gardens of its size in Britain (2 acres).

DRUMMOND CASTLE GARDENS (Earl of Ancaster)
Gardens only are open.

MUSEUMS AND GALLERIES

THE ANGUS FOLK MUSEUM, Kirkwynd Cottages, Glamis (National Trust for
Scotland)
Collection of early furnishings, clothing, domestic utensils and agricultural
implements from the former County of Angus.

ARBROATH ABBEY MUSEUM, Arbroath (Secretary of State for Scotland)
A small collection of architectural and other exhibits primarily connected with the
Abbey.

ARBROATH ART GALLERY, Public Library, Hill Terrace, Arbroath (Arbroath Town
Council)

General art collection, emphasis on local artists. Collection of pastels and watercolours by J. W. Herald.

BARRACK STREET MUSEUM, Ward Road, Dundee
Museum of Dundee shipping and industries.

BRECHIN MUSEUM, Mechanics Institute, Brechin (Brechin Town Council)
Local antiquities.

BROUGHTY CASTLE MUSEUM, Broughty Ferry, Dundee
Relics of local and military history. Natural history of the Tay. Whaling gallery.

CAMPERDOWN HOUSE MUSEUM, Camperdown Park, Dundee

CITY OF GLASGOW MUSEUMS AND ART GALLERIES

ART GALLERY AND MUSEUM, Kelvingrove
Extensive collection of old master paintings. 4 galleries of British paintings from the 16th century to the present day and a gallery of 19th-century French paintings which includes all the great names. European and Oriental Art objects including silver, porcelain, glass, bronzes and costume.

ARCHAEOLOGY AND HISTORY: Neolithic, Bronze Age, and Roman material now shown in Archaeology Gallery; items from Egyptian, Greek and Cypriot Collections; Scottish bygones.

ARMOUR: The Scott Collection of Arms and Armour. The Whitelaw collection of Scottish Arms.

BURRELL COLLECTION: Tapestries, furniture, porcelain, stained glass, silver and other art objects; contains outstanding treasures of Gothic art. Collection of pictures with special emphasis on 19th century French.

ETHNOGRAPHY: Implements, clothing, weapons, religious and ceremonial objects relating to primitive and civilised societies.

NATURAL HISTORY: A series of large groups showing animals of Scotland, Polar Regions, Africa, India and Australia; The British Bird Gallery; Geology Gallery; and general Zoological Gallery.

TECHNOLOGY: Engineering exhibits and a collection of ship models.

DUNBLANE CATHEDRAL MUSEUM, The Cross, Dunblane (Society of Friends of Dunblane Cathedral)
Large collection of pictures of Cathedral before restoration. Very large collection of Communion tokens. Collection of reproductions of Bishops' seals. Leightoniania, medieval carving, library, archives room, local history.

DUNDEE MUSEUM AND ART GALLERIES, Albert Square, Dundee
Regional collection of archaeological, historical, natural history, botanical and geological material. Flemish, Dutch, French and British paintings particularly Scottish schools.

GLENESK MUSEUM, The Retreat, Glenesk
Presents the local scene with emphasis on the immediate past. General display with available historical records; examples of farming and trades, domestic interiors, costumes, music and children's interests. Sound recently installed.

HAGGS CASTLE, 100 St Andrews Drive, Glasgow
A new museum of history for children being developed with work space for children's activities.

THE HUNTERIAN MUSEUM, Glasgow University, Glasgow
Collections include geological, archaeological, historical and ethnographical material; the Hunterian coin cabinet; books and manuscripts; and the fine art collection of the University.

THE MEFFAN INSTITUTE MUSEUM, Forfar
Collections of archaeological, historical, geological and natural history material.

MEIGLE MUSEUM, Meigle (Secretary of State for Scotland)

25 sculptured monuments of the Celtic Christian period. An outstanding collection of Dark Age sculpture.

MUSEUM OF COSTUME, Aikenhead House, King's Park, Glasgow

MUSEUM OF TRANSPORT, 25 Albert Drive, Glasgow

Examples of land transport. 7 Glasgow tramcars from 1894 horsedrawn to electric 1952. Many veteran and vintage cars with emphasis on Scottish motor production up to present day. Passenger and commercial horsedrawn vehicles. The development of the bicycle. Railway locomotives. Model railway.

MONTROSE MUSEUM, Panmure Place, Montrose (Montrose Natural History and Antiquarian Society)

Regional collection of archaeological, historical, natural history and geological exhibits, including sculptured stones and collection of Scottish coins and medals. Reference library founded 1785. Fully modernised.

OLD GLASGOW MUSEUM, People's Palace, Glasgow

Provides a visual record of the rise and development of Glasgow.

ORCHAR ART GALLERY, Broughty Ferry, Dundee

Oil paintings and watercolours mostly by Scottish artists of the 19th century. Etchings including 36 by Whistler.

PERTH ART GALLERY AND MUSEUM, George Street, Perth (Perth and Kinross District Council)

Art collection is mainly of the Scottish School. A fine regional natural history Museum. Ethnographical geological and antiquarian exhibits; tropical aquaria.

POLLOK HOUSE, Pollok Park, Glasgow

House built 1752 designed by William Adam. Contains Stirling Maxwell Collection of paintings.

PROVAND'S LORDSHIP, 3 Castle Street, Glasgow (Provand's Lordship Society)

Mainly of 17th and 18th century; furniture and domestic articles.

ST MARY'S TOWER, Nethergait, Tower of St Mary's Church, Dundee

Site Museum.

ST VIGEANS MUSEUM, Arbroath (Secretary of State for Scotland)

Sculptured monuments of the Celtic Christian period, including the Drosten stone.

THE SIGNAL TOWER MUSEUM, Ladyloan, Arbroath (Angus District Council)

Once the shore base of the Bell Rock Lighthouse, the Signal Tower contains displays which illustrate the history and development of Arbroath and its district, including the building of the famous lighthouse.

TOLLCROSS MUSEUM, Tollcross Park, Glasgow

A children's museum: zoology, pictures and dolls.

WALES

CLWYD
HISTORIC HOUSES AND CASTLES

BODRHYDDAN HALL, Nr Rhyl (Col the Lord Langford)
17th-century manor house of historic interest. Famous portraits, armour, furniture; garden.

CHIRK CASTLE, Nr Wrexham (Lt-Col Ririd and Lady Margaret Myddleton)
Built 1310. Exterior is a unique unaltered example of a border castle of Edward II's time, inhabited continuously for 660 years. Interesting portraits, tapestries, etc. Gardens.

MUSEUMS AND GALLERIES

PLAS NEWYDD MUSEUM, Llangollen (Llangollen Urban District Council)
Black and white house and home from 1780–1831 of the 'Ladies of Llangollen' eccentric blue stockings.

WREXHAM EXHIBITION HALL, Public Library, Wrexham
Various exhibitions normally changed monthly.

DYFED
NATIONAL PARKS

BRECON BEACONS (part)
PEMBROKESHIRE COAST

HISTORIC HOUSES AND CASTLES

CILGERRAN CASTLE, Nr Cardigan (National Trust)
13th-century ruin, an inspiration to many artists, including Turner.

MANORBIER CASTLE, Pembrokeshire
Birthplace of Giraldus Cambrensis. Castle built between the 12th and 14th centuries.

PICTON CASTLE, Haverfordwest (The Hon Hanning and Lady Marion Philipps)
Home of the Philips family since the 12th-century. Shrub and walled gardens.

TUDOR MERCHANT'S HOUSE, Tenby (National Trust)
An example of a merchant's house of the 15th century and National Trust information centre.

GARDENS

CYMERAU, Glandyfl (Major-General Lewis Pugh)
Gardens in superb country with fine panoramic views, rhododendrons, azaleas, unusual shrubs, herbaceous borders.

THE HALL, Angle (Major and Mrs J. N. Allen-Mirehouse)
On banks of Milford Haven: woodland, shrubs, roses, walled garden, greenhouses.

MUSEUMS AND GALLERIES

THE CASTLE MUSEUM AND ART GALLERY, Haverfordwest (Pembrokeshire Museums)
New and developing regional museum with collections of archaeology, folk-life, local industry and works of art. Changing displays and frequent temporary exhibitions.

THE COUNTY MUSEUM, Carmarthen (Carmarthenshire County Council)
Stone Age relics, Romano-British and Ogham inscribed stones. Collection of Roman gold, jewellery and other antiquities.

THE NATIONAL LIBRARY OF WALES, Aberystwyth
Collection of books, manuscripts and records relating to Wales and the Celtic countries, topographical prints, maps, drawings, etc, of historical interest. A copyright library.

PARC HOWARD MUSEUM AND ART GALLERY, Llanelli (Llanelli Corporation)
Collection of Llanelli pottery. Exhibits of Welsh artists. Items of local interest.

PENRHOS. Havefordwest (Pembrokeshire Museums)
Traditional Welsh cottage, furnished. Branch museum and information centre near Preseli Hills.

SCOLTON MANOR COUNTRY PARK MUSEUM, Scolton, Nr Havefordwest (Pembrokeshire Museums)
New regional museum and nature trail, study centre, etc.

TENBY MUSEUM, Castle Hill, Tenby
Collections of local geology, archaeology, history and natural history, maps, pictures and bygones.

UNIVERSITY COLLEGE OF WALES GALLERY, Aberystwyth
Visiting exhibitions of painting and sculpture. Small display of museum art objects, pottery, etc, in gallery. Remainder of collection by appointment.

MID GLAMORGAN

NATIONAL PARKS

BRECON BEACONS (part)

MUSEUMS AND GALLERIES

ART GALLERY AND MUSEUM, Cyfarthfa Castle, Merthyr Tydfil
The collections cover paintings, ceramics, coins and medals, silver and other art objects, natural history and local history. There is a small Welsh kitchen.

GWENT

NATIONAL PARKS

BRECON BEACONS (part)

OUTSTANDING NATURAL BEAUTY

WYE VALLEY (part)

HISTORIC HOUSES AND CASTLES

CHEPSTOW CASTLE, Chepstow (Department of the Environment)
Great Tower dates from late 11th century.
LLANVIHANGEL COURT, Abergavenny (Colonel and Mrs Somerset Hopkinson)
16th-century manor house. Front rebuilt 1559, internally remodelled 1660.
SKENFRITH CASTLE, Nr Monmouth (National Trust)
Norman castle built as defence against the Welsh; a keep stands on the remains
of the motte; 13th-century curtain wall with towers.

MUSEUMS AND GALLERIES

ABERGAVENNY AND DISTRICT MUSEUM, Castle House, Abergavenny (Monmouth
District Council)
Antiquities of town and district. Border farmhouse kitchen, saddler's shop,
archaeology, costumes, postal history, smoking items, playbills and Father Ignatius
relics.
LEGIONARY MUSEUM, Caerleon
A branch archaeological gallery of the National Museum of Wales. Displays of
objects found on the site of the Roman legionary fortress of Isca.
THE MUSEUM, Bridge Street, Chepstow
The Chepstow Society collection of local antiquities, prints and photographs.
NELSON MUSEUM, The Market Hall, Priory Street, Monmouth
Relics of Admiral Lord Nelson, his contemporaries and Lady Hamilton. Local
history centre, archives, exhibits, maps, etc.
NEWPORT MUSEUM AND ART GALLERY, John Frost Square, Newport (Newport
Corporation)
Collections of natural history; art, specialising in Early English watercolours,
Roman remains from Venta Silurum (Caerwent); folk-life including Pontypool
Japan ware. Temporary art exhibitions.
RURAL CRAFTS MUSEUM, Llanvapley
Old agricultural tools, items from the farmhouse kitchen and the implements used
in country crafts such as thatching, smithing, milling, etc.

GWYNEDD
NATIONAL PARKS

SNOWDONIA

OUTSTANDING NATURAL BEAUTY

ANGLESEY LLEYN

HISTORIC HOUSES AND CASTLES

BODYSGALLEN HALL, Llandudno (Mr and Mrs T. Andersen)
Elizabethan house incorporating a medieval tower. Open as a private hotel and
restaurant.

BRYN BRAS CASTLE, Llanrug (Mrs M. Gray-Parry and R. D. Gray-Williams, Esq)
Lawns, woodland walks, stream, waterfalls and pools, mountain walk. Castle built
in 1830s around an earlier structure built before 1750.

CAERNARFON CASTLE (1283–1322) (Department of the Environment)
The most important of Edward I's castles. Museum of the Royal Welsh Fusiliers is
housed in the Queen's Tower.

CONWAY CASTLE (1283–9) (Department of the Environment)
Built by Edward I to command Conway Ferry.

GWYDIR CASTLE, Nr Llanrwst (Richard Clegg, Esq)
Historic royal residence, magnificently furnished Tudor period, beautiful grounds,
over 50 famous peacocks and many tropical birds.

HARLECH CASTLE (Department of the Environment)
Built 1283–9 by Edward I. Concentric plan.

PENRHYN CASTLE, Bangor (National Trust)
The 19th-century castle is a unique and outstanding example of neo-Norman
architecture. The garden and grounds have exotic and rare trees and shrubs.
Industrial railway museum; exhibition of dolls, and a natural history display.
Extensive grounds; Victorian formal garden.

PLAS-YN-RHIW ESTATE (National Trust)
Small manor house, part medieval, with Tudor and Georgian additions;
ornamental gardens. Open permanently: Porth Ysgo, Rhiw, a sheltered cove:
Mynydd-y-graig, Rhiw, rising 800 ft from the sea with a hill fort; Cilan, a
renowned view point; the Porth Orion cliffs at Aberdavon; Foel Fawr Mynytho,
an old windmill on a hill.

GARDENS

BODNANT GARDEN, Tal-y-Cafa (National Trust)
Laid out in 1875 by Henry Pochin. The garden is among the finest in the country.

GILFACH, Roewen, Conway Valley (Miss I. Gee)
Small garden specialising in shrubs.

PLAS NEWYDD, Isle of Anglesey (National Trust)
18th-century house by James Wyatt. Fine spring garden. Rex Whistler's largest
wall painting. Military museum.

PORTMEIRION, Gwyllt Gardens, Cardigan Bay (Sir Clough Williams-Ellis)
Wild gardens and woodlands, famous for rhododendrons, azaleas and sub-tropical
flora.

MUSEUMS AND GALLERIES

BANGOR ART GALLERY AND MUSEUM OF WELSH ANTIQUITIES, Bangor (University
College of North Wales)
Art Gallery: monthly exhibitions of contemporary paintings and sculpture.
Museum: illustrates history of North Wales. Collections of Welsh prehistoric and
Roman antiquities, furniture, domestic objects, textiles and clothing.

FESTINIOG RAILWAY MUSEUM, Harbour Station, Porthmadog (Festiniog Railway
Company)
Museum illustrating the past history and present activity of the Festiniog Railway.

MUSEUM OF CHILDHOOD, Water Street, Menai Bridge
Dolls and educational toys, paintings and needlework, money boxes (savos),
wind-up toys, pottery and glass depicting children and commemoratives and audio
and visual pastimes.

THE NARROW GAUGE RAILWAY MUSEUM, Tywyn (The Narrow Gauge Railway Museum Trust)
Locomotives, rolling stock, and exhibitions illustrating the narrow gauge railways of the British Isles.

NORTH WALES QUARRYING MUSEUM, Llanberis (Administered by the National Museum of Wales in conjunction with the Department of the Environment)
Machinery and equipment associated with the local quarrying industry.

PLAS MAWR, Conwy
Finest example of an Elizabethan town mansion in Wales (1550–80). Headquarters of the Royal Cambrian Academy of Art. Exhibitions of art.

RAPALLO HOUSE MUSEUM AND ART GALLERY, Fferm Bach Craig-Y-Don, Llandudno
Collections of prints, watercolour drawings, pastels and oil-paintings; porcelain, sculpture and bronzes; armour and weapons, Roman relics and a Welsh kitchen. Ornamental and secluded garden.

SEGONTIUM ROMAN FORT MUSEUM, Caernarvon (Administered by the National Museum of Wales in conjunction with the Department of the Environment)
The museum is on the site of the fort and contains mostly material excavated there.

POWYS
NATIONAL PARKS

BRECON BEACONS (part)

HISTORIC HOUSES AND CASTLES

POWIS CASTLE, Welshpool (National Trust)
General aspect of 13th to 14th-century castle, although reconstructed in early 17th century. Fine plasterwork, murals, furniture, paintings and tapestry. Historic terraced garden; herbaceous borders, rare trees and shrubs.

TRETOWER COURT AND CASTLE, Crickhowell (Department of the Environment)
One of the finest medieval houses in Wales.

MUSEUMS AND GALLERIES

BRECKNOCK MUSEUM, Brecon (Powys County Council)
Local and natural history of Brecknock. Archaeology, agriculture, domestic material, pottery, porcelain and lovespoons. Assize Court reconstruction, library and archive collection.

LLANDRINDOD MUSEUM, Temple Street, Llandrindod Wells
Archaeological material mainly from Castell Collen excavations (Roman). Paterson Doll Collection.

MUSEUM OF LOCAL HISTORY AND INDUSTRY, Market Hall, Llanidloes (Powys County Council)
Articles of local interest and industry.

POWYSLAND MUSEUM, Welshpool (Powys County Council)
Material of folk-life, archaeology and historical interest relating to the area.

THE ROBERT OWEN MEMORIAL MUSEUM, Broad Street, Newtown
Numerous books, documents, relics, etc, relating to Robert Owen.

SOUTH GLAMORGAN

HISTORIC HOUSES AND CASTLES

CARDIFF CASTLE (Cardiff City Council)
Begun 1090 on site of Roman Castrum. Rich interior decorations. Location for Cardiff Searchlight Tattoo.
CASTELL COCH, Whitchurch (Department of the Environment)
13th-century castle, restored on original lines for the Marquess of Bute in 19th century and made habitable.
ST FAGAN'S CASTLE, Cardiff (Welsh Folk Museum)
16th-century house built within curtain wall of 13th-century castle. Extensive folk museum.

MUSEUMS AND GALLERIES

THE NATIONAL MUSEUM OF WALES (Amgueddfa Genedlaethol Cymru), Cardiff
Collections and exhibitions in archaeology, art, botany, geology, industry and zoology. The Reardon Smith Lecture Theatre is used for concerts, lectures, and other events arranged by the Museum and is hired by other bodies.
TURNER HOUSE, Penarth (National Museum of Wales)
A branch art gallery of the National Museum of Wales.

WEST GLAMORGAN

OUTSTANDING NATURAL BEAUTY

GOWER

MUSEUMS AND GALLERIES

GLYNN VIVIAN ART GALLERY AND MUSEUM, Alexandra Road, Swansea (Swansea City Council)
British paintings, drawings and sculpture, old and contemporary ceramics including Welsh pottery and porcelain; glass. Loan exhibitions.
INDUSTRIAL MUSEUM OF SOUTH WALES, Victoria Road, Swansea
Industrial relics and displays of local industries covering steel, copper, aluminium, oil, light industries and transport.
ROYAL INSTITUTION OF SOUTH WALES AND UNIVERSITY COLLEGE OF SWANSEA MUSEUM, Victoria Road, Swansea
Collections of antiquarian interest; archaeology; ceramics. Welsh folk culture, ornithology, botany, zoology, geology, art, industry. Library.

APPENDIX 2 A Select List of Conservation and Amenity Societies

This list does not claim to be exhaustive but merely seeks to give the more important national societies.

ADVISORY BOARD FOR REDUNDANT CHURCHES   Fielden House, Little College Street, Westminister, London SW1P 3SH (01-930 1603/4)

ANCIENT MONUMENTS SOCIETY   33 Ladbroke Square, London, W11 3NB (01-221 6178)

ARBORICULTURAL ASSOCIATION   59 Blythwood Gardens, Stanstead, Essex CM24 8HH (027-971 3160)

ASSOCIATION FOR INDUSTRIAL ARCHAEOLOGY, 3 The Wharfage, Ironbridge, Telford, Salop TF8 7RE (095-245 3522)

ASSOCIATION FOR THE PROTECTION OF RURAL SCOTLAND   20 Falkland Avenue, Newton Mearns, Renfrewshire G77 5DR (041-639 2069)

BRITISH ASSOCIATION FOR THE CONTROL OF AIRCRAFT NOISE   30 Fleet Street, London EC4 (Horley 4200)

BRITISH CYCLING BUREAU   Greater London House, Hampstead Road, London NW1 7QX (01-387 6868)

BRITISH ECOLOGICAL SOCIETY   Hon Council Secretary: Dr E. A. G. Duffey, Monks Wood Experimental Station, Abbots Ripton, Huntingdon PE17 2LS (Abbots Ripton 381)
Hon Meetings Secretary: Dr J. A. Lee, Department of Botany, The University, Manchester, M13 9PL (061-273 3333)

BRITISH TOURIST AUTHORITY   64 St James's Street, London SW1A 1NF (01-629 9191)

BRITISH TRUST FOR CONSERVATION VOLUNTEERS   Zoological Gardens, Regent's Park, London NW1 4RY (01-722 7112)

CENTRAL COMMITTEE FOR THE ARCHITECTURAL ADVISORY PANELS   4 Hobart Place, London, SW1W 0HY (01-235 4771)

CENTRAL COUNCIL FOR RIVERS PROTECTION   Fishmongers' Hall, London, EC4R 9EL (01-626 3531)

CENTRAL RIGHTS OF WAY COMMITTEE   Suite 4, 166 Shaftesbury Avenue, London WC2H 8JH (01-836 7220)

CIVIC TRUST   17 Carlton House Terrace, London SW1Y 5AW (01-930 0914)

CIVIC TRUST FOR THE NORTH EAST   34–5 Saddler Street, Durham (0385 61182)

CIVIC TRUST FOR THE NORTH WEST   56 Oxford Street, Manchester M1 6EU (061-236 7467)

CIVIC TRUST FOR WALES/TREFTADAETH CYMRU   c/o Wales Tourist Board, Welcome House, Llandaff, Cardiff CF5 2YZ (0222 567701)

CLEAN AIR COUNCIL Department of the Environment, Queen Anne's Chambers, 28 Broadway, SW1H 9JU (01-930 4300 Ext 396)

CLEAN AIR COUNCIL FOR SCOTLAND Scottish Development Department, Government Buildings, Pentland House, 47 Robb Loan, Edinburgh (031-443 8661)

COMMISSION FOR THE NEW TOWNS Glen House, Stag Place, London SW1E 5AJ (01-834 8034)

COMMITTEE FOR ENVIRONMENTAL CONSERVATION (COENCO) 29-31 Greville, London EC1N 8AX (01-242 9647)

COMMONS, OPEN SPACES AND FOOTPATHS PRESERVATION SOCIETY Suite 4, 166 Shaftesbury Avenue, London WC2H 8JH (01-836 7220)

CONFERENCE ON TRAINING ARCHITECTS IN CONSERVATION (COTAC) Hon Secretary: 19 West Eaton Place, London SW1X 8LT (01-245 9888)

CONSERVATION SOCIETY 34 Bridge Street, Walton-on-Thames, Surrey KT12 1AJ (Walton-on-Thames 41793)

COUNCIL FOR BRITISH ARCHAEOLOGY 8 St Andrew's Place, Regent's Park, London NW1 4LB (01-486 1527)

COUNCIL FOR NATURE Zoological Gardens, Regent's Park, London NW1 4RY (01-722 7111)

COUNCIL FOR PLACES OF WORSHIP 83 London Wall, London EC2M 5NA (01-638 0971)

COUNCIL FOR SMALL INDUSTRIES IN RURAL AREAS Advisory Services Division, 35 Camp Road, Wimbledon Common, London SW19 4UP (01-946 5101)

COUNCIL FOR THE PROTECTION OF RURAL ENGLAND 4 Hobart Place, London SW1W 0HY (01-235 4771)

COUNCIL FOR THE PROTECTION OF RURAL WALES/CYMDEITHAS DOIGELU HARDDWYCH CYMRU Meifod, Powys, SY22 6DA (Meifod 383)

COUNTRY LANDOWNERS' ASSOCIATION 16 Belgrave Square, London SW1X 8PQ (235 0511)

COUNTRYSIDE COMMISSION 1 Cambridge Gate, Regent's Park, London NW1 4JY (01-935 5533)

COUNTRYSIDE COMMISSION FOR SCOTLAND Battleby, Redgorton, Perth PH1 3EW (0738 27921)

CROFTERS COMMISSION 4-6 Caste Wynd, Inverness IV2 3EQ (0463 37231)

DUKE OF EDINBURGH'S AWARD SCHEME 2 Old Queen Street, London SW1H 9HR (01-930 7681)

ENGLISH TOURIST BOARD 4 Grosvenor Gardens, London SW1W 0DU (01-730 3400)

ENTERPRISE YOUTH 49 Melville Street, Edinburgh EH3 7HL (031-226 3192/6412)

FARM BUILDINGS ASSOCIATION Roseleigh, Deddington, Oxford OX5 4SP (Deddington 234)

FARMERS' UNION OF WALES Llys Amaeth, Queen's Square, Aberystwyth SY2 3EA (0970 2755)

FEDERATION AGAINST AIRCRAFT NUISANCE 60 Beckenham Place Park, Beckenham, Kent

FORESTRY COMMISSION 22 Savile Row, London W1X 2AY (01-734 0221)

FRIENDS OF FRIENDLESS CHURCHES 12 Edwardes Square, London W8 6HG (01-602 6267)

FRIENDS OF THE EARTH LIMITED 9 Poland Street, London W1V 3DG (01-437 6121)

GEORGIAN GROUP   2 Chester Street, London SW1X 7BB (01-235 3081)
GREEN BELT COUNCIL FOR GREATER LONDON   1-4 Crawford Mews, London W1H 1PT (01-262 1477)

HIGHLANDS AND ISLANDS DEVELOPMENT BOARD   Bridge House, Bank Street, Inverness IV1 1QR (0463 34171)
HISTORIC BUILDINGS BUREAU   Department of the Environment, 25 Savile Row, London W1X 2BT (01-734 6010)
HISTORIC BUILDINGS COUNCIL FOR ENGLAND   25 Savile Row, London W1X 2BT (01-734 6010)
HISTORIC BUILDINGS COUNCIL FOR SCOTLAND   Argyle House, Lady Lawson Street, Edinburgh EH3 9SF (031-229 9191 Ext 402)
HISTORIC BUILDINGS COUNCIL FOR WALES   St David's House, Wood Street, Cardiff CF1 1PQ (0222 397083)
HISTORIC CHURCHES PRESERVATION TRUST   Fulham Palace, London SW6 6EA (01-736 3054)

INLAND WATERWAYS AMENITY ADVISORY COUNCIL   122 Cleveland Street, London W1P 5DN (01-387 7973)
INLAND WATERWAYS ASSOCIATION   114 Regent's Park Road, London NW1 8UQ (01-586 2510/2556)
INSTITUTE OF FORESTERS OF GREAT BRITAIN   Newton House, Newton of Falkland, Freuchie, Fife KY7 7RZ (Falkland 291)
INSTITUTE OF LANDSCAPE ARCHITECTS   12 Carlton House Terrace, London SW1Y 5AH (01-839 4044)
INSTITUTE OF PARK AND RECREATIONAL ADMINISTRATION   Lower Basildon, Reading, Berkshire RG8 9NE (Goring-on Thames 3558)

KEEP BRITAIN TIDY GROUP   First Floor, Circus House, New England Road, Brighton BN1 4GW (0273 691217)

LANDSCAPE RESEARCH GROUP   Longmoor, 8 Cunningham Road, Banstead, Surrey (Burgh Heath 55932)
LIGHT RAILWAY TRANSPORT LEAGUE   64 Grove Avenue, London W7 3ES
LOCAL AUTHORITIES AIRCRAFT NOISE COUNCIL   Bristol and West House, 173 Friar Street, Reading RG1 1JB (0734 55911 Ext 302)

MEN OF THE STONES   The Rutlands, Tinwell, Stamford, Lincolnshire PE9 3UD (0780 3372)
MEN OF THE TREES   Crawley Down, Crawley, Sussex
METROPOLITAN PUBLIC GARDENS ASSOCIATION   4 Carlos Place, London W1Y 5AE (01-493 6617)
MUSEUMS ASSOCIATION   87 Charlotte Street, London W1P 2BX (01-636 4600)

NATIONAL ASSOCIATION OF PROPERTY OWNERS   14-16 Bressenden Place, London SW1E 5DG (01-828 0852)
NATIONAL CARAVAN COUNCIL   Sackville House, 40 Piccadilly, London W1V 0ND (01-734 3681)
NATIONAL COUNCIL ON ISLAND TRANSPORT   Woodside House, High Road, London N22
NATIONAL FARMERS' UNION   Agricultural House, Knightsbridge, London SW1X 7NJ (01-235 5077)

NATIONAL FEDERATION OF HOUSING SOCIETIES 86 Strand, London WC2R 0EG (01-836 2741)

NATIONAL FEDERATION OF WOMEN'S INSTITUTES 39 Eccleston Street, London SW1W 9NT (01-730 7212)

NATIONAL HERITAGE 202 Great Suffolk Street, London SE1 1PR (01-407 7411)

NATIONAL MONUMENTS RECORD (ENGLAND) Fortress House, 23 Savile Row, London W1X 1AB (01-734 6010)

NATIONAL MONUMENTS RECORD (SCOTLAND) 52-4 Melville Street, Edinburgh EH3 7HF (031-225 5994)

NATIONAL MONUMENTS RECORD (WALES) Edleston House, Queen's Road, Aberystwyth, Dyfed SY23 2HP (0970 4381/2)

NATIONAL PLAYING FIELDS ASSOCIATION 57b Catherine Place, London SW1E 6EY (01-834 9274/5 and 01-828 8151)

NATIONAL SOCIETY FOR CLEAN AIR 136 North Street, Brighton, Sussex BN1 1RG (Brighton 26313)

NATIONAL TRUST 42 Queen Anne's Gate, London SW1H 9AS (01-930 0211)

NATIONAL TRUST FOR SCOTLAND 5 Charlotte Square, Edinburgh EH2 4DU (031-226 5922)

NATIONAL WATER COUNCIL 1 Queen Anne's Gate, London SW1 (01-930 3100)

NATURAL ENVIRONMENT RESEARCH COUNCIL Alhambra House, 27-33 Charing Cross Road, London WC2H 0AX (01-930 9232)

NATURE CONSERVANCY COUNCIL 19-20 Belgrave Square, London SW1X 8PY (01-235 3241)

NEW TOWNS ASSOCIATION Glen House, Stag Place, London SW1E 5AJ (01-828 1103)

NOISE ADVISORY COUNCIL Secretariat: Queen Anne's Chambers, 28 Broadway, London SW1H 9JU (01-930 4300)

NOISE ABATEMENT SOCIETY 6–8 Old Bond Street, London W1 (01-493 5877)

PILGRIM TRUST Fielden House, Little College Street, London SW1P 3SH (01-839 4727)

RAMBLERS' ASSOCIATION 1-4 Crawford Mews, London W1H 1PT (01-262 1477)

REDUNDANT CHURCHES FUND St Andrew-by-the-Wardrobe, Queen Victoria Street, London EC4V 5DE (01-248 3420)

RESCUE: A Trust for British Archaeology 15a Ball Plain, Herts ATR TSD

ROYAL COMMISSION ON ANCIENT AND HISTORICAL MONUMENTS IN WALES Edleston House, Queen's Road, Aberystwyth, Dyfed SY23 2HP (0970 4381/2)

ROYAL COMMISSION ON ENVIRONMENTAL POLLUTION Church House, Great Smith Street, London SW1P 3BL (01-222 6991)

ROYAL COMMISSION ON HISTORICAL MONUMENTS (ENGLAND) Fortress House, 23 Savile Row, London W1X 1AB (01-734 6010)

ROYAL COMMISSION ON THE ANCIENT AND HISTORICAL MONUMENTS OF SCOTLAND 52-4 Melville Street, Edinburgh EH3 7HF (031-225 5994)

ROYAL FINE ART COMMISSION 2 Carlton Gardens, London SW1Y 5AA (01-930 3935)

ROYAL FINE ART COMMISSION FOR SCOTLAND 22 Melville Street, Edinburgh EH3 7NS (031-225 5434)

ROYAL FORESTRY SOCIETY OF ENGLAND, WALES AND NORTHERN IRELAND 102 High Street, Tring, Hertfordshire HP23 4AH (0442 82 2028)

ROYAL INSTITUTE OF BRITISH ARCHITECTS 66 Portland Place, London W1N 4AD (01-580 5533)

ROYAL SOCIETY FOR THE PROTECTION OF BIRDS   The Lodge, Sandy, Bedfordshire SG19 2DL (0767 80551)

ROYAL SOCIETY OF ARTS   John Adam Street, Adelphi, London WC2N 6EZ (01-839 2366)

SALTIRE SOCIETY   Gladstone's Lane, 483 Lawnmarket, Edinburgh EH1 2NT (031-225 7780)

'SAVE THE VILLAGE POND' CAMPAIGN   111-13 Lambeth Road, London SE1 (01-582 0185)

SCOTTISH CIVIC TRUST   24 George Square, Glasgow G2 1EF (041-221 1466)

SCOTTISH COUNTRYSIDE ACTIVITIES COUNCIL   15 Main Street, Dundonald, Kilmarnock, Ayrshire KA2 9HF (056 385 406)

SCOTTISH GEORGIAN SOCIETY   39 Castle Street, Edinburgh EH2 3BH (031-225 8391)

SCOTTISH RIGHTS OF WAY SOCIETY   32 Rutland Square, Edinburgh EH1 2BZ

SCOTTISH TOURIST BOARD   Administration Offices: 23 Ravelston Terrace, Edinburgh EH4 3EU (031-332 2433)

Information Centre: 2 Rutland Place, Edinburgh EH1 2YU (031-332 2433)

SMALL INDUSTRIES COUNCIL FOR RURAL AREAS OF SCOTLAND   27 Walker Street, Edinburgh EH3 7HZ (031-225 2846)

SOCIETY FOR ENVIRONMENTAL EDUCATION   33 Mallory Crescent, Fareham, Hants (Fareham 6469)

SOCIETY FOR THE PROMOTION OF NATURE RESERVES   The Green, Nettleham, Lincoln LN2 2NR (0522 52326)

SOCIETY FOR THE PROTECTION OF ANCIENT BUILDINGS   55 Great Ormond Street, London WC1N 3JA (01-405 2646)

SOCIETY OF ARCHITECTURAL HISTORIANS OF GREAT BRITAIN   8 Belmount Avenue, Melton Park, Newcastle upon Tyne NE3 5QD (Wideopen 2524)

SOCIETY OF INDUSTRIAL ARTISTS AND DESIGNERS   12 Carlton House Terrace, London SW1Y 5AH (01-930 1911)

SOIL ASSOCIATION   Walnut Tree Manor, Haughley, Stowmarket, Suffolk IP14 3RS (044 970 235)

SOLICITORS' ECOLOGY GROUP   c/o The Law Society's Hall, 113 Chancery Lane, London WC2A 1PL (01-242 1222)

SPORTS COUNCIL   70 Brompton Road, London SW3 1EX (01-589 3411)

TOWN AND COUNTRY PLANNING ASSOCIATION   17 Carlton House Terrace, London SW1Y 5AS (01-930 8903)

TRAFFIC TRUST   5 New Bridge Street, London EC4V 6HL (01-353 3112)

TRANSPORT AND THE ENVIRONMENT GROUP   Rosenmullion, Holmesdale Road, South Nutfield, Surrey (Nutfield Ridge 2351)

TREE COUNCIL   Secretary: Room C10/06, 2 Marsham Street, London SW1 (01-212 3876)

TREES FOR PEOPLE   38 High Street, Watford, Herts WD1 2BS

ULSTER ARCHITECTURAL HERITAGE SOCIETY   30 College Gardens, Belfast BT9 6BT (0232 660809)

ULSTER SOCIETY FOR THE PRESERVATION OF THE COUNTRYSIDE   West Winds, Carney Hill, Holywood, Co Down BT18 0JR (Holywood 2300)

VICTORIAN SOCIETY   29 Exhibition Road, London SW7 2AS (01-589 7203)

WATER RESEARCH CENTRE Ferry Lane, Medmenham, Marlow, Bucks SL7 2HD
(049 166 282)
WORLD WILDLIFE FUND Panda House, 29 Greville Street, London EC1N 8AX
(01-404 5691)

APPENDIX 3 Conservation—Current Law and Practice

1 1971 TOWN AND COUNTRY PLANNING ACT

This Act consolidated the law by drawing together all the legislation affecting town and country planning since the War and including the new measures of the 1968 Act.

It requires the Secretary of State to compile lists of individual buildings of architectural or historic interest; a copy of the list is sent to the local authority and made available for inspection, and notification is also sent to individual owners, who are not consulted beforehand.

It repeats the important clause of the 1968 Act which for the first time gave positive protection to listed buildings. Previously, an owner had only to notify the local authority of his intention to alter or demolish, and unless the authority imposed a Building Preservation Order within 6 months, he could proceed. Now, however, listed building consent must be obtained from the planning authority before a building can be altered or demolished, and notice of application for consent must be advertised, the procedure being designed to ensure that the case for prevention is fully considered. An authority must inform the Secretary of State before granting consent. He can, if necessary 'call in' the proposal and decide it himself.

It gives protection to unlisted buildings by enabling the local authority to serve a building preservation notice which gives protection for up to 6 months (until it can be listed).

It enables the local planning authority to serve a listed building enforcement notice if it appears that works are being undertaken without consent. Under s 114–115, a repairs notice can be served if the owner is not taking reasonable steps to maintain a listed building and, if it is not complied with, compulsory purchase powers are available.

It ensures that if the owner deliberately neglects the building in order to develop the site, the local authority can acquire it at a price which excludes the value of the site for development. This provision, in the 1968 Act, closed an important loophole in the law, since councils had been reluctant to pay the large sums of compensation required towards the theoretical development value of the site.

The Act also included a number of minor improvements: if permission to demolish was granted, the RCHM[1] should have time to record the building first; local authorities were required to consult amenity societies before allowing

[1] Royal Commission on Historical Monuments.

245

demolition or alteration; if an owner did demolish a building without permission, the authority could compulsorily acquire the site; penalties for contravention of the law were all increased, and the fine for demolition of a listed building without consent was linked to the financial gain obtained by the owner.

2   1972 TOWN AND COUNTRY PLANNING (AMENDMENT) ACT

This Act introduced two important provisions affecting conservation areas. Sections 8 and 9 gave local planning authorities in England, Scotland and Wales powers to control the demolition of unlisted buildings in conservation areas, extending to them the provisions of the 1971 Act concerning listed buildings. This gave for the first time positive protection to buildings which, although individually not of sufficient merit to be listed, contributed to the character of an area. The local planning authorities are empowered to give a direction that specified buildings within a conservation area should be subject to control in the interests of the character and appearance of the area. Such a direction must be confirmed by the Secretary of State.

The other important provision, Section 10, made available grants to be administered through the Historic Buildings Council for buildings within a conservation area of outstanding architectural or historic interest. These 'conservation grants' are of major importance for the improvement of the environment, particularly in urban areas of historic interest, since they are available for unlisted as well as listed buildings within the conservation area.

A third major clause, Section 7, closed a loophole in the 1971 Act by empowering the local planning authority to bring a building preservation notice into effect by attaching it to a building rather than trying to serve it on the owner. This was directly inspired by the notorious Wheathampstead case, where the St Albans Council had been unable to serve the preservation order on the owners of the fifteenth-century farmhouse because their address could not be found; it was subsequently demolished for speculative building.

3   1974 TOWN AND COUNTRY AMENITIES ACT

This followed Lord Duncan-Sandys' Civic Amenities Act, 1967 and was a private member's measure introduced by Mr Michael Shersby, substantially incorporating the provisions of Sir John Rodgers' Town and Country Amenities Bill 1973–4 which had been through its committee stage before falling as result of the February 1974 dissolution of Parliament. The Act is described by its Sponsor as 'Parliament's contribution to European Architectural Heritage Year' and it widens the scope of the 1971 and 1972 Acts by further extending the powers of local authorities in dealing with conservation areas and historic buildings.

Conservation Areas: Section 1(1) re-enacts Section 277 of the 1971 Act

(designation of conservation areas) and adds two new sections – 277A (replacing
s 8 of the 1972 Act) which brings the demolition of all buildings in a conservation area under control (in contrast to the previous situation where only
those unlisted buildings specified by the authority were protected); and 277B
which requires the local planning authorities to prepare and make public schemes
for the preservation and enhancement of their conservation areas, thereby
taking a more positive attitude which requires public participation. The new
section also requires the authorities to consider whether to designate further
conservation areas, and empowers the Secretary of State to designate them himself
as a last resort. Section 3 gives increased control over advertising within
conservation areas.

Listed Buildings: Section 4 requires local planning authorities to give publicity to any proposal which affects the setting of a listed building and this
could include the immediate surroundings or land some distance away. Section 5
re-enacts s 101 of the 1971 Act (urgent repairs for the preservation of unoccupied listed buildings) and makes provision for the authorities to recover from
the owner of an occupied listed building any expenses incurred by them in
exercising their powers to carry out urgent works for the preservation of the
building; this power is now extended to an unlisted building of particular
importance in a conservation area.

Section 6 changes the basis of compensation in the case of compulsory
acquisition of a listed building; compensation by the local authority is only to
be assessed on the value of the building, and not as before on the value of the
site with the automatic assumption that listed building consent would have been
granted for redevelopment. Section 7 widens the powers of the Secretary of
State by making it necessary for every application for listed building consent
to be made to him by the local authority; previously this was only necessary in
respect of a building owned by the authority.

Finally, the Historic Buildings Councils are empowered to make grants towards
the preservation of gardens of outstanding interest, whether or not they are
associated with an historic building; and wider protection is given to trees.

4   THE LISTING OF BUILDINGS

Under the 1947 Act, the statutory list to be compiled by the Ministry's
investigators consisted of three categories of building:

GRADE I   Buildings of outstanding interest which are too important to be
destroyed.
GRADE II   Buildings of special interest which should be preserved as far as
possible. A subsequent II* category was made within this grade to mark
buildings of particular interest in it.
GRADE III   Buildings of interest, or which contribute to the general effect.
This grade formed a 'supplementary' list, without legal effect. In 1969, the
category was abolished, since it afforded no actual protection, some of the
buildings being upgraded to II and others being notified to their local authorities
to form an unofficial supplementary list.

In choosing buildings for listing, special attention is paid to: (a) good examples of a particular architectural style or piece of planning, or good illustrations of social or economic history; (b) technological innovation; (c) association with well known characters and events; (d) group value, and examples of planned layout.

In practice, any building dating from before 1700 is listed automatically, and most buildings between 1700 and 1840. Between 1840 and 1914, only those of definite character and quality are included; certain selected buildings between 1914 and 1939 are now also being listed.

The first listing programme ran from 1947 to 1968 and the total of buildings listed in England and Wales was:

GRADE I	4,351
GRADE II	111,300
GRADE III	136,752
TOTAL	252,403

After the reassessment of the abolished Grade II category, the total given for England by December 1971 was 137,000.

A second programme is now under way, and, it is hoped, will be completed by 1985; owing to the pressure of urban development, some priority is being given to boroughs and urban districts, and the current rate of additions to the Grade II list is approximately 25,000 buildings a year. Listing is seen as a continuing process, reflecting current needs and changing ideas, and the second programme is wider than the first, including late Victorian, Edwardian and even more recent buildings. When complete, the lists should contain an estimated 250,000 buildings.

The rate of demolition of listed buildings has dropped considerably in the past few years, showing the effective increase of planning control. Although official figures were not kept, an estimated rate of demolition in 1965 was 400 to 500 a year (*The Care of Old Buildings Today*, D. W. Insall, 1972, p 13). Current figures show a percentage, if not an actual decline, although the list for European Architectural Heritage Year (Appendix 6) makes very grim reading.

5   CONSERVATION AREAS

There are now (May 1976) over 3000 conservation areas in the United Kingdom of which approximately 300 have been designated as 'outstanding'; and new areas are being designated each month. Whether an area is 'outstanding' or not is decided by the appropriate Historic Buildings Councils on application from the place involved. The rate of demolitions within a conservation area has not been monitored in the past, and so it is not possible to tell whether the provisions of the 1972 Act, giving protection to all buildings within the conservation area, have made any difference. There is still considerable imbalance in the lists, reflecting different approaches by local authorities, some preferring to list many small areas and others fewer but larger ones. But some low figures come from architecturally rich areas such as Norfolk, Northumberland, Shropshire and Somerset.

In a letter to the author in April 1976, the Parliamentary Under Secretary of State at the Department of the Environment (Baroness Birk) indicated that the following authorities at that date had not designated any conservation areas:

ENGLAND: Blackpool, Castle Point, Chester-le-street, Crawley, Forest of Dean, Nuneaton, Oadby and Wigston, Oswestry, St Helens, Scunthorpe, Slough, South Ribble, Walsall, Wigan.

WALES: Blaenau Gwent, Islwyn, Meirionnydd, Rhondda, Torfaen.

An Outline History of Architectural Conservation in the United Kingdom

The Town and Country Planning Acts of 1971–2, and the Town and Country Amenities Act of 1974, provide measures of protection for historic buildings and areas to an extent which would have been unimaginable even a decade ago. Increasing threats have been countered by new laws, but the history of architectural conservation in the United Kingdom goes back for over a century.

1854   John Ruskin proposed to the Society of Antiquaries that an association should be formed to make and constantly revise a record of buildings of interest threatened by destruction or restoration.

1855   The Society of Antiquaries established a conservation fund to finance the formation of a catalogue of existing monuments and buildings of interest.

1873   Sir John Lubbock, Liberal MP for Maidstone (subsequently 1st Lord Avebury) also a member of the Society of Antiquaries, introduced his National Monuments Preservation Bill. This sought to establish a national monuments commission and a schedule of monuments to be protected by the commission. Its purpose was to provide time in which the nation or local authority might buy a threatened monument, and it was immediately inspired by the attempted sale for building land of part of the Avebury stone circle. On this occasion, and for the next six years when he introduced it, the Bill was blocked by property interests. (Lord Francis Hervey, 1875: 'Were the absurd relics of our barbarian predecessors who found time hanging heavily on their hands and set about piling up great barrows and rings of stones to be preserved at the cost of infringement of property rights?')

1877   William Morris founded the Society for the Protection of Ancient Buildings, initially to advise on the correct restoration of old buildings, his aims being the same as Ruskin's over twenty years earlier.

1882   Under the new Liberal Government, Lubbock's Bill was passed as the Ancient Monuments Protection Act (c 73). It had an initial schedule of 21 monuments which the State could purchase or take into guardianship in the event of any threat to them; but it provided no element of compulsion or any power over the owner.

1895   The increasing spread of railways over the countryside was a major factor in the founding of the National Trust, whose original rôle was to acquire and manage open spaces for the benefit of the nation.

1900   The Ancient Monuments Protection Act (c 34) allowed county councils to acquire monuments and established the principle of public access to scheduled ancient monuments.

1907   Parliament gave the National Trust the right to hold land 'inalienably'. This meant that no one might acquire National Trust property without permission from Parliament. The Trust soon widened its scope to include the purchase of neglected historic buildings.

1908   The idea that making a list of interesting monuments might help to preserve them was exemplified in the foundation of the Royal Commission on Historical Monuments (RCHM), which was to make and publish an inventory of ancient and historical monuments and constructions and specify which seemed most worthy of preservation; but it was given no power to do so.

1913   It had become apparent that the 1882 and 1900 Acts were ineffective and, as they did not cover inhabited monuments, a number of fine buildings had been destroyed. The Ancient Monuments (Consolidation and Amendment) Act (c 32) created preservation powers for the first time by providing that the Commissioner of Works could make a preservation order in respect of a scheduled monument; this order would fall unless it was confirmed by an Act; it also established the right of pre-emptive purchase in giving the Commissioner first refusal when an owner sold.

1931   The Ancient Monuments Act (c 16) extended control a little further by providing that preservation orders did not have to be confirmed by an Act unless there was an objection to them; it also established the principle of protecting a whole area (later enshrined in the Civil Amenities Act, 1967) by establishing 'preservation schemes' to protect the territory around a scheduled monument.

1932   The Town and Country Planning Act (c 48) allowed local authorities to make a preservation order in respect of any building of special architectural or historic interest in the area and abolished the principle that a building of historic interest must be inhabited.

1944   As the Royal Commission had only reported on eight counties since 1908 and since there was no way of checking how many distinguished buildings had been destroyed by bombing, the Town and Country Planning Act (c 47) introduced the statutory listing of buildings of architectural and historical interest, whether or not they were inhabited, giving for the first time a comprehensive list of historic buildings in Britain.

1947   Town and Country Planning Act (c 51). This was a landmark in the history of town planning legislation, repealing all other enactments and laying the foundation of the present land use system. In respect of historic buildings, it incorporated the listing provisions of the 1944 Act and introduced building preservation orders to be made by local planning authorities or by the Minister of Housing and Local Government when a building of architectural or historic interest was threatened. This thereby introduced the principle of central government intervention, first used in respect of uninhabited ancient monuments in the 1913 Act, to cover the far wider field of inhabited buildings.

1950   The changed economic conditions of the post-War years meant that an increasing number of historic buildings came under threat and the Gowers Committee Report recommended financial assistance to the owners through Government grants, tax relief and the power of compulsory purchase.

1953   The Historic Buildings and Ancient Monuments Act (c 49) incorporated one of the main recommendations of the Gowers Report by establishing Historic Buildings Councils for England, Scotland and Wales who would advise the Minister of Works on making grants and loans for the repair and upkeep of buildings of outstanding historic or architectural interest.

1962   Town and Country Planning Act (c 38) renewed the provisions of the 1947 Act concerning historic buildings. Also, in 1962, Parliament passed a private member's bill, introduced by Mr Paul Channon, the Local Authorities (Historic Buildings) Act (c 36) which empowered local councils to make grants towards the upkeep of any historic building. This was intended to help those owners whose properties were not sufficiently outstanding to qualify for a government grant from the Historic Buildings Council.

The Preservation Policy Group

By the mid-1960s, it was increasingly obvious that not only individual buildings but whole areas of historic towns were at risk. The Preservation Policy Group was set up in 1966 within the Ministry of Housing and Local Government in order to coordinate pilot studies to be made of four historic towns – Bath, Chester, Chichester and York – with the overall aim of examining how conservation policies could be sensibly implemented. The individual town studies were published in 1968 and the Group also published its own general recommendations in 1970, arising from its experience of the action necessary to preserve the character of historic towns and suggesting some of the improvements that could be made legally, financially and administratively for the preservation of historic buildings and areas. Many of these recommendations were incorporated into the 1972 Town and Country Planning Act.

1967   Civic Amenities Act (c 69). This was a private member's bill introduced by Mr Duncan Sandys, President of the Civic Trust, with the support of the Government. For the first time, it introduced the concept of protection for whole areas (as distinct from individual buildings) of cities, towns or villages.

Part I of the Act required local planning authorities to designate 'Conservation Areas' (it has now been replaced by s 277 of the 1971 Town and Country Planning Act, a consolidation measure). It gives a positive direction that the authority shall 'from time to time determine which parts of their area are areas of special architectural or historical interest, the character or appearance of which it is desirable to preserve or enhance and shall designate such areas as conservation areas. The Secretary of State can also direct the authority to take this action, if necessary. Applications for planning permission which could affect the character of a conservation area must be fully publicised and the public given the chance to comment within a set period.

It also brought improvements in the control over listed buildings: six months' notice instead of two had to be given for proposals to alter or demolish a listed building, and penalties were introduced for unauthorised works. Local authorities were given the power to serve a repairs notice on the owners of buildings urgently in need of repair, and, if necessary, to carry out the repairs themselves. Compulsory purchase powers were extended to cover all listed buildings in the event of an owner failing to comply with a repairs notice.

The Act also introduced further environmental improvements by requiring the local authorities to plant and protect trees, to improve refuse facilities and to remove abandoned cars from the streets.

1968   Town and Country Planning Act (c 72). Part V, on buildings of Architectural or Historic Interest, was based on the work of the Preservation Policy Group and introduced important reforms in the protection of listed buildings which had been shown to be increasingly necessary over the past few years. These included much higher fines for unauthorised demolition and radical changes in the building preservation order and development value compensation procedure. These measures were consolidated by the 1971 Town and Country Planning Act.

APPENDIX 5 A Random Selection of Valuable Past Gifts to Museums from Individual Collections

This list is reproduced by courtesy of the Standing Commission on Museums and Galleries and was attached as an appendix to their evidence to the Select Committee on the Wealth Tax.

No mention is made here of objects acquired through such funds as the Chantrey Bequest, the Duveen or Courtauld Funds, or trust funds, or from individual financial benefactions, or from public appeal, nor acquisitions through the National Art-Collections or Gulbenkian Funds or the Contemporary Art Society etc (which also in turn originate mainly from private collections).

BIRMINGHAM

CITY MUSEUM AND ART GALLERY   J. R. Holliday Collection of Pre-Raphaelite drawings; David Cox Collection; Tangye Collection of English ceramics; Barnett Bequest of jewellery; Ellis Greenberg Collection of Matthew Bolton silver plate; John Feeny Silver Collection; E. T. Cook Bequest: Claude landscape.

BRIGHTON

MUSEUMS AND ART GALLERY   Henry Willet collection of ceramics, old master paintings, natural history (basis of museum's collections); Booth Bequest – natural history.

BRISTOL

MUSEUMS AND ART GALLERY   Schiller Bequest of oriental art (later added to by further gifts).

CAMBRIDGE

FITZWILLIAM MUSEUM   Fitzwilliam Foundation Bequest and building.
WHIPPLE MUSEUM   Whipple Foundation Bequest.

CARDIFF

NATIONAL MUSEUM OF WALES   Pyke Thompson Collection of watercolours; W. S. de Winton Collection of ceramics; Goscombe John Collection of Edwardian Sculpture. Percentage of total collection in form of gift (or loan) from individuals: Chinese jades 100%; European and Oriental wares 100%; Ceramics 95%; Glass 90%; Modern French paintings and drawings 50%; Sculpture 87%; Old masters paintings 70%; British 18–19th-century paintings 50%; Impressionist and modern paintings 85%; Modern British paintings 41%.

EDINBURGH

NATIONAL GALLERIES OF SCOTLAND Paintings–two thirds of collection by gift. Lady Murray paintings by Watteau and the bulk of Alan Ramsay's surviving drawings; Coats Gift painting by Vermeer; Prints and drawings: 6 bequests account for over two thirds of collection; D. Y. Cameron Bequest of etchings by Rembrandt; portraits: 4000 D. O. Hill photographs (2 gifts); Lothian Bequest (eight 17th-century portraits); Vaughan Bequest: Turner collection.

NATIONAL LIBRARY OF SCOTLAND Substantial collections of books and manuscripts; Lord Rosebery Collection of Scottish books; Fergusson Collection of Scottish books.

IPSWICH

MUSEUMS Extensive Natural History collections (one valued at £30,000).

LEEDS

CITY ART GALLERY Sam Wilson Bequest (1925)–large collection of paintings, oriental porcelain, sculpture and furniture; individual bequests form most of the rest of the collections.

TEMPLE NEWSAM HOUSE Frank Fulford gift (1939), and Mrs Fulford and Mrs Jackson Gifts (1944) 86 gold and silver etui and boxes (second only to V and A collections). Ceramics: R. T. Walker (1901), H. C. Embleton (1938), Mrs A. S. Bulmer (1934) and Mrs Arthur Smith (1938) Collections.

LEICESTERSHIRE

MUSEUMS AND ART GALLERIES Total of collection valued at £3m received as gifts, apart from £50,000 spent on purchases in past 10 years (99% of numbers of specimens).

LIVERPOOL

MERSEYSIDE MUSEUMS A. Jones and A. Ridyard early African ethnography collections; Joseph Mayer's Foundation Gift and Bequest (1867)–antiquities and decorative arts; Derby Foundation gift in natural sciences; The Benas Jackson and Stopford Collections of European, American and other coins (1873–1904); Crossfield Collection of antiquities (1861) including important Egyptian material; Lady Elizabeth Pilkington Gift of 39 French POW ship models; Robert Gladstone Gift and Bequest of ship models and maritime paintings.

WALKER ART GALLERY Roscoe Collection, one of the first collections of early Italian art to be formed, including works by Simone Martini; many bequests of pictures; Sudley house (1944) with Holt collection of paintings and sculpture including 3 oil paintings by Turner.

LONDON

BRITISH MUSEUM *Coins and Medals:* Sloane and Cotton British and European coin collections formed basis of collection (1753); among many pre-War benefactions, 22 supremely important gifts were received between 1799 and 1935. *Greek and Roman Antiquities:* Among 10 highly important benefactions since 1760 were: R. Payne Knight Bequest (1824) laid the foundation of the Museum's collection of Greek Etruscan and Roman bronzes; Sir William Temple Bequest

(1856): collections of terracottas and vases; Felix Slade Bequest (1869): unequalled collection of glass.

Western Asiatic Antiquities: A number of significant gifts from King Edward VII, Lord Aberdeen, Lady Howard de Walden, etc. the most important being the Oxus Treasure from Sir A. W. Franks.

Oriental Antiquities: Franks Gift of Chinese and Japanese porcelain; Bridge Gift of Indian Sculpture (still four-fifths of Museum's holding); Raffles Gifts (two) of Javanese art; Lady Browning Gift: unique Sinhalese bronze Tara; Mrs Tucker Gift of Sanchi Bracket figure.

Medieval and Later Antiquities: Waddesdon Bequest of Renaissance jewellery, silver etc; Sutton Hoo burial.

BRITISH LIBRARY Sloane Collection; Cotton Collection; Royal collections; Crackerode Collection; Thomason Collection.

COURTAULD INSTITUTE, UNIVERSITY OF LONDON Lord Lee of Fareham's Gift (1931) of old master paintings; Mr Samuel Courtauld's Gift (1931) of French Impressionist paintings; Mr Samuel Courtauld Bequest (1947) of further paintings; Roger Fry Bequest (1933) of 20th-century English and French paintings; Lord Conway of Allington: photographic library.

GEOLOGICAL MUSEUM Donations of a large part of the mineral and gemstone collections over the years.

HORNIMAN MUSEUM F. J. Horniman gift (1901) of building, collections and library, including outstanding ethnographical and musical instrument collections.

IVEAGH BEQUEST, KENWOOD Lord Iveagh Bequest (1927), house and collections.

NATIONAL GALLERY Wynne Ellis Gift; Lord Duveen's Gift including Correggio and Hogarth paintings; Holford Family gift of Lotto's 'Lucretia'; Lord Lansdowne's gift of self portrait by Salvator Rosa; Salting, Layand and Mond Bequests; Cook Bequest: Portrait of a woman by Titian.

TATE GALLERY Before the War, 89% of acquisitions were by gift, as was the Gallery itself.

Historic British Collection: Sir Henry Tate Gift (1897) 65 works mainly by Victorian artists; Robert Vernon Gift (1897): 143 paintings including works by Gainsborough, Wilson, Constable and Turner; Henry Vaughan Gift (1900–06): 55 works including 12 paintings by Constable; J. M. W. Turner Bequest (1906) 276 paintings bequeathed by the artist; George Salting Gift (1910) 28 works including 13 paintings by Constable; Gifts of work by Blake include 22 works from Mrs J. Richmond (1922), 21 works from W. G. Robertson (1939–49), 16 works from Miss A. G. E. G. Carthew (1946).

Modern Collection: Lord Duveen Gift – 24 works; Wertheimer Family Gifts – 5 works by J. S. Sargent; C. F. Stoop Gift: 20 works by Gaudier Brzeska and bequests of 17 paintings all of very high quality by Van Gogh, Modigliani, Cezanne, Matisse, Picasso and Braque; Montague Shearman Bequest – 7 paintings by Sisley, Toulouse-Lautrec, Utrillo, Matisse, Rouault and Vuillard; Sir Hugh Walpole Bequest: 9 works by Renoir, Tissot, Cezanne, Sickert, Steer and Augustus John; Lady H. Cavendish-Bentinck Bequest: 16 works by Sickert, S. F. Gore and Augustus John; Earl of Sandwich: 2 gifts and 4 bequests including works by Bonnard, Gauguin and Lehmbruck.

VICTORIA AND ALBERT MUSEUM Among major benefactions were: The Sheepshanks Collection (1857) (containing Constable sketches); Townshend paintings (1868); Constable Gift (1888) (comprising the bulk of his work); Ionides paintings, prints and drawings (1900); Mrs S. S. Joseph miniatures (1941); Alexander Dyce collection of books, prints, drawings and watercolours (1869); Dalton Bequest of drawings (1919); The Jones Bequest of furniture, prints and paintings (1882);

The Blore Gift of architectural drawings (1879); The Phene Spiers collection of architectural drawings (circa 1906–19); The Salting Bequest of sculpture and other artefacts (1910); The Farquharson Bequest of arms and armour (1927); The Crofts-Lyons Bequest of important continental church plate (1926); The Waldo-Sibthorpe Bequest of jewellery (1898); The Forster Library (including notebooks with drawings by Leonardo da Vinci).

WALLACE COLLECTION   House and collections.

MANCHESTER

CITY ART GALLERIES   Thomas and Mary Greg Gift (1904): collection of English pottery; Miss Anna M. Philips Gift (1906): collection of Wedgwood black basalt and jasper ware; Charles Lambert Rutherston: gifts of works by living English artists between 1910 and 1925 (oil paintings, sculptures and prints and 400 water-colours); James T. Blau Bequest (1917) of paintings including watercolours by Turner and contemporaries and 19th-century academic paintings; Leicester Collier Bequest (1917) of oriental and European porcelain and glass–also paintings and old master prints; Professor Frank E. Tylecote Bequest (1965) of 250 items of 18th- and 19th-century glass; Dr David Lloyd Roberts Bequest (1970): collection of 18th-century prints and early 19th-century watercolours and oils; Frederick Behrens Bequest (1933) of 157 colour prints and drawings; John Edward Yates Gift (1934): 138 pieces of jade and semi-precious stones; John Edward Yates Bequest (1934): oil paintings, watercolours and prints mainly by Victorian artists including Holman Hunt's 'Lady of Shalott' and collections of Greek, Roman and Egyptian gold jewellery, Egyptian bronzes and vases, and Oriental ivories and enamels; Mrs F. C. Dykes Gift (1948) of Worcester porcelain; Harold Raby Bequest (1958): collection of English enamels (about 500 items) and porcelain.

MANCHESTER MUSEUM   Jesse Haworth: major Egyptian collections, excavated by Sir Flinders Petrie (worth today over £1m); Charles Bailey: British and European herbarium; Cosmo Melville–rest of world herbarium; Leo Grindon–historical and illustrative herbarium; (These three combined make the Manchester Herbarium into one of the six most important in the world.)

OXFORD

ASHMOLEAN MUSEUM   Building on the original gift by Elias Ashmole of the Tradescant Collections and his own, and such gifts as those of Dr Penrose (1834) of 25 pictures, of Mr Chambers Hall (1855) of 60 paintings and a collection of old master drawings and Greek and Roman bronzes, of John Ruskin (1861) of 36 watercolours by Turner, of Mrs Bennett Combe (1893) of 21 pre-Raphaelite paintings, the collections in this Museum have been very largely made up of gifts and bequests. In addition important gifts include: Farrer Collection of paint-ings and Huguenot silver. In the Departments of Eastern Art and of Coins and Medals gifts account for 90% of the collections. Sir Arthur Evans Cretan Collections.

PITT RIVERS MUSEUM   A benefaction brought this museum into being, and it has been added to subsequently by numerous important gifts. Some single items of such material today are worth tens of thousands of pounds.

PLYMOUTH

CITY MUSEUM AND ART GALLERY   The Cottonian Collection: Gift (1853) and Bequest (1862): Paintings, old master drawings, prints, rare books and manuscripts and objets d'art; Bignell Collection Gift (1910) Natural History (important collection of insects); de Pass Collection: Gift (1928) – paintings and drawings; Carpenter Collection: Gift (1934) – English ceramics (mainly earthenware); Hurdle Collection – Gift (1937) – Oriental and English ceramics.

READING

MUSEUM AND ART GALLERY W. I. Palmer Bequest (1896) of paintings (200–300 works late 19th-century English); Keyser Collection: Gift (1917) – 12th-century carved stone capitals from Reading Abbey cloister, internationally important; Knox Collection (1930) of 500 Baxter coloured prints.

NEWCASTLE UPON TYNE

LAING ART GALLERY AND MUSEUM Sir Gainsborough Bruce Gift (1906) of 60 of the watercolour drawings by Henry Burdon and Charles Richardson recording the Roman Wall in 1848; John G. Joicey Bequest (1920s) of pottery, porcelain, silver, watches and jewellery, etc then valued at £50,000 (plus a larger sum for the provision of a building); Higginbottom Gift (1920s) of over 1500 examples of Japanese works of art; Parker Brewis Collection: Gift (1940) of weapons from the Bronze Age and 17th- and 18th-centuries, Japanese and ethnological collections; H. E. P. Taylor (Whickham) collection of 500 examples of arms and armour; John Lamb Bequest (1909) of watercolour drawings, etc; Holliday Bequest (1927) of watercolour drawings; Matthew Bell Collection of local glass (1925–8); George Henderson Gift and Bequest (1937) of oil paintings, watercolours and drawings, including Alma Tadema's 'Love in Idleness'.

APPENDIX 6 Buildings for which Consent to Demolish Was Granted in 1975— European Architectural Heritage Year

This is a list given to the author in answer to a Parliamentary Question.

It should be pointed out that some of these buildings were past saving. Equally, this list does not represent the sum total of buildings lost. Some were demolished following consent the previous year, others were pulled down without official sanction. A list of this length, containing as it does so many much loved local buildings of little individual national significance, points to the need for local vigilance.

GRADE 1

NIL

GRADE II

173, 185-91 (odd) and 219-23 (odd) Hoxton Street, London N1
Bothey, Hazel Eall, Pond Land, Peaslake, Guilford, Surrey
New Fairlee Farmhouse, Staplers Road, Newport, 10W
21 High Street, Lymington, Hants
Glen Spey, Lower Ashley Road, New Milton, Hants
Yew Tree Cottage, 97 Lymington Road, New Milton, Hants
Church Hill House, East Ilsley, Berks
Dunsters Mill House, Tilehurst, Reading
Barn at Corpus Farm, Sandford Road, Littlemore, Oxford
Barns at Yew Tree Farmhouse, Stoke Mandeville, Bucks
19-23 Station Road, Lawford, Essex
Baptist Tabernacle, Swindon, Wilts
The Barn, Shillingham, Cornwall
42 St Thomas Street, Weymouth, Dorset
The Coach House, 16 Barnwood Road, Gloucester
Elmfield, Stanley Road, Leicester
Gibfield Cottage, Gibfield Lane, Belper, Derby
13 High Street, Daventry, Warks
18-20, 26, 27 Newhall Hill, Birmingham
2-3 New Street, Worcester
7 North Church Side, Hull
5-11 Whitehouses, Bolton, Lancs

Toll House, Halfpenny Bridge, Saltburn, Cleveland
Cottage west of Millbank Arms, Barningham, Co Durham
60 High Street, Yarm, Cleveland
1331 and 1333 High Road, Whetstone, London N20
9 and 12 Bridewell Place and 13 New Bridge Street, London EC4
13, 14 and 15 Hawks Lane, Canterbury
77 Castle Street, Canterbury
108 Bellevue Road, Bournemouth
Cedar House, 14 Boston Road, Holbeach, Lincs
49-53 Sheep Street, Northampton
48 St Owen Street, Hereford
11-15 Waterloo Place, Lewes, Sussex
29 Aston Street, Stepney, London E4
Old Barn, Ockenden Road, Upminster, Essex
The Dairy, Popes Lane, Gunnersbury Park, London W3
Viaduct at Lewes Road, Brighton
17 London Road, Horsham, Sussex
Beaumont Barracks, Aldershot, Sussex
Windmill Inn, High Street, Misterton
Church Hall, St Sampsons Church, York
9 Bridewell Place, London EC4
19 Round Street, Wendover, Bucks
17-18 Norfolk Road, London NW3
37-8 Gerrard Street, London W1
40 Dock Street, London E1
Central Foundation School for Girls, Spital Square, London E1
Anchor Brewery, Mile End Road, London E1
Avenue Chambers, Vernon Place, London WC1
9-10 Fleur-de-Lys Street and former police station, Commercial Street, London E1
291 Streatham Street, London WC1
Barn at Tillage Farm, Fisherman's Lane, Aldermaston, Berks
19 The Parade, Margate, Kent
The Towers, Yarmouth, 10W
107 High Street, Winchester
36-8 Welland Street, Peterborough
Archway to Dean's Court, Cathedral precinct, Peterborough
Malthouses, High Street, Mistley, Essex
Barn East of Clapgate Farmhouse, Marley Lane, Wymondham, Norfolk
15-16 Market Place, Great Yarmouth, Norfolk
Bay Tree House, Dubbridge, Stroud, Glos
15-25 How Street, Wooton under Edge, Glos
36 Slad Road, Stroud, Glos
8 and 9 Richmond Terrace, Clifton, Bristol
42-4 Hillesdon Road, Torquay, Devon
Little Jordon, Mill Green, Lyme Regis, Dorset
16 Dorchester Road, Weymouth, Dorset
Mount Braddon Hotel, Braddon Hill Road, Torquay, Devon
43 Gold Street, Kettering, Northants
75 High Street, Boston, Lincs
3 Cooper Street, Manchester
24 Pilgrim Street, Newcastle-upon-Tyne
210 High Street, Tonbridge, Kent

Spurrell's Lodge, Bishopsgate, Norwich
Murley House, West Chinnock, Somerset
1-18 and 20a-23 Boar Lane, Leeds
1-7 New Station Street, Leeds
18-23 and 27 Briggate, Leeds
3 and 5 Alfred Street, Leeds
Uckfield House, Uckfield, Sussex
8-10 Harefield Road, Uxbridge, Middlesex
Public Lavatories at clock tower complex, Herne Bay, Kent
19-21 Snook's Hill, Newport, IOW
1-3 Railway Road, Downham Market, Norfolk
35 South Street, Bourne, Lincs
97 High Street, Bromsgrove, West Midlands
5 Sherford Street, Malvern, Worcs
Old Watermill, Waterside Road, Barton-on-Humber, Lincs
Harrogate Hall Farm, Bilton, Harrogate
Chairgate Mill, Glastonbury, Somerset
50 Culver Street, Saltash, Cornwall
59-61 Southbroom Street, Devizes, Wilts
2 Castle Street, Barnstaple, Devon
69-87 Park Road, London N8
Goods Yard, Pickering Station, Yorks
19-21, 24-6 Watling Street, London EC4
6-8 Folgate Street, London E1
Old Malt House at 2 Queen Street, Arundel, Sussex
Barn at Manor Farm, Brown Candover, Hants
'The Stores', Church Street, Nonnington, Dover
51 Pyle Street, Newport, IOW
5 Melville Street, Ryde, IOW
Speen Lodge, Speen Lane, Newbury, Berks
Upper Roughway Farmhouse, Plaxtol, Kent
23-5 Williams Street, Windsor
Cedar Cottage, Needham Road, Stowmarket, Suffolk
42-4 High Street, Haverhill, Suffolk
15-16 Market Place, Great Yarmouth, Norfolk
21 Cambridge Street, Aylesbury, Bucks
Barn at rear of 26 Lake Street, Leighton Buzzard, Bucks
58 Church Street, Mevagissey, Cornwall
39 South Street, Wellington, Devon
48 North Street, Taunton, Devon
61 Market Place/2 Strait Bargate, Boston, Lincs
11-12 and 14-16 St Mary's Hill and
31-3 St Mary's Street, Stamford, Lincs
107-13 High Street, Pershore, Worcs
Yeóvil House, Westbury Street, Leominster, Herts
Pillar Box Cottage, Castlethorpe, Nr Brigg, Humberside
Wray House Farm, Marishes, Pickering, Yorks
Cottage at Foxhouse Farm, Uppergate Road, Stannington, Sheffield
Cardigan Arms, Hough Lane, Bramley, Leeds
1-2 Drury Lane, Knutsford, Cheshire
First Church of Christ Scientist, Village Road, Oxton, Birkenhead
58 Saddler Street, Durham

42 Clissold Crescent, London N16
1 and 2 Davies Court, Esher, Surrey
21 and 23 High Street, Witney, Oxon
Former Co-operative Shop, Fowlmere, Cambs
2-4 Market Place, Warminister, Wilts
15-21 St Paul Street, Bristol
Coromandel House, Camden Row, Bath
Tanyard Farmhouse and Granary, Tanners Lane, Coventry
42-8 (even) Redmans Road, London E1
Howard Buildings, Deal Street, London E1
Eden Engineering Works at 818-22 Uxbridge Road, Hayes, Middlesex
Coopers School, Hawkwood Lane, Chislehurst, Bromley, Kent
Highgate Methodist Church and Hall, Archway Road, London N6
4-6 South Street, Braintree, Essex
55A Lee Crescent, Edgbaston, Birmingham
36-9 Wright Street, Small Heath, Birmingham
Methodist Church, Mill Street, Kidderminister, Worcs
18-20 Kirkgate, Bridlington, Yorks
2-16 (even) Church Street, Dagenham, Essex
120, 122a and b, 124 and 126 South Street, Bridport, Dorset
Granary, College Lane and Warehouse, S Quay, King's Lynn, Norfolk
Old Burleigh Farmhouse, Charing Heath, Ashford, Kent
5-7 Southgate Street, Launceston, Cornwall
Barn at White Lion Hotel, Banbury, Oxon
93-4 High Street, Lymington, Hants
44 Oxford Street, Woodstock, Oxon
3-4 King Street, Sudbury, Suffolk
Manor House, Field Dalling, Norfolk
8-13 Great Stanhope Street, Bath
51 High Street, Glastonbury, Somerset
Frome Hall, Bath Road, Stroud, Glos
5 Bridgewell Street, Bristol
Upper Grant, Lovedays Mead, Folly Lane, Stroud, Glos
The Gothic Temple Chillington Hall, Staffs
Cottage, west of Highley Farm, Whitburn
Cottage next to Marquis of Granby, Wellingore, Lincs
Westbourne Lodge, 13 Combit Road, Spalding, Lincs
28-42 Agard Street, Derby
215 Uppertown Street, Bromley, Leeds
28-32 St Pauls Street, Leeds
Church of St Augustine, Queens Road, Hull
Addison House, Daisy Bank Road, Manchester
Old Boiler House, The Old Mill, Mill Green, Congleton, Cheshire
6-8 Glasgow Street, Liverpool
266 Lowther Street, Whitehaven
Ivy Cottage, Cowren, Bewley, Cleveland
Herringthorpe Hall and Stables, Rotherham, Yorks
265 High Street, Uxbridge, Middlesex
18 North Street, Leighton Buzzard, Beds
1a Mount Beacon Row, Lansdown, Bath
St John's Vicarage, Vicarage Road, Moordown, Bournemouth
Wykes Court, The Grove, Rox Lane, Bridport, Dorset

16-18 North Road, Bideford, Devon
18, 19, 19A George Street, Tamworth, Staffs
38-38A Bolebridge Street, Tamworth, Staffs
Blagden Farm, Blagden Lane, Newsome, Huddersfield
Driffield House, 209 Anlaby Road, Hull
Boundary Wall, Silver Street, Glastonbury, Somerset
1-7 Pritchard Street, Bristol
Ship Tavern, 27 Lime Street, London EC3
Cheese House, Boreham Road, Great Leighs, Essex
Tor School House, Chilkwell Street, Glanstonbury, Somerset
Washington Works, Wellington Street, Sheffield
Whitwell Place and Barn, Wistons Lane, Elland, Yorks

Bibliography

I hesitate to dignify this booklist with the title of 'Bibliography', as it is, of necessity, selective. Anyone interested in the heritage will find a subscription to *Country Life* a necessity. The articles on the heritage and the environment by Marcus Binney, John Cornforth and others are essential reading and notable at once for their content and for their authors' felicity of style. *Built Environment* is another journal which repays regular study, as does *Apollo, The Connoisseur*, and especially the *Burlington Magazine*. In the realms of the daily press, the *Guardian, The Times* and *Daily Telegraph* together with the *Sunday Times* and the *Observer*, act as splendid watchdogs on behalf of those for whom the heritage and its defence are matter of prime concern. Among the books which I have found most useful are the following:

Aldous, T., *Battle for the Environment* (Fontana, 1972)
Amery C. and Cruickshank, D., *The Rape of Britain* (Elek, 1975)
Barker, Sir Ernest, *The Character of England* (Oxford University Press, 1947)
Barr, J., *Derelict Britain* (Penguin, 1975)
Beazley, E., *The Countryside on View* (Constable, 1971)
Booker, C. and Lycett-Green, C., *Goodbye London* (Fontana, 1973)
Braun, Hugh, *Parish Churches; Their Architectural Development in England* (Faber, 1970)
Buglar, Jeremy, *Polluting Britain* (Pelican, 1972)
Cantucazino, ed, *Architectural Conservation in Europe* (Architectural Press, 1975)
Christian, Garth, *Tomorrow's Countryside* (Murray, 1966)
——, *A Place for Animals* (Lutterworth, 1958)
Civic Trust, The, *Heritage Year Awards* (Civic Trust, 1975)
Condy, William, *Woodlands* (Collins, 1974)
Cooper, ed, *Great Private Collections* (Weidenfeld & Nicholson, 1963)
Cornforth, John, *Country Houses in Britain; Can They Survive?* (Country Life, 1974)
Cullen, G., *Concise Townscape* (Architectural Press, 1971)
Cullingworth, J. B., *Problems of an Urban Society*, Vol 3 (George Allen and Unwin, 1973)
——, *Town and Country Planning in Britain* (George Allen and Unwin, 1972)
Dutton, R., *The English Country House* (Batsford, 1935)
Edinburgh University Press *The Conservation of Georgian Edinburgh; the Proceeding and Outcomes of a Conference* (1972)
Fedden, Robin, *The National Trust; Past and Present* (Cape, 1970)
Fergusson, Adam, *The Sack of Bath* (Compton Russell, 1973)
Gregory, R., *The Price of Amenity* (Macmillan, 1971)
Gresswell, Peter, *Environment; an Alphabetical Handbook* (Murray, 1971)

Harrod, Lady, ed, *Norfolk County Churches and the Future* (Norfolk Society, 1972)

Harvey, J., *The Conservation of Buildings* (J. Baker, 1972)

——, *The Medieval Craftsman* (Batsford, 1975)

Hayward, J. and Watson, M., *Planning, Politics, and Public Policy* (Cambridge, 1975)

HMSO, the following Countryside Commission Publications; *The Planning of the Coastline* (1970); *The Coastal Heritage* (1970); *New Agricultural Landscapes* (1974)

    Four Studies in Conservation published in 1968 – *York, Bath, Chester* and *Chichester*.

    The Report and Proceedings of the Select Committee on the Wealth Tax, 1975.

Hoskins, W. G., *The Making of the English Landscape,* Vol 1 (Hodder and Stoughton, 1955)

Insall, Donald *The Care of Old Buildings Today* (Architectural Press, 1972)

Kennet, Wayland, *Preservation* (Temple Smith, 1972)

MacEwan, M., *Crisis in Architecture* (RIBA, 1974)

Nicolson, Nigel, *Great Houses of Britain* (Weidenfeld & Nicholson, 1965)

Nuttgens, P., *York* (Studio Vista, 1971)

Page, Robin, *The Decline of an English Village* (Davis-Pointer, 1974)

Patmore, J. Alan, *Land and Leisure* (Pelican, 1970)

Peel, J. H. B., *An Englishman's Home* (Cassell, 1972)

Richards, Raymond, *Old Cheshire Churches* (Moreton, 1974)

Robertson, C., *Bath: An Architectural Guide* (Faber, 1975)

Smith, D. L., *Amenity and Urban Planning* (Crosby, Lockwood, Staples, 1974)

Strong, Binney and Harris, *The Destruction of the Country House* (Thames & Hudson, 1974)

Taylor, Alec Clifton, *The Pattern of English Building* (Faber, 1972)

——, *English Parish Churches as Works of Art* (Batsford, 1974)

Taylor, R., ed, *Britain's Planning Heritage* (Croom Helm, 1975)

Wallwork, K. L., *Derelict Land* (David and Charles, 1974)

West, Trudy, *The Timber Frame House in England* (David and Charles, 1971)

Williams-Ellis, C., *Britain and the Beast* (Dent, 1937)

UNESCO, *The Conservation of Cities* (Croom Helm, 1975)

Index